SECOND SON
THE MAN IN THE IRON MASK

SARAH B. MADRY

Contents

Acknowledgements		v
Introduction – The Case For The Panoramic View		ix
1	**THE WHITE BLACKBIRD**	**1**
1	The Arrest Of Eustache Dauger	3
2	The King's Search For Eustache Dauger	27
3	Leaks, Speculations, And Suspicions	39
4	The Valet	63
2	**SQUIRRELS, LIZARDS, AND SNAKES**	**71**
5	Fouquet And Colbert	73
6	The Jailers: Louvois And Saint-Mars	83
7	The Prisoners	103
8	Pignerol And Exilles	127
9	Sainte-Marguerite And The Bastille	149
3	**THE HABSBURGS, THE MEDICI, THE BOURBONS**	**163**
10	Queen Anne Of Austria And Cardinal Jules Mazarin	165
11	Louis XIV	179
12	Louis XIII: A Medical Examination	195
13	Secondary Plan Of Nature	211
14	The Case For The White Blackbird	233
15	The Clue Of The Missing Apostrophe	251
16	Oger The Dane	263
17	Madame De Sévigné's Clues	277
18	Beaulieu And The Lhoste	295
4	**IT WILL BE BY THE LADY, NO DOGS WILL BARK**	**309**
19	A Footed Bowl	311
20	Philippe D'Orléans	333
Medical/Clinical References		339
History, Sociology, Cultural References		345
Endnotes		367

Credits & Copyright

Second Son: the Man in the Iron Mask

by Sarah B. Madry

COPYRIGHT © 2024 LEGACY SECTOR, AN IMPRINT OF LOCATE PRESS INC.
ISBN: 978-1-998414-00-0

Direct permission requests to info@locatepress.com or mail:
Locate Press, B102 5212 - 48 ST. Suite 126
Red Deer, AB, Canada, T4N 7C3

Editor   Tyler Mitchell
Interior Design   Based on Memoir-LaTeX document class
Cover Design   Tyler Mitchell & Sarah Madry
Publisher Website   http://legacysector.com
Image Sources:

1. Cover - Medal. "Anne d'Autriche, mère de Louis XIV, protectrice du Val-de-Grâce," J. Warin, 1645. Bronze.
2. Cover - Safe. Château de Langeais. J.M. Laugery. Collection de l'Institut de France. 17th century. Wrought iron over wood.
3. Part 1 - "The White Blackbird" - Created by Sarah Madry
4. Part 2 - Detail of the Fouquet heraldic symbol on the Vaux-le-Vicomte cour d'honneur ornamental facade. Photo by the author.
5. Part 3 - Profile image of Emperor Charles V. Daniel Hopfer. 1521? USA National Gallery of Art. Public domain.
6. Part 4 - A bas-relief detail on the cornice of the Hôtel de Beauvais inner courtyard that is perhaps a likeness of Anne of Austria. Photo by the author.

No part of this work may be reproduced or transmitted in any form or by any means, electronic or mechanical, including photocopying, recording, or by any information storage or retrieval system, without the prior written permission of the copyright owner and the publisher.

Acknowledgements

In honor of those who freshen the edges, then bring one side together with the other.

Special thanks to Dr. Stephen Hooper, Ph.D., Chairman of the Department of Allied Health Sciences, School of Medicine, University of North Carolina at Chapel Hill

and

The Craniofacial Center, Adams School of Dentistry, University of North Carolina at Chapel Hill

and

Jesse Coleman, Los Angeles, California, Proof Reader and Editor of this volume

David Anderson, Chapel Hill, North Carolina

Francesca Allegri, Health Sciences Library Head of User Services, University of North Carolina at Chapel Hill

Brigitte APPAVOU, archivist, Centre des Missions Etrangères, Paris, France

Robert BONFILS sj (Societas Jesu), archiviste, Jésuites de la Province de France

Paul Brandes, Ph.D. †

Claire Williams Bridgwater, Ph.D., Research Professor, American University, Washington, D.C., USA

Marilyn A. Cohen, Administrative Director & Patient Care Coordinator Regional Cleft Palate-Craniofacial Program Cooper University Hospital

Dr. Carole Crumley, Ph.D., Professor Emeritus, University of North Carolina at Chapel Hill

Court Cutting, M.D., Professor of Plastic Surgery, New York University Medical Center

Elise DUTRAY-LECOIN, Co-commissaire de l'exposition "L'Enfer des vivants, 2010, Bibliothèque de l'Arsenal, Paris

Jean-Luc DAUPHIN, Amis du Vieux Villeneuve-sur-Yonne †, Bourgogne-Franche-Comté

Marie-Pierre DEMARCQ, Bibliothécaire, Service Recherche, Musée Marine, Paris

Patrice DE VOGÜÉ, Vaux-le-Vicomte, Maincy, Seine-et-Marne

Alexis DONETZKOFF, Conservateur du patrimoine, Archives départementales du Nord, Lille, France

Joëlle DUCOS, Professeur de linguistique et de philologie médiévale, Sorbonne Université, Paris, France

Aurélia DUPLAN, Directrice Bibliothèque Municipale, Montbrison (Loire)

James P. Evans M.D., Ph.D., Bryson Distinguished Professor of Genetics and Medicine, Department of Genetics, School of Medicine, University of North Carolina at Chapel Hill

Georges FETERMAN, Président de l'association ARBRES, Associate Professor of Natural Sciences, Université Paris 8, Vincennes-Saint-Denis, France

Madame Nathalie GAUT, Chapel Hill, North Carolina

Madame Sophie GUET, Hôtel Demoret, Moulins, France

Frédérique HAMM, Director Archives départementales du Loiret, Orléans, France

François JACOB, Institut et Musée Voltaire, Genève

Dr. Elizabeth Anne Jones Ph.D., University of North Carolina at Chapel Hill

Lucretia Kinney, Ph.D., Carrboro, North Carolina

Maarten H. D. LARMUSEAU, Ph.D., Professor of Human Genetic Genealogy at University of Leuven, Belgium

Joanne LAUZON, Bibliothécaire, Direction de la Collection nationale et des services spécialisés, Bibliothèque et Archives nationales du Québec

Christophe LEBLAN, archivist, Beauvais, France

Jean-Luc LESERVOISIER, Emeritus, Conservateur des manuscrits du Mont Saint-Michel et responsable du Fonds ancien, Avranches, France

Nicolas LE TUTOUR, Brittany, France

Professor Donatello LIPPI, Ph.D., University of Florence Faculty of Medicine

Daniel MARTIGNY, Historien, Départment de l'Oise

Cybelle H. McFadden. Ph.D., Associate Professor of French and Francophone Studies, University of North Carolina at Greensboro

Stéphane MALTÈRE, Ph.D., Professor of Modern Letters, University of Clermont-Ferrand, France

Samantha Meltzer-Brody, M.D., M.P.H., Director, UNC Perinatal Psychiatry Program, UNC Center for Women's Mood Disorders, Chapel Hill

Sébastien NADIRAS, Centre d'Onomastique, Centre d'accueil et de recherche des Archives Nationales (CARAN,) Paris, France

Dr. Joe Pelton and Dr. Eloise Pelton, Arlington, Virginia, USA

Sophie PIERRESTÉGUY, Département des patrimoines culturels, Direction générale – AP-HP

Tatiana PUTILINA, Paris, France

Jean-Manuel RIEU and Véronique RIEU, Paris, France

Madame Claudine RIEU, Paris, France †

François ROGNON, Musée–Archives, Bibliothèque, Grande Loge de France

M. Bruno ROLLET, Archives départementales de Seine-et-Marne

Clotilde ROMET, Directrice des Archives départementales de l'Oise

Clément SAVAYR et Lucile VILLEY, Secrétariat administratif Saint-Sulpice, Paris, France

Roland SEENÉ and Anne LEJEUNE, Archives départementales de la Somme, Amiens, France

Dr. Nancy L. Segal, Ph.D., Professor of Psychology and Director, Twin Studies Center, California State University, Fullerton, C.A.

Daniel L. Smith, J.D., Special Collections Librarian, Health Sciences Library, University of North Carolina at Chapel Hill

Jay M. Smith, Ph.D., Professor of History, Department of History, University of North Carolina at Chapel Hill

Dr. Margot Stein, Ph.D., Adams School of Dentistry, University of North Carolina at Chapel Hill

Ruud Stelten, Archaeologist and Interim Director, Saint Eustatius Center for Archaeological Research, Saint Eustatius, Caribbean Netherlands

Brigitte TAILLIEZ, Historienne et anciennement documentaliste au musée du Louvre

Dr. Jenny VAN DONGEN, Ph.D., Department of Biological Psychology, Vrije Universiteit Amsterdam, The Netherlands

Michael Venutolo-Mantovani, Chapel Hill, North Carolina

Olivier VERMESCH, Administrateur de la SDHA (Société Dunquerquoise d'histoire et de archéologie)

Jean-François VINCENT, Bibliothèque Universitaire de Médicine (BIUM), Service d'histoire de la médecine.

Jean-Louis VINCENT, Curé de la paroisse Saint Austremoine au pays d'Issoire

Valentine WEISS, Conservateur du Centre de Topographie, CARAN, Paris, France

Professor Bailey K. Young, Ph.D., Distinguished History Professor Emeritus, Eastern Illinois University

Dr. David Zajac, M.A., Ph.D., Adams School of Dentistry, University of North Carolina at Chapel Hill

Barry M. Zide, M.D., D.M.D., Professor of Plastic Surgery, NYU Medical. Center, New York, New York

Sarah Zimmerman, Ph.D., Professor of English, Fordham University, New York, New York

I am grateful to the staff of the following libraries who have helped me with my research in France the Bibliothèque Nationale (Paris Mitterand and Richelieu); the Service Historique de la Défense; the Archives de Paris; the Bibliothèque de l'Histoire de Paris; the Bibliothèque Sainte-Geneviève; the Archives des Affaires Etrangères; the Centre d'Accueil et de Recherche des Archives Nationales (CARAN); the Centre des Missions Etrangères; the Centre d'Etudes Supérieures de la Renaissance (Tours); the Archives départementales of the following departments in France: Seine-et-Marne, Loiret, Somme, Pas-de-Calais, Oise, and Nord; the Saint Eustatius Center for Archaeological Research in Saint Eustatius in the Caribbean Netherlands; and the Bibliothèque et Archives Nationales du Québec.

Introduction – The Case For The Panoramic View

> Reading these perfectly authentic documents conserved in the archives, one has the disagreeable impression that one is in the bottom of a basket of crabs. But these crabs are those that made the grandeur of France which we proudly show to school children and attendees of the greatest lycées of France as our noble French patrimony.
>
> —Jean Markale

Register Of Death And Burial Of Eustache Dauger From The Parish Church Records Of Saint Paul, Rue Saint-Paul, Paris:[1]

> On November 19, Marchiali, about forty-five years of age, died in the Bastille; his body was buried in the parish of Saint-Paul, his parish, the 20th of that month in the presence of Mr. Rosarges, major of the Bastille, and Mr. Reilh, surgeon.[2]

Report Of The Longtime Prisoner's Death Entered Into The Bastille Prison Official Roster of Prisoners By The Lieutenant Of The Bastille, Etienne Du Junca:

> This same day — Monday the 19th of November 1703 — the unknown prisoner, always masked with a black velvet mask that Monsieur de Saint-Mars, governor, had brought with him from the St Marguerte islands, that he had guarded for a long time; who had felt a little sick yesterday when he left mass, died today at ten in the evening, without any warning signs — the event could not have been slighter. Monsieur Girault, our almoner, who confessed him yesterday and who was taken by surprise by his death, did not get the sacraments to him in time but exhorted him a moment before he died and this unknown prisoner guarded for such a long time was buried on Tuesday at four in the afternoon—the 20th—November in the Saint Paul cemetery,

our parish. On the mortuary register they wrote an unknown name and Monsieur de Rosarges and an old surgeon signed the register.

I learned since that the name placed on the register was Monsieur de Maresiel[3] and that 40 *livres* were paid for the burial.[4]

It was reported by a great nephew of Saint-Mars that acid was poured on the face of the decedent before he was abandoned in the trench of layered corpses that was currently open in the Saint-Paul cemetery. He had not appeared outside of his cell in the last years of his life without his black mask. Acid was the final mask that he wore into eternity.

A Jesuit priest named Henri Griffet (1698–1771), the Bastille's almoner and confessor from 1745 to 1764, became interested in the mysterious prisoner whose story he had heard from guards and officers who were always ready to talk about the masked prisoner of forty years ago. On Tuesday, February 19, 1750, Griffet went a few blocks down the rue Saint-Antoine from the Bastille to enquire at the Saint-Paul church about the prisoner's death certificate created in November 1703. He saw the certificate and asked the vicar, named Poitevin, to make him a copy. In 1769 Griffet published a book in Brussels in which he gave the contents of the death certificate and also the comments written in a journal about the prisoner's death by the lieutenant in charge of keeping the records of prisoners, Etienne du Junca, that Griffet had access to because he was an employee of the prison. In du Junca's description Griffet learned the moment of death, the premonition of it by a slight malaise the day before, and the embarrassed *nota* that the prison chaplain did not arrive in time to give the expiring prisoner the sacraments, a serious diversion from the way things should have gone, according to strict Catholic rules about deathbed rites. In 1850 a historian named Marius Topin (1838–1895) located the certificate in the archives of the Paris City Hall and paraphrased it in his book on the Mask.[5]

The original death certificate was unfortunately burned in 1871 with thousands of other birth, death, and marriage records when the Commune of Paris, a rabid group of insurrectionists if there ever was one, set fire to the City Hall, the Tuileries palace, the Sainte-Chapelle, Notre Dame cathedral, and many other monuments.

These two photos were taken from the same geographic coordinates. The French verity, "*Plus ça change, plus c'est la même chose*" describes the history of the entrance to the cemetery.

Introduction – The Case For The Panoramic View

Figure 1: At left, entrance to the public playground built over the Saint-Paul cemetery. Photo by the author, 2012. At right, photo of the entrance and gate to the cemetery in 1912 just before the cemetery was destroyed. Attribution: Jean Bary mort depuis plus de 70 ans, CC BY-SA 4.0, via Wikimedia Commons.

I Go Down The Passage Saint-Pierre

In 2008, in the French history stacks of my university library I saw on the spine of a book *The Man in the Iron Mask*. Similarly to many other scholars, military officers, historians, playwrights, filmmakers, and amateurs before me, I found that the mystery was a velcro gold coin that could not be put down.

After reading one book on the Mask, I proceeded to read all that my library had on the subject. I continued to find other books[6] in online stores and read them too. Each time I opened the first page, I hoped that this author had answered at least one of three critical questions: what was the Man in the Iron Mask doing from his birth until the end of July 1669 when he was arrested by King Louis XIV?; why did he wear a mask over the top of his face?; why did the king of France arrest him and keep him in prison for thirty-four years until his death in 1703?

I considered the events of this man's incarceration as they related to signal events in the lives of a small number of people who have traditionally been considered candidates for the Mask and concurred with the decision of twentieth-century researchers that, out of the more than twenty candidates that historians examined, the prisoner named Eustache Dauger was the Man in the Iron Mask. I studied the facts of Dauger's arrest and imprisonment, excerpts of important letters between his jailers, the few physical descriptions that exist, and the many reports about him from scoundrels and saints, purported first-hand witnesses, and third-hand reporters.

Soon, reading library books was not enough. I went to France to read some of the archival material on the life of the Man in the Iron Mask held in the National Library of France, the Archives of the Ministry of Exterior Relations, the Archives of the Ministry of Defense, the Archives of Paris, the Library of the History of Paris, the Sainte-Geneviève library, and the National Archives of France, as well as some French departmental archives. My first research trip was 2010 was just after Professor Michel Vergé-Franceschi had published a new book on the Mask mystery and I was impatient to get a copy. In a bookstore on the rue Saint-Antoine near the *Masque de fer*'s burial place I asked a saleswoman if they had a copy of the professor's book. *Madame* could see I was a foreigner and possibly did not understand I was in a bookstore where only new books were sold. "We don't sell *livres d'occasion* (used books) here, *Madame*," she told me. I did not know what "*livres d'occasion*" meant, so, not wanting to enter into a discussion with her that I would certainly not understand any better than "*livres d'occasion*" I mumbled, yes, sorry, and left the shop. I mention this only to show immediately that this mystery is, in many peoples' minds, even French booksellers' minds, a very old story that was solved a long time ago as unsolvable, and despite her shop being across the street from the Mask's graveyard and a few blocks from the marker of the destroyed Bastille prison where he died in 1703, she had no interest in a new book about it. I finally got up the courage in another bookstore to ask for the book and buy it.

I respect and admire the authors who have applied themselves to this mystery. The past two centuries have seen thorough research and posing of possible candidates by *Père* Griffet, Théodore Iung, Frantz Funck-Brentano, Roger McDonald, John Noone, Marcel Pagnol, Jules Loiseleur, Jean Luizet, Gaston Rohn, Jean-Christian Petitfils, Roux Fazillac, Marius Topin, Maurice Duvivier, Georges Mongrédien, Jean-Etienne Riga, Madeleine Tiollais, Marie-Madeleine Mast, Michel Vergé-Franceschi, and Paul Sonnino, to name only a few of the authors of the ninety-two titles that one gets when "*masque de fer*" is entered for a search in the Bibliothèque Nationale general catalog. They all chose a candidate that they thought identified a man whose name was not spoken, whose furniture and belongings were burned immediately after his death at the same time that the floor tiles of his room were removed and the walls were debrided to make sure no written message was hidden, whose face was perhaps dissolved with acid in his grave, whose death certificate signed in the church of Saint-Paul[7] just off the rue Saint-Antoine bore a false name and age, who had no family, no friends, no mourners.

Second Son has found some solutions and posed some theories that have never been proposed because historians that have written on this subject have never thought carefully about some descriptions given by first-hand witnesses of Dauger that, if followed, lead to a medical diagnosis. This book is medical sleuthing in search of a solution to an important French mystery on a background of seventeenth-century France and the courts of Louis

XIII, Anne of Austria, and Louis XIV, especially their cultural and religious rules. No investigator had ever pinned up a map of seventeenth-century historical events and cultural practices side by side with a map of Eustache Dauger's mystery. The crossroads between Dauger and the political events of Louis XIV's reign had been somewhat explored, but where were the links between Dauger and the social expectations and prejudices of France in the seventeenth century?

My search for new information about the identity and life of the Man in the Iron Mask became a fifteen-year research project using French archival primary and secondary sources, fieldwork in France, and, in a dramatically different approach from the entire previous body of writing on the mystery, personal consultation with geneticists and craniofacial specialists at major universities in the United States, France, and Belgium. This book is not a typical entry on the long list of books on the Mask because to attempt to "find" Dauger I have made a cross-disciplinary examination of the influencing factors of culture, history, religion, medicine, and recent scientific discoveries in genetics. That has never been done before.

The first chapters of this book describe Louis XIV's arrest of Dauger and give the testimonies of a very small number of people who saw him or had interactions with him. Chapters then begin to describe his life in prison and the lives of people who had control over him; a theory that he had a craniofacial birth defect is presented and supported by clinical texts. In the closing chapters Madame de Sévigné gives clues to Dauger's location before he was arrested in a *jeu des portraits*, a word game like those that were so popular in upper class social circles of the seventeenth century.

I Walked On The Parquet Floor

In *Ancien Régime* France, when Parlement met in the Gran'Chambre (omission of the "d" is traditional) overlooking the Seine where it decided judicial cases, only the king and the highest ranking dukes were allowed to cross the parquet floor obliquely; all others had to walk around the square perimeter of the sides of the room, treading on the corners. I took this strict rule as an ideal for my research. I did not believe what I read until I had walked around the edges more than once and stalked the mystery using archival documentation. I agree with Harry Thompson who said in his book on the Mask, "...it is a story that requires careful historical consideration, because some famous reputations are at stake."[8]

The story of the Man in the Iron Mask is a cold case mystery about a mysterious person and his relationship to seventeenth-century France's royal family. It is in some ways a missing person's story, because Louis XIV did all he could to erase the man he arrested at Calais in 1669; his background, appearance, and his name.

There are some cautions that usually apply in detective work that I followed.

First, I kept in mind that the mystery is about secrets held by very important, rich, powerful people. I read their actions as indicators, as texts that I had to be astute enough to parse, keeping to the testimonies left to us by first- or reliable second-hand witnesses.

I kept watch for any evidence or testimony that sounded too good to be true. I ignored testimony that I deemed deficient. I paid attention to what was being left out...to what did *not* happen when the situation required it. Very few people knew the whole truth about Eustache Dauger. There were many who thought they knew the truth, many who made up truth, who exaggerated truth, who twisted truth, who misunderstood truth. If I was told Monsieur de X knew the truth or the comte de Y knew the result, I was careful and suspicious. I reserved judgment.

Using inference from the actions of the characters in this drama to make decisions about them was not a reliable tactic. "If she did this, she must have thought that," or "If he said this, he must have been there." Our present irritations, fears, and remedies may not have been those that affected the actions of people in past centuries and I could not ascribe to them the solutions we would use today without looking carefully at context. Therefore inferring anything about Eustache Dauger was not a smart way to know him, at least until I had a very broad understanding of his actions, of the people who directed his fate, put these into the time zone in which he lived, and put a stern check on my desire for quick judgements.

Conjecture, in some parts of this mystery, is necessary, because the mystery is very old, has hundreds of books (almost all in French) in its library, has its own authors who had their own guesses and theories, and as any detective must, those must be listed, judged anew, and added to with new information. And the next writer on the Mask will build on that. However the history of seventeenth-century cultural rules, which I have shown give evidence to Dauger's history and position, are not conjecture, or at least they are conjecture that has been studied by scholars over hundreds of years.

During my research, as I began to learn more about how Dauger was arrested, the character of his chief jailer Saint-Mars, and his experiences in four different prisons, I had an increasingly uncomfortable suspicion that one question had not been addressed at all by past authors and it was the most important question; *why* did Louis XIV put the man in prison in such secure conditions for his entire lifetime? Why didn't he kill him? Because he stayed with Saint-Mars in super cells made just for him until his death means there was a taboo against killing him. What was the reason for the intense scrutiny that was given to the prisoner by the king's most servile and damned minister of state, the marquis de Louvois? In the final chapters of the book I try to make some sense out of the extremely secure incarceration of a man described as quiet and devout. He must have had a relationship with the king or have had importance to the king and I present an extraordinary explanation of what that link might have been. The path of investigation I chose to follow was the name of the prisoner: Eustache Dauger. I could make a case for anthroponomastics, the study of personal names, as the key to this mystery. Testimonials of contemporaries almost all say that a hallmark of all records and memories of the masked prisoner was that his name was non-existant, was unspeakable... a voicing of it would be followed by quick death. His name, Eustache Dauger, was, for Louis XIV, equivalent to the cryptic pronouncements of the Oracle of Delphi in ancient Greece; to hear her and then interpret her could lead to death or worse: humiliation, decline, removal from memory, the advent of darkness. The king did not want anyone to hear the Oracle. Names of people, both first names (*prénoms*) and last names (*noms de famille*) in old French texts were spelled differently from day to day. In an age where adding or omitting letters and apostrophes in people's names was not a *faute*, the essential requirement being that the agglomeration of letters and context should label the person even if the spelling varied in documents, mistakes often happened. Spelling of names proved to be both a help and hindrance in deciphering the Mask's story.

I did not intend to hear the Oracle, and I resisted hearing it for a while because this would be a simpler story if it was just about Eustache Dauger's identity, but I could not avoid a creeping suspicion that the underlying mystery was about Louis XIV's identity. The evidence was *incontournable*, a rhapsodical French word meaning something one can't turn away from. It describes why Louis XIV's extreme solution was his only choice and why he did not, could not, kill Eustache Dauger.

From three hundred years' distance, the well managed silence imposed by the people in charge of the prisoner—organized, purposeful, intentional silence— is still in command. It is the object of this book to take the rod of governance out of the fist of Louis XIV and give it to the reader and those who will continue to study this mystery in the future. I have tried to resist approximations and guesses. But until we find reliable documentation of Eustache Dauger's life before he was imprisoned, we must either guess or stay silent, and once the story of the Man in the Iron Mask enters consciousness, we are compelled to do the first and are quite unable to do the second.

Part 1

THE WHITE BLACKBIRD

1. The Arrest Of Eustache Dauger

"But I doubt we will ever get to the bottom of this mystery: it was so deftly, so insidiously and so jealously contrived."
—Maurice Duvivier, Le Masque de fer

A Crowned King Signs A Warrant For The Arrest Of The Man In The Iron Mask

In the center of Paris next to the central food market in the summer of 1669, stonemasons destroyed the south stone arcaded wall of the largest public cemetery in Paris, the Cemetery of the *Saints-Innocents*,[9] to make way for a road widening, and with each strike of the hammer, pieces of a mural that had been painted on that wall in 1425 crumbled and fell in chunks on the floor of the old covered walk, above which, as on the other three sides of the cemetery, was an attic stacked tightly with bones of previous residents of the cemetery, who, after the cemetery staff guessed that they had been in the ground long enough, had been disinterred, any remaining flesh burned off, and the cleaned bones artfully placed in the unwalled gabled attic, the permanent depository of the dead, open to the air and the eye, numbering in the hundreds neatly beside and on top of other deceased inhabitants of Paris. The creative arrangement of the bones had long been a tourist attraction. Cemetery ground was limited in Paris and so continual reuse of the precious square meters of cemetery dirt was a regular practice for almost all cemeteries. The cadavers, usually in shrouds, not in caskets, which were an expensive luxury, were in the ground only as long as the worms took to clean them, and then it was time for someone else's wife or child to undergo a temporary earthly dunking. This practice made room for the recently dead.

The mural's[10] subject was the *Dance of the Dead* (*La Danse Macabre*), which consisted of poems and pictures having to do with death.[11] The people who came to see the bones in the attic of the arcades also spent time looking at the mural cartoons and reading the cautionary poems.

Saints-Innocents cemetery was ancient, revered, and had a *cachet*: the dirt, all 7,000 meters squared of it, was believed to have been transported from the Holy Land because it could consume a body within nine days. (It might have seemed more in line with Biblical teaching about immortality in the Holy Land to arrange the myth to be that bodies wouldn't decay at all in Jerusalem dirt, but that wouldn't have fit the purpose of the cemetery, so we'll leave it the way the Parisians had it.) By the end of the seventeenth century the cost of a burial in a *Saints-Innocents charnier* (a little more costly than the interior field), was 18 livres.[12]

Figure 1.1: Charnier at Saints Innocents Cemetery. The cartoons of the *Danse Macabre* can be seen through the open arcades. 1424-1425. Theodor Josef Hubert Hoffbauer (1839-1922). Creation date unknown. Public domain. Wikipedia.

The removal of the ten arcades of burials and their crown of stored bones was to make way for an enlargement of the rue de la Ferronnerie, then approximately thirteen feet (four meters) wide, that ran parallel to the cemetery to its south. King Henri IV (1553–1610),[13] the first Bourbon king of France, was assassinated in the rue de la Ferronnerie on May 14, 1610, because the busy street was very narrow. A traffic jam forced the king's carriage to halt in the street, and a religious fanatic named Ravaillac, who had been following him, put a knife through Henri twice, stepping up on the

CHAPTER 1. THE ARREST OF EUSTACHE DAUGER

running board on the outside of the carriage and striking the king through the open window, so that the comrades of the king in the carriage were unaware of what had happened until blood began running out of Henri's mouth. The widening of the rue de la Ferronnerie, despite a regicide having taken place there due to its small breadth, made 1669 the year of the fix, fifty-nine years after Ravaillac's crime and punishment.[14]

The *Saints-Innocents*, perhaps annoyed by their famous mural being scratched to the ground, gave posterity a tenacious mystery on the summer day of July 28, 1669; one could speculate, if unearthly decisions can be accepted to have bearing on historical certainties, that they pronounced a curse on the Bourbon family, because that was the day that Henri IV's grandson, Louis XIV, signed an arrest warrant for Eustache Dauger.

There was a warning on the *Danse Macabre* that was addressed to any and every king but possibly it was appropriate particularly for King Louis XIV. On a central panel, Death's skeleton, seizing the king's ermine mantle and pushing him with his knee from behind, said to the king:

> Come to me crowned king Renowned for force and power. In the past you lived With pagentry and great nobles. But now all your glory Disappears/ you will not be alone. Of those with you now The richest will have only a shroud.[15]

My Approach To The Investigation

There are four bases that have supported my study of Eustache Dauger:

First, a good detective will start investigation of a crime by reviewing all the facts that have been found and verified up to the present. In this chapter the official and respected documents of the historical record about Eustache Dauger's arrest and life in prison will be examined, as all other books on the Mask have done, because in order to understand any theory about who he was and what he represented to King Louis XIV, the chronology of his prison life and comments by his jailers have to be known... one cannot play chess without knowing where all the pieces are... what the *Père* Griffet, one of the first investigators of the mystery, called the "traditions," such as the dates of his imprisonment, his companionship of Nicolas Fouquet in Pignerol, and the text of Louis XIV's *lettre de cachet* ordering his arrest.

Second, based on the belief that any story, especially one as complicated as this one, must be viewed in the framework of the society in which the story takes place, the political, religious, and military constructions in that society, I set out to see what I could find in French seventeenth-century history that might bear on the motive of Louis XIV to permanently imprison a quiet, hitherto unknown, pious bookworm; more specifically, what were the predominant economic, social, and political movements and habits of early seventeenth-century Europe? I committed myself to volume after volume of seventeenth-century history to see what was trending, as we say today, in the broadest sense: the Thirty Years War, the War of the Spanish Devolution, the Peace of Westphalia, the Treaty of Aix-la-Chapelle, the territorial ambitions of Spain and France, the Spanish and Austrian Habsburgs, the Counter-Reformation, Jansenism, the Jesuits, the *dévots*,[16] the convents, the prisons, Cardinal Richelieu, Louis XIII and his wife and queen, Anne of Austria, Louis XIV and his brother Philippe, Cardinal Mazarin, Louis XIV's disgraced minister of finance Nicolas Fouquet, the new *salon* culture, the court and administrators of Louis XIV, the Fronde and other French rebellions, the colonial and financial opportunities available in the New World, the decline of feudalism, the rise of Dutch economic ventures and the French hatred of Dutch smarts and their industry, pirates, alchemy, poisoning scandals, cultural influences from Italy, and the maneuvering for control of the Alpine passes from Brussels to Milan by the French, the Spanish, the Habsburgs, the Germans, the Swiss, the Savoyards, and the Italians.

Third, I used modern medical and genetic science, some of which has only recently been published, to support explanations of mood, health, and difficult behavior that some of the characters display.

Fourth, I looked at a much larger universe of cultural, political, and societal norms of the seventeenth century than previous Mask authors, particularly the treatment of marginalized people, such as prisoners, orphans, and people with physical abnormalities. My aim in surveying these large areas of human life and business was to create a comprehensive background for Dauger's life, in part to compensate for the paucity of factual information we have about him, especially during the first half of his life before arrest.

Does Eustache Dauger's story have anything to tell us about the change that took place between 1550 and 1650 in the way people thought about their families, about war, about their allegiances? Dauger was arrested in 1669. Was his arrest the moment that the Modern Age began? Or would that go too far? I rephrase that question. Does Eustache Dauger have anything to do with modernity? Better...does Eustache Dauger have anything to do with us?

CHAPTER 1. THE ARREST OF EUSTACHE DAUGER

Dauger Became A Symbol Of Despotism After The French Revolution

When Henri IV was assassinated by a religious fanatic in 1610, France went into deep mourning. He had been loved, at least by the people who believed his conversion from Protestantism to Catholicism was real, and admired for his daring and successful military and civic leadership, his program to bring manufacturing to France and restore her financial stability after years of civil religious wars fought over whether Christ wore red or brown. He was called *Henri le Grand*. But the following reigns of Louis XIII, Louis XIV, Louis XV, and Louis XVI produced wars, debt, and procrastination about bettering the lives of the Third Estate, i.e. the people who paid taxes whereas the first two estates, the church and the nobles, did not. The taxpayers were poor, often hungry, were threatened with arbitrary imprisonment for slight offenses, and strangled by political and financial bureaucracies that had become hopelessly frozen.

By 1789, the first year of the French Revolution, the Man in the Iron Mask had become a symbol of the old regime's secrecy and blunt force. The absence of any crime ever recorded for him made the Mask the ultimate representative of the unfairly imprisoned French citizen. Unfair imprisonment—being denied freedom while living in somber and dangerous conditions when you have not committed a crime is a fearful horror. Maybe it is for this reason that the story of the Man in the Iron Mask refuses to submerge. It rises above whatever is put on top of it: fire, water, smoke, floor tiles, ceiling plaster, velvet masks, lies, darkness, iron, acid, bones, earth. The *Masque de fer* still whispers a soft plea for justice denied for three hundred years.

When an angry gang of rioters broke into the Bastille prison on July 14, 1789 after months of increasing political and economic tensions in Paris, one of the secrets they wanted to expose first was the identity of the Man in the Iron Mask. Facts about the Mask's life before he was arrested in late July 1669 are not known. This lack of information is due partially to the order of Louis XIV that neither the prisoner nor anyone should speak about his life or his name on pain of death, a rule that was as vital in 1703 when the prisoner died as it had been in 1669. No one knew the names of the masked prisoner's parents, where or when he was born, where he lived before his arrest, if he was ever married, if he ever owned property, why he was arrested, why he was never released, but, exactly because of these unknowns, former prisoners and Bastille staff had kept his memory alive by telling each other their memories of the prisoner or repeating the memories of others who had spent time in the Bastille. The whispers had reached the general population.

Simon Schama, historian of the French Revolution, said that by 1789 the hated Bastille had accumulated a mix of true and imagined history:

> Such was the symbolic power of the Bastille to gather to itself all the miseries for which 'despotism' was now held accountable, that reality was enhanced by Gothic fantasies as the building was ransacked. Ancient pieces of armor were declared to be fiendish 'iron corsets' applied to constrict the victim and a toothed machine that was part of a printing press was said to be a wheel of torture. Countless prints from the workshops of the rue Saint-Jacques, which had cranked up their production to service the acute hunger for news, supplied suitably horrible imagery, featuring standing skeletons, instruments of torture and men in iron masks.[17]

A 2010 exhibition on the Bastille's history at the Arsenal library in Paris acknowledged this fact. From the exhibition catalog: "[The story] furnished the plot of an adventure novel. So many speculations over the years made the prisoner "*au Masque de fer*" a true symbol of the secret state, which functioned by imprisoning in the Bastille those who opposed it."[18]

The hooligans who barged into the Bastille central records office were not accountants. They knew nothing of spreadsheets or notarial stamps of approval. They were people who suddenly had a vision of something that they had been forbidden to see for a very long time, a view into a secret garden; they were not respectful, they proceeded to tear down what they had been denied.

By evening they had killed the governor of the prison (Bernard René Jourdan de Launay, 1740–1789), who had been pursued to the city hall, and also the Prévôt des Marchands, Flesselles. The invaders suffered 98 dead and 73 wounded.[19] While the governor's head was being pumped up in the air on a long pike at the head of a band of joyous rioters in procession down the rue Saint-Antoine, a few of the newcomers had stepped over the bodies of three murdered soldiers, found the interior interrogation room, and began throwing fistfuls of prisoner and administrative records into the moat below the lowest cells, the *cachots*. Into the moat also went archives that had been stored at the Bastille: records of the Paris lieutenant general of police and all the transcripts of the secret royal trials of special importance to kings of France.[20] Those who pitched the records to the breeze must have had a wonderful thrill to see them fan and flutter to the ground. Anger was the primary emotion that day and so the impulse was to destroy the records of the prison which was a symbol of their hardships; for four hundred years the Bastille's eight towers, their walls ten feet thick and over seventy-eight

CHAPTER 1. THE ARREST OF EUSTACHE DAUGER

feet high, had stood on the east edge of the city, its soldiers on the top parapet that connected the dark cylinders, looking down every minute of each day at every man, cart, and beast below that drove both into and out of the Saint-Antoine arched, stone city gate below the northern-most tower of the Bastille, where the road went toward Melun, Charonne, Saint-Maur and farther to Flanders.

But the leaders of the new government thought saving the registers of the inmates would serve better than mayhem to break down the wall of secrecy that had been dividing the people from their human rights. Telling the former prisoners' stories would honor them and some mysteries might be solved. On that first day restraint was impossible—tempers were too hot.[21] Almost immediately, calmer heads prevailed and ordered that these muddied papers be retrieved and put with the records that had not been ditched. These were soon turned over to editors assigned to put them in order. Some bonfires on the evening of the 14 July probably ate a good bit of Bastille history, but there was enough left to form a multi-volume work by the reviewers.

Figure 1.2: Model of the Bastille on display at the Museum of the History of Paris. Photo by the author.

Monsieur Pierre-Hubert Charpentier was appointed within days of the riot to publish the Bastille records, and he did so in stages, a work eventually called *La Bastille devoilée* (*The Bastille revealed*) with co-author Louis-Pierre Manuel (1751–1793). The authors listed and described the prisoners who had been in the Bastille, including the mysterious, masked prisoner.

The appointees of the new government, Monsieurs Charpentier and Manuel, did the logical thing one would do if one were searching for information on former Bastille prisoners: they went to the *Great Register* of the Bastille that was the official record of prisoners with details relating to their imprisonment, which luckily was not lost during the riot. The book was enclosed in a locked briefcase of red Morocco leather with the word "Bastille" embossed in gold on the front and an engraving of the arms of the king on the back. There were 280 pages. Inside the book the data on the prisoners were recorded in spreadsheets each having eleven columns and row after row of prisoners. Here is what was written at the top of each column:[22]

1. Names and social rank of the prisoners
2. Date of their entrance
3. Names of the Secretaries of State who co-signed the orders
4. Volumes
5. Pages
6. Date of end of detention
7. Volumes
8. Pages
9. Reason for detention
10. Observations
11. Notes

When Charpentier and Manuel examined the *Great Register* they found that the page that would have had the record of the Mask's entry to the Bastille and the record of his death in 1703 was missing.

What We Know About Eustache Dauger And His Life

Dauger's life before he was arrested is a mystery, but as to his life *after* he was arrested near Calais[23] in July 1669 we have archival documents and testimonies that describe the prisoner quite well; these sources tell about his jailers' relationships with him, what his life was like in prison, and how he sustained thirty-four years of imprisonment. We must, to use an astronomical simile, study him as if he were a stellar black hole whose size and character is mostly known by the signals around him. We have: his arrest warrant signed by Louis XIV and the king's most trusted aide, Minister of War Michel Le Tellier; some reports from a few people who claim to have seen the man or heard his voice; a few mentions of him in memoirs; two full pages of descriptive journal entries written by the military officer who reg-

CHAPTER 1. THE ARREST OF EUSTACHE DAUGER

istered his entrance and death at the Bastille; a copy of his death certificate; and some letters about the rules he had to follow and the special security procedures and cells that were created especially for him in all the prisons in which he lived. This particular man had no birth certificate or at least no record of his birth has ever been found, despite the fact that baptizing a child was a legal and moral duty for parents and in the absence of parents, for the person who assisted the birth or found the child abandoned. In France at that time, or at any time, only family members with power to deviate from staunchly held religious and legal practices would have been able to eliminate, steal, or avoid records of a birth and baptism. Some logical reasons that could explain the inability to find the birth certificate are: if he was born in Paris, his baptismal records could have been destroyed when the city hall was set on fire by rioters in 1871, and if he was born in the area where he was arrested, near Calais, his documents could have been lost on the *jour de débarquage*, D-Day, June 6, 1944, the day the World War II American invasion of France started when forty-five percent of the archives of the department of *La Manche* were destroyed by bombs dropped by the Americans. In any case, we don't have a record of his birth.

The difficulty in describing the prisoner's life and character can be pictured by the metaphor that Madame de Sévigné (1626–1696),[24] one of France's great letter writers and contemporary of Louis XIV, used in one of her letters to her daughter on October 18, 1671, when describing a remote memory: her thoughts, she said, were similar to "*la mousse*," the Celtic, folkloric, undefined spirit of the ethereal air that bears down upon the Brittany coast and passes into its interior. This unquiet, drenched white air, like foam, appeared to her one night while she was walking in her own woods at her property in Brittany, *Les Rochers*.

> But I come back to your story. I made fun of the tale of La Mousse[25] but I'm not joking about this one. You told it so well, that indeed I shivered when I read it. This Auger, in fact, is a boy that I have seen and talked to and he naively told this same story to me. There can be no mistake about it; it was a spirit, I am sure.[26]

An Arrest In Calais

On July 28, 1669, Louis XIV (1638–1715) was in residence at Saint-Germain-en-Laye near Paris, principal palace of the king.[27] It was Sunday. At some point between the chanted mass in the morning and the late afternoon Adoration of the Holy Sacrament,[28] the king asked his oldest and most trusted advisor, the minister of war since 1643, Michel Le Tellier, a seasoned operative who was the holder of many secrets in the king's mother's regency, to come to his private chamber to do him a favor: co-sign a *lettre de cachet*, a letter from the king that ordered the arrest of a man in Calais.

Figure 1.3: Michel Le Tellier (1603–1685). Father of the marquis de Louvois. Minister for War and Chancellor of France in Louis XIV's early reign. Co-signer of the arrest warrant for Eustache Dauger. Photo of a bust of Michel Le Tellier in the Bibliothèque Sainte-Geneviève, Paris, by the author 2022.

The warrant was addressed to Captain Alexandre de Vauroy (d. 1703), the sergent-major of the port town and citadel of Dunkirk, very near Calais. Louis XIV ordered Vauroy to arrest Eustache Dauger and take him under guard to the prison of Pignerol (Pinerolo, Italy, then controlled by France) located within the citadel of Pignerol in the Alps near Turin (Torino, Italy). The king demanded that Vauroy return to Saint-Germain afterwards and relate to him what had occurred on the trip and how the transfer to Saint-Mars had gone, then he could return to Dunkirk.

The Arrest Warrant

The official *lettre de cachet* that Vauroy carried with him to Calais as his authority for arrest, signed by Louis XIV and co-signed by Le Tellier, is today

CHAPTER 1. THE ARREST OF EUSTACHE DAUGER 13

in the French National Archives. In the body of the letter, "Eustache Dauger" is written as the person to be arrested but is in a different handwriting from the rest of the letter indicating that the letter writer and the name writer were two different people.

In addition to the original, a draft of the *lettre de cachet* is today in the archives of the Historical Service of the French Department of Defense.[29] In normal procedures for issuance of orders for arrest, a draft was created, usually by dictation to a secretary, the author would read it, the secretary would rewrite the draft with any changes wanted by the author, put it in an envelope, stamp it with a wax seal, send it off for delivery to the recipient, and the draft was usually kept by the issuing agency to keep a record of the arrest, thus becoming what we might call a copy-to-file. The copy of Eustache Dauger's arrest warrant omits the name "Eustache Dauger" in the sentence that would seem to require it to keep the name from being seen by the secretary.

Here is the translation of Dauger's arrest warrant signed by Louis XIV:

> At Saint-Germain on 28 July 1669
>
> Capp^{ne} de Vauroy, being dissatisfied with the conduct of the man named [blank on the draft and Eustache Dauger on the master], and wishing to take him into my custody, I write you this letter to tell you that as soon as you see this man you will seize him and arrest him and take him yourself under great security to the citadel of Pignerol to be guarded there in the care of Capp^{ne} de Saint-Mars to whom and to the governor [the marquis de Piennes] of the place [town of Pignerol] I write these attached letters, so that the said prisoner is received by him [Saint-Mars] and guarded without difficulty. After which, you will come back to me to describe to me how you have executed my order, having no other business to tell you...[30]

Normally, the Secretary of the House of the King, Jean-Baptiste Colbert (1619–1683), would eventually have seen notice of the arrest because Colbert would have to record the arrest, but Louis XIV must not have wanted the document to be seen by Colbert or by anyone else because notice of the arrest does not appear in any official House of the King register.

One underlying reason for this secretive process was a competition for the favor of the king between Michel Le Tellier and his son the marquis de Louvois, and Colbert. Maybe the king wanted to keep this strictly a Le Tellier business. That would be reasonable, given the jealousy that Louis XIV encouraged between the two families up to Colbert's death in 1683. Or perhaps it was that Louis XIV didn't want *anyone* to know about this arrest. He must have had someone's help to find Dauger, probably Le Tellier's and Louvois' help, and he needed Vauroy to carry out the arrest; it was beneath the king's dignity to arrest people himself. And the chief officer of the prison, the chevalier de Saint-Mars (Bénigne Dauvergne 1626–1708), had to know about the arrest because he received the product of it, but that was Louis' limit for witnesses.

Also on Sunday 28 July 1669, Louis XIV signed a letter addressed to Saint-Mars for Vauroy to deliver when he got to Pignerol with the prisoner. In this letter his majesty told Saint-Mars to prepare a cell for the prisoner named Eustache Dauger (the name was written) and his majesty would, in a separate document, write to the marquis de Piennes, governor of the town of Pignerol, telling Piennes that he should give Saint-Mars whatever help he might need in any matter having to do with this prisoner.

Many of the documents having information about Eustache Dauger are located in the archives of the Ministry of Defense because the functionary who was in charge of overseeing Dauger's incarceration was the minister for war in Louis XIV's regime, the marquis de Louvois, even though Dauger did not have any connection with France's wars or the military.

The official *lettre de cachet* and the letter of instructions from Louis XIV to Saint-Mars, both of which have Eustache Dauger's name written into the text and both signed by Louis XIV, are today in the French National Archives only because Saint-Mars received them at Pignerol, they remained in Saint-Mars' possession with all of his papers relating to his duties in the king's service, and at the time of the French Revolution these were filed in the National Archives with all of the documents having to do with business of the king.[31] Saint-Mars was meticulous about the security of his prisoner and keeping those two documents was true to his nature. He kept them because it was the usual rule to keep the arrest warrants of his prisoners and he fastidiously followed all rules, and that was a quality the king and Louvois liked. Since Saint-Mars had no orders to destroy the letters, it was normal for Saint-Mars to keep them. Maybe it did not occur to the king that these instructions would become part of the official state record. The king's understanding of "fastidious" would have been that the *lettre de cachet* and the letter to Saint-Mars would have been destroyed because they had the name of the prisoner on them but the king and Saint-Mars had different opinions of the name "Eustache Dauger." To Saint-Mars the name was anodine, one more name, one more arrest, but to the king the name must have meant something much more important, and that is proved by the fact that he kept Dauger in prison for the rest of his life. Saint-Mars kept these two documents and other letters from Louvois about the prisoner and

CHAPTER 1. THE ARREST OF EUSTACHE DAUGER

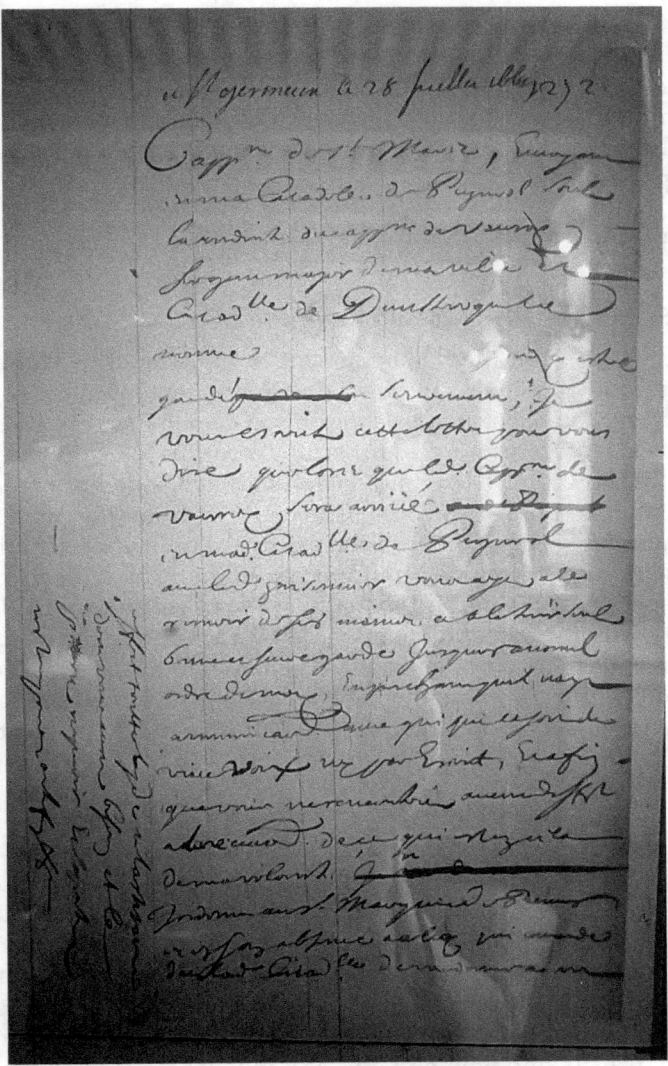

Figure 1.4: Draft of the king's letter to M. de Saint-Mars in the archives of the French Ministry of Defense, Vincennes, written July 28, 1669. The space for the prisoner's name to be written on the final copy is blank in this draft. Image by the author 2015. 1669–Minutes–Juillet–Aoust–Volume. SHD serie A1, vol. 234, f. 272.

no one thought about them again until historians started looking through the old papers of the House of the King and the Ministry of War after the French Revolution. We owe Saint-Mars our gratitude for holding onto the two letters the king signed, one to Vauroy and one to himself, because these documents give us the name of the prisoner and the approximate date of his arrest. Saint-Mars was perhaps proud of possessing personally autographed letters by the king addressed to him. Very rare documents to have. Maybe he considered them to be prized mementos. Louis XIV, however, if he had known these letters with Eustache Dauger's name on them would eventually be high and dry in a box of state papers somewhere, would have had an apoplectic fit.

The letter from the king to Saint-Mars says:

> At Saint-Germain on 28 July 1669
>
> Capp^{ne} de Saint-Mars, having sent to my citadel of Pignerol, under the guard of capp^{ne} [sic] de Vauroy, sergent-major of my town and citadel of Dunkirk, the person named Eustache Dauger to be guarded securely, I am writing you this letter to tell you that when Capp^{ne} de Vauroy arrives at my Citadel of Pignerol with the said prisoner, you will receive him from [the captain's] hands and keep him under good safeguard until you hear otherwise from me, keeping him from communicating with anyone, by speech or writing, and so that you do not encounter any difficulty with the execution of my order, I am ordering the marquis de Piennes [governor general of Pignerol] and, if he be absent, whomever is commanding the citadel, to give you all the assistance you will need and require. And at present having no other business...[32]

Further, Vauroy was ordered by Louis XIV to keep his mission a secret. An accompanying document, written by the marquis de Louvois, was supplied for Vauroy to show to the governor of Dunkirk, Godefroy d'Estrades (1607–1686), giving a false pretense for Vauroy's temporary absence from Dunkirk. The lie to d'Estrades was that Vauroy and his men had been asked by the king to chase down some remnants of the Spanish army loose in the region. The recent War of the Spanish Devolution having just been handily concocted, waged, and won by Louis XIV in what is now the far northeast of France and the western part of Belgium, and boundaries drawn between the French and the Spanish possessions, Louis XIV must have thought that accusing those pesky Spanish of chasing down some of their deserters in his patch of ground was something d'Estrades would accept without question.

> From the marquis de Louvois to Captain Vauroy
>
> At Saint-Germain on 28 July 1669
>
> Monsieur [Vauroy], I've been told that Spanish officers have come into the king's territory to track down deserters from their army.

CHAPTER 1. THE ARREST OF EUSTACHE DAUGER

> They must be stopped from doing this. His Majesty wishes that you capture any officers who are taking or conducting deserters.
>
> Louvois[33]

Louvois also wrote a two-sentence letter to the governor of Dunkirk, d'Estrades, asking him to excuse Vauroy temporarily from his post. He included a copy of the letter he had just written for Vauroy.

> From the marquis de Louvois to the governor d'Estrades
>
> At Saint-Germain on 28 July 1669
>
> Monsieur [d'Estrades], The sieur Vauroy has business that obliges him to be absent. I very humbly ask you to give him leave.
>
> Louvois[34]

This lie to comte Godefroy d'Estrades irritated Marcel Pagnol (1895–1974), member of the French Academy and filmmaker, in his book on the Mask,[35] and I agree with him that it is surprising and egregious given d'Estrades' reputation, rank, and sterling service to the French crown as ambassador to Holland and London and the chief negotiator for the return of Dunkirk to France from England in 1662. The count negotiated the Treaty of Bréda (Breda 1667) with the king of Denmark and the Treaty of Nimègue (Nijmegen 1678) with the Dutch. He was eventually marshal of France in 1675. In his retirement he was a tutor to Louis XIV's nephew, Philippe II d'Orléans. Pagnol wrote, "This faithful servant of the regime certainly had known and kept many political and military secrets much more important than one involving a petty criminal. It would have been logical to write, 'M. de Vauroy is assigned to arrest a criminal and take him to Pignerol, and I beg you to give him leave.'" Pagnol did not understand why an outright lie was told to d'Estrades. Vauroy must have been embarrassed, Pagnol says, to be forced to tell such a lie (*à jouer une comédie humiliante*) to the distinguished man he reported to.[36] The deception might be explained by d'Estrades' alliance with Colbert with whom he was studying solutions for the renovation of the French navy. D'Estrades had been a friend of Nicolas Fouquet (1615–1680), the superintendant of finances that Louis XIV prosecuted and jailed almost immediately after taking personal control of his government in 1661, making d'Estrades suspect to the king, but d'Estrades' negotiated retrieval of Dunkirk from England quieted suspicions of his loyalty. As was said above, this arrest was to be kept a secret from Colbert and therefore from anyone who might tell Colbert about it.

The briefcase of documents for Vauroy to carry with him was taken from Saint-Germain to Dunkirk by a messenger, who presumably left Saint-Germain-en-Laye on the 28th, arrived at Vauroy's door probably on the 29th or 30th, and Vauroy, reading through these papers, saw the importance and urgency of his assignment and arrested Dauger between the 30th of July and the 1st of August.[37]

Stanislas Brugnon[38] found at the Bibliothèque Nationale a travel reimbursement order for the period late July to early August 1669 in the amount of 3,000 *livres* for four men from Dunkirk to Calais (presumably Vauroy and three soldiers), and for five men from Calais to Pignerol (Vauroy, the three soldiers and the *Masque de fer*); then 3,000 additional *livres* for four men from Pignerol to Calais (Vauroy and his three soldiers, returning to their home base in Dunkirk).[39] That is proof that the mission occurred, that it was to Calais, and it ended in a journey to Pignerol and back to Dunkirk. The only part of the journey that was not mentioned in this travel account was Vauroy's stop at Saint-Germain to report to the king on his completed mission, but perhaps that leg of the trip was not known by the accountant.

Arrival At Pignerol

We have no details about the trip to Pignerol, only that the five men arrived at Pignerol on August 21.[40] We don't know if Dauger walked, rode a horse, or was carried in a litter or a wagon. A deduction that he rode a horse would be proposed in this way: it is certain the soldiers rode horses... soldiers on such a mission would not ride in a carriage, and we have information in the travel reimbursement that there were only three soldiers with Vauroy, which doesn't allow for carriage drivers or litter carriers. If Dauger walked while the soldiers rode, the mission would be slowed down considerably, taking much longer than twenty-one days to get from Calais on the northeastern seacoast to the Italian Alps. He must have ridden a horse or a mule.

Saint-Mars reported their arrival on the day of its occurence:

> Saint-Mars to Louvois
>
> 21 August 1669
>
> M. de Vauroy delivered the man named Eustache d'Auger[41] to me. As soon as I placed him in a secure place, one I picked out to be temporary quarters for him until the special cell is ready, I told him in the presence of M. de Vauroy that if he spoke to me or anyone else of anything except his necessities, I would put

CHAPTER 1. THE ARREST OF EUSTACHE DAUGER

my sword through his stomach...I will never fail, on my life, to carry out punctually your orders."[42]

The sword through the stomach threat is a sempiternal utterance of Saint-Mars but never so fierce as this first announcement to his just arrived prisoner. Many times I read this particular oratory and put it to Saint-Mars' love of exaggeration and drama. But instead, it was another of his personal qualities that was in play: servility to the utmost. Louvois had written to Saint-Mars on July 19 to alert him that a new prisoner would soon be sent to him and the instructions on how to handle his future arrival told him to be "very severe" in threatening death if Dauger said anything about himself. The word in the 19 July letter that tells the jailer how to instruct Dauger is "*tousevi.*" The sentence is, "...and that you will never listen, under any conditions, what he wishes to tell you, menacing him very severely ("*tousevi*") to kill him if he ever opens his mouth about anything other than his necessities."[43] General Theodore Iung's 1873 transcription of this letter, which has never been challenged, said the adjective was "*toujours,*" which would make the sentence, "Do not fail to always remind him that you will kill him if he speaks about himself." But the original letter plainly shows that an *i* complete with its dot is at the end of the word, so the translation of "*toujours*" cannot be right. "Very severely" is the English translation of "*tousevi,*" which, properly written, would be "*tout sévi.*" Even though the secretary's handwriting is far better than most, this particular word has been hard for researchers to decipher, perhaps because the secretary left off the acute accent on the *e* in "*sévi.*"

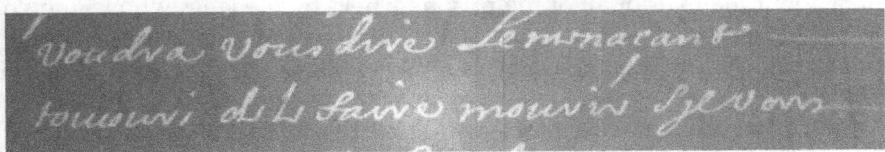

Figure 1.5: Detail from Louvois' July 19, 1669 letter to Saint-Mars. French National Archives. Image by the author 2016. The two lines are: "...voudra vous dire le menaçant tousevi de le faire mourir sil vous..."

Once in Saint-Mars' supervision, Dauger never left it for the rest of his life. He was truly Saint-Mars' prisoner. Only Saint-Mars was deemed trustworthy enough to hold this special person, and, imagining the king's thoughts on the matter, unless Saint-Mars made a huge mistake in handling the prisoner, it didn't seem worth the trouble and risk to train anyone else in the needs and special rules of this captive's handling.[44] Over thirty-three years, from 1669 to 1703, Saint-Mars, his turnkey Ru, and Lieutenant Rosarges were almost the only three people Eustache ever interacted with. Doctors came into his cell from time to time to treat him—he talked to them, although he always had his mask on when he was with a doctor—and he had two companions at different times that we know of.

No documents mention that he was masked in 1669 but by the time he died in the Bastille in 1703 the official report said he was "always masked." The mask was made of black cloth and was worn over the top of his face any time he left his cell and any time any person other than his three jailers came into his cell. His incarceration was ended by his sudden natural death at ten o'clock at night on November 19, 1703, in his room in the Bastille, and he was buried the next day a few blocks away in the cemetery of the Saint-Paul[45] church on the rue Saint-Paul at four o'clock in the afternoon. The church is no longer standing and the bones buried in the churchyard were moved when Saint-Paul was closed in 1791, because for centuries there had been so many decaying bodies buried so close to the surface that they were causing bad odors in the apartments nearby and the putrid air was changing the color of the neighbors' drapes, but some of the bones may still be under what is now an urban public playground.[46] It is also possible that not all of the bones were removed from the east portion of the cemetery before apartment buildings were built on top of it.[47]

The Name Of The Prisoner Is Important To Solving The Mystery

Many hundreds of writers have written many thousands of pages about *le Masque de fer*. Eighteenth- and nineteenth-century historians collected data about the lives of all of the prisoners held by the jailer who is known to have been the Mask's only jailer, the ex-musketeer Saint-Mars, marking their dates of birth, death, incarceration, their crimes as described by those who imprisoned them, and then proposing likely explanations for the overlaps of place, time, and activity in these men's lives and the schedule of events in the Mask's life as told in the narratives of witnesses. But those witnesses are suspected, most of them, of having incorrect information, of exaggeration, of misunderstanding what they saw or heard, and of muddying the waters for various reasons, personal and political. So it was quite a long search by many researchers to filter out the masked man from Saint-Mars' other prisoners in this nest of detours and traps.

Finally there came to be a consensus by Mask scholars that one prisoner had all the right qualifications, and the rest of the people on the list were put aside. In 1932, Maurice Duvivier in his book, *Le Masque de fer*, summed up the catalog of all the prisoners held in the prisons governed by Monsieur de Saint-Mars, by declaring, "The person who, in 1698, was taken, masked, from the Sainte-Marguerite prison to the Bastille, where he died in 1703,

CHAPTER 1. THE ARREST OF EUSTACHE DAUGER

could not be other than the one arrested in 1669, Eustache Dauger."[48] Up to the present time, scholars agree on this fact but they disagree about whether this was his *real* name—*real* as in, his name on his birth certificate, which we don't have and which may not ever have existed—because it was common practice in Louis XIV's government to deceive everyone, even prison staff, about prisoners' identities, but the name written in the arrest warrant that still exists in the French National Archives is "Eustache Dauger," and so at least for the events surrounding his arrest, that is the name which identified him to the king and the soldiers who took him prisoner. In this instance, the simplest explanation is most likely the right one. Paul Sonnino, American historian and author of a book on the mystery, is convinced that the name Eustache Dauger was truly the name of the masked prisoner based on the reasoning that if his name was not Eustache Dauger, whoever directed that the false name of "Marchiali" (or possibly the spelling is "Maresiel") be put on his death certificate would not have bothered to fake a name.[49] "Marchiali" for a very long time persuaded searchers to direct their attention to another prisoner of Saint-Mars with a similar name, Mattioli. Despite the reluctance by researchers to believe the writing on the arrest warrant, nevertheless, the name on the warrant is valid, or at least if the name was assumed, it was Dauger himself who had assumed it, not the king.

No Name

But having his supposed name doesn't answer the question, who was Eustache Dauger. After his arrest warrant was served, his name rarely ever appeared in any correspondence or notes created by his handlers. The rule was that the prisoner should never say his name, never say who he was, where he had come from or where he had lived before he was imprisoned, and if he did he would be immediately killed. The close companion of this rule was that no one else should speak the man's name either, with the same consequence for violation of the rule. All of the bureaucrats and jailers who entered data about the prisoner into the official records which are left to us, including Lieutenant Etienne du Junca who recorded his death in 1703 in the Bastille register, did not know what his name was. Not even a false name was created, as was usually done. The normal routine was that *Jean* would be dubbed "*Antoine*," and *Blanc* would be named "*Noir*." Not so here. The jailers sometimes had a nickname for Eustache so that they could make clear which prisoner they were talking about in a practical situation, but it is obvious in reading the written references that these are the jailers' inventions. In the rare instances when identifying the prisoner was unavoidable, the speaker would refer to "the one whose name is not said aloud" or "the ancient prisoner" or "the man who was brought by sergent Vauroy." At a certain stage of his life in prison he was called "*La Tour*," which was a quick way to say "the prisoner of the lower tower,"[50] although there may have been another meaning in this nickname which will be discussed later. If we ask what Louis XIV was most anxious about in relation to Eustache Dauger, it was his name. Such extreme care was taken that Eustache's name be unspoken that perhaps it is a clue to the mystery.

The estimable corps of nineteenth-century researchers who threw out a dragnet for the Mask's identity quickly caught a contemporary character who had this name: Eustache d'Auger de Cavoye, soldier and childhood playmate of Louis XIV through his father having been Cardinal Richelieu's chief of Guards and his mother a lady in the queen's circle. But Eustache d'Auger de Cavoye had a sad, dissolute life and died in Paris' Saint-Lazare prison at a verifiable date well before the death date of Eustache Dauger at the Bastille. De Cavoye's relatives had put him in detention because he was a heavily indebted alcoholic, a common action for families to take with their annoying black sheep.

The King And The Valet

Despite the fact that the arrest warrant was written on July 28 and carried out less than a week later, we know that the king was aware of the general location of Eustache Dauger nine days before July 28 because his henchman Louvois, the son of Le Tellier, sent a letter to Pignerol on July 19 telling Saint-Mars that a new prisoner, Eustache Dauger, would soon be arriving at Pignerol and to prepare a cell which must be expressly made to an ultra secure design.[51] This letter has great importance in the mystery because Louvois stereotyped the prisoner as a *"valet"* in the letter, and since that was the only description of his place in society that we have ever had, the attribution stuck, and those trying to decipher the mystery began to suspect only people who had been valets, either a house valet or a man who was what we would call a business manager or accountant for someone—in France at that time the word used for such an office worker was often *"intendant,"* a supervisor of the details of the household, farm, or office, but *"valet"* is also a word used in general for a helper of any kind.

Louvois' 19 July letter shows that he knew where Eustache Dauger would be in a few days:

> 19 July 1669
>
> From Saint-Germain-en-Laye
>
> Monsieur,
>
> The king, having commanded me to have the person named Eustache Dauger escorted to Pignerol, I instruct you that it is of the utmost service to the king that the prisoner be guarded in great

security, that he cannot communicate anything about himself in any way, neither talk to any person whatsoever. I am giving you advance notice, so that you can begin to make a secure cell for him... I am sending directions to sieur Poupart to work night and day on your design for the cell and you will bring in furniture that is necessary for the person that will be brought to you, keeping in mind that, as he is only a valet, he will not need anything of value, and I will see that you are reimbursed for his furniture and whatever you think you need for his food."[52]

This July 19 letter is the only artifact in a void that, were it filled by even the slightest message, would tell where Eustache Dauger was just before and at the point of his arrest, information that would lead to other facts perhaps: his identity, his occupation, his domicile. But we can ask some questions, as long as we adopt Mask author Pierre-Marie Dijol's attitude about studying this mystery: "[We] must muck about in the swamps of an uncertain chronicle and dive bravely into the ocean of hypotheses."[53] The only assumption that can safely be made is that Louis XIV arrested Dauger because he was a problem in some way; maybe we can go so far as to say a threat to something the king valued. If Dauger was not a thorn in Louis' side, then logically he would not have arrested him and kept him prisoner for thirty-four years.

Return Of The Great Register Notes

We left the editor of the Bastille registers, Charpentier, in 1789 staring at the place in the register of prisoners where there should have been the Man in the Iron Mask's true name and the reason for his arrest but seeing only a ragged edge of a missing page in the spine. "The man of the mask had come to represent the essential cursed victim"[54] of all the kings and queens of France; not being able to find his name seemed like a victory for his royal tormentors and this made the new *citoyens* all the more sure that the prisoner had been someone important.

Charpentier and his committee had reluctantly accepted the absence of the notes on the masked prisoner and had begun to publish their first volumes, starting at the beginning of the first register. Volume one was published in 1789, and then a second volume in 1790. More editions followed, going to press gradually as the Bastille's files were transcribed.

After multiple volumes of the *Bastille dévoilée* had been printed, the page 120 of the *Great Register* containing the notes on the registration of the prisoner with no name suddenly appeared. It was not the original, but a copy, entirely written by the chief military officer of the Bastille from 1749 to 1783, Major Henri-Godillon Chevalier (d. 1783). M. Duval, a former secretary of police, "found" a copy of the page, and it was assumed to be authentic, therefore when Charpentier created a new volume of his *Bastille dévoilée*, he included the "found" information.

Major Chevalier had been the resource for Louis XV and Louis XVI when they wanted information about the mysterious ex-prisoner. These two kings, descendants of Louis XIV, were, in this matter, shoulder to shoulder with the rest of a growing number of people who had heard of the prisoner and wanted to know more about him. Chevalier, at the request of Malesherbes (Guillaume-Chrétien de Lamoignon de Malesherbes, 1721–1794), opened the register of prisoners and made bibliographical notes for some of them. Here is what he wrote for the Man in the Mask, referencing a journal essay written by the official who admitted him to the prison, Lieutenant du Junca, in 1698. Chevalier wrote:

> This was the famous man of the mask that no one ever knew. He was treated with great distinction by M. the governor and was seen only by M. de Rosarges, major of the [Bastille] château, who alone took care of him; he was sick for only a few hours before he died suddenly. Buried at Saint-Paul [cemetery] on Tuesday 20 November 1703 at four o'clock in the afternoon under the name Marchiergues.
>
> *Nota*: he was wrapped in a new white sheet that the governor gave, and all that was found in his room was burned, his entire bed, chairs, tables and other utensils, or melted, and all thrown into the latrines.[55]

The *Nota* is Chevalier's own addition to du Junca's journal entry of 1703. Chevalier also added that in 1775 he tore the pages that had information on the masked prisoner out of the official register at the order of Monsieur Malesherbes because Louis XVI (1754–1793) and his wife Marie-Antoinette (1755–1793) had wanted to know who the Man in the Iron Mask was and had asked Malherbes to look for the files concerning this prisoner and tell them what he found.[56]

Historian Théodore Iung said it was his opinion that the document found by Monsieur Duval was not an exact copy of the extracted page. On each page in the *Great Register* there are eleven columns, while the page "found" by Citizen Duval has only ten columns, the column missing being, "Names of the Secretaries of State who co-signed the orders." The "found" page was the creation of Major Chevalier, says Iung, whether he made the document up entirely or whether he copied from the original page with modifications made by his superiors.

However Iung thought that we can rely on these pages to a certain extent. He thought that they are factual in the filling in of the columns, and that what was taken out were the observations and notes.[57]

Here is the recreated registration data for the Mask:

- **Names and social rank of the prisoners:** Old prisoner from Pignerol, obliged to always wear a black velvet mask,[58] whose social rank was never known.
- **Dates of their entrances:** 18 September 1698 at 3 o'clock in the afternoon.
- **Volume:** du Junca [59]
- **Page:** V. 37 ("V" means *Verso*, which indicates the information is on the reverse of page 37 (in du Junca's journal).
- **Dates of their deaths:** 19 November 1703.
- **Volume:** du Junca
- **Page:** V. 80 (in du Junca's journal).
- **Reasons for the detention of the prisoner:** It has never been known.
- **Observations:** left blank [60]

The missing column, "Names of the Secretaries of State who co-signed the orders," is significant. One of many unusual aspects of Dauger's arrest is that no record of the arrest appears in the official register of arrests carried out by the House of the King for the year 1669. Jean-Baptiste Colbert, Secretary of State for the House of the King, should have officially placed the arrest in the king's papers by signing the report of it, but there is no report. The name of Michel le Tellier, who co-signed the order for arrest, is not mentioned.

Even more flagrant abuse was done to Colbert's power to sign documents for his jurisdiction: in 1669 Colbert and Louvois, Le Tellier's son and heir to his father's minister of war post, had divided between them the major administrative posts of France. Louvois received power in full passed from his father for minister of war, *Secrétaire d'Etat de la Guerre*, and Colbert, among other departments, took the ministry of the *Marine* (the navy) which carried authority from Calais to Bayonne, the Mediterranean, and the fortifications called *l'ancien domaine du roi*, Champagne, Alsace, the "Three Bishoprics" (Metz, Toul, Verdun), Bourgogne, the Dauphiné, Provence, and Languedoc. An arrest by a *lettre de cachet* in a geographical area of Colbert's authority, Calais, was Colbert's official business.[61]

The permanent disappearance of the original page that showed this omission and the appearance of a copy of it that did not have a column in the spreadsheet for this category could have been purposefully arranged by someone, perhaps Chevalier or more likely one of the ministers for Louis XVI who reviewed the page that Chevalier had torn out of the Great Register and thought the lack of required documentation for the arrest was irregular, and since this arrest was attracting attention and might do so again in the future, it might be better to omit the column.

Seven Questions

Louis XIV had a reason for putting Eustache Dauger in prison. He never explained that reason to posterity, but he must have had one. Dauger was never accused of a crime or put on trial. Dauger had to have been a threat to Louis XIV. Chevalier wrote that just after Dauger's death the order was given to burn all his possessions. We have another testimony[62] that as soon as they had done that, they completely destroyed the room he had lived in, including taking up the stone floor tiles and scraping the walls down, presumably looking for writing he may have hidden. If Louis XIV, after having received word of the death of a devout old prisoner who loved books and never having even the slightest evidence in thirty-four years that he was trying to leave his identity behind, tore up the plaster walls and stone floor of his room, he was scared of him. Why did Eustache Dauger scare Louis XIV?

My first attempt at answering this question took the form of another question: I asked, what would Louis XIV most fear losing? I arrived at these seven things:

1. His throne (including all perquisites and possessions);
2. His heirs' rights to inherit the throne;
3. His life;
4. His reputation;
5. His soul, i.e. his ability to be absolved by his confessors from his sins at the end of his life;
6. His good standing as a devout Catholic (he would want to avoid excommunication);
7. The cohesion of the kingdom.

I believe that Louis XIV thought all of these were at risk if Eustache Dauger had been free to live where he pleased and talk to whom he pleased about whatever he felt like discussing.

2. The King's Search For Eustache Dauger

> He is the first Passenger among passengers, that is to say the prisoner of the passage. And the land from which he leaves is not known, no more than the land where he once more sets foot. He only has his truth and his country in the lonely space between two spots of land which, neither of them, can belong to him.
>
> —Michel Foucault

Where Was He?

It is time for investigators of this seventeenth-century cold case to start proposing theories about Dauger's life and location before his arrest. But that task is very hard because we have no hints in archival documents or memoirs that suggest where he was before he was arrested near Calais between July 30 and August 1, 1669. But he *did* exist, and if he existed he *was somewhere*, and there is bound to be a clue to where that was. Where did he live as a baby and young child? Did he move to a different place when he became an adult? In the beginning, we have to use circumstantial information, even to guess, to find a sign of life to hang onto, but the creativity must be based on familiarity with the characters and above all, be guided by the social, cultural, medical, religious, and military rules of the seventeenth century.

How And When Did Louis XIV Find Dauger?

When did Louis XIV learn of the existence of Eustache Dauger and when did the king decide to arrest him? These are probably two different dates. Somehow, Louis XIV learned that Dauger would be at Calais at the end of July, but although everything from how wig makers gave fine tone and sheen to wigs by baking them inside a loaf of bread to the negotiations of the Treaty of Nijmegen that ended the Dutch War has been researched for understanding the *Grand Siècle*, yet we know nothing about the king's search for Eustache Dauger.

The king might have known of Dauger's existence for many years before July 1669, knew where he lived, and did not consider Dauger a threat, but something occurred that caused Louis to suddenly act. The corollary is, why did the king begin to see him as a threat and was this a gradual or sudden judgement? Or the king might have known of Dauger's existence for many years before July 1669 and *did* consider him a threat but didn't know where he was. The king might *not* have known before July 1669 that a person named Eustache Dauger existed or that he was affiliated in any way with himself, but he suddenly found that Dauger existed, was a problem for him, and he decided to arrest him.

Even more difficult than the length of time that Dauger had been in the mind of the king as a target of arrest is the question of whom Louis asked to do the footwork to find out where Dauger was and how he could be approached. One of his chief subordinates, such as Le Tellier or Louvois? They were top-level ministerial secretaries of the war office but these two were also called on for a lot of things that had nothing to do with war. "*On le[s] mettra à toutes les sauces*," says a biographer of the father and son.[63] A subordinate as yet unknown to history? Louis' chief of guards? Louis' confessor? His mother, his brother, his mistress? Did Louis find Dauger by actively searching for him or did he find him by accident?

Someone in the king's family or circle must have told the king about a person of interest, the one he would eventually arrest. He had a network of informants, and the longer he reigned, the longer the list of spies grew. He had an inordinate need for knowing everything that was happening in his realm. This was perhaps because in the early years of his mother's regency he had experienced the humiliation and fear of being turned out of his house by the parlementary judges and the nobles of Paris during the Fronde, a serious and widespread revolution against the crown in 1649 that lasted four years. The effect on him was everlasting suspicion of everyone. But a less sinister reason for ubiquitous spies might be that he loved knowing titillating details about his friends' lives that they didn't know he knew: whose husband was sleeping with his cousin's lady-in-waiting, the *conseiller* in the parlement who had just been ruined at the card table, the duke whose budget for a new town house in Paris had been decimated by the cost of the gilded ceilings installed by a minor Genoese decorator now gone back to Genoa with the ceiling unfinished because he hadn't been paid. Some people love hearing gossip. Also, the only way to run any government, ancient or modern, is to know what is happening in the capital and the provinces. Spies are statecraft. For many reasons, Louis XIV was an avid secret listener of secrets. So perhaps Louis found Eustache through a seasoned spy or just a person in one or more degrees of separation from Louis who knew something the king would like to hear.

CHAPTER 2. THE KING'S SEARCH FOR EUSTACHE DAUGER

Louvois' July 19 letter to Saint-Mars contends for the theory that Louis had been looking for Eustache for at least some months to years before July 19, 1669 but could not find him. Suddenly Dauger's sure location was identified and the arrest was carried out immediately.

An alternate theory is that, while having known of Dauger's location for some time but not having any or much concern about him, Louis suddenly received intelligence that something in Dauger's life had changed and the king thought arrest was now a good idea. I favor this last theory because it is consistent with a particularly strong pattern in Louis' relationships with important people in his close circle.

Despite being of very strong character and will, beneath his exterior pompous, steel control, Louis XIV had, as many people who outwardly flout their fearlessness, a lot of fear. He displayed both shyness and abrupt rudeness in his youth and these two partnered more as he grew up until finally, because of nearly losing power in the Fronde and the emergence of his sexuality, which was very strong, these two characteristics merged on a stage where he was alone. He sculpted his roughness and shyness into a perfectly formed statue for public display whose arm and leg movements, not to mention the mental workings of this creation, were observant, patient, stilted, and dry. He was patient for people who were in his way to die before moving directly and speedily to his own agenda. When the most important people in his life, his mother, his godfather Cardinal Mazarin, Colbert, or Louvois, obstructed his plans he did not have the courage to openly override their wishes while they lived; he could not courageously contradict these people, thwart their versions of reality to insert his own, and go about his day and his reign, leaving disappointments and chasms in his relationships if necessary. His father Louis XIII could do this, but Louis XIV could not. One might be tempted to say he was too sly or sneaky to put his own preferences forward. But those adjectives, although used often by historians to describe Louis XIV, are not words that describe this pattern of delaying his actions when he didn't want to cross someone in his family or his entourage. He preferred to wait for the disappearance of the person restricting his forward motion rather than initiate a direct confrontation.

For instance, during Louis' boyhood, an Italian Cardinal put on the high council as consultant to Anne of Austria by Louis XIII just before he died, Jules Mazarin, was commander of his mother, of the state, of the juvenile king's spending money, of whether he got new linens for his bed, and a restriction from finery was kept even after Louis' coronation when he was thirteen. His mother had needed Mazarin to advise her and run state business after Louis XIII died in 1643 and Mazarin was happy to do that and kept her hypnotized (she was willing) while he stole the state blind. Louis, not being hypnotized, knew that he was stealing egregious amounts of money from the treasury, from the troops, from the poor, from the rich, from foreigners, from his mother. He knew the cardinal's business manager, Colbert, was helping him do this and taking his share, yet he did not stand up and fight them off. He put up with it until March 1661, when the cardinal was *in extremis* in his bed at Vincennes castle in the front room while Colbert rewrote his will a few times in the back room, both of them down to the wire trying to figure out how to hide this diamond encrusted estate, thirty-nine to forty million livres,[64] from the world and allow it to slide to Mazarin's heirs.[65] Immediately, a few hours after Mazarin's last breath on March 9, Louis announced to his gaggle of first-minister-want-to-bes that they could take a back seat, the king was in charge and would not have a first minister now or ever. At first he wasn't believed. Courtiers, nobles, parlementarians, bureaucrats, the queen mother, all supposed that announcement would be reversed in about two weeks, but they were wrong; Louis personally oversaw the administration of France until his death on September 1, 1715. He did not expose and/or imprison either Mazarin or Colbert, rather he waited for Mazarin to die and then took Colbert into his service as chief for finances so he couldn't work for anyone else who might want to steal from the king. If Colbert became greedy, Louis would be down on him before too much damage was done, and if he stole from the state in small ways, Louis could and did ignore it as the price to be paid for keeping this financial tumbler to himself.

Given Louis' tendency to patiently wait for a human obstacle to die or retreat before setting up his own priorities on their former projects, a case could be made that Louis knew of Eustache for some time but that Eustache had a person with him whose disappearance Louis was waiting for before he ordered the arrest. This person might have died or been incarcerated or become ill or disappeared from Dauger's life in some other way, finally making way for Louis to take him under his own control. Who might that person have been? A servant? A teacher? A priest?

There could have been a fortuitous discovery of Dauger in the year 1667 or 1668 by Louis XIV's soldiers and his engineers who were assessing the lands east of Calais in Spanish Flanders just acquired by the French in the War of the Spanish Devolution: Charleroi, Audenard, Courtrai, Lille, Douai. In May 1669 Louvois and Sébastien Le Prestre de Vauban (1633–1707), a fortification genius and a long associate of d'Estrades, the governor of Dunkirk, traveled to the new possessions in Flanders and Artois to assess the existing fortifications and begin plans for repairs and additions.[66] D'Estrades might have given Louvois or Vauban a lead that enabled them to find Dauger. Remember that at the point of arrest, d'Estrades was not only uninformed but duped, so if d'Estrades had given a clue about Dauger to Louvois in May, it was unwitting. If d'Estrades' (hypothetical) revelation to Louvois proved to

CHAPTER 2. THE KING'S SEARCH FOR EUSTACHE DAUGER   31

be the goal he was looking for, Louvois might have told Captain Vauroy in May the location of the future prisoner. "Wait for word from the king. When you receive the order, you can find the man you will be looking for at...." Colbert de Croissy (Colbert's brother and ambassador to England), Louvois, Vauban, or someone anonymous might have come across an odd bit of news that the king was interested in. Everyone knew that the king happily devoured details about people and events in his kingdom, especially things that seemed to be out of routine.

Setting aside the king's knowledge for a moment, did Vauroy know about Dauger before the end of July 1669? There is not a calendar of Vauroy's activities of the year of 1669 for us to look at. The only facts we have are that the king signed the letter of arrest on 28 July and Vauroy and the prisoner (with a guard of three soldiers) arrived at Pignerol on August 21, 1669.[67]

The sergent-major, Captain Vauroy, being familiar with the area surrounding Calais (in 1669 Vauroy had been sergent-major of Dunkirk since 20 December 1662, and since 21 October 1667 he had also been captain of the hunt in the districts of Dunkirk, Bergues, and Furnes, which would have made him familiar with the terrain and residents in the area between Dunkirk and Calais and the area slightly south of those two towns),[68] might have had knowledge about Eustache Dauger's existence and location and knew where he could be found without having to be told. The short period of time between Vauroy receiving the warrant and its being served could mean that Vauroy knew where he was before the king contacted him.

The tempting passage through the problem of how Vauroy knew where to find Dauger is to guess that Dauger was arriving or departing from the port of Calais or Dunkirk, the principal harbors for ships coming from England, but also from the Low Countries (Holland and Belgium), other foreign places, and other French ports. An imagined instruction to Vauroy might be, "Be at the docking of the ship *l'Hirondelle* on Monday in Calais," or "Meet the *Grand-Danois* in Dunkirk on the 1st." Unfortunately, records of ship arrivals and departures, passengers, and sailors were not recorded for incoming ships until many years after 1669. I learned this by calling the archives of Dunkirk, and the archivist, stupified at receiving an overseas call from an American lady about ship arrivals in 1669, was polite but brief. *N'existe pas.*

Two other unknowns about the arrest are whether the soldiers took Dauger by force and whether he knew they were coming for him in advance. Given that only three soldiers were seconded from Vauroy's staff at Dunkirk for the mission, it is likely the interaction was predicted to be and was peaceful. Dauger might also have been aware that soldiers were coming to take charge of him and he did not try to flee. He never protested his imprisonment so he probably did not protest the official act that started it.

The fact that there is no document, at least none in the places in the archives where there should be, that points to a prequel to Dauger's arrest, and at this point, with all the research done over the last two centuries in the military archives, the foreign service archives, and the Bibliothèque Nationale, it would have turned up, means that the search, if there was one, was by Louis XIV himself and perhaps one other person who remained permanently quiet. Louis didn't describe the man in a letter to any military or civil authority, he didn't write to anyone about his need to find this man. The lack of evidence of a search for Dauger can be added to the list of things in this murky mystery that lead one to think this was Louis XIV's own secret, not a secret of state, not a secret of international diplomacy.

Foreign Travel

During the fifteen years that I researched the mystery of the Man in the Iron Mask and the history of France, I wrote down ideas that came to me every once in a while about the possible life of Dauger before he was imprisoned. At first I wanted to sail him off to distant lands, not because the record shows he traveled (it does not show he *didn't* either), but because at that time in Europe, sailing across the ocean to Canada or the West Indies, an ambitious and unusual undertaking, to harvest salt, start communities, convert natives to Catholicism, fish and trap for profit, and raid Spanish ships of gold and silver were very good ways to disappear forever, which presumably Dauger and his protectors, if he had any, would desire.

I was influenced to consider ocean travel when I read *Histoire de la folie à l'âge classique* by the French twentieth-century author Michel Foucault who wrote about marginalized populations in what a later chapter of this book will call nowhere places, either forced or chosen, hospitals, monasteries, convents, and prisons. In these retreats the excluded person stays still and steady in one place and cannot get out. The opposite strategy that society uses to cope with people who are considered by society to be abnormal is to maneuver them to a permanent life of travel, a "departure" as Foucault calls it, for another place, at which they immediately embark again to go somewhere else that also doesn't belong to them. A forced wandering existence of a madman or a stigmatized person is useful to the people in the center because it sends the affected person on a voyage by road, canal, or ocean, and even if he doesn't stay on the circuit permanently, he is less of a problem for a while for those who fear him and are trying to manage his disorder. In medieval Europe, they put madmen on boats in the care (an optimistic word) of sailors. Foucault uses this ancient practice to make a parable to explain exclusion in modern society. The parable prompted me to wonder if Eustache traveled to foreign countries such as Canada, the Antilles, Cabo Verde, or another foreign place. Sending him on a voyage to a new, permanent, foreign home would eliminate him forever from Europe. He might have been on a ship's crew or he might have been in a group of Europeans who went to Africa, North and South America to start communities, to trade, or start religious conversion programs, hospitals, and schools.

One path of investigation in this direction again brought up the inevitable Fouquet clan. Jacob du Quesne was a business collaborator of the Fouquets, a main actor in the commercial activities on the high seas in the 1600s. He was a brother of the famous sea captain Abraham du Quesne (1610–1688) and their father had worked closely with Nicolas Fouquet's father François Fouquet (1587–1640) to plan and create France's first international shipping companies for Richelieu. Cabo Verde is an island country in an archipelago of ten volcanic islands in the central Atlantic Ocean, now a part of West Africa. It was an area of activity, mercantile and slaving, in 1648 by Jacob du Quesne while he was under contract to Portugal, which had owned Cabo Verde since Portugal discovered it in the middle of the fifteenth century, and it was the native country of Guillaume La Rivière, Nicolas Fouquet's (1615–1680) servant at Pignerol. Nicolas Fouquet's father François had personally founded three international trading companies: the Companies of Senegal, of Cabo Verde, and of Gambia. Looking at these facts all together makes it reasonable to guess that La Rivière had come from Cabo Verde to France with Jacob du Quesne or another sea captain;[69] maybe he had been orphaned or was just confident that he could make a better life in France than at home. However it happened, the young La Rivière came to Madame Fouquet, Nicolas' mother. She often shared her home with homeless people. Her own mother, Marie Morély, had been known for this practice.[70]

As usual in the personal and business affairs of the Fouquets, saintly intentions of some members of the family are countered with greed for solid silver coin either legally or illegally gained: Nicolas Fouquet had bought ships to start commerce in fishing and shipping he hoped would bring him millions of *livres*; Jacob du Quesne was a captain who worked for the highest bidder and neither of them had scruples about renting their ships and expertise to pirates flying the Portuguese flag to raid ships of France's allies. Business relationships like this one, especially if they involved pirates, were the dark side of the new maritime opportunities. Ships require sailors. Maybe Dauger had a place in Fouquet's navy?

A more spiritual group of brave Frenchmen was also traveling to Canada. Richelieu's niece and heiress of a portion of his wealth, the duchesse d'Aiguillon (1604–1675), had been her uncle's hostess and after his death was a mainstay of the *dévot* community. "In addition to Madame de Gondi and Mademoiselle Legras, admirable women, it was Madame d'Aiguillon, said Bonneau-

Avenant, who contributed most to all the works founded by Saint-Vincent-de-Paul."[71] She was also, in 1643, a friend of Anne of Austria. One of Madame d'Aiguillon's charitable interests was colonization and evangelization of Québec in the land called New France. She funded a hospital for the French colony that her uncle Cardinal Richelieu had founded in Québec, Canada. Many ladies of the court donated money to build the hospital. A group of Ursulines, a teaching order of nuns, went across the ocean to the Saint Lawrence Valley to aid the Jesuit fathers who were there already and had started a Jesuit college, a seminary for Indian boys, and a convent school, where they proselytized the Catholic faith and established an infrastructure for administration and health. The duchess funded another series of voyages, this time to create Ville-Marie, the future city of Montréal. By 1659, the executors of the movement to create the town and a hospital funded by the duchesse d'Aiguillon, among other wealthy donors, had achieved the goal.[72] In the course of the founding of the town and hospital and the institution of civil police brigades to protect the colonists from Indian attacks, many religious and lay men went to Canada with the priests as support staff: Mance, Bourgeois, and Maisonneuve. Dauger might have been with them.

Another route to Canada for Dauger might have been the Seminary for Foreign Missions in Paris[73] founded in 1663 that began sending priests to Québec soon after. Jean-Marie Lhoste, one of Fouquet's lawyers at his trial, was a founder of the Seminary for Foreign Missions, a school to train missionaries who wanted to work overseas.

The close friendship and working relationships between the Fouquets, the duchesse d'Aiguillon, and high-ranking members of the Paris Parlement whose wives also funded the Québec voyages and settlements, could have produced a solution for Dauger's young adulthood.

Paris?

Or... perhaps he never was out of France... maybe he never left Paris? The old leprosy hospital at Saint-Lazare on the road to Saint-Denis, long since emptied of lepers, was given to Vincent de Paul (1581–1660) in 1631 for his charities' use. He started a school where were held classes for young people who wanted to go to Canada. During the Fronde (1649–1652) the Saint-Lazare facility was an operations center for distributing food all over Paris to poor people, many of whom were refugees from the countryside. In the parish of Saint-Paul they fed 5,000 poor.[74] Did Eustache live at Saint-Lazare?

CHAPTER 2. THE KING'S SEARCH FOR EUSTACHE DAUGER

Two Incidents In 1666

Dauger was not arrested on August 1, 1669 by magic. Human activity planned and carried out the arrest. The fact that there is silence in the records of daily activities of the king and his staff about anything that could possibly be a plan for the arrest can be interpreted as one of two things: the arrest was of an insignificant valet whose story was not worth mentioning then or now—we have been duped into believing an hallucination because some prison governors told idle tales; or it was an arrest of a man who had such an important secret that the king took meticulous care to cover up his searches for Dauger. To believe the former would be to trivialize the massive effort that Louis XIV made to secure Dauger permanently and keep his existence and his name a secret. The latter scenario is more likely. Previous research on the mystery of the Mask has not looked for hints in the historical record that might indicate a search for Dauger, but the search for the search must begin because learning even one small clue about the tracking of Dauger's location would be helpful. We haven't been able to find Dauger but the king found him and we should look for his path.

To that end, I began to look for signals in the official record of the king's personal and military actions for the years between 1666, when Louis XIV's mother died, and 1669, when Dauger was arrested, that were departures from the usual procedure, things that Louis XIV seemed concerned enough about to risk an odd reaction or action.

Paul Pellisson, Fouquet's Secretary, Suddenly Released From The Bastille

Why is his mother's death date important for speculating on the king's search for Dauger? Because Anne of Austria had an important relationship with Dauger and had been sending money for his pension, food, and expenses. I speculate that on her deathbed in January 1666 Anne of Austria told her oldest son for the first time about Dauger. Previous to that day, it was her secret alone and she protected Louis by keeping it, not even having told Mazarin, although he probably knew anyway through his spies—I have a high regard for Richelieu's and Mazarin's spies—but now that she would be gone, the king had to know about Dauger in case anything should happen to disturb the heretofore quiet waters and to take over the movement of funds for his living expenses.

The king released Paul Pellisson (1624–1693), Fouquet's personal secretary, from prison in January 1666, the month Anne died. Pellisson had been imprisoned at the same hour as Fouquet, September 5, 1661. Could Paul Pellisson have traded his freedom for information about where Dauger was living? Pellisson knew all Fouquet's secret codes, the identity of the recipients of thousands of *livres*, and the details of the most sensitive problems that Fouquet helped his clients solve. If Dauger was the queen's secret, and if she had asked Fouquet's help with locating safe housing and supplying money to pay Dauger's bills, then Pellisson would have known everything about him. I theorize that the king, via one of his appointees, offered Pellisson a swap... Pellisson would be set free in return for going through Fouquet's files that had been confiscated the afternoon of Fouquet's arrest and were in Colbert's possession, and digging out the information on Dauger's location and other data that the king could use in the future. And if the *monsieur* was not able to do this, he could stay in prison forever. Pellisson was a poet, among other things, and the sound of "forever" rhymed with endeavor to get out of the Bastille.

Pellisson was emancipated in more ways than one after January 1666. The king welcomed him into his court. He became the king's historiographer, converted to Catholicism, got rich, and was a respected fixture in the court social scene until his death. Court observer Primi Visconti said an interesting thing about Pellisson in his journal: "Pellisson was smug and mysterious at times, hinting that he was knowledgeable about the secrets of the king, but that was not probable."[75] There were some things, however, that Primi did not know, and the reason for Pellisson's freedom, fame, and fortune might have been one of them.

The Fortress On Tombelaine

Another suspicious action of the king that I noticed in my research also occurred in 1666 and was also connected to Nicolas Fouquet. Fouquet wanted a place or places to headquarter his new shipping business.[76] He bought the rocky islet of Tombelaine in the Bay of Mont-Saint-Michel in 1658 not long after he had bought Mont-Saint-Michel. Saint-Michel abbey was a busy pilgrimage destination on the border between the Normandy and Brittany coasts and Tombelaine island was nearby but smaller and more remote. On 27 June 1659, Fouquet made an inspection tour of his purchases. He asked about the island of Tombelaine and was told it was deserted except for an old couple who lived in a fortress that had been built long ago. Fouquet wanted to remedy this and named his relative and friend, the marquis de La Garde-Fouquet, to rehabilitate the two places. Nicolas never saw the islands again.

La Garde-Fouquet and Claude-Jean Le Clair, Sieur du Fresne, an old captain of the *gardes du roi* and friend of Fouquet, put Tombelaine's fort back in order and appointed a garrison of eight guards. "Du Fresne consolidated the walls, enlarged the buildings, put through a series of windows in the

CHAPTER 2. THE KING'S SEARCH FOR EUSTACHE DAUGER

chateau and constructed living quarters that had a little oratory...they restored the place as a base in Brittany for friends and relatives of the family. All this was under the instructions of Fouquet."[77]

In 1666 Louis XIV ordered the last governor of Tombelaine, the Sieur de la Chastière, to destroy the fort and the small chateau that were on Tombelaine.[78] This act is suspicious because it was unnecessary and went against the usual attitude toward newly acquired fortresses. Why did the king want these buildings on Tombelaine destroyed? Why were these structures taken down on an almost deserted island? There was no military activity on Tombelaine; no other structures were planned or built; the fort had just been modernized and made comfortable at someone's else's expense; no reason was given for the demolition. The trend in 1666 was for the crown, if it obtained new fortresses by hook or crook, to enlarge and repair them. Tombelaine's little chateau, fort, and chapel could have been a useful lookout, if staffed with soldiers, on the northern coast for a young king who was seeking conflict to show his power. Generally, the only reason to destroy an existing fort was to punish a former owner or keep someone else from occupying it.

Tombelaine would have been a perfect place to hide a man away from the prying eyes and ears of the world, a pious man who could not be in public because he had a facial abnormality but who could be protected by the dependable community of monks and the caretakers of Mont-Saint-Michel who could regularly bring medical care and provisions.

He might have spent time at the abbey working in the famous library. In May 2012 I went to the Avranches public library and spoke with M. Jean-Luc Leservoisier, curator at that time and author of books and articles about Mont-Saint-Michel, about what work, if any, was done on the ancient manuscripts of Aristotle, medieval missals and Bibles, and commentaries on the works of Saint-Augustine and other fathers of the church housed at Mont-Saint-Michel abbey across the bay from Avranches. He told me that there was always work to do on the books and manuscripts that were kept on the second floor of the refectory...the dining hall of the monastery, which they had partitioned into two floors. Monks in the late Middle Ages up to the revolution, he told me, constantly worked on the rebinding of many of the manuscripts whose covers had suffered over centuries and millenia from cold, dust, and mildew.[79] At the French Revolution, all the manuscripts were moved to the Avranches public library.

If Louis XIV had discovered that Dauger had recently or in the past lived on Tombelaine, would he have wanted the house, chapel and garrison quarters destroyed? He would have if he was worried that the man he was looking for might try to return home.

3. Leaks, Speculations, And Suspicions

The press, naturally, took up the question. It had ceased to be a solidly held state secret and had crept into the public sphere, where the great interest in it attracted a swarm of writers whose theories and alarms grew like mold. The Mask thus became the soap opera hero that he still is today.

—Maurice Duvivier

The Rue Saint-Antoine

In Paris, I always stayed, in my childhood, in a hotel on the corner of the rue Saint-Honoré and the rue Saint-Roch because my father, a scholar of the rhetoric of the French Revolution, with whom I first experienced France, wanted to unpack in what I much later found out was the virtual location of the riding academy where Robespierre and Danton had made speeches that brought sweat, blood, and tears to the king's "good town" of Paris at the end of the *Ancien Régime*. The academy and the quiet monasteries and convents on the rue Saint-Honoré became, after July 14, 1789, the halls where cocky speechmakers successfully disenfranchised a wealthy and elite estate of monks, nuns, bishops, and clerics by declaring all their vast properties transferred to the state. And the journalists and lawyers who were responsible for the hubbub, finding themselves needing buildings in which to conduct business, make lists, and set dates (even revolutionaries have to have lists and calendars), proceeded to squat in the riding academy and the monasteries and use the libraries and oratories for offices and conference rooms.

Until I began my research on the mystery of the Man in the Iron Mask nothing could take the first *arrondissement's* place at the top of my list of Paris neighborhoods. But at the end of his life the Man in the Mask lived in the Bastille prison on the rue Saint-Antoine on the east side of the city where I had rarely ever been, so, my bags packed, I hovered over the rooftops of the Hôtel de Ville and the Saint-Gervais church and then down into the small streets between the rue Saint-Antoine and the Seine, much as we change locations in Google Earth—a lift, a jump, and a downward swoop into a new place, to the third and fourth arrondissements. The area is called the *Marais* and is where Madame de Sévigné, Nicolas Fouquet, Louis XIV's great general Turenne, the courtisan Ninon de l'Enclos, the duc de Sully, Madame Françoise Scarron and her first husband[80] Paul Scarron the playwright, lived. King Henri IV built one of the greatest residential urban spaces in Paris, originally called Place Royale and renamed Place des Vosges after the Revolution, on the grounds of the ruined Palais des Tournelles on the north side of the rue Saint-Antoine. The little towers that were a feature of the surrounding walls of the Tournelles gave way to a large square with contiguous, identical facades under which arcades protected the entrances to fine townhouses.[81] The Place Royale was a popular *rendezvous* for the centuries-old practice of dueling that by the beginning of the seventeenth century had begun to considerably lower the population of the male nobility and their retinues. A subtle slur at a garden party, a sour glance during a wedding celebration was enough for calling out the seconds to back up the principals in broad daylight, swords and pistols drawn, each having *"la tête près du bonnet."*[82] Cardinal Richelieu and Louis XIII on May 12, 1627 announced a legal prohibition against it that was not popular or obeyed, partly because the musketeers of the king and the guards of the cardinal were frequent opponents and king and cardinal happily kept a scorecard of their wins and losses.

Eustache Dauger's burial in the Saint-Paul cemetery, the parish church of the Bastille, took place within view of the place des Vosges, across the street, in fact, on the rue Saint-Paul. The rue Saint-Antoine, which is a very wide old Roman road, very straight, running along a natural ridge that is safe from flooding when the Seine overflows, was appropriated in the fourteenth century to serve sometimes as an entertainment field for the nearby royal Hôtel des Tournelles and the royal Hôtel Saint-Pol, each on either side of the road. Jousting, parades, and celebrations required a field big enough for the sporting events and the Christian crowds that climbed onto the temporary wooden grandstands and milled around the plaster arches of triumph and temples to the Roman gods that were built as temporary scenery for the parties.

The rue Saint-Antoine is pinned to the neighborhood by many narrow, quiet side streets; as you walk from the Seine up the rue Castex or the rue Saint-Paul, the sound of your footsteps gradually becomes less audible and then you emerge in the noisy, sunny *grande rue*. Near the carousel beside the Saint-Paul subway exit, students and shoppers appear from underground to join the combustible atmosphere of the rue Saint-Antoine. On a hot summer evening in 2012, when I had been at the Bibliothèque Nationale earlier, I was buying my supper from a street vendor near the carousel when I turned and saw, barrelling down the street on skates, with two comrades also on

CHAPTER 3. LEAKS, SPECULATIONS, AND SUSPICIONS

skates, the calm young lady who had renewed my library card on the rue de Richelieu a few hours before. They were going pretty fast, in and out of the traffic. I think they may have been going to the wide park on the south side of the place de la Bastille where skaters gather when there isn't a protest going on.

For a long time there were only planted fields and marshes (thus the name "*Marais*") on either side of the big road; the Sainte-Catherine-du-Val-des-Ecoliers and the Annonciades Célestes nuns tended their vegetable gardens on the north side of the rue Saint-Antoine, the Célestins and the Filles de la Visitation Sainte-Marie lived between the south side of the rue Saint-Antoine and the Seine. The Saint-Paul church with its cemetery on the rue Saint-Paul was about midway to the Seine; at the river end of the rue Saint-Paul there was a small port for offloading goods from barges. The church was torn down in 1799; only a vestige of its west tower remains, a sad golden ruin of what had been the parish church for the royal families who had lived in the Hôtel des Tournelles and the Hôtel Saint-Pol in the fourteenth and fifteenth centuries.

Walking east on the rue Saint-Antoine, once halfway around the circle of the place de la Bastille (whether on skates or on foot), you will then be on the rue du Faubourg Saint-Antoine, which many authors say is the neighborhood where most Parisian uprisings have occurred.[83] If you keep walking, before you reach the Vincennes castle a little over three miles away, you will pass the Saint-Antoine Hospital, where the old convent of Saint-Antoine-des-Champs used to be.[84] A fountain commissioned by the nuns in 1643 is still on the street across from the main entrance.

The place de la Bastille is a round, wide, urban chasm between the end of the rue Saint-Antoine and its faubourg extension, stabbed in its center with a 705-foot-tall banded column commemorating the Paris July 1830 uprising. The *place* was hollowed out by the destruction of the Bastille, an eight-towered block of masonry that was begun in 1370[85] by King Charles V and his administrator, Hughes Aubriot. It was a formidable hold against invasion from the east bolstered by a continual defensive wall from the fortress to the Seine and from the Seine to the Philippe-Auguste wall (1220) at the Tour Barbeau on the quay of the Célestins. The hulk blocked the end of the rue Saint-Antoine, and its gates, dependencies, and what was left of the medieval protective ditches filled with sour water, spread out over the north and south sides of the fortress, forcing travellers who wanted to exit the city toward the east to take a jog to the north where the fortified Saint-Antoine gate was. The Bastille was overwhelming, threatening, and dark.

The revolutionaries that conquered the Bastille fortress on July 14, 1789 immediately began to dismantle it so that by the beginning of October it was a variegated ruin, some parts of the walls almost gone and partly dismantled towers betraying the interior cells' configurations. Some of the stones were used to build the pont de la Concorde across the Seine connecting the place de la Concorde and the Left Bank, and some were cut into small pieces to make eighty-three models of the prison that were sent, one each, to the eighty-three departments of France "to keep the memory of the horror of despotism alive."[86] The shattered towers were the sentries for an illuminated evening dance held at the site to celebrate the first anniversary of the prison's capture.[87]

The Man in the Iron Mask lived in the Bastille from September 18, 1698 to November 19, 1703, his death date, and so his fate was attached to the prison. The two symbols of rigid, insensitive, capricious, harsh governance, the prison and its most famous prisoner, became one.

What follows are relations of the very first public statements that refer to Eustache Dauger and a quick reference about who made them...where they had accurate information and also where they were mistaken.

One purpose of writing these testimonies is to accurately record the details of the witnesses' statements to serve future historians as basis for their own research. Previous books on the Mask have also related these stories, but as time passes, more information is found and so new authors, new detectives, must correct wrong information and post recently obtained data and gather and summarize the testimonies.

Voltaire

Remarkably, the person who surpassed all other pre-French Revolution writers about this mystery was Voltaire (François-Marie Arouet, 1694–1778), an eighteenth-century *Philosophe* and playwright whose installment comments on the mystery between 1738 and the end of his life in 1778 were responsible for making the masked prisoner a public possession. Voltaire is known for his cynical criticisms of politicians and religion but he also wrote non-fiction political history. By the time he was thirty-two in 1726, Voltaire had already made a name for himself as a sharp critic of the church and the regent for King Louis XV.

Voltaire first talked about the *Masque de fer* in a letter to a historian friend, the abbé Dubos,[88] on 30 October 1738, writing that he had knowledge of "*l'homme au masque de fer*"—that he had spoken with people who had served him,[89] which means that his informants might have been either workers in the prison, those who cleaned or cooked, or prison guards in the Bastille who passed along stories they had heard from previous guards, and since

Figure 3.1: Voltaire. Life-sized statue of the *Philosophe* in one of the stairwells of the Bibliothèque Nationale, Paris, rue de Richelieu. Workshop of Jean Antoine Houdon (French, Versailles 1741–1828 Paris). Image by the author 2015.

the positions were often passed from family member to family member, they may have heard them from a father or uncle; and who does not believe his father or uncle in such an important matter?[90] The stories, mixed with errors, passed from person to person as fact.

Voltaire wrote a history of the reign of Louis XIV.[91] This book, *Le Siècle de Louis XIV* (*The Century of Louis XIV*), brought the Man in the Iron Mask to the public's attention in its first edition, published in 1751 in Berlin. Voltaire had heard of the masked prisoner when he was in the Bastille,[92] and his informants, whomever they were, must have had fascinating stories to tell, because he put a short description of the prisoner at the end pages of the book, which were the first in a steady speculative chatter in his articles and books, some of the references added to otherwise unrelated writing on history and philosophy and some in direct replies to his critics, who came forward in print to say they knew this or that fact that Voltaire got wrong and usually adding the criticism that the philosopher was overreacting and overreaching. The mysterious prisoner became more well known with each challenger's literary boxing match with Voltaire, who always portrayed himself as the chief watchdog of the mystery. By reading what he wrote and critiquing it we can acquire a familiarity with the timeline and actions of the characters that were important in the life of Eustache Dauger.

After a scholarly three-hundred-page review (which is still admired and used today by historians) of Louis XIV's wars with most of the countries of Europe, the reasons for them, the results of them, and the peace treaties that ended them, Voltaire placed this statement at the very end in a postscript titled, "Miscellaneous anecdotes of the reign of Louis XIV." It has the veneer of an afterthought: "*Oh, messieurs, mesdames, I have just remembered...*" But do not be deceived. It is not an accident that the startling story of a mysterious masked prisoner was placed at the hind end of his book. Voltaire knew what could happen to people who published news and opinions that the authorities did not like, and although he was obviously thrilled to know this story, he did not know if it was of importance to the crown, so he decided to leave it in a little bag at the back door of his book and see what happened.

Here is the full quotation about the masked prisoner from *Le Siècle de Louis XIV* (1753 edition). The doctor he refers to is Dr. Fresquière, a physician who treated Dauger in 1703, who had passed along this information to his son-in-law, the doctor for the duc de Richelieu, and it is from the duke that Voltaire learned about Fresquière's interactions with Dauger.

> A few months after the death of this head of state [Cardinal Mazarin[93]] a totally unparalleled event occurred, and, what is very strange, no historian has ever mentioned it before.
>
> In the highest secrecy, an unknown prisoner was sent to the prison of the island of Sainte-Marguerite in the Sea of Provence. He was above average height, was young, and was of a handsome and noble stature. The prisoner, on the journey to Sainte-Marguerite, wore a mask which had a chinpiece of steel with springs so that he could eat while he had the mask on. If he took the mask off, his guards had orders to kill him immediately.
>
> He was a prisoner at Sainte-Marguerite until a trusted officer, named Saint-Mars,[94] governor of Pignerol, having been named governor of the Bastille in 1690, came to take him to the Bastille, always masked. The marquis de Louvois visited him at Sainte-Marguerite before he was moved.
>
> The mysterious prisoner was led to the Bastille where he was given good lodgings. He was not refused any request. His greatest interest was in extraordinarily fine linen and lace. He played the guitar. They fed him well and the governor rarely sat down when he was with the prisoner.
>
> An old doctor who treated patients at the Bastille, who had often given medical help to this singular man when he was sick, said

he had never seen his face, even though he had often examined his tongue and the rest of his body.

He had an admirable physique, said this doctor: his skin color was a little on the brunette side; he was interesting by virtue of the singular tone of his voice; he never complained of his situation and never gave any hint of who he was.[95]

Some of the information given to Voltaire was wrong because Dauger lived in the Bastille for only the last five years of his thirty-four-years in prison and those who "served" him knew almost nothing about his previous years of incarceration at other prisons, so they added some of their own guesses and presumptions to their recollections. The history of the Mask is overloaded with volunteered assumptions that about half the time were made thinking them to be helpful and true, based on the speaker's own knowledge of history and politics. We have to forgive the other half because no other story tempts the teller so severely to proud elaboration as this one. It has been too hard to leave well enough alone and too tempting to claim exclusive knowledge.

There are a few minor errors in this relation but the following items in Voltaire's description are true:

- He did not protest his incarceration;
- Since he died a natural death it is logical that he never said anything to anyone about his life before prison or his identity.
- Maybe he really was taller than usual and maybe his body was normal, or perhaps he was solidly built. Some people are. Eustache Dauger might have been. Voltaire's critics must have thought that only a skeletal man with a gimpy leg could be authentic. Voltaire was stating in a romantic way the same thing the doctor said. The doctor said he had an "admirable physique"... Voltaire goes to *"la figure la plus belle et la plus noble."* Yes, that is somewhat poetical but Voltaire had the basic information that the man's body was at least normal, even better made than normal, and so he put a lyrical swagger on it.
- He received good treatment in prison; he was given everything he wanted except the ability to speak about himself or leave prison.
- The matter of the linen and lace (*linge et dentelles*) comes up in other references. It suggests (at least it did to Voltaire) a link with Queen Anne of Austria, Louis XIV's mother, whose fondness for fine lace and fabrics was well known. Was Voltaire suggesting the prisoner might have been her son? Yes. For a long time I dismissed this talk about fine

linen, but it is mentioned by more than one testimony, and Eustache, although we get the impression that he was gruff, was able to read and was given books in prison. If he grew up with books he could have grown up accustomed to nice clothing. And if he was from Calais or from the United Provinces (Holland) or from Flanders (Belgium), all places where lace was manufactured and where good cloth was easily found, then maybe this is right. As to Anne of Austria's love for fine cloth, the love of lace is not in DNA, as far as we know.

- He played the guitar. This is possible, but we do not know this for certain.

- *La plus grande chère...* he was well fed. We know, although he may not have had the elegant meals of noble prisoners, that he was adequately fed and money for his necessities was freely forthcoming from state funds.

- As for the governor rarely sitting down in front him, it is impossible to know if this is true. We have numerous testimonies, however, that the governor had great respect for Dauger.

- He wore his cloth mask when doctors examined him.

Voltaire's *Siècle* poked the fire, as was his intent, and some corrections and rebuttals flared up in the newspapers from people who had had secondhand contact with Dauger and wished to correct Voltaire's version of events. Most of the information we have on Dauger's appearance comes from these jealous refutations of Voltaire's repeated references to the Man in the Iron Mask.

Bishop Louis Fouquet And Madame La Duchesse D'Orléans

Ironically, it was the prisoner's chief jailer, Saint-Mars, who was responsible for the first descriptions of the prisoner. Saint-Mars was the only person in charge of Dauger over thirty four years; Saint-Mars was appointed as governor of the Sainte-Marguerite prison in April 1687 and he took Dauger with him.

The populations of Pignerol and Exilles, two small walled towns in the Italian Alps[96] about thirty miles from each other, had better things to do than wonder who was imprisoned in the Pignerol prison. In any case, they already knew that a very important state prisoner had resided there since 1665, the former chief manager of the realm's finances, Nicolas Fouquet (1615–1680). The story of the king's accusations against the *surintendant* Fouquet of treason and stealing state funds had been publicized thoroughly

CHAPTER 3. LEAKS, SPECULATIONS, AND SUSPICIONS 47

during a four-year trial in Paris that ended in a verdict of guilty and a life sentence in Pignerol, a finish that had been arranged by the king through the suborning of Fouquet's judges. Other prisoners, whomever they might be, were boring next to that very exciting criminal and the residents of Pignerol thought nothing about them. In 1680 Fouquet died and Saint-Mars and the Mask moved to the nearby Exilles prison, and in 1687 Saint-Mars was given a promotion from the bleak and isolated fort of Exilles to the post of governor of the prison on Sainte-Marguerite island in the Bay of Cannes in the geographical area that some call the French Riviera.[97] Cold, windy, silent Exilles lay just below the tree line of the lower Alps, but the prison-fort of Sainte-Marguerite looked out over a warm pebbled coastline, Cannes only two miles away to the north on the mainland coast, and Africa quite distant and unseen to the south; sunshine, blue water, and sky between.

Saint-Mars, in his usual fastidious and energetic mode of obedience that always accelerated when he had direct orders from his immediate supervisors the marquis de Louvois and the king to follow, carefully planned his strategy for the trip to Sainte-Marguerite, writing Louvois that he thought the best way to transport Dauger unnoticed was to hire porters to carry him in a fully closed traveling chair.[98]

Fine. As long as you guarantee that no one will be able to set eyes on the prisoner, said Louvois, who, as minister of war, was busy with the War of the League of Augsburg and was therefore possibly distracted from thinking reasonably about this small plan of the fussy Saint-Mars. At that moment Louvois had the maximum number of troops in the field that the *Ancien Régime* had ever had: 340,000 men.[99]

Saint Mars writes to Louvois on arrival at Sainte-Marguerite on 3 May 1687, that the prisoner was not seen by anyone on the trip:

> I made the trip in only twelve days because my prisoner was sick; he told me that he could not get enough air. I can assure you, Monseigneur, that no one saw him, and the way in which I guarded him and conducted him during the trip made everyone wonder who my prisoner was. The bed of my prisoner was so old and broken, like all the things he had, table linen and furniture, that it wasn't worth the trouble to transport them and I sold them for thirteen écus. I paid to the porters who brought traveling chairs from Turin for me and my prisoner to carry us here, 203 livres.[100]

The soldiers, prisoner, porters, and Saint-Mars and his family left Exilles on April 17, travelled to Oulx and Briançon, then through the pass of Mont-

Genèvre. They reached Grasse and finally arrived at Cannes on April 30. As they progressed, there were people who saw the parade of cavaliers surrounding a traveling chair supported by porters and covered with a waxed cloth[101] so that the person inside the chair was totally hidden. And nearly suffocated, too. It was reported by Saint-Mars that Dauger protested that he couldn't breathe in this carton, the only complaint he ever made that was recorded.[102]

But unnoticed? Saint-Mars' strategy on how to make his prisoner incognito was faulty because the group was the opposite of invisible as it passed through towns and beside farms... lots of soldiers, a completely closed vehicle probably holding an important prisoner (otherwise he would be walking) in a part of the country where almost nothing was completely closed due to the hot climate. To the contrary, the passage of such a well-outfitted group attracted attention. The communities through which the prisoner passed could not resist, and no one told them to resist, speculating on why he or she was being escorted through the provinces in style.

Bishop Louis Fouquet's Letter – 1687

We don't know eactly when rumors started about a mysterious masked prisoner because the first rumors were quiet ones told to each other by guards and staff of the prisons where he lived, but around the time of his relocation to Sainte-Marguerite in 1687 these stories escaped the prisons and dropped into a letter written by Bishop Louis Fouquet (1633–1702), a younger brother of the, by then, deceased Nicolas Fouquet. Cardinal Mazarin, during the time that Nicolas was working for His Excellence,[103] had gratified Louis Fouquet in 1658 with the bishopric of Agde[104] on the Mediterranean coast west of Marseilles, but after Nicolas Fouquet's fall he had to leave that post and was ordered to exile in Villefranche. The letter, written on 4 September 1687 from Paris, four months after Saint-Mars' group reached Sainte-Marguerite prison, was found by a biographer of Monseigneur Louis Fouquet, the abbot Xavier Azéma, doctor of theology and professor at Petit Séminaire de Montpellier. There is no name of recipient. Was this an ecclesiastical "*étrange bouffée de l'esprit méridional*"? The letter says:

> M. de Cinq Mars (sic) transported by order of the King a state prisoner from Pignerol to the Iles Sainte-Marguerite. No one knows who he is and there is an interdiction to say his name and an order to kill him if he pronounces it. Others have been taken to Pignerol and this one is no doubt a similar sort. A man killed himself there. This one was enclosed in a traveling chair carried by porters having a mask of steel on his face and all that any-

one could know from Cinq Mars (sic) is that the prisoner was at Pignerol for a long time and all the people that the public thinks are dead are not. Remember the Tower of Oblivion of Zerabi[105] that Procopius wrote about?[106]

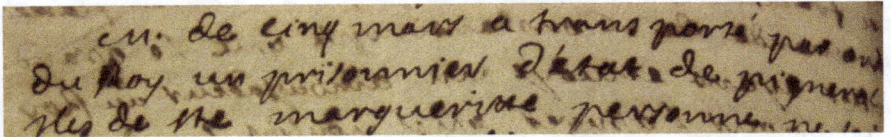

Figure 3.2: Detail of Bishop Louis Fouquet's letter describing Saint-Mars' prisoner. Image by the author 2022. Courtesy Bibliothèque Sainte-Geneviève.

Madame's Letter To The Electress – 1711

Four years before Louis XIV died, a letter floating a rumor about a masked prisoner who had recently died at the Bastille was delivered in [what is now] Germany, and it survived because it was from Louis XIV's infamous German sister-in-law, many of whose letters were saved and published. Elisabeth-Charlotte, duchesse d'Orléans (1652–1722), the manly wife of the queer brother of King Louis XIV (Philippe d'Orléans), wrote one of the first descriptions about the Mask. *Madame*—the traditional official title at court for the wife of the king's brother—was a magnificent independent woman and a prolific letter writer of insider information on the French court in its stark truth roped up with strings of adjectives that would do a sailor proud.[107] These letters were to her German family in the Palatinate, particularly her Aunt Sophie-Dorothée, the Electress of Hanover and to her half-brothers and sisters in Heidelberg.

Madame told the Electress on 10 October 1711 that she had recently heard a rumor about an unknown masked prisoner who had died in the Bastille in 1703. He had been threatened with instant death if he said his name or anything about himself, ate his meals and slept at night with his mask on, had been well treated and well lodged, was very devout, and read a lot of books. He was not masked as a punishment, she confided,[108] and a few days later she wrote to her aunt again to say the man was the Duke of Berwick, an English noble said to have been implicated in a plot to assassinate King William III of England in 1696.[109] We do not know the identity of her informant.

As determined as she was to reject customs that were not to her liking and as suspicious as she was about a lot of other things she was told over the years, she swallowed whole the rumor about the mysterious prisoner. Madame's acceptance of the story without challenge is typical of the gullible character of almost everyone who has ever written about the Mask or read books or articles about him, and this ungirdled passion to join the ranks of the initiated has caused a lot of confusion and misinformation.

We do not know how Bishop Louis Fouquet and the duchess of Orléans heard about Dauger, but both had essential information, although each report shows the effect of time on rumors: facts were eroded as the story was passed from one person to another. Fouquet's letter was wrong on the spelling of the name of Saint-Mars, although it's clear that he was referring to Dauger's jailer; he related an assumption, probably wrong, about what the mask was made of; but he was right about the enclosed traveling chair, right about his having been at Pignerol for a long time and that he would be shot if he said his name. Madame also was certain about the "speak and be killed" warning, and she knew Dauger was well treated but she thought he slept and ate with his mask on, which he did not.[110] She was right about his love of books, which evidently Bishop Fouquet didn't know about, not surprising because what he knew was from someone familiar with the road trip to Sainte-Marguerite. And Madame was right about his being very devout. Her informant was someone who was familiar with Dauger's day-to-day life in the Bastille.

The Fouquet 1687 letter has an important communication from Saint-Mars, and it sounds perfectly congruent with other teasers about his special prisoner that Saint-Mars occasionally blurted out: "...and all that one could learn from Saint-Mars was that the prisoner had been for a long time at Pignerol and that perhaps some people who are thought to be dead...are not."

The source of the description of the prisoner during his voyage is unknown. We wish we knew more about the origin and chronology of the leaks but we have only a few anonymous second-hand (also third-hand) reports of French southerners. Did the source of Louis Fouquet's information come from people who viewed the caravan on the highway? But how could Dauger's mask have been seen by a witness who only saw the line of troops from a distance? The group had to stop each night so perhaps someone at an inn saw the mask on Dauger? The use of a fully enclosed transport chair was to keep anyone from seeing the person being carried. But Fouquet's source not only knew the stringent directions that the prisoner had to follow but also he knew that under the waxed cloth sat a person who had a spring-operated device on his face. The report must have come from someone very close to the business of transporting the prisoner. Furthermore, knowing that the prisoner was forbidden to say his name and would be killed if he did says again that the source was not a shopkeeper in Oulx or Castellane or any of the overnight stops on the way to Cannes. More likely his source

CHAPTER 3. LEAKS, SPECULATIONS, AND SUSPICIONS 51

was an official of the town of Grasse or Cannes who would have received leaked information from one of the members of Saint-Mars' staff... or from Saint-Mars. Saint-Mars, who was hired to be an absolutely silent sentinel over the secret, was not silent; in fact he was talkative. In general, we know more about Dauger from Saint-Mars and the soldiers in his company and their descendants than from any other source.

De Palteau's Letter To The Editor – 1768

Most of what is known about Eustache's physical appearance comes from a letter written in 1768 by Guillaume-Louis de Formanoir de Palteau (b. 1712), son of Guillaume Formanoir, nephew and lieutenant of Saint-Mars (d. 1740). De Palteau was a middle-aged farmer, a member of the Royal Society of Agriculture of the generality of Paris. In 1768 he wrote a letter to the editor of a magazine called *l'Année littéraire* (*The Year in Literature*). He had previously published some observations on agriculture in this journal, but his second submission to the magazine was more personal than his previous thoughts on new farming techniques. He wrote to the editor of *l'Année littéraire* to refute the statements of Voltaire and of a certain Monsieur de Saint Foix (Germain-François Poullain de Saint-Foix, 1698–1776)[111] both of whom had recently raked up the, by then, old story of Louis XIV's mysterious masked prisoner. Who better than he, Guillaume-Louis de Formanoir de Palteau, the son of a soldier who had been one of the Mask's jailers, would be more able to tell the truth of this matter?

Guillaume Formanoir, de Palteau's father, had inherited the farm of Palteau from his uncle Saint-Mars. Guillaume had two brothers, Louis (d. 1724) and Joseph Formanoir (1672–1731). The three brothers, all nephews of Saint-Mars, had been members of Saint-Mars' small personal company of soldiers. Monsieur de Palteau, the son of Guillaume and his heir, therefore the owner of Palteau in 1768, related to the editor of *l'Année littéraire* what he had been told years ago by his uncle Joseph Formanoir, the sieur de Blainvilliers. Blainvilliers had scouted this information, not from his sighting of the prisoner during the day, but during a midnight, secret (that is, without Saint-Mars' permission) stake-out from a perch outside the prison near the prisoner's cell window that we are unable now to find. Maurice Pagnol said because there is now no gallery under the windows of Dauger's cell at Sainte-Marguerite, he believes this personal spying must have taken place at Pignerol.[112] But I hesitate to question Blainvilliers' story. There could have been a structure there that is now gone that would permit this nightwatch. At the Bastille there was for a time a walkway of planks around the prison that guards used for their regular rounds built on the earthen counterscarp. They could see in the cell windows that faced the dry moat in front of them.[113] The wooden sidewalk disappeared before the Bastille was destroyed, which shows that architecture, even of prisons, is subject to change or destruction at any time, so there could have been such a walkway attached to the side of the Sainte-Marguerite prison that disappeared and we have no record of it.

Seated at his desk at his chateau of Palteau in the Yonne department of Burgundy, the son of Guillaume de Formanoir wrote this letter about the Man in the Iron Mask:

> Monsieur,
>
> Since I see that the *letter of M. de Saint Foix*, recently published in your journal, shows that the Man in the Iron Mask still today exercises the imagination of our present day writers, I will tell you what I know of this prisoner. He was only known at the Isles Sainte Marguerite and at the Bastille as *La Tour*. The Governor and the other Officers thought highly of him. Whatever could be given to a prisoner, he received. He often walked about with a mask on his face. I had not heard of the mask being of metal until M. de Voltaire's *Siècle de Louis XIV*; maybe my informant forgot to tell me this fact; but he only wore the mask when he went out for a walk or when he was obliged to see a stranger.
>
> The Sr de Blainvilliers, Infantry Officier, who served under M. de Saint-Mars, Governor of the Isles Sainte Marguerite and afterwards the Bastille, told me many times that because *La Tour* interested him very much, to satisfy his curiosity, one night he dressed in a soldier's uniform and took a weapon and posed as sentinel in a walkway under the windows of the prisoner's room at Isles Sainte Marguerite; he said from that position he watched him all night; that he could see him very well; that he did not have his mask on; that he had a white face, was tall and well made, with his lower legs a little thick, and white hair, although he was in the prime of life; the prisoner passed the night pacing in his room. Blainvilliers added that he was always dressed in brown, that he was given beautiful linen and books, that the Governor and the Officers stayed standing before him with their hats off until he gave them permission to put their hats on and sit down; that they went often to keep him company and to eat with him.
>
> In 1698 M. de Saint-Mars left the Government of the Isles Sainte Marguerite to be Governor of the Bastille [taking his masked prisoner]. On the way, M. de Saint-Mars stayed with the prisoner at his property of Palteau in Burgundy. The man in the mask arrived in a litter that preceded that of M. de Saint-Mars;

CHAPTER 3. LEAKS, SPECULATIONS, AND SUSPICIONS 53

they had many men on horseback with them. The peasants presented themselves to their Seigneur; M. de Saint-Mars ate with his prisoner, who had his back to the window of the dining room which faced the courtyard; the peasants that I talked to said they could not see if he ate with his mask on; but they saw very well that M. de Saint-Mars, who was at the table across from the man, had two pistols beside his plate. They were served by only one *valet-de-chambre* who brought the food that was brought to him in the antichamber, closing very carefully behind him the door of the dining room. When the prisoner crossed the courtyard he had his black mask on his face; the peasants said they could see his teeth and his lips; that he was tall and had white hair. M. de Saint-Mars slept in a bed that they set up for him beside that of the man in the mask. M. de Blainvilliers told me that when the prisoner died in 1704 [sic] they buried him secretly at Saint Paul [Saint-Paul church cemetery in Paris], and that they put drugs in the coffin to consume the body. I never heard it said that he had any foreign accent.

You will make, Monsieur, the use that it pleases you of these notions that to me seem not to have any relation to the conjectures that have been considered up to the present on the state of this unhappy prisoner.

I have the honor to be, &c.

Your very humble and very obedient servant,

PALTEAU

At the Château de Palteau near Villeneuve-le-Roi, this 19 June 1768[114]

Joseph Formanoir de Blainvilliers' story is proved true, at least in part, by his description of the prisoner pacing all night. Prisoners in solitary confinement pace, which gives veracity to Blainvilliers' memory of the nightwatch.[115] It is reasonable to assume that the other descriptions Blainvilliers gave of the prisoner are also true, with this reservation; Blainvilliers was in the dark watching from a distance and there was probably little light in the cell where Eustache was pacing. Blainvilliers' descriptions, like the details of the face, hair color, and size of calves, do not seem unreal but should be taken with caution because they are, after all, the result of an illegal, independent venture spurred by vigorous curiosity in the middle of the night.

The scene that de Palteau says occurred in 1698 in his own courtyard[116] is tagged as information he got directly from one or more of the chateau staff who were present on the day Eustache Dauger arrived in his own litter followed by Saint-Mars's litter and an escort of cavalry on an overnight stop during the trip from Sainte-Marguerite to Paris. A litter, in this case, would be a small coach-like box with curtains to hide the passenger carried by porters using poles attached under the box.

The prisoner and his jailers went to their rooms immediately and rested before dinner. Saint-Mars sat across from his prisoner during their evening meal with two pistols on the table, which were probably to menace or kill anyone who would enter the room to attempt to take Dauger away. The staff member or members who watched the prisoner cross the courtyard, enter and leave the mansion saw his "lips and teeth" and said that he wore a black mask and was dressed in black. He was tall, they said, and had white hair. A cot was set up for Saint-Mars to sleep in, and the prisoner, it can be assumed, slept in a bed. He mistakenly said the prisoner died in 1704, but then said something fairly astounding: he said that at the prisoner's burial, acid was poured onto the body "to consume it" before covering it.

Louis XIV had tried to deny Eustache Dauger his life. Did he also try to deny Dauger a decent burial? De Palteau, a reasonable, landed gentleman farmer, obviously believed this testimony about acid, or he would never have given it to the public. Whether Blainvilliers was being dramatic in his stories to the young Guillaume-Louis, adding an untrue gruesome description that couldn't be checked, we will never know. However there is a possibility that the acid story may be true. A historian of Parisian cemeteries and burials, Vanessa Harding, says that by 1670 many Paris cemeteries were burying well over a thousand bodies a year.[117] The way they managed to accommodate so many bodies is neatly explained by the early twentieth-century Paris historian Lucien Lambeau in an article on the Saint-Paul cemetery:

> The [Saint-Paul] cemetery was 674 toises all together. For twelve centuries this little rectangle of 60 meters [196 feet] x 40 meters [131 feet], according to the map of Jaillot, took all the dead of the parish. It destroyed the bodies very fast. The ditches were 30 feet deep by 20 feet wide. They put the bodies very close together in rows... Once full, one foot of earth was put over to close it. Then they would open another ditch.[118]

After a period of time that was judged necessary for the soil and microclimate of the cemetery to remove the flesh from the bones, the trench would be opened, the bones taken out and stacked in unwalled buildings around the cemetery. If Dauger's face and body had not been eaten by acid put over him at the time of burial, someone could have come into the cemetery just after the burial and seen his face or seen part of his remains years later.

CHAPTER 3. LEAKS, SPECULATIONS, AND SUSPICIONS 55

Saint-Mars had obeyed orders from his superiors for thirty-four years about keeping anyone from seeing the ancient prisoner, so this may have been the last act of a long series of acts to hide Dauger, his face, his body, and his name.

New Facts About Dauger At Palteau

I went to Villeneuve-sur-Yonne to take photos of the manor house of Palteau, which I knew to be still standing and owned by a pony club that holds summer riding classes for private students, and after my husband successfully steered us to the house of Saint-Mars which is on a long road up the hill above the river Yonne, we took photos; then I returned to the village below and stopped at the tourist office where I found, as I had hoped, a booklet on the history of the area. It was written by a local historian, Jean-Luc Dauphin, and there was a chapter on the overnight stay of the *Masque de fer* at Palteau. I got the contact information for Monsieur Dauphin[119] and he sent me some other writing about the Mask that he had authored in a regional historical journal. In that way I discovered that there was more to the effort of M. Guillaume-Louis Formanoir de Palteau to expose the story of the prisoner and Saint-Mars than he wrote in the letter in 1768 to *l'Année littéraire*. Six years previous to his letter to *l'Année littéraire*, M. de Palteau wrote directly to Voltaire about the passage of Saint-Mars and the Mask through Villeneuve-sur-Yonne and the night they stayed at Palteau on the way to the Bastille in 1698. This letter was mentioned by Mongrédien in his book *Le Masque de fer*[120] and was enlarged upon by Monsieur Dauphin in the provincial historical journal *Etudes Villeneuviennes* in 2008.[121] Monsieur Dauphin had received from a trusted friend, M. Bonneville de Marsangy, a transcription of the letter de Palteau wrote to Voltaire in 1762. It had been transcribed by a certain M. Jacques Alexandre Augustin Hesme in 1856.[122] Hesme reported that he and his family were friends of de Palteau and his uncle Joseph Formanoir de Blainvilliers, who lived at Palteau.

Hesme's grandfather, M. Bonneville, lived many years with Guillaume Louis de Formanoir de Palteau, and before he died, Bonneville gave a copy of the 1762 Voltaire letter to Hesme and Hesme transcribed the letter, which ended up in Jean-Luc Dauphin's hands.

Hesme was often at the house and remembered vividly "the room hung with tapestries with mythological subjects, with its high posted bed and high backed chairs. The room bore the name *'chambre du Masque de fer.'*" Those who frequented the house always were impressed by the story, said Hesme, and gave many different guesses as to who the masked man had been. Hesme also remembered seeing, in an armoire at Palteau, the official certificates (*brevets*) of Saint-Mars' post assignments to Pignerol, Ex-

Figure 3.3: Entrance to the Palteau courtyard. Photo by the author 2018. The sign on the gate at the entrance to the farm is "Poney Club de Formanoir."

illes, Sainte-Marguerite, and the Bastille, and handwritten letters by Saint-Mars' two nephews who had been guards of the prisoner, Guillaume de Formanoir, who inherited the manor in Saint-Mars' will, and his brother, Joseph Formanoir de Blainvilliers.

The information that Guillaume Louis de Formanoir gave to *l'Année littéraire* in 1768 is slightly different from his previous 1762 letter to Voltaire. In the latter, the arrival at Palteau, the description of the prisoner (white hair, tall, lips and teeth), the scene at dinner with Saint-Mars' two pistols next to his plate, the name of the prisoner as La Tour, are almost word-for-word identical to his letter to the editor six years later, but there are three additional data points, one of them startling. In the 1762 letter to Voltaire, dated 15 March, the seigneur of Palteau said that the Mask and Saint-Mars had stayed *two* nights at the house. Since Saint-Mars owned Palteau at the time of the stay, perhaps business of the estate required two days' time. He also told Voltaire there had been sixty servants at Palteau who lined up to greet Saint-Mars in 1698, and de Palteau said he had personally known thirty of these servants, and in 1762, one of them was still living.[123]

De Palteau's letter to Voltaire said that Joseph Formanoir de Blainvilliers,

CHAPTER 3. LEAKS, SPECULATIONS, AND SUSPICIONS 57

who was on the staff of the Bastille when the Mask died in 1703, said Dauger was "buried secretly in the choir of the Saint-Paul church and that drugs had been put in the casket to consume the body."[124] The treatment of the corpse with acid was already part of the accepted (gruesome) story but the assertion that Dauger was buried in the choir of the Saint-Paul church is, if true, evidence that Saint-Mars had high respect for the prisoner. Or, Saint-Mars may have thought that the chance of the casket being opened in the chapel would be less than the chance that someone in the cemetery might have seen his face before other bodies were stacked on top of him. The Saint-Paul church was destroyed a few years after the French Revolution. If Dauger's body was buried in the choir and disintegrated by acid, the workers who took apart the church in 1799 probably shrugged at the sight of an empty casket, and thought little of it.

Should the chapel burial story be believed? De Palteau did not put this detail in his 1768 letter to Elie Fréron, the editor of *l'Année littéraire*. Maybe he had forgotten the place of burial, maybe he began to doubt that his uncle de Blainvilliers had been telling a true story, maybe he thought putting this detail in a public journal would be the wrong thing to do... that it would result in the burial being disturbed or in finding, upon digging in the choir of Saint-Paul church, that no body was there and then the public faction that was loud at the time in saying that the *Masque de fer* was a hoax would have support. De Palteau knew the Mask was not a hoax. That was why he wrote to Voltaire and to *l'Année littéraire*.

More Testimonies From Father Henri Griffet And Lieutenant Du Junca

The Jesuit Father Henri Griffet (1698–1771) had been a confessor and almoner[125] on the Bastille staff from 1745 to 1764, a theologian, historian, professor of literature at the *Collège Louis-le-Grand* and an admired orator. He published a book called *Treatise of Various Proofs That Establish Truth in History* in 1769, which was a landmark in the Mask mystery because he printed in this book three famous documents that were truly, in the spirit of the title of his book, proofs. Two of these proofs he found, while he was on the staff at the Bastille, in a journal written about fifty years previously by one of the Bastille's lieutenants,[126] Etienne du Junca (d. 1706).[127] These two documents may be the most important and reliable documents we have about the identity of the Man in the Iron Mask.

When du Junca, a former soldier from Bordeaux, became second in command of the Bastille under Besmaux (François de Monlezun, sieur de Besmaux, d. 1697, previously chief of Mazarin's guards) in 1690, eight years before Dauger got there, he looked at the spreadsheet format of the Great Register which he was responsible for keeping, and it didn't suit him; he wanted to keep a textual record in addition to the Great Register. Lieutenant du Junca's *Journal* contained far more information about the prisoners who entered and left the Bastille than the Great Register did, and it is obvious when looking at the two volumes of this journal that he took great care to be fully explanatory about each prisoner he received.

Here are du Junca's comments that he wrote on the day that Dauger arrived at the Bastille in company with Saint-Mars (18 September 1698) and his free company and on the day Dauger died (19 November 1703).

Du Junca's Journal Entries

Subtitle of Volume I

"Information on the prisoners who have been sent by order of the king to the Bastille, starting with Wednesday, the eleventh of October, when I began to serve as lieutenant of the king in the year 1690." The journal covers the time period 24 October 1690 to 26 August 1705.

Entry of 18 September 1698

On Thursday 18 September 1698 at three in the afternoon, Monsieur de Saint-Mars, governor of the château of the Bastille, arrived for the first time, coming from his government of the islands of Sainte-Marguerite Honorat, bringing with him in a litter an old prisoner that he had at Pignerol that he kept always masked and whose name is not spoken, and we put him, when he descended from the litter, in the first room of the tour de la Basinière to wait until nightfall so that I, myself, at nine at night, with M. de Rosarges, one of the sergents that monsieur the governor had brought with him, moved him into the third chamber of the tour de la Bertaudière, alone,[128] that I had furnished with everything a few days before his arrival and I received the order of M. de Saint-Mars that the prisoner is to be served by M. de Rosarges and monsieur the governor will provide the cost of his food.[129]

Subtitle of Volume II

"The accounting of the prisoners who left the Bastille, starting with the eleventh of the month of October, when I started my position in the year 1690." 24 October 1690 to 15 July 1705.

Entry of 19 November 1703

CHAPTER 3. LEAKS, SPECULATIONS, AND SUSPICIONS 59

This same day — Monday the 19th of November 1703 — the unknown prisoner always masked with a black velvet mask that Monsieur de Saint-Mars, governor, had brought with him from the St Marguerte islands, that he had guarded for a long time; who had felt a little sick yesterday when he left mass, died today at ten in the evening, without any warning signs — the event could not have been slighter. Mr Girault, our almoner, who confessed him yesterday and who was taken by surprise by his death, did not get the sacraments to him in time but exhorted him a moment before he died and this unknown prisoner guarded for such a long time was buried on Tuesday at four in the afternoon — the 20th — November in the St Paul cemetery, our parish. On the mortuary register they wrote an unknown name and monsieur de Rosarges and an old surgeon signed the register.

[Postscript]

I learned since that the name placed on the register was Mr de Maresiel and that 40 *livres* were paid for the burial.[130]

"The sum of forty *livres*, although modest, is a fee for burial in the same cemetery that represents twice the cost for the burial of Saint-Mars' *porte-clefs* Rû on January 21, 1713 (17 *livres*, 10 *sols*)," says historian Vergé-Franceschi. "We don't know the reason for the unusual expense: a purchase of *chaux vive* quicklime to dissolve the body? The *petit-neveu* of Saint-Mars said that the body was dissolved but he didn't say how or why. Special burial precautions? What were those?"[131]

Father Griffet had been told by staff members and guards about the mysterious masked prisoner who used to live in the Bastille and, like them, he must have been interested in the lore because when he discovered du Junca's journal and the entries in the two-volume journal for both the day the Mask entered the Bastille in 1698 (page 37 of the first volume) and the day he died in 1703 (page 80 of the second volume),[132] he copied them for his own possible future use, closed the books and put them back where he found them.

That must have angered Louis XIV's ghost because allowing this literature professor to scavenge old Bastille records, not to mention make copies, was dangerous to the silence he had imposed on Eustache Dauger. Du Junca's journal entries are irrefutable evidence of the existence of the prisoner, that he was not a figment of someone's imagination, that he wore a black mask, a loup that covered only the upper part of his face including his nose, when outside his room during the five years he was in the Bastille, that he died on November 19, 1703.

François-Joseph De Lagrange-Chancel

In addition to du Junca's journal entries, Father Griffet, to support his portrait of the Man in the Mask in his *Treatise of Various Proofs*, also referred to a magazine article by François-Joseph de Lagrange-Chancel (1677–1758) that had been published in *l'Année littéraire* in 1759.

Lagrange-Chancel was a prisoner at Sainte-Marguerite from around 1718, which means that he arrived at the Sainte-Marguerite prison twenty years after Dauger had left it. He was a literary antagonist, satirist, playwright, and poet who was imprisoned because he aimed some of his barbs at Regent Philippe II d'Orléans (1674–1753), caretaker of the French kingdom after his uncle Louis XIV died.

Lagrange-Chancel felt compelled to write to *l'Année littéraire* to correct Voltaire's previous assertions about the Man in the Iron Mask that had been printed in Voltaire's history book about Louis XIV's reign. He had information from three informants on the Mask which would correct Voltaire's story. Parts of this letter were published by *l'Année littéraire* in 1759 and 1768.[133]

Griffet, former almoner of the prison, wrote that the officers of the Bastille told him things about the Mask they had personally witnessed and stories that had been told to them by their predecessors, such as what the masked man looked like when he crossed the interior courtyard of the prison to attend mass, that he was an unknown person of an unknown social status and unknown name, that no one interacted with him except the governor and his closest staff.

> [M. de Launay], when he came to the Bastille to take a position in the general staff, recounted that many of the Officers, Soldiers, and Servants of the Bastille remembered the prisoner, and those that had seen him cross the courtyard with his mask on to go to mass, said that there was an order given, after his death, to burn everything that he had used, such as linens, clothing, mattress, bed covers, etc; and that they had even sanded down and repainted the walls of the room where he lodged.[134]

Griffet summarizes his data with a firm rebuttal of the prisoner's connection with Anne of Austria.

CHAPTER 3. LEAKS, SPECULATIONS, AND SUSPICIONS

> This Prisoner was not, then, a son of Queen Anne of Austria, who hid his birth so well that the Public never knew anything about it. If that were the case he wouldn't need to conceal his face from the entire universe. Thus this supposition, which for other reasons anyway is devoid of any truth, is not worth discussing.[135]

Finally, Griffet remembers clearly (and let this not discourage us) that:

> Monsieur de Launay said that Monsieur d'Argenson, Lieutenant de Police [of Paris], who often went to the Bastille, because he had much business there, knowing that the guards still talked about this Prisoner, asked one day of the Officers what the rumors were: and after the Officers told him of the many versions of the story that were passed around, he only responded: *We will never know the truth about that.* [Italics are Griffet's.][136]

Griffet's report that Dauger's belongings were obliterated just after he died was independently confirmed by the lawyer and journalist Simon Nicolas Henri Linguet (1736–1794), friend of Pierre-Hubert Charpentier, the man appointed in 1789 to collect the papers of the just vanquished Bastille. Linguet had heard the story about the demolition of Dauger's belongings and cell walls while imprisoned at the Bastille for a short time and he told this to an official of Louis XV's household, M. Jean-Benjamin de La Borde,[137] a composer, violinist, and member of the *Fermiers Générale* tax collectors.

Whether Voltaire knew of and read du Junca's journal entries that were printed in Griffet's book in 1768 is not known. Voltaire never mentioned the Griffet material, which was banned in France. He could have known of the content of the book, though, and kept silent about it to protect himself or to protect his status as the chief *patron* of the rumors.

During the daylight hours of November 20, before Rosarges and Reilh put Dauger's body on the litter that they would accompany a few blocks down the rue Saint-Antoine to the Saint-Paul cemetery, Monsieur de Saint-Mars gave to the two men a new white winding sheet that, according to the notes of Chevalier, he donated for wrapping Dauger's cadaver.

We have heard witnesses say that the governor had respect for Eustache. He had known and lived with him for thirty-four years. The donation of a new white shroud by Saint-Mars accentuates how alone both men were, but particularly how alone Dauger was. He had no family, no one had ever come to the authorities to look for him or advocate for him, he had never asked to make a will, showing he had no possessions other than those in his room and they belonged to the prison, not to him. If Saint-Mars had not given a cloth to cover the prisoner, he would have gone nude into the cold ground. Of all we have said and will say about Saint-Mars, this gift of a shroud says more about the currents and aspirations of his life than anything else. Saint-Mars and Dauger, in that last moment together in the Bastille, the one a dead prisoner on the way to the Saint-Paul cemetery and the other a jailer, before too many years to be on his own passage to the same cemetery, were of equal authority.

4. The Valet

> Colors are important, clubs bearing more positive indications, hearts next and their meaning is *"douceur, joie, libéralité."* The diamonds (*carreaux*) mean a quarrel or delay... these come next, and lastly the spades which are the signs of sickness or sadness.
> —Un initié Mystères des sciences occultes, 1894

"He Is Only A Valet"

In the first chapters of this book the life story of Eustache Dauger was told, at least his story after he was arrested. And we heard the testimonies of people who saw the prisoner and those that knew to a small degree his behavior in prison, his pasttimes, and, most importantly, we paid special attention to the facts we know about his change of prisons, forced changes at the time of Saint-Mars' promotions; when Saint-Mars was awarded an advancement at a new prison and a higher salary, Dauger always went with him. Luckily for historians, the movements on these overland trips of soldiers and baggage were witnessed by people who recorded surprise at a state prisoner under tight guard being traipsed around the countryside in a closed transport, making weak points in the secrecy that Louvois and Louis XIV wanted to maintain about the prisoner.

Before other prominent characters are added to the case in ensuing chapters—Louis XIV and his servants who watched over Dauger, Louis XIII and Anne of Austria, the parents of Louis XIV—it would be helpful to subtract one character in particular whose presence in the mystery has been unhelpful and undisciplined: the Valet.

When attempting to solve a mystery, after getting comfortable with the story, a detective can come to consider certain roadblocks more critical than others. In this mystery the spelling of certain words and their different meanings to different characters in the story can be confusing. When reading about a place or person in seventeenth-century sources we often have a kaleidoscope of spellings that change from book to book or even from page to page. To further complicate things, some spellings are used in some countries and not in others, in certain time periods and not in others; seventeenth-century Frenchmen spelled words in various ways, usually according to how the name sounded to them when they last heard it spoken;

and, most challenging, we sometimes have to cross purposefully laid traps to understand descriptions because the raging Paris fashion in upper-class society in the 1600s was playing word games, the mechanics of which were created by those who attended *salons*. Invitations to the *salon* of Catherine de Vivonne, Mme de Rambouillet (1588–1665) were the most sought after, and if one became a regular guest at her weekly gatherings at her *hôtel* in the rue Saint-Thomas-du-Louvre, you were called a *Précieuse*, one who followed the unwritten rules and vocabulary of the group. Some, not all, of these people would merit being called pretentious as well as precious.

Readers of seventeenth-century letters and memoirs, whether about the Mask or any other subject, have to be prepared for navigating a *Précieuse* allusion or riddle because eventually the fashion for coded poetry and prose decipherable only to a limited set of insiders became popular and ubiquitous. Like a rock with mica sprinkled through it, the riddle sparkles but one has to turn it fifty different ways to see each glint of gold, and then step back to admire the whole. We find phrases in personal letters, in particular, that use *Précieuse* license to joke and deceive, and they turn up suddenly without warning because stealth was one goal of the game.

I believe this is the case with the word "valet," which the marquis de Louvois, the administrative overseer of the Mask's incarceration, wrote in his letter of July 19, 1669, to Saint-Mars, the senior jailer at Pignerol, informing him of the imminent arrival of an important prisoner to Pignerol.

This 19 July letter was found in the French national archives by Father Joseph Delort when researching his book *Histoire de l'homme au masque de fer*, published in 1825. Ever since that year, writers have, while wondering in footnotes if the use of the word "valet" *might* have been a deliberate deception by Louvois, decided that Louvois was speaking factually—that he was inside the king's confidence on the prisoner Eustache Dauger who was certainly a "valet." Since that was the only occupation ever associated with Dauger during his imprisonment, after 1825 those trying to decipher the mystery began to suspect only people who had been valets. Attempts to solve the mystery have all tried to find a servant or middleman to accuse. Fouquet's great biographer, J. Lair, did so. "Who was this person and why was he arrested? He was French, Catholic, a valet."[138] The most recent books by professional scholars limit their research to valets of one sort or another.

One of the reasons that Louvois's valet designation was taken so seriously is because we have known Louvois as a mastermind of the dark side of the reign; if you will, Louis XIV's valet for secret operations. In view of these crimes, writers had absolute confidence that he would know all about this matter in 1669 that became the greatest secret, and possibly the great-

CHAPTER 4. THE VALET

Figure 4.1: The word "valet" in the letter from Louvois to Saint-Mars, July 19, 1669, shown in the microfiche copy of the original letter in the French Archives Nationales. Photo by the author 2016.

est crime of all. Yet other authors have questioned whether Dauger was a valet in his life before prison. Jean Markale in his book on the Mask offered the simple question, "Why such secrecy for a simple servant?"[139] Excellent question that in seven words becomes rhetorical.

I am firmly convinced that the "valet" is not a characterization of the prisoner, but the "valet" is a pun on the prisoner's surname which sounds like the name of the knight of Charlemagne, Oger the Dane (sometimes spelled Hogier or Ogier), who was regularly pictured and named on the third picture card in the suit of spades. In English this card is called the Jack of Spades, sometimes the Knave of Spades,[140] and in French it is *Le Valet de Pique*.[141]

Just as the *Précieuses* had their special culture of word usage, the designers of decks of cards had theirs, and to decorate the picture cards they applied historical or mythical personas to them and printed the names on the cards to add the reputations of past kings, queens, emperors, and knights to the fun of the game. Assigning names of heroic and historical characters to the picture cards in decks of playing cards had been conventional in Europe for a long time. In December 1581 the French king Henri III and the French parlement had regulated the design of playing cards and in 1613 a rule was made that card makers had to put their names, surnames, seals, and devices on the *Valet de Trifle* (Knave of Clubs) in each pack of cards.[142] In French decks, the chief picture card often bore the names of rulers with whom the royal Capet family identified: King David, King Solomon, Alexander the Great, Caesar Augustus, and Charlemagne.[143] Queens might be marked Argine (anagram for Regina), Rachel (the *Bible's* Rachel), or Pallas (Pallas Athena), and their *Valets* might be labeled La Hire (*nom de guerre* of Etienne de Vignolles, knight of Charles VII of France), Hector (Hector de Galard, captain of the guard to Louis XI of France, although sometimes he is also the Trojan warrior); and the Knave of Spades was frequently Oger.[144]

Figure 4.2: Valet de Pique issus de jeux de cartes au portrait de Paris. 1732. Artist unknown. Estampe. Courtesy Bibliothèque nationale de France.

So not only was it conventional in the seventeenth century, and long before, that Oger the Dane was the person represented on the "*Valet de Pique*" (the English and American Jack of Spades), but his name was always printed next to his picture. Anyone at the French court who fanned open a hand of newly dealt cards at one of the gambling tables at Fontainebleau and Saint-Germain-en-Laye, and the soldiers at Pignerol who played cards in their off-duty time, would know that Oger was the equivalent of *Valet*.

CHAPTER 4. THE VALET

The structure of the joke is that the prisoner's last name sounds exactly like the historical character (Oger) anthropomorphized on *Valet* (Jack, Knave) playing cards. Eustache Dauger does not need extravagant furniture because he is only *"un valet."*

Linguists call this arrangement of words a homophonic heterograph which is a pun that makes a link between words that sound the same but are written differently, in this case, d'Auger, Dauger and Oger. Before even getting that far with this particular pun though, you have to know another connection that is not a sound-alike set of words but which is a set of interchangeable words: *Valet* and Oger. One of the *Valets* in a deck of cards is customarily Oger.

> We find at this period (1698) the marquis de Cavoye luxuriously occupying the fifth pavilion at Marly that he shared with the maréchal de Créquy. Is it necessary to add that the grand maréchal was in most of the hunting parties and other amusements, and that his love of gambling, that we have referred to elsewhere—totally excusable because the valet de pique was one of his ancestors—earned him a place often at the king's card table?[145]

Triple Jeopardy

The pun was a triplicate play on words because Louvois was also making a spontaneous, antagonistic joke on the name of his rival for the sexual favors of a young girl, a contest he had lost. In French a *"valet"* usually would mean a male servant or low-level helper; *"valet"* could be pejoratively used to describe someone deemed a lackey who unhesitatingly did the bidding of his master. Louvois was, that summer of 1669, frustrated that Louis d'Auger de Cavoye (1639–1716) had bested him in a contest for the flesh of Marie Sidonie de Lenoncourt, marquise de Courcelles (1650–1685). Louis d'Auger de Cavoye was one of the most handsome men at court, said the memoirist Saint-Simon, so he could take his leisurely pick from the loveliest of the *filles* who were social handmaidens at the houses of noblility and royalty.

In the previous summer of 1668, Marie Sidonie, a teenage newlywed, hosted the dashing Cavoye for an afternoon at her husband's house when he wasn't home.[146] In fact Cavoye may well have been her companion for more than one afternoon as he eventually rented a house she owned on the rue des Saints-Pères in Paris that he finally bought, enlarged, lived in with his future wife (not Marie-Sidonie), and died in in February 1716.

After Cavoye left the Courcelles house, Hortense Mancini, niece of

Mazarin and previous lover of Cavoye, who had seen Cavoye's carriage on the street in front of the hôtel de Courcelles, told the marquise's husband that his wife had a visit from the gentleman Cavoye during his absence. Courcelles taunted Cavoye into a duel, which we know did not result in the death of either one because not too long after the duel they were imprisoned in July 1668 in cells in the *Conciergerie* next to the *Palais de Justice* on the *île de la Cité*, because dueling was illegal.[147] This particular incident of casual adultery, common in Paris and in all the universe at all times, had an unusual consequence: a noxious effect on the mystery of the Man in the Iron Mask.

The marquis de Louvois had been trying to force the teenage Marie Sidonie into double adultery with him since she had married the marquis de Courcelles in 1667. He had set one of his spies on her, Langlée, a man of low reputation but who hoped to rise in "the game," as Saint-Simon put it, by informing Louvois about his prey, whether young girls or other targets. Marie Sidonie was interested in sex, but not with Louvois. She dallied with the handsome François de Neufville de Villeroy (1644–1730) and simultaneously with the *abbé* d'Effiat, who was so handsome that Louis XIV almost had him removed from court because he was making the *demoiselles d'honneur* of the court swoon, but her affair with the *abbé* was not known to de Villeroy, who was sleeping with Madame de Monaco, previously a girlfriend of the comte de Lauzun and the king. Marie was always happy to see Louis d'Auger de Cavoye at her door, who had, like de Villeroy, been a childhood friend of Louis XIV. Louvois was embarrassed and angry that these pretty men, Cavoye and the others, were being invited into the bedroom of a girl who would not allow him past her front steps.

By 19 July 1669 when Louvois wrote his "valet" letter to Saint-Mars, Marie Sidonie had become pregnant, had been sued and pursued in court for adultery by her husband, had been put in confinement, and she had just given birth on 5 July 1669 to a baby that died a few weeks later. Louis d'Auger de Cavoye's name is similar to Eustache Dauger's name, so the pun on Oger, Dauger, and d'Auger was wrapped up with a seasoning of vengeance that portrayed d'Auger de Cavoye as a weakling lackey who was in jail in the Conciergerie.

The valet conundrum has been the gatekeeper, the sentinel, standing in the way of productive progress on the mystery. Historians have limited themselves to suspects who were servants or people who were not interesting on their own accord but had value merely as the accomplice of someone else who *was* interesting.

The *valet* joke also shows that Louvois didn't know who Eustache was or why he'd been arrested. The war minister's insertion of a pun in the in-

CHAPTER 4. THE VALET

structions about how to handle a new prisoner shows he had no idea that the prisoner was very important to Louis XIV and whose treatment and length of incarceration would blossom into the most secretive and mysterious event of the Old Regime. Making a joke about this new prisoner was dismissing him (and Louis d'Auger de Cavoye) as negligible; important prisoners of state would be more respected in a letter to the king's jailer when ordering a cell prepared. For instance, "the *Comte de* ... will have his servant with him who will require an accommodation," or "the *per diem* of the *maréchal de* ... will be forty *livres* and you should purchase furniture for him commensurate with his rank." Louvois must not have noticed the irregularity of an unknown individual with no rank being sent to Pignerol, a prison for safekeeping of the highest state officials of the realm. It would take Louvois many years to question the discord between the king's orders for Eustache Dauger's meager provisions, his food and furniture, and the level of security that Louis XIV insisted on for him, which, in the course of thirty-four years, increasingly perplexed Dauger's jailers, and in the next three hundred years the researchers of the mystery of the Man in the Iron Mask found themselves wondering the same thing the jailers wondered: why such permanent secrecy and security for an obedient, pious, quiet man, whose name, as it said on his death notice in the Bastille register, was "never known."

The Valet obstacle has been eliminated. In his absence, many things point to a connection between Dauger and the royal family and as future characters are introduced the architecture for this theory will become clear. Dauger was certainly not a valet. Louis d'Auger de Cavoye was not a valet, but Louvois was a valet of Louis XIV, a servant required to do exactly what he was told from sunrise to the last party of the late evening. He was dancing in the shadow of the king, not knowing, for a while, that the king had another shadow to partner with.

Part 2

SQUIRRELS, LIZARDS, AND SNAKES

5. Fouquet And Colbert

[Fouquet] was sensitive and perceptive. He discovered the genius of Molière and La Fontaine, Le Nôtre and Poussin, Puget, Le Brun and La Quintinie...he was the most magnificent and the most curious man of his time, attractive, political, experienced in business, he had the eye, the passion, the power and the fortune, all the gifts that make the grand philanthropist.

—Edmond Bonnaffé

Nicolas Fouquet (1615–1680)

A subordinate topic of the Man in the Iron Mask mystery could be said to be burials; at least where Nicolas Fouquet and Eustache Dauger are concerned. Who was Nicolas Fouquet and why is the location of his burial a question that the city of Paris cannot answer...or would rather not answer?

Monsieur de Chamillart, Louis XIV's secretary for war late in his reign, to stop people from begging him for the identity of the Man in the Iron Mask, which people assumed had fallen to him as manager of the Mask's dossier from the laps of the dead Louvois and his son Barbezieux, responded to inquiries by stoically pronouncing that the prisoner was "a man who had all the secrets of Monsieur Fouquet." The unknown secrets of Nicolas Fouquet were a favorite subject for fantasizing about the famous *surintendant* of finances therefore this statement by Chamillart is vainglorious posing rather than fact. Chamillart, like the rest of Louis XIV's court, had no idea who the prisoner was.

It might be more true to say that Fouquet knew all the secrets of Dauger. They were both prisoners at Pignerol between 1669 and 1680, supervised by Saint-Mars. The theory that Nicolas Fouquet helped Anne of Austria with the logistical side of Dauger's life is not farfetched. Fouquet could have been the person who found places for him to live that were appropriate for his condition and invented methods to direct untraceable money for his needs. Fouquet had lots of clients who hired him to wash money and get it to the caretakers of children and adults that the clients wanted to hide. That sort of thing is exactly what Fouquet did for people: he helped them out in their darkest moments, when their world was falling in on top of them, and he stopped the fall, or at least he was the conduit for the money that paid off an adoptive parent, a wetnurse, an assassin, the police... in return for something that he would ask for later. He bought people by fixing their problems. Anne of Austria herself said that Fouquet helped her get funds for her charities, so we know that the queen, Fouquet, and money had joined more than once.

Nicolas Fouquet's and his family's presence in the mystery of the Mask could be compared to an electromagnetic spectrum of visible and invisible colors. They appear suddenly in blue or red and then give way to other players but they never entirely disappear. Fouquet's younger brother Louis penned the first sighting of the prisoner traveling through Provence in a closed litter with a metal mask on his chin. Fouquet's mother was admired by Anne of Austria because she was a member of the devout Counter Reform community in Paris; the queen asked her to use her skills as a home nurse to treat Queen Marie-Thérèse for seizures following a delivery of a royal baby. Basile Fouquet, who looked very much like his famous older brother, was Mazarin's[148] chief of secret police.

At this moment, we can look at the basic, black and white story of Fouquet's duel with King Louis XIV and the king's new chief minister for finance—Colbert, who replaced Fouquet as chief for finances after the king and Colbert had ruined Fouquet and put him in jail. Fouquet's and Colbert's animosity to each other nurtured and validated the king's dislike of Fouquet. The consequences of the hatred were disastrous for Fouquet and influential to the life of Dauger. In 1675 Louvois gave permission for Eustache Dauger to serve as Fouquet's valet in Pignerol prison when Fouquet's valet was sick. That made Fouquet the only person to interact with Dauger in any social way other than Saint-Mars and Rosarges. Dauger had a vial or box of medicine on him when Fouquet was found dead in his cell at Pignerol of a sudden heart attack or stroke in March 1680.

Nicolas Fouquet was a charming, erudite man, smart, ambitious, well educated, a good lawyer and writer; he gave space in his country retreat at Saint-Mandé east of Paris near Vincennes to scientists and physicians for their research, including laboratory space, and had a natural sensibility for art and beauty. Jean Markale in his *La Bastille et l'énigme du Masque du Fer* drew Fouquet as having a "refinement, a sense of compromise, but was not compromised; these made him a superlative actor of the modern political world, alert to opportunities, able to work adeptly in a wide range of affairs, and gain with grace the confidence and services of people he thought to be valuable."[149] He held two very important positions: king's chief attorney general in the Paris parlement and concurrently, as of 1653, chief of the country's finances, *surintendant des finances*, the highest financial officer in the kingdom. The king was his only overseer.

CHAPTER 5. FOUQUET AND COLBERT

It was Fouquet who first saw the worth of the artists who later worked for Louis XIV. Fouquet hired André Le Nôtre (1613–1700) to design his gardens, hired Louis Le Vau (1612–1670) to design his palace at Vaux-le-Vicomte,[150] hired Charles Le Brun (1619–1690) to paint the walls and canvasses that praised the *surintendant* with naked cherubs, floating mythical figures, and many squirrels, the Fouquet mascot, holding penants that waved the motto of the owner to every visitor: *Quo non ascendet*? How far will he climb?[151]

Vaux-le-Vicomte suffered a long history of neglect, but is now restored, a stone monument that bristles out of the flat terrain, proud and solid, an effect due partially to the very attenuated lateral wings extending forward from the main house. Fouquet and Le Vau used an architectural device found at the royal palace of Madrid in Paris: a *sous-sol* extending up to the terrace on the front side. This partially underground passage had service rooms, a kitchen, wine caves, offices, and dormitories for house servants.[152] Fouquet's personality and his daring show of wealth, not of old money but of money recently acquired by family connections in government positions, a practice that bourgeois families in France had been using for generations to rise to noble status, can be felt viscerally at Vaux when standing on the expansive steps on the back of the château looking out into the garden, the magnificent oval mouth of the two-storey *salon* behind, with its painted interior dome over the floor of the room that is easily imagined as a *parterre* of tables spread out for dinner with Fouquet's gold plates, his crystal and silverware, double- and triple-tier comports overflowing with rare fruits, and servants passing like small waves of water among the diners pouring fine Burgundian wines. The guests would, in pretty weather, be able to pass directly into the garden through tall doors all around the front of the oval, making it a transitional clairvoyant precursor to the garden in front of them, which was an aesthetic feast greater than the edible luxuries Fouquet provided.

Louis XIV was outraged that this suave, wealthy government official made him look, he thought, poor, provincial, and inferior; the *surintendant's* innate grace and seductive smile infuriated Louis XIV. Fouquet's natural glow of savoir-faire and his almost professorial command of the textual and visual arts of the Baroque era was totally opposite to the essential character of Louis XIV, who was cool, ultra courteous, but without giving of himself. Louis was cautious, cunning, above personalities. He reined himself in. Fouquet had a sweetness about him, a cordiality, and he must have been one of those people who, when you are telling your story, you feel as if you are being heard, that the listener has your best interests at heart and will ally with you if he possibly can. These two personalities were so opposite that the clash was too much for Louis, especially since Fouquet had control of all his money.

Jean-Baptiste Colbert 1619–1683

Les Halles, the old central Paris food market, was a bright acreage, the iron roofs over the hundreds of stalls of vegetable and fish sellers quite high over the ground, letting in a lot of light, even on a rainy or cloudy day. It was the busiest part of Paris in the center of the old town, where, there not being as many little grocery stores scattered in each neighborhood as now, many Parisians went each day to find their daily meals of cabbage, of canteloupes, of lamb and trout that they carried home in string bags and ate that night, the restaurant chefs having already been there at dawn to buy *crème fraîche* and oysters and potatoes for their dinner clients. In 1969 the city, having long ago decided that the market needed to go elsewhere, destroyed the iron skeletons supporting the market roofs and replaced them with underground shopping malls and gardens above ground, but fifty years later the space seems still to be waiting for its destiny.

Above the expansive carved out space of the old *Halles* is the south facade of the Saint-Eustache church on the north perimeter of the marketplace. Gothic straightness and points of stone are the first presentations of the church, but it has subtle Greco-Roman features that can be spotted on a thoughtful tour of the interior. It is not a cathedral, but is as big as one; it is a huge parish church, finished in 1640, which served the neighborhood on the east side of the rue de Richelieu for baptisms, funerals, religious services, and community aid.[153] It is dedicated to Saint Eustache, a legendary and possibly invented Roman soldier who converted to Christianity during the first century after seeing a burning Holy Cross spread between the antlers of a deer in the forest. In the legend, he and his family were tortured and killed in 118 A.D. because they were Christians. His saint's day is September 20 and he is invoked for the protection of hunters, firefighters, sword makers, the communities of Madrid and Paris, and anyone facing adversity.

The nave and its choir and chapels are dark, despite the repeated sets of beautiful gilded colonettes with blue and red diagonal stripes next to others that have golden festoons swirling around rosettes and green pea vines climbing skyward. It is darkest on the north side of the chancel where stands the tomb of Jean-Baptiste Colbert (1619–1683), formerly a parishioner, Louis XIV's minister for construction, finances, the rebuilding of the French navy, the operation of the king's house, possessions, staff, chateaux, a man of many responsibilities, always at work for the king at all hours each day of the week.

His tomb, designed by Charles Le Brun and sculpted by Antoine Coysevox and Jean-Baptiste Tuby, has the same contrast of bright light and darkness that the surroundings and interior of the church have; his kneeling, life-sized image is made of bright white Gennes-Val-de-Loire marble posed on

CHAPTER 5. FOUQUET AND COLBERT

top of his black marble casket, his hands placed together in prayer, his eyes looking neither down nor up, but straight ahead at a little angel holding a Bible, but the angel was destroyed in a raid on the church by revolutionnaries in 1789 or soon after, so Colbert is staring at something that was taken away from him, a fitting visual epitaph for his twenty-two-year wrestling match with Louis XIV. Strangely, he wears clothing that was in style a century before his death: a sixteenth-century doublet and trunk hose with a short semicircular cloak and stockings held by prominent garters. The carved female grieving figures of "Abundance" and "Fidelity" are at his left and right, and "Fidelity's" dog, her symbol, is enclosed within her hemline, in retreat while he watches the churchgoers and the tourists, most of them probably not knowing or caring who Jean-Baptiste Colbert was and certainly not knowing that he had to be put in his casket at night in secret because he had been so hated that the *doyens* of the church were afraid they might have some trouble getting him settled if it had been daylight. I have not looked closely enough at the sarcophagus to see if his family crest mascot, the *couleuvre* (French for grass snake), is present.

Most of Colbert's body was thrown in a ditch when the little angel was tossed away in 1789. No one but God knows if there is anything left of him in the huge dark black sarcophagus that his white body kneels on.[154] Colbert was Nicolas Fouquet's enemy and from that pose, imitating the snake on his family crest, he terrorized, bit, and killed the small, poised, overly happy Nicolas Fouquet whose family's arms showed a squirrel.

Jean-Baptiste Colbert had been Mazarin's money manager, quite a successful one because with Colbert's aid Mazarin collected in nine years the largest fortune of the Old Regime. It was not very hard to steal money from the state because as architectural historian Hilary Ballon wrote, in French seventeenth-century state finances there was an
"...erosion of boundaries between one investment and the next, one pocket and the other."[155] Changing the rules for borrowing money to suit their circumstances, filling bankrupt lines of credit with funds that had money in them that were supposed to go to a different purpose and feeding off the cantering interest rates that resulted, these actions were available to Fouquet, Colbert, and Mazarin. Mazarin greedily siphoned government provisions for the army and sold them to make a profit on the black market. Colbert was methodical; he was the ultimate wizard in spreadsheets. Mazarin, an Italian, would recognize the Italian word *equivoco*[156] as fitting to describe their alliance. When Mazarin died in March 1661 Colbert had gathered his own little fortune from their joint ventures but he was facing unemployment.

Colbert wanted Fouquet out of government (preferably carried out in a casket) because he knew that Fouquet knew at least half of what had been pilfered because Fouquet had been the manager of the funds from which thousands of *livres* were regularly disappearing; Fouquet could see what was happening—he said so at his trial—but under the circumstances (the country was at war), it would have been disloyal to the state to interrupt the process, however damaged, and complain in public or to the king. The man doing the stealing was Louis XIV's godfather and stepfather; what point would there have been?

Here is an example of a fundraiser by Colbert to Mazarin in 1653:

> I think we should cover ourselves for the loss we've had because of the lowering of [the value of the *livre*] by convincing the king that he needs a loan from us for 150,000 to 200,000 *livres* at fifteen percent interest, and we'll reimburse ourselves next June by passing the debt through some good accounts [those with money in them] like the convoy from Bordeaux or the salt taxes from Languedoc and Lyon which are starting to come in now."
>
> Mazarin wrote his consent: "I approve for 150,000 *livres* under a false name.[157]

To look straightforwardly at the details leads to an agreement with one of Colbert's biographers, Inès Murat, that Fouquet had been drawn into the larceny and was not innocent.

> [Fouquet] also had the same cleverness of financing that Mazarin had. He was a superior trader, deal-maker. It was thanks to his personal caution that he gave to the state a lot of money to finance the war with Spain. How to reimburse himself ? It was up to him.[158]

When the Peace of the Pyrenees ended the Spanish war in 1659, Colbert feared that if Fouquet was allowed to continue as superintendant of finance he might expose Colbert's crimes to the king. Colbert told the king that Fouquet had continued his juggling of state accounts to find money to fund the broken state (which had been his ordained responsibility for the last eight years) despite the king having had a serious talk with Fouquet about ceasing his irregular practices now that the war was over.

The king and Colbert wanted Fouquet beheaded so that he would be out of their way permanently but to achieve a death sentence Colbert and the king needed more than a charge of financial mismanagement—they had to charge Fouquet with a crime meriting death. Conspiring to overthrow the king's authority would make the case. Colbert arranged for a spy to be sent under cover to Belle-Ile, an island near the peninsula of Quiberon[159] that Fouquet had been asked by Cardinal Mazarin to buy to get it out of the hands of the rebellious Retz family, and where Fouquet was building an independent maritime shipping center, although details were few; Fouquet had sealed the operation from public view, no visitors were allowed, and the letters of the nuns who ran the medical clinic were reviewed before they left the island.[160] The spy came back with a map of the island and the glad news that there were 1,500 workers at Belle-Ile, a guard of 200 men, 400 pieces of cannon of which 100 in cast-iron and 300 in iron, a lot of bombs and firepower in storehouses, five artillery pieces of iron, guns and provisions for 6,000 men. There were large stores of wine and wheat.[161] That certainly looked like treason. Someone who hated Fouquet a little less could have also made the case that the fortifications and armed men might have been prudent and necessary purchases for the start of a shipping company that would have both colonization and trade as goals, seeing that the seas were battlegrounds where the Dutch, the Portuguese, the English, the Spanish, and the pirates were experienced defenders of fabulous wealth coming through their own maritime companies. Seizing islands to make colonies, that princes all over Europe were discovering to be political bargaining chips and for which their warships were already under sail from Canada to the African Gold Coast and were never happy with intruders, was on the rise. One could say Fouquet might have needed half the four hundred cannons just to defend his ships against the pirates alone. Colbert would never have made that case; for Colbert, the activity at Belle-Ile was a sign that Fouquet wanted to become master of Brittany and northern overseas trade, undermining the king's power: treason.

Colbert and Louis XIV proceeded to arrest Fouquet in Nantes (Charles Ogier de Batz-Castelmore, the Musketeer d'Artagnan (1613–1673) was the arresting officer, personally chosen by the king), on the king's birthday in 1661, imprison him, accuse him of stealing state funds and committing treason, seal and confiscate all his properties and papers, exile all his family members, including two brothers who were bishops, to the four corners of France. He separated his young children from their mother and allowed them to be sent to their grandmother only because Anne of Austria begged Louis for this favor, put many of his close associates in jail, such as his secretary, Paul Pellisson (1624–1693), set up a special chamber of justice that over four years the king and Colbert manipulated into a bare majority vote of guilty, and when to their immense anger and humiliation the sentence was exile and not death, the king aggravated that sentence to life in prison in Pignerol, where Fouquet was taken by d'Artagnan and a company of musketeers in December 1664.

Paul Morand, author of a small, intensely sensitive book on Fouquet that is closer to poetry than prose in some paragraphs, asked the same question that all historians ask about Fouquet's arrest: why was Fouquet so sure he would not be arrested even though many of his friends and informants had told him that he should flee the house at which he was staying in Nantes[162] where the king had requested his presence for a government council meeting, by use of its underground tunnel to the riverside and board one of his ships that would take him to his own island harbor of Belle-Ile where he had soldiers and fortifications? "The inertia of Fouquet before this imminent danger is incomprehensible." He asks if there was a secret of the king held by Fouquet that he thought would give him immunity from arrest, perhaps that of the *Masque de fer*?[163]

Figure 5.1: The garden (south) facade of Vaux-le-Vicomte, designed by Louis Le Vau and built between 1658 and 1661. The chateau could be passed through from one side to the other without obstacles. The protruding entrance to the two-story "salon" on this side originally could be closed with iron gates but later doors of glass were installed. The hall from the front to the back opened on this south side to a view of a magnificent garden with entirely new garden styles and a canal one kilometer long ending in a grotto. The gardens were begun in 1641 and were designed by André Le Nôtre and gardeners before him whose names we are not sure of. Photo by the author 2010.

After the arrest all Fouquet's papers became Colbert's papers,[164] Colbert buried himself in them looking for anything that he could use in his legal actions against Fouquet: secret allowances, bribes, and fraudulent business transactions. Here is one item, not fraudulent but curious because it had to do with the queen mother, Anne of Austria: Henri de Grave de Villegargeau, formerly governor of Monsieur,[165] admitted having given the

CHAPTER 5. FOUQUET AND COLBERT

queen considerable sums of money. The marquis de Grave was involved in an account found in Fouquet's papers as having received 152,800 livres for secret and private uses (*affaires secrètes et particulières*)."[166]

Colbert not only wanted to know how Fouquet had moved money around, he also studied the *surintendant's* ideas for financial reforms and maritime ventures for France, made them his own, and proceeded to create the reputation of a reliable minister of state spouting a fountain of service to France at a crucial period in her history, the maker of France's renewed economy, the builder of the French navy, the intellect behind France's accentuation on luxury goods production, the creator of the academies of science, architecture, and music, among others.

Colbert's tomb, majestic in white and black and peaceably on view for eternity in his parish church, contrasts violently with Nicolas Fouquet's burial on the rue Saint-Antoine in the chapel of the order of the Visitation, Notre Dame des Anges.[167] The government of France questioned many years ago whether Fouquet's body was actually in the Fouquet family vault of the Chapel of the Visitation due to the delay of the delivery of the body to the family, and despite the church's official record of his burial in their church they took away the plaques that testified to the interment, covered and sealed the cave, and there is now no trace whatsoever of Nicolas' burial, of his mother's and father's, of his brother's. The Paris archives has in storage (not in the chapel) only the plaques of the first wife of Nicolas and one of his infant children. The rest of the plaques could not be found by the archives in 2017. (Personal communication to the author from the Museum of Paris, June 20, 2017.) There is no memorial to the four sisters of Fouquet who were Visitandine nuns, nor a reminder of his father's and mother's founding contributions for building the church.

Fouquet's burial is at least inside a church that remains standing. *The Masque de Fer* was buried just down the street from Notre-Dame-des-Anges in the cemetery of the Bastille's parish church, Saint-Paul, dropped on top of other recent burials underneath him and under new bodies that would soon be arriving; cemeteries buried bodies in common graves in ditches, filling them with bodies and then covered them with dirt long enough for the cadavers to decay, at which time they took up the bones, burned them or displayed them in a charnal house outside the church, and used the ditch again. In 1750 the cemetery was receiving around 600 bodies each year. Saint-Paul church, located where now are #30 and #32 rue Saint Paul, was closed in 1791 when all other churches were closed by the order of the revolutionary government, sold in 1794, and demolished in 1796. The cemetery was destroyed in 1910 and the historian Jacques Hillairet said that, "Houses were built on its place before all the bones were taken up so that some of them may still be in the ground."[168]

Only a few blocks away is the church whose official records state that Nicolas Fouquet and his mother were buried there on the same day. It is ironic that both Fouquet and Eustache Dauger were interred without markers within a few hundred yards of each other.

6. The Jailers: Louvois And Saint-Mars

None are more hopelessly enslaved than those who falsely believe they are free.

—Johann Wolfgang von Goethe

Eustache Dauger's Jailers

The only people allowed to see or talk to the prisoner were the governor of Pignerol, Saint-Mars, his closest aide, Rosarges, and the keeper of the keys, Ru. This was ordered by the king through the marquis de Louvois and from him to the former musketeer and soldier, Saint-Mars. Doctors who treated him saw him only with his mask on; the priest who did mass for the prisoners did not see him. Saint-Mars created for this prisoner (as well as for some others) small cubicles in which the prisoner inside could see the host when it was held up during the service and he could hear the mass but neither could see each other. Since the marquis de Louvois and Saint-Mars brought Dauger his meals, gave rules for even his smallest necessities, ordered medical care, and oversaw the security of the prisoner, checking his room carefully each day and sometimes searching him, one of the few ways we can "know" Dauger is to know these two men, Louvois and Saint-Mars, and from their actions, told to us in letters between the two that were saved in France's military archives. Louvois was the powerful minister for war during most of Louis XIV's reign, rich, feared, born to the post, and able to fill it with a smooth grasp of organization of the military which was supported by a dark, gritty, self satisfaction and an ability to do illegal and merciless acts without flinching. Saint-Mars was his lowly underling, although in the prisons he governed he was the highest authority. They spoke to each other weekly in letters. By the time Saint-Mars and his prisoner went to the Bastille in September 1698, Louvois had been dead for seven years.

The Marquis De Louvois (1641–1691)

Letter to the marquis de Louvois from Madame Nallot d'Aubray, 16 July 1673: "Monsieur de Louvois: I am taking the liberty to tell you that my brother is dead, and that in his last moments he told me to tell you of this and he told me where to find the things he has been keeping for you. Please write to me about these items. He ordered me not to talk about this with anyone and to keep the same reserve and commitment that he had. Monsieur Chauvelin and Monsieur de Carpatry came to my door to ask me if my brother had left some things that belonged to you. I did not answer. I await your instructions."

Letter from Louvois to Duclos, "I will appreciate it if you will keep until I return the box (*cassette*) that the sister of the deceased Nallot has for you, and Carpatry will bring you a bed cover that you must keep until my return and be absolutely sure that you don't screw it up."[169]

The marquis de Louvois was Louis XIV's liaison to the Man in the Mask; he conferred with the king on all important questions about Dauger's treatment and passed on the king's orders to Saint-Mars, the jailer in charge of the prisoner. This relationship between the three jailers, Louis XIV, Louvois, and Saint-Mars, is evident in Louvois' letters to Saint-Mars, now in the archives of the French defense department, although it has been suggested that Louvois never consulted the king at all, and that the king really had very little to do with the Mask and had no interest in him, that the minister held him for life out of anger or fear that some plot of Louvois would be revealed if the masked prisoner was released.

There are many problems with this proposition, not the least of which is that the regime of Saint-Mars and Dauger, with the same threats, the same allowances, the same secrecy, continued after Louvois died in July 1691. And as powerful as Louvois was, he was not in a position to ask for and receive the sort of obedience that he got from the personnel at the prison, the citadel, and the town of Pignerol for his own personal project over such a long period of time. If he did occasionally write instructions to Saint-Mars of his own inclination, or fail to tell the king about an action of the jailer or his staff that was less than meritorious, it was to protect his own reputation with the king. Otherwise, I think Louis XIV was in charge of Dauger, just as he was in charge of thousands of other seemingly small items in his house, his gardens, his wars, his money, and the minute details of the lives of all the thousands of people that lived with him at Versailles. Louis didn't do much delegating. It was not his habit or his nature.

But we were with Nallot's sister as she went looking for the hidden *lit blanc*, as she called it, that her brother had warned her had a connection to Louvois, an item that should be returned to him with absolute secrecy.

Jacques Nallot (d. 16 July 1673) was general treasurer of the brotherhood

CHAPTER 6. THE JAILERS: LOUVOIS AND SAINT-MARS

of Saint-Lazare but he was also a secret agent of the marquis de Louvois. Certainly not the only one, for Louvois had spies and henchmen all over Europe, but this particular agent's sudden death from poison in July 1673 was described and saved because it had to do with the so-called "Affair of the Poisons," an epidemic of poison making, buying, selling, and using in Paris in the 1670s, and it gives us an opportunity to look inside one of the marquis de Louvois' duties at Louis XIV's court.

Figure 6.1: François-Michel Le Tellier, marquis de Louvois. After Jacob Ferdinand Voet. Oil on canvas. Musée des Plans Reliefs, Les Invalides, Paris, France. Photo by Scott Madry 2024.

Louvois was the liaison between the king and the chief investigators and prosecutors of the community of poisoners, black mass performers, and abortionists in Paris that came to the notice of the king and the police after a *marquise* named Brinvilliers (1630–1675) had efficiently and rapidly poisoned her father and brothers, subsequent to testing her recipes on patients at the Hôtel Dieu, the Paris hospital next to Notre Dame cathedral. She poisoned her father in 1666 because he was opposed to her new lover, tried to poison her husband in 1668 but he was alert and took an antidote to save himself, and then in 1670 killed both of her brothers. After her lover, Gaudin de Sainte-Croix, died[170] she insisted that a certain box be returned to her from his apartment and the box, containing evidence of her crimes, was examined. She fled to England and was finally arrested in Liège (Belgium), extradited to Paris, and burned on a pyre in front of the Hôtel de Ville in 1675. Quiet inquiries and trials about the very widespread use of poison to eliminate rivals and husbands were begun around 1670, but the public was not told until 1680. Louis XIV shut down the investigation when it became clear that people close to him, specifically his official mistress, the marquise de Montespan, might be guilty of having used poisons to get their hearts' desires.[171] Louvois' agents, including Nallot, were assigned to question the accused after arrest. He was very active in the investigation of the marquise de Brinvilliers and the inventory of her lover's possessions. It was following one such session with the abbot Colombier in July 1673 that Nallot became suddenly mortally ill and died at home in a few hours.[172] Then followed Nallot's sister's letter to the marquis de Louvois, who was supervising the siege of Maëstricht (the Netherlands) at the time, and then Louvois' instructions to his factotums Duclos, Chauvelin, and Carpatry in Paris to get immediately from Nallot's sister the box and the mysterious *lit blanc*.

A *lit blanc* translates literally into English as white bed, but if we imagine the *messieurs* Carpatry and Chauvelin struggling to lift a white bed in a wagon to hide for Louvois, the thought comes to mind that this can't be right. If we refer to French dictionnaries for the words "*lit*" and "*blanc*" we get a different meaning. The dictionnary *Le Grand Robert de la Langue Français* gives this definition of "*lit*": "A set of fabrics that are for the bed. One would say that a woman prepares her bed for her childbirth, that means the sheets, the bed cover, the valence, the bed curtains of the bed."

In French dictionaries for the word "*blanc*" I found these entries: "*De but en blanc*" means point blank. "*Mariage blanc*" means a marriage not consummated. "*Vers blanc*" is blank verse. In addition, the stipulation that the fabric was white could mean that Madame d'Aubray was saying the "*lit*" was clean, white being the equivalent of clean when talking about fabric.[173] Carpatry tells Louvois he unfolded ("*déployer*") the *lit* and found the "*pièces*" inside. I came to the conclusion that this *lit blanc* was not a white bed but was an empty bed cover which normally holds a stuffing of goose feathers, closed up by buttons. Note that only Madame d'Aubray calls it a "*lit blanc*." Carpatry calls it a "*lit*." She is giving a description of the bed cover—that

CHAPTER 6. THE JAILERS: LOUVOIS AND SAINT-MARS   87

it was not in use, it was clean, and saying the cover's stuffing is not there, only the "*pièces*" are there, which must mean pieces of paper, which is generally meant by "*pièces*" except when the reference is to rooms, but there is no possibility that "*pièces*" means rooms in this context.

These papers (hidden in a very good hiding place) that belonged to Louvois but that he did not want in his own house, may or may not have something to do with the Man in the Iron Mask, however, the story illustrates that Louvois was the perfect man for "...a process [that] needed a blunt, fearless, scoundrel to uncover and disturb the evil matrix that had been discovered in Paris."[174] These were the same qualities that Louis XIV wanted in an overseer of Eustache Dauger.

Buried

It is to Louvois that France owes the Hôtel des Invalides on the left bank of Paris, a great mass of square, brown buildings protected by a church with a gilded dome that masters the downriver Seine *arrondissements*. For many reigns previous to Louis XIV's a retirement and rehabilitation center for military veterans had been discussed, and Louvois achieved it. He wanted to be buried there and was...but Louis XIV moved his remains on January 22, 1699 to a mausoleum on the place Vendôme in the monastery of the Capucins.[175] When that monastery was torn down, he was buried in a hospital created in 1293 by Marguerite de Bourgogne (1250–1308), countesse of Tonnerre and wife of the King of Sicily Charles d'Anjou, Notre-Dame de Fontenilles of Tonnerre, a county[176] Louvois had bought in 1684. I have been to Tonnerre. It is quiet, and the small church where Louvois lies was locked up that day. This war minister had a baton only slightly shorter than Louis XIV's, but the king did not like to be compared, so he made sure the marquis was buried in the backwater Burgundy cow country.

Michel Le Tellier (1603–1685), war minister in the high royal council, who co-signed Eustache Dauger's arrest warrant, had secured the devolution of his post to his son, François-Michel Le Tellier (1641–1691) and had provided him a title by buying him the marquisat of Louvois, south of Reims in Champagne, in 1656. In 1669 Louvois had already been an apprentice for the post under his father and Louis XIV. As he merged into his father's ministerial post he also grew in Louis XIV's esteem as a man naturally suited to perform the necessary secret and illegal acts of the reign. This he did until his death in 1691, while with his right hand building Louis' army to a powerful, efficient force. He was smart, a great builder and reformer of France's military, but he was also a cheat, a liar, a womanizer, and a brazen, arrogant facilitator of many illegal and cruel actions of Louis XIV's reign. The Le Tellier family crest bore a lizard.[177]

The ambassador from the court of Brandebourg, Ezéchiel Spanheim (1629–1710), wrote a final report to the Elector of Brandebourg, for whom he worked, that gave clear, insightful, and honest portraits of people at Louis XIV's court. The following is part of what he said about Louvois to the Elector of Brandebourg after his term as envoy in France was over (1689).

> I won't take long on his exterior. I will content myself with saying that it wouldn't promise all the activity, vigilance, and competence that he has and that one would not have expected of a portly person, nor of an air naturally rude and without reflection, nor the brusque and high-handed manner that one sees in him. That temperament is opposite to that of the chancellor, his father. But it is logical that his star rose. He is the same age as the king. His father passed to him the position of secretary of state for war and he began carrying out those duties at a very young age.
>
> His haughty attitude often annoyed both Le Tellier and the king and sometimes Louvois tried to ameliorate his manners but he never managed very well to do so.
>
> At the time of writing, Louvois is still in his post and does not seem to be in danger of losing it. But his health has been bad for some years and might give problems in the future. He has an indisposition of the leg,[178] gets frequent attacks of fever, for which he uses quinquina. He doesn't eat properly, especially in the way of melons and fruits in their season and has a body overweighted in bile;[179] those attributes and actions can limit his days or make him retire sooner than he wants to.[180]

Ambassador Spanheim's appraisal subtly says Louvois was overweight, an unusual physique at the time. His portraits show him in a large black flowing wig with a direct look, full jowls, and a well formed nose.

One of the posts that Louvois held in addition to his oversight of the war office was director of the postal system from 1669 to his death in 1691.[181] He made reforms that increased efficiency of mail delivery—and was able to decrease the efficiency of mail delivery or divert the mail when the king's business required it. Roujon's book on Louvois quotes a letter from Louvois to the prince de Condé about a diversion he ordered to buy time for Condé to secretly move troops into place. Louvois had ordered that the letters in question would not arrive at Dijon until after Condé's departure. The courrier whose schedule ordinarily had him leave on Saturday at noon was told not to leave until Sunday morning, and a package they also wanted to

CHAPTER 6. THE JAILERS: LOUVOIS AND SAINT-MARS

arrive late would not get to Dijon before it had made visits to a few other French cities, Lyon, Besançon and Dôle, while a package for Lyon would be sent to Dijon to make it appear that there had been an innocent misunderstanding. Time that the prince needed to achieve his military aims would be gained while the confusion was wallowed in.[182] In his book on the *Cabinet Noir*, Eugène Vaillé gives a dark description of opening and reading letters by postal officials that was common and had been for some time: "The rattle tap-tapping of the *chef-conseil* of the mails is felt throughout France and even outside of France when he uses his smoldering wick. He has unlimited power to do as he likes; he harasses, hits, stings, bites, and strips away skin and hair."[183]

Louvois' wife was the caretaker of two of Louis XIV's illegitimate children by Madame de Montespan, Françoise-Marie, Mademoiselle de Blois, and Louis-Alexandre, comte de Toulouse, born in 1677 and 1678. The duty came to her because the widow Scarron, later Madame de Maintenon, who had been nursemaid to the king's first babies sired with Madame de Montespan, said she would not take on another baby after Louis had sworn to his confessor on Easter 1675 that he would terminate his double adulterous relationship (the king had a wife and Montespan had a husband) with Montespan and then gave proof—twice—that he did not keep his word to God or to her. So Anne de Souvré, the marquise de Louvois, raised the children until they reached an age to be left with a governor and governess. The children might have been supervised at the Paris town house of Louvois and his wife on the rue de Richelieu that they bought from Basile Fouquet, the brother of the disgraced superintendant of finances in 1669,[184] or at their home at Saint-Germain-en-Laye.

The habit of the times was to send away babies and children at loose ends... any young children, as a matter of fact, that disrupted their busy parents' activities at court or in the literary salons or at the hunt; in short, most children of families who could afford to, sent their children into the country to be cared for by competent, caring, or incompetent, ferocious paid sitters. Those who had the worst experiences in this system—orphans, disabled children, the blind, the deaf, children with neurological or genetic deformations—were sent off to fates that were morally abhorrent; scholars of child treatment in the European early modern age say that many children were taken advantage of, that they were ignored, crippled on purpose to make them more credible beggars, underfed, murdered, left alone, left sick to die. Madame de Montespan's babies, however, were not of this population. Madame de Louvois had a staff that kept the children safe (we don't know whether happy).

Secret and illegal matters migrated to Louvois because it was a family tradition; since 1643 his father had been an unerring master at clearing away problems for the royal family that could not come into the open, and also because Louvois could calmly meet evil deeds with his own evil eye. One of the tasks that fell into this category was the management of the life of the Mask. The marquis did not realize that this chore would be the one for which he would be most remembered (at least by Mask researchers) because at first, in July 1669, the task of giving orders for the Mask's arrest and his prescribed treatment by Saint-Mars seemed simple and orderly. Many people were arrested by *lettre de cachet*, this man would be, his jailer needed instructions, it was assumed he would be in custody for a few months to years and then set free. Typical. So he must have been surprised when his majesty demanded in summer of 1670, about a year after Eustache Dauger had been placed in Pignerol, that Louvois go over the Alps to the prison in company with his agent Nallot and the sieur Sebastien Le Prestre de Vauban (1633–1703), siege master, fortress builder, and military engineer *extraordinaire*. A trip of this sort was not an easy matter at the time. This was an order that would take the minister away from his duties at court and there was never a good time for that as Louvois was a very busy man with the challenge of building the French army on his shoulders. Louvois made the trip there and back in two weeks, an extremely fast roundtrip of half the length of France including a difficult jog across the Alps.[185] There were reasons for this trip from Paris to Pignerol, one of which was Louvois' need to appear at Pignerol to vacate the five-year judicial sentence to the galleys of a man named Valcroissant who had tried to help Nicolas Fouquet escape from Pignerol, however Valcroissant had been an informant for Louvois, which Louvois had to explain in person to the tribunal. Another reason was to inspect the Pignerol citadel and prison fortifications for the purpose of strengthening them. A large amount of stored ammunition had blown up half the prison just a few months after Nicolas Fouquet got there in 1665 and possibly the rebuilding done at that time needed Vauban's inspection.

Another reason for the August 1670 trip might have been to see Eustache Dauger and to make sure he was properly watched and locked in. There had been notice to Louvois that Dauger was not as secure as the king had ordered him to be.

> From Louvois to Saint-Mars
>
> Saint-Germain-en-Laye 26 March 1670
>
> Monsieur,
>
> I have received your letters of the 8th and 15th of this month, by which I see that you have decided to take the *sieur* Honneste yourself to the tribunal at Pignerol, when the judges call for him to be brought; that is good, and when there is a decision made

CHAPTER 6. THE JAILERS: LOUVOIS AND SAINT-MARS 91

about him, His Majesty orders that he be informed of the decision to see if he approves of it.

I have been told that the *sieur* Honneste, or one of the other valets of monsieur Fouquet, spoke to the prisoner that was brought to you by the major of Dunkirk, and he, among other things, asked him if he had anything to tell him, to which he responded that he wished to be left in peace: he probably said this because he thought you had set someone up to ask him about himself to test him and see if he would reveal something; by this you can see that you have not taken enough precautions to keep him from talking to anyone; and, as it is very important to the service of His Majesty that there be no communication between him and anyone else whatsoever, I desire that you visit carefully the inside and the outside of the place where he is and to make sure that the prisoner cannot see or be seen by anyone and cannot talk to anyone or hear what anyone has to say to him.

I am, monsieur,

Your very fond servant,

De Louvois[186]

That Dauger had been questioned by an associate of Fouquet, in spite of many precautions taken by Saint-Mars that this not happen, probably worried Louvois. Whether this breach of security was reported to the king is unknown, but why would Louvois tell the king anything that would reflect badly on himself?

The letters that Louvois wrote to Saint-Mars did not have the open animus that his letters to many other subordinates had because Saint-Mars' sister-in-law was his mistress. This may be why Saint-Mars didn't lose his job when he made bad mistakes. Louvois perhaps didn't even tell Louis XIV what the mistakes were, just as he didn't tell him that he had been lying to the king about the mass conversions of Protestants to Catholicism. These never happened, but Louvois knew the king would be impressed with such a magnificent tribute to the minister's savage, military terrorism of the Protestant population, so he made up the conversions, and Louis XIV was very happy to know he was saving so many souls.

Nevertheless Louvois must have told the king some things that reflected badly on everyone else in the garrison of Pignerol and its surroundings because just after his minister of war returned from Pignerol his majesty ordered a complete change of the supervisory personnel at the town and the citadel. Vergé-Franceschi quotes a letter from Louvois to Monsieur de Loyauté, the army intendant:

> At this time his majesty has decided to stop the story-telling immediately and to put his administration at Pignerol on a good footing. I hereby tell you that the king has decided to take away Monsieurs de la Bretonnière [governor of the town of Pignerol], Saint-Jacques [governor of the citadel of Pignerol], Lestang, and de la Moransane [both high-level officials].[187]

Louvois added that Loyauté should not tell anyone because his majesty wants this done secretly.[188] The departure of these senior officers meant that their junior staff of about thirty-five officers and all their troops had to be replaced.[189] Saint-Mars and his free company were not replaced.

What does Louvois mean by "storytelling"? The staff were evidently talking among themselves about the prisoners (there were two, Fouquet and Dauger—Fouquet had two valets who lived with him). Here we see a comedy playing; the king and Louvois at the very beginning of their monumental struggle to keep Eustache Dauger a secret from every human being inside and outside the prison were zero for two... at least. Prisoners inside were whispering to Dauger through the walls and rumors were so rampant among the staff of the prison and the citadel that everyone had to be removed and replaced.

Louvois' death occurred at Versailles twenty-one years later on July 16, 1691. He was fifty years old. Poison was rumored, but probably a heart attack was the cause; had not Spanheim predicted it? However we know that by July 1691 Louvois feared that Louis would disgrace him, put him in the Bastille or Vincennes, even assassinate him. The king was coming to an end of his tolerance for the minister, ever more ugly in mood, manners, and appearance as he aged. Madame de Maintenon, Louis' second, secret wife that he married in 1683, had had her limit years before. The *abbé* de Choisy, in his memoirs, said:

> ...fifteen days before his death, he [Louvois] knew his fall from grace was coming. He said as much to one of his friends who told it to me. 'I don't know,' he said,'whether he will just fire me or put me in prison; it's all the same to me if I am no longer the master.' His friend, who is M. le premier (Beringhen) tried to reassure him, saying to remember that for the last ten years he had said this twenty times. 'It is different now!' said M. de Louvois. 'In the past we have had a hundred very severe arguments after which he was very angry; and the next day when I came in to meet with him, he was gracious again. But for the last fifteen

days he always has a wrinkled brow; he has decided against me and all that is left is how he will deliver the verdict.'[190]

The memoir writer Saint-Simon's famous description of Louis' frozen and perturbed demeanor at the news of Louvois' instantaneous death that had taken place moments after leaving a work session with the king and his wife has been interpreted in many ways. I think the shock of being outwitted by the Holy Ghost, who snapped Louvois up before the king was able to, left Louis XIV irritated with God, and that sensation frightened the king. His prey had been caught by Someone Else (or even by *someone else*—for although *we* know Louvois wasn't poisoned, Louis didn't) and that wasn't familiar to Louis. For a rare moment, the man who concealed his inner self completely, the never uncovered masked player, was unable to fully manage his expression, leaving it bare for Saint-Simon to look at.

The Chevalier De Saint-Mars (1626–1708)

Louvois took orders about Eustache Dauger from Louis XIV and passed them on to the chevalier de Saint-Mars, the man directly in charge of Dauger's life and death from 1669 to 1703.

John Noone's book *The Man Behind the Iron Mask* closes with Noone's thesis that the prisoner was entirely made up by Saint-Mars, that Saint-Mars felt he needed to show possession of a high-ranking prisoner to enlarge his credit and importance with the king and Louvois. He put a mask on his imaginary prisoner, says Noone, as a stage prop to make his captive interesting because he knew the mask would be a lure to those nosey onlookers whose loose talk could make or break a career.[191] Deciding that he was an invention of Saint-Mars to get a higher salary or a better post is an unseemly conclusion about the identity of the Mask. Surely Noone could not really have believed this.

There is no question that, in the beginning, Saint-Mars was proud to have such an important prisoner, even though he didn't know who he was. Louvois and the king seemed to think he was very important, and that was good enough for Saint-Mars, being a soldier whose loyalty to the king was extreme.

Bénigne Dauvergne was born in 1626 in the commune of Montfort-l'Amaury in the Yvelines department not far from Paris to Louis Dauvergne, an officer of the pantry of the king (Louis XIII), and Marie Garrot. Dauvergne was a small child when his parents died and he was raised by Marie Garrot's sister who was married to Zachée de Byot, sieur de Blainvilliers. One of their children, his cousin, would later be in his "free company" of soldiers.[192] Although the name Dauvergne suggests that he was from the geographical region of the Auvergne (d' = from + Auvergne), instead the etymology of his name comes from the word *verne* (alder trees), the same origin that similar family names in France have such as Lavergen, Duverne, Dauverne, Vergneau, Vernay, Desvernes, etc.[193] Since he was sent off to the army at age eleven (1637), it might have been that his aunt and uncle wanted this orphan out of the house as soon as possible. He was *"enfant de troupe"* from that age and continued in the army until 1650 when he was received as a Musketeer, *à la première compagnie de mousquetaires de la Garde*. It was ten years before he received a promotion to brigadier of the Grey Musketeers[194] (1660).

Like most other fighters, he took a *nom-de-guerre*, "Saint-Mars," much as a boxer today takes on a title that is used for promoting him- or herself.[195]

> One sees in a text of a novel of the 15th century titled *Le Jouvencel* that the surnames were very common in the Middle Ages, above all among the professional soldiers, and often became proper names. Jouvencel received from his captain the permission to keep the name, under which he had at first been known. "You must know," the captain said to him, "that generally the captains and *chefs de guerre* are not named by their family names, unless these names are really short, as Galiot, Salzard, Gascon, Poton, Blosset, Talbot, Floquet, etc. But sometime they are named by the name of the lands owned by their families, as Montgascon, Gaucourt, Wilby, Scales, Dunoys, etc. Or they name them by the name of the region that they are from, as l'Aragonais, le Navarrot, le Galois, le Barrois, le Béarnais and others; or they are named for the imperfections that they have, as Le Bègue [stutterer] de Vilaines, Jehan le Baveux [drooler], le Manchot [one-handed], le Borgne [one-eyed] Clisson, le Borgne Foucault, and many others. I saw a captain who, in his infancy, had the name Etienne de Vignoles and always from then he had the *nom de guerre* La Hire." [The captain was naming himself after the famous knight Etienne de Vignolles, one of Joan of Arc's comrades-in-arms, whose *nom de guerre* was La Hire.][196]

Saint-Mars was in the unit led by musketeer Charles Ogier de Batz-Castelmore, who called himself d'Artagnan, a name of a property owned by his mother's side of the family. D'Artagnan, who had been a secret agent of Louis XIV's godfather and mentor, Cardinal Jules Mazarin,[197] was assigned by the king to arrest Nicolas Fouquet, vicomte de Vaux, marquis de Belle-Ile, and superintendant of finances, at the chateau of the dukes of Brittany in Nantes on 5 September 1661. Saint-Mars was the rear guard standing on the back

CHAPTER 6. THE JAILERS: LOUVOIS AND SAINT-MARS

of the carriage that carried Fouquet out of Nantes to his first prison cell in the fortress of Angers.[198]

D'Artagnan was Fouquet's guard for the four years that it took Louis XIV and Fouquet's nemesis, Jean-Baptiste Colbert, to arrange a guilty verdict just before Christmas 1664, after which he was immediately transported by one hundred soldiers commanded by d'Artagnan to Pignerol. The musketeer that Alexander Dumas made famous in his novels was much as Dumas described him: a man of honor and courtesy, a soldier of fortune, a brave and easily offended warrior. He had carried out his duties efficiently and honorably as jailer for Fouquet during his trial at the express order of Louis XIV but he had no interest in taking a permanent post at a prison. When Louis XIV said he needed a reliable man who would obey orders diligently and without question to keep the offender Fouquet under safe guard, d'Artagnan recommended his fellow musketeer Saint-Mars, and Louis consequently appointed him Marshal of Lodging and commandant of Pignerol prison in 1664. Saint-Mars hired his free company, including, his cousin Zachée de Byot (the son of the aunt who took him in as an orphan, d. 1682), his nephew Guillaume Formanoir, sieur de Corbé (the son of his sister, d. 1740), and a soldier who was not a relative, Jacques Rosarges (d. 1705). Also with Saint-Mars from January 1664 were lieutenants Saint-Martin, Dufresne, and Dupleissis. La Prade joined the staff at Pignerol in 1673, and the captain of the gates, the sieur Lécuyer, was hired in 1670.

Saint-Mars was promoted to the position of governor of Pignerol prison in 1665 and became governor of three other prisons during his lifetime, Exilles prison, Sainte-Marguerite prison, and the Bastille, where he died in 1708. Eustache Dauger had become his second prisoner at Pignerol on August 21, 1669. The king, as one of his many gifts to Saint-Mars for his service, gave him letters of nobility in 1673, from which time he was entitled to be called the chevalier de Saint-Mars.[199]

From 1664, he could be found somewhere in the battlements of his responsibility, the prisons Louis XIV put him in charge of; spying on his prisoners, overseeing the design of new cells, filling out paperwork, or handling personnel issues, just as any administrator must. He rarely got any time off, was overwhelmed at times by his duties although he was proud of them, had to suffer the insults and escape schemes of some of his prisoners, although never of Eustache Dauger, and had the disappointment at the end of his life to realize, despite holding the highest post in the prison system of France, that he had abandoned his military career to be a tool of politicians he never understood and didn't really like. He is said to have been always grasping for money but I wonder if it was really money or something else he wanted: respect.

Soon after his appointment at Pignerol he married a woman his own age (he was thirty-eight, she thirty-nine), Marie-Antoinette Collot. She had been, like Bénigne himself, forced to become an adult at age eleven when her mother died and she took her mother's place as housekeeper for her father, Antonin Collot. Captain Louis Damorezan, with whom Saint-Mars worked closely, high-ranking official of the citadel of Pignerol, had married a daughter of Antonin Collot, and the Monsieur Collot had two other daughters, Marie, who had made a good marriage with Elie du Fresnoy, an operative for Louvois in the war office, and Marie-Antoinette.[200] Bénigne married Marie-Antoinette and they had two children, both boys, André Antoine (1672–1693) and Bénigne Antonin (1679–1702). Louvois was André's godfather. The children grew up in the Pignerol citadel, and around 1687 they both went into the army, as their father had done as a boy.[201]

Marie-Antoinette's sister Marie was beautiful and became both the wife of du Fresnoy and the mistress of Louvois,[202] so that Louvois and Saint-Mars, while not related by blood or marriage, were related by the *boudoir*, and perhaps that made their friendship more cordial than it would have been if they'd been actual brothers-in-law.

In September 1681 Saint-Mars was appointed governor of Exilles prison not far from Pignerol only a year and a few months after Fouquet, his first prisoner, had died of a heart attack. Saint-Mars was ordered by Louvois to take with him only Dauger and the ex valet of Fouquet, La Rivière. In April 1687, after he had complained for years of the cold and silence at Exilles, he was sent to govern the Lérins islands' prison of Sainte-Marguerite, within view of the Cannes harbor. Dauger went with Saint-Mars but La Rivière died just before they left Exilles.

Saint-Mars bought for his oldest son a very expensive regiment of dragoons.[203] André was the colonel of the unit. As for Bénigne, Louvois (as head of the army) refused to make him colonel-lieutenant as he was too young, so he served under his brother as the cornette, *le porte-drapeau*.[204] At the battle of Neerwinden (1693) André was killed at age twenty. His brother was seriously wounded in the same battle at age seventeen. Madame de Saint-Mars died soon afterwards and it was said the cause was grief from these losses. Only men without wives or whose wives did not live with them were eligible to be governor of the Bastille, so Saint-Mars' wife's death made him a candidate, and he was offered the post in 1698. He arrived in Paris in the late afternoon of September 18, 1698, with his much reduced free company who joined the soldiers already in place at the Bastille and with his old prisoner.

At Paris Saint-Mars took care of his youngest son, whose injuries were not

CHAPTER 6. THE JAILERS: LOUVOIS AND SAINT-MARS

healing well. He wanted to buy him a regiment, but the war minister, Barbezieux, who did not have the reasons that his father (Louvois) had had to be nice to him (the *boudoir* connection), only gave him a *sous-lieutenance* in a regiment of *gendarmerie*. Bénigne married the daughter of an important protocol officer at Versailles, but four years later in a battle near Landau in the Palatinate in summer 1702, the youngest son of Saint-Mars was killed.[205] His "longtime prisoner" died in 1703. So Saint-Mars, an old man, was alone in the governor's quarters of the Bastille. The governor had inherited the house and grounds of Palteau near the town of Villeneuve-sur-Yonne on the Yonne river from his uncle, Cantien Garrot de Fontenelle, seigneur of Palteau and governor and administrator of Sens and Villeneuve-sur-Yonne.[206] André and Bénigne having died, he willed Palteau to his nephew and former lieutenant, Guillaume Formanoir. To Guillaume's brother Louis Formanoir (d. 1724) he willed the *seigneurie* of Dixmont, a castle near Palteau that had been given to him by the king in 1703.[207] As for the youngest Formanoir brother, Joseph Formanoir (1672–1731), who told the young boy de Palteau about his memories of seeing Dauger, the will says he had been given the fief of Blainvilliers in 1686 and would receive the sum of 500 livres. Saint-Mars' inventory dated 2 October 1708 states that Saint-Mars died the Jour de Saint-Louis previous, i.e. 25 August 1708.[208] He was buried in the Saint-Paul cemetery on the 28th of September, the same cemetery in which his *ancien prisonnier*, Eustache Dauger, had been buried five years previously.

A Man Of (What) Quality?

For historians, most of the mystery of the Man in the Iron Mask has consisted of a guessing game with around two dozen serious candidates spread on the board and a calculator of dates, places, and incidents being the only aid allowed. It's important to remember that Saint-Mars played this game too, and eventually Louvois played it, because I do not think that either Louvois or Saint-Mars knew who Eustache Dauger was any more than we do. We think we are ill used that we must struggle in a mire of nobles, magistrates, and illegitimate sons of kings to get clarity on the Mask's identity, but Saint-Mars and Louvois also lacked information on Dauger's identity and rank in society, and that was unsettling for them. Their careers and maybe their lives depended on showing a proper attitude toward this prisoner but that required knowing his social status, his *qualité*, which for all people in France at that time, no matter what their social rank, was the most important thing to know about someone, because the *qualité* of a person was the determining factor for what tone of voice and vocabulary should be used, if eye contact could be made or held for any period of time, what food was served, and whether it was served on porcelain or tin. Prison was not a leveler; these social rules applied to prisoners. Transgressing social laws by treating a prisoner who was a member of the noble class with indifferent language and disrespectful deportment was absolutely forbidden. For instance, the word "*lèse-majesté*," meaning treasonous conduct, is translated literally as an attack on the dignity of the king or a lack of the full version of the dignity due him. Everyone from the king to a stable boy had a *qualité* that governed all social interactions. Not knowing Eustache's social status was a conundrum for Saint-Mars and Louvois and anyone else who interacted with the prisoner. Was the man a "*misérable*" (Louvois' description of him on July 19, 1669), or was he a literate, polite man who had the respect of the governor and his soldiers?

If Saint-Mars had been well informed, we wouldn't see him fishing for Dauger's identity in the years just after Dauger came to Pignerol. Louvois' lack of information is shown more subtly and over a longer period of time in his actions and phrasing. I firmly believe that Louvois gave Saint-Mars false stories when he (Louvois) didn't know the truth any more than Saint-Mars did. Louvois and Saint-Mars were dealt the same cards by Louis XIV that we were dealt: a mysterious man, unknown crime, unknown history. Saint-Mars assumed that his superior, Louvois, knew the prisoner's identity and his *qualité*...because...Louvois was war minister...high-ranking servant of the king...the director of the prisoner's case. To prod Louvois into telling him who the prisoner was, Saint-Mars began to write to Louvois some purposefully annoying guesses in a teasing, self-satisfied, superior tone, thinking surely Louvois would react by explaining who Dauger was. Here is one written just ten days after Dauger arrived at Pignerol:

> From Saint-Mars to Louvois
>
> 31 August 1669
>
> A lot of people around here think [my new prisoner] is a marshal of France and others think he is a president.[209]

And also:

> From Saint-Mars to Louvois
>
> April 12, 1670
>
> I get all kinds of questions about my prisoner and people want to know why I am adding so much new security in my prison. I tell them big, fat lies about him and they believe them, which makes me laugh.[210]

CHAPTER 6. THE JAILERS: LOUVOIS AND SAINT-MARS

If Saint-Mars had known who the prisoner was, he would never have ventured any hint about his identity. That he threw out these not so subtle brags shows his ignorance about his captive. He was curious, very curious, as might be imagined. Very good treatment had been ordered for the new prisoner... immediate medical care in case of illness, liberal access to mass and confession, a private cell but one which had to be built to specific instructions from Louvois with extra security features. And most extraordinary of all, Saint-Mars himself must serve all his meals.

Saint-Mars was fastidious, the side of him that the king and Louvois saw when they hired him to manage their prison, but he was a proud man with ambition; he loved drama, and he desperately wanted to know who his prisoner was. He couldn't ask Louvois point blank because it wouldn't have been prudent to show his boss that he wanted knowledge beyond his station, so after a while, he fantasized about who his prisoner might be, and he couldn't help bragging about some of his made-up characters. This was flagrant disobedience of orders. These stories got back to the king and Louvois via spies at the prison, but instead of firing him, which he deserved, they went to the trouble of telling him a lie to keep him quiet. Saint-Mars' hint about the prisoner's identity that was reported in Louis Fouquet's letter ("people not being dead when they have been advertised to be") shows that Louvois or the king must have invented a false identity shortly before the move to Sainte-Marguerite because Dauger was treated much better at Sainte-Marguerite and at the Bastille than he had been at Pignerol and Exilles. In the south of France and at the Bastille he was said to be greatly respected by the governor and his staff; that they occasionally shared meals with him but they did not sit down unless he gave permission, a sign of their acknowledgement that he had a higher social position than they did. It was reported that Saint-Mars once called him "prince."[211] What we know about his time in Pignerol and Exilles fits with the treatment that would be expected for any prisoner: a cell, few contacts with others, day after day of almost no daylight, little news from the outside world, illness in silence, and hopelessness.

If we are looking for the lie they gave Saint-Mars, we can think of people whose decease was thought by insiders in government to have possibly been invented, which could mean that the king and Louvois told him the prisoner was the duc de Beaufort, supposedly killed in battle in 1669 on approximately the same day that Dauger was arrested. Or they might have said the man was Eustache d'Auger de Cavoye, older brother of Louis d'Auger de Cavoye whom we mentioned above, a cashiered soldier with a grey past who was useful to the authorities as a fog, which it has been for sleuths in trying to decipher this mystery because Eustache d'Auger de Cavoye and Eustache Dauger had very similar names. Who knows what Louvois came up with? The dark, curly-haired Louvois had a sinister imagination and knew the inside of all the mean stories of Louis XIV's government, so he could have used the name of a real person or he might have pieced together a character.

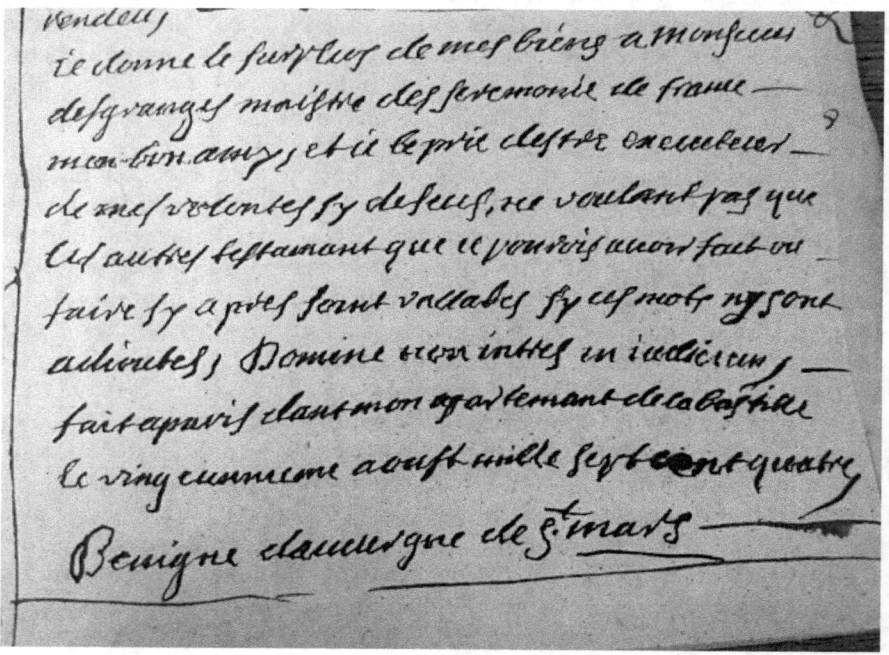

Figure 6.2: Detail from the will of Saint-Mars showing his signature. Photo by the author 2018 at the National Archives of France. Minutes de Louis DU- RANT (MC/ET/XCVI/191 - MC/ET/XCVI/301). Minutes. 1708, juil- let–1708, septembre (MC/ET/XCVI/203). Archives Nationale MC/ET/X- CVI/203.

Saint-Mars, at the time of leaving Exilles for Sainte-Marguerite, was happy that he finally knew the secret, and he was so proud that he hinted that his prisoner was a man the rest of the world considered dead, showing to his new neighbors that he was inside the circle of confidence of the king and his minister. Poor Saint-Mars. He was so badly used, even though they gave him an increasingly large salary and many showers of *livres* from time to time to assuage his avowed (maybe not sincere) desire to get out of prison governance and go back into the army, but he wouldn't have received the pay he got as governor of a prison. Prison managers had a salary and various benefits and always made a lot of money from their prisoners' accounts because it was accepted that they skimmed from the top of the prisoners' food and clothing allowances. His income never did him any good, though. He never got out of prison to spend it. What was important to Saint-Mars was belonging to the royal club, and he never did, although Louvois tried to convince him he was a member. I think that the knowledge that he was being lied to was more evident to Saint-Mars as time went on, certainly by the time he was at the Bastille. In thinking it over, he realized he really didn't know who this man was, and if he didn't know, if he'd been lied to, then the man must really be someone important, noble or royal. He by then mistrusted everything that was said to him by the authorities in Paris and reluctantly accepted that he would never know who Dauger was....but he really respected him, even liked him.[212] And he saw that the prisoner had a refined quality about him, an infallible devotion to his religion, a temperment that was out of the ordinary. Despite having had his life taken away from him, Dauger kept an elevated bearing...a noble bearing; quiet, devout, shy, but obedient, forgiving, knowledgeable (we may assume from his interest in reading) perhaps about history, maybe philosophy. Maybe his reading included travel books about faraway places; perhaps he knew by heart the poems of the Latins or studied Aristotle's books. Or he could have read only the *Bible* and books by ancient and modern Church Fathers.

Would Saint-Mars have followed the order of his master and killed Dauger if he spoke his name or about his past? Here are his words again just after Dauger was delivered to him: "I told him in the presence of M. de Vauroy that if he spoke to me or anyone else of anything except his necessities, I would put my sword through his stomach...I will never fail, on my life, to carry out punctually your orders."[213] We can imagine Saint-Mars drawing his sword with a sweeping move and waving it in the air. This is not a calm, steely-eyed guardian who might really be capable of calmly slicing up Dauger's abdomen if he thought he needed to; this is a man for whom the drama of the moment is nourishing to his sense of self.

Saint-Mars was certainly obedient, he was fastidious in his chores, he followed his superiors' instructions with blazing speed and was proud of his ideas on how to arrange transportation and cells for his prisoner. But whether he really could have killed Dauger is another question. Was he made of that? Or was he more theater than threat? If Dauger had voiced "Dau..." would Saint-Mars have killed him? In front of Vauroy in 1669, probably. But on a quiet early June morning a few years later when Saint-Mars delivered his food for the day and set it on his table? What would "I am Eustache Dauger" have brought?

7. The Prisoners

> Prisoners have no history: there is no describing their monotone days; their complaints have no echo; their suffering is seen by no one except those who make them suffer; no one hears their hearts. Only poets understand and sing the winsome woes of captivity.
>
> Marius Topin, L'Homme au masque de fer

Pignerol

> From Louvois to Saint-Mars
>
> Saint-Germain-en-Laye 14 July 1665
>
> We all agree with you that monsieur Fouquet was very fortunate to have been spared in the major disaster produced by lightning setting fire to the gunpowder stored in the château of Pignerol, and you were very right to have feared that he and his valet were buried in the rubble.
>
> I cannot tell you just now what decision the king will make on the purchase of [new] furniture and belongings of monsieur Fouquet or for the loss of your personal possessions until I have your response to my letters that the *sieur* d'Artagnan gave you from me, nevertheless I assure you that I am always, *monsieur*,
>
> Your very affectionate servant,
>
> De Louvois.[214]

The *commissaires* who oversaw the munitions storage at the fortress within the citadel of Pignerol had been told to relocate the gunpowder.

The explosion must have been louder than any noise made in the Alps for a very long time... louder than cannon fire, which had been known in the past to breach Alpine silence in Pignerol during the many times it was fought for by the Italians, the Savoyards, the French, and the imperial Habsburgs. As happens when munitions explode, there were multiple highlights of the event; the first big boom when a mass of powder stored in one of the towers caught fire and a *segué* of continuing explosions as barrels of the powder let loose their energy one by one when the fire reached them. The heights of the lower Alpine slopes provided ridged ground for the reverberations to pass across great distances, and the falling rocks and rubble of the crippled towers must have been like the underlying notes of a base instrument keeping time to the blasts.

Fouquet and his valet were indeed fortunate that they were standing in a salient window alcove watching the storm when lightning struck in June 1665 and the explosions of powder began, because the room and the tower that the window had been part of were blown away, leaving Fouquet and his valet standing above the wreckage of half the prison. The tower and much of the prison had to be rebuilt, and Fouquet was temporarily moved to a nearby small fortified house until July 1666.

Here are descriptions of the citadel and the prison of Pignerol, the latter existing within the former:

> Pignerol was a fortified frontier town of Piedmont, which was for some time French property, half bought and half stolen from Italy. It stands on the lower slopes of the southern Alps, twenty miles from Turin, fifty from Nice and ninety east of Grenoble. It was a stronghold of the princes of Savoy, capable of effective defense, with a small red-roofed tower and many tall *campaniles* gathering round an inner citadel, raised on a commanding height. This central keep is a mass of rambling buildings with solid buttressed walls, essentially a place of arms... It was a French garrison town inhabited largely by Italians. There was a French governor in supreme command, also a king's lieutenant who was commandant of the citadel, and the head gaoler, who held the prison proper; and these three officials constituted a sovereign council of war.[215]

> The *donjon* had its own gateway, through which prisoners could be brought or taken away without anyone in the citadel knowing, and it consisted of various buildings and two towers which were the actual prisons. These towers were known as the Upper Tower and the Lower Tower, the upper being the more comfortable and the lower the more secure. Distinguished prisoners were given rooms in the Upper Tower. Each tower had three stories with one large chamber on each floor. The top floor of the Upper Tower contained a chapel which was divided into separate compartments so that the prisoners could not see each other. The apartments of the Governor were so placed that he could overlook both of these towers. No prisoner of Saint-Mars succeeded in escaping.[216]

CHAPTER 7. THE PRISONERS

Pignerol is on a road that the ancient Romans built that commands the exit of the chief pass to Italy from the region of the French *Dauphiné*. Thirty-nine years before Dauger came to Pignerol, the citadel was taken from the duke of Savoy by a company of the French army led by Cardinal Richelieu in March 1630 at a point that was a crossroads in his relationship with Louis XIII. Without having donned armor, crossed the Alpine Mont Cenis pass in January and February, and taken Pignerol, Richelieu might very well have been the loser to Marie de Medici, Louis XIII's mother, later that year when she made a savage "him or me" ultimatum to her son the king, and Louis XIII chose...him. France might have been swallowed by the Habsburg dynasty if pro-Spanish Marie de Medici had been victorious over Richelieu.

At the end of the first phase of the Dutch War, in December 1672 and January 1673, Louis XIV had land troops of 120,000 men. While they decided how to attack the Dutch again (on the first attempt the Dutch opened their flood gates that held back the sea and forced Louis' army to retreat in wet muck) they kept 8,000 men in Roussillon on southern frontier, 5,000 to 7,000 in Lorraine, and 1,000 men in Pignerol.[217] Pignerol was a prosperous place if 1,000 soldiers were there, buying things in the town, proudly posing in streets in the citadel. Saint-Mars was not in command of these 1,000 soldiers, only of his own company in the prison, but he coordinated his priorities with the military and civil authorities of the town and citadel so he had a lot of business to do every day.

Guillaume La Rivière

When the explosion occurred at Pignerol prison in June 1665, La Rivière was still a young man, about thirty-five years old. He was part of the Fouquet family, having been unofficially adopted by François and Marie Fouquet almost certainly through some link (that we don't know) to François Fouquet's Cape Verde Company because La Rivière was from Cape Verde. He was in the news for one day in February 1661 because his baptism was announced in the *Gazette* newspaper on February 12, 1661.

> On 6 February was baptised at Notre-Dame-de-Pitié, a Turc, about thirty years old, native of the town of Maison in Africa. The First President of Parlement honored him by serving as his godfather, with the Dame Fouquet [as godmother], mother of the Superintendent of Finances, and he was named Guillaume; and the Abbé de Nesmond, Doctor at the Sorbonne, having preached on the subject, performed the ceremony after which there was a very solemn procession where this convert was led, dressed in white: the turban, the sabre, the vest and the tunic were dis-

played in front of him as a sign of victory of our religion over Mohamedism.[218]

He was not Turkish and not from Africa either, but the name "Turc" was used to characterize anyone of the Islamic faith, no matter where they were from. His "town" is actually a little island called Maio in the Republic of Cabo Verde, a set of islands in the middle of the Atlantic Ocean in the same volcanic system as the Canary Islands and the Azores. His first name Guillaume was given to him at the ceremony in honor of his godfather, Guillaume de Lamoignon, First President of the parlement at that time, a naming tradition that was often followed and encouraged by the church, godfathers having a significant influence in their godchildren's lives. Possibly his last name was a reference to a topographical feature at the island of Maio, or it could be that, as servants were often named after geographical features or areas (two of Fouquet's other servants were Champagne and La Forêt), they picked La Rivière as suitable because it fell into that category. Vergé-Franceschi says that he was one of many members from colonized countries in the Fouquet household. "They had at that time an impressive group of exotic emigrants, Blacks, Moors, and Indians from Canada, where Fouquet *père* had commercial interests."[219] As was said above, Marie de Maupeou took people into her home who needed a refuge.

Prisoners of means could have, if the king allowed, one or two valets to serve them in prison to help them dress, brush and fold their clothes, make their beds, serve their food, and generally look after them; they could even have a cook and their wives with them, all who shared the same accommodations and restrictions as the prisoner and who sometimes even had separate living spaces close to their masters. Fouquet, right after he was arrested, was given a valet by the name of La Vallée, who soon got sick and was replaced by La Rivière who went with him when he was sent to Pignerol in December 1664, but La Rivière was shell shocked by the explosion of the powder magazines in 1665 and left the prison to convalesce for a while during the time Fouquet was in a temporary prison, and Saint-Mars provided a valet, presumably someone from the neighborhood of Pignerol. When Fouquet was moved to the rebuilt Pignerol upper tower in 1666, La Rivière returned and another family valet, Champagne, came also to help Fouquet withstand the rigors of imprisonment. Life for Fouquet was miserable during his first ten years at Pignerol; worse than the four years he had spent in various prisons during his trial. He was not allowed to see any members of his family nor communicate with them or with anyone. He received no news at all, was watched and regularly searched by Saint-Mars. He tried, sometimes successfully, to make his own pens, ink, and paper, and was irritated and rebellious until after some years his physical ailments and the oppression he was subject to made him milder.

The Letters In The Military Archives

The team appointed by the Commune of Paris and the Assembly of Electors on 16 July 1789 to sort through the Bastille records didn't know that the most valuable and reliable trove of documents having to do with the Man in the Iron Mask were not in the Bastille but in the archives of the French Ministry of War,[220] in which are almost all the letters that remain from a weekly correspondence over twenty-nine years[221] between Saint-Mars and the director of Fouquet's and Dauger's incarceration, the marquis de Louvois, who died in 1691 and left the chore to his son, Barbezieux (1667–1701), the inheritor of the post of war minister. At Barbezieux's death in 1701, the comte de Pontchartrain, Secretary of State, communicated with Saint-Mars because the Bastille was in his purview.

Many of the letters were printed in two volumes by Joseph Delort in 1829 in *History of the Detention of Philosophes and Men of Letters in the Bastille and Vincennes, Preceeded by that of Fouquet, Pellisson, and Lauzun, with All the Authentic and Unpublished Documents*. As the title suggests, in the book there are also communications about Fouquet's and Lauzun's prison rules and a few letters from Paul Pellisson, a secretary of Fouquet's who had been arrested with Fouquet in 1661.

Louvois wrote from wherever the court was sitting, usually at the chateaux of Saint-Germain-en-Laye or Fontainebleau, and Saint-Mars wrote from Pignerol and the other prisons he commanded. They are trustworthy documents, communications between state officials. The writers, Louvois and Saint-Mars, generalized and obfuscated as much as possible to avoid putting on paper any details about Eustache that would indicate his preferences, his character, or the nature of his illnesses. Any letters that contained specifics were burned after reading or else hidden in a hole so dark and deep that they have never shown up. The letters left to us, full of bland directions and comments that say almost nothing, are frustrating to read because we know that the writers could have told us what we want so badly to know, but they keep their secrets.

A sample of letters from Louvois to Saint-Mars during that time shows the disharmony between Fouquet and Saint-Mars.

> From Louvois to Saint-Mars
>
> Saint-Germain en Laye 26 July 1665
>
> Monsieur
>
> I have received your letters of the 8th and 15th of this month and another one without date with the notes written by M. Fouquet

and with a book. The king wanted all of this and was not surprised to see that he is doing his utmost to get news from the outside and that you are doing your best to see that he doesn't achieve his aim.

As he is using things we cannot deprive him of to make writing tools, like chicken bones to make a pen and wine mixed with sweat to make ink, it is really difficult to stop him. You are right to be dissatisfied with the valet that you put in his service who did not alert you to the papers that you sent me and those that were hidden in the back of the chair. You must instruct him to be more faithful to you from now on. Monsieur Fouquet may make pens and ink but they won't do him any good unless he has paper. The king wants you to search him and take away from him anything you find and tell him that if he continues to make new efforts to corrupt your staff you will be obliged to search his person every day and guard him more strictly than ever. You must try to find out from his valet how Monsieur Fouquet wrote the four lines that appeared in the book when heat was put to it and what he used to write them with.

I am, monsieur,

Your very fond servant,

De Louvois[222]

From Louvois to Saint-Mars

Paris 21 August 1665

Monsieur,

Your letters of the 1st and the 8th of this month were delivered with the two pens and the bit of paper that you seized from Monsieur Fouquet. It is expected that you will prevent him from writing anything, and be sure to keep pressure on his valet to give you information or else it may well be that you will be outsmarted.

I am, monsieur,

Your very fond servant,

De Louvois

There is a postscript.

You previously told me that you found many papers of Monsieur Fouquet in the back of his armchair and that you would send them to me; please do so, the king wants to see them.[223]

Louvois to Saint-Mars

Fontainebleau 4 June 1666

I received your letters of the 8th and 15th of the past month. You do well to sometimes talk with the confessor of Monsieur Fouquet and remind him of the loyalty he owes to the king, and to help him stay in the same frame of mind, his majesty wants to give him 300 livres that I will send you for him.[224]

Eustache Dauger Arrives At Pignerol 21 August 1669

When Eustache Dauger arrived at Pignerol on August 21, 1669, Saint-Mars had learned to cope with Fouquet's artful dodging and was probably expecting the same slippery behavior from his new prisoner. The first letters between Louvois and Saint-Mars about Dauger, written just after his arrival in August 1669, are perfunctory comments and instructions, an overview for Saint-Mars as to what the prisoner's experience should be. Louvois tells Saint-Mars how often he can be confessed, that he can hear mass when it is performed in the prison chapel but he must be isolated from other prisoners, that if he is ill a doctor can be called without having to write to Paris first for permission. These letters do not show the prisoner's name, and that is common, because the government kept secret the names of people they had arrested and the mail system, although under Louvois' oversight and mostly locked down, still could be violated and so putting a name of an inmate, or even an inmate's servant, in a letter to or from a prison was not often done. There would be a nickname applied or the reference to the individual might be, "... the valet of M. Fouquet[225] who is ill..." or, "... the one you recently threatened with harsh punishment whose behavior has greatly improved..." In chapter 1 we gave a few of the workaround names that the staff created for Dauger: "the one whose name is not said aloud" ("*le nom ne se dit pas*"), or "the longtime prisoner," or "the man who was brought by sergent Vauroy." For a long time the prison guards called him "*la Tour*" (the Tower).

Louvois ordered a special cell built for Dauger. Its primary characteristic, to our knowledge, was that it should have two locking doors far enough apart so that a servant could bring the dishes of food and the daily clean chamber pot, put them on a table, Saint-Mars, Rû, and
Rosarges, the only three people who could see Dauger, took these, then unlocked the inner door, and brought Dauger his food and his "necessi-

ties." Such a special cell was also built at the Exilles prison and the Sainte-Marguerite prison when Saint-Mars and Dauger had to relocate.

Here are Louvois' first instructions to Saint-Mars:

> From Louvois to Saint-Mars
>
> Saint-Germain-en-Laye 10 September 1669
>
> Monsieur,
>
> I received your letters of the 24th and the last day of the past month. You can give to your new prisoner a book of prayers, and if he asks you for other books, give them to him also. You can allow him to hear the mass that is given for Monsieur Fouquet on Sundays and saints' days, however they are not to be in the same room, and you will make sure that during that time your guard will be such that he cannot escape or speak to anyone; you can also allow him to take confession three or four times a year, if he desires, and not more, unless he develops a serious illness. I heard that you told Monsieur de la Bretonnière that you were about to receive a prisoner, but I am confident that cannot be at all true.[226] I will send you at the earliest possible time documents that grant reformed lieutenancies for those of the cadets in your company that have had posts in the infantry.
>
> I am, monsieur,
>
> Your very fond servant,
>
> De Louvois[227]

On 25 September 1669 Louvois writes to Saint Mars that permission is not required for the new prisoner to have medical care; it should be given if he needs it.

> From Louvois to Saint-Mars
>
> Chambor[d] 25 September 1669
>
> Monsieur,
>
> I learned, by your letter of the 4th of this month, about the indisposition of Monsieur Fouquet and the opinion of the doctors; and that the prisoner that was brought to you is also sick; if he needs to be bled to recover his health there is no problem with that, and when in the future similar things happen, you should have him treated and medicated without a special order for it,

only keep me informed of what has happened, as you are accustomed to do.

I am, monsieur,
Your very fond servant,

De Louvois[228]

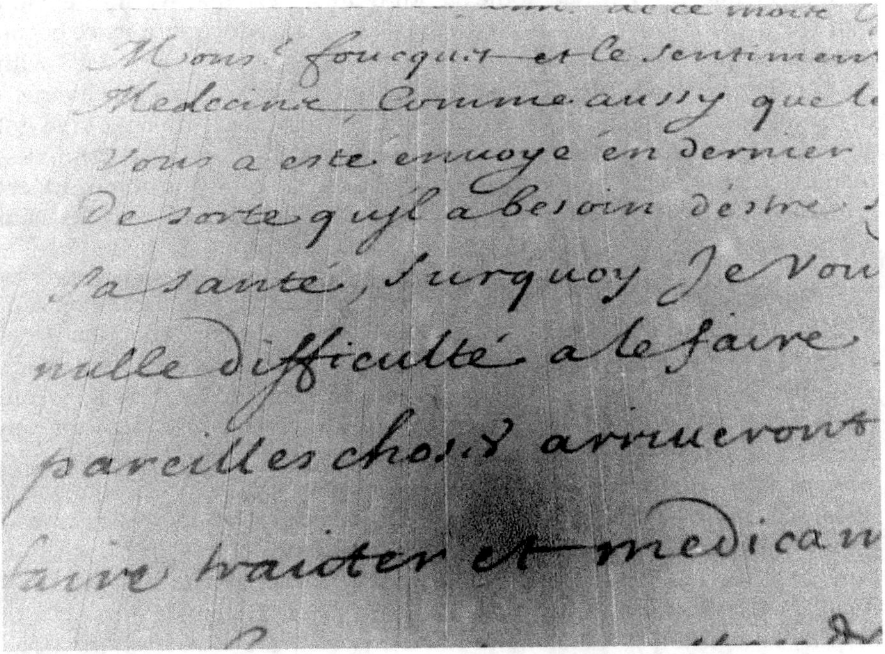
de ce mois
Mons.r fouquet et le sentiment
Medecins, Comme aussy que l
Vous a este envoye en dernier
De sorte quyl a besoin destre
sa sante, surquoy Je vou
nulle difficulte a le faire
pareilles chos.s arriueront
faire traiter et medican

Figure 7.1: A detail of the microfiche in the French National Archives showing Louvois' 25 September 1669 letter to Saint-Mars. Photo by the author.

From Versailles on 27 November 1672 Louvois wrote a reply to Saint-Mars' complaint that the prisoner brought by Vauroy was sick and the illness was forcing Saint-Mars to do extra work, perhaps because he had to visit his cell more than once a day, his usual routine. At any rate, Louvois tells Saint-Mars: "While the sieur Logier [*sic*] is sick you can put him in a healthier lodging than that he is in so he can get better quickly and as a result he will not be a bother to you long."[229]

Besides confirming the lack of consistency of spelling of the era (Logier is an approximation of Dauger...Ogier is another way to spell Auger), we see that Louvois has forgotten how to spell Dauger's name, and possibly he is repeating a misspelling that Saint-Mars made in his letter to him, so both of them are absent-minded about the prisoner. Possibly Saint-Mars had placed

Dauger in a damp, out-of-the-way cell and rather forgotten about him except for bringing him his food, wine and water each day. Finally Dauger got very ill and Saint-Mars had to begin more extended contact with him. Dauger is not an exotic prisoner at this early part of his incarceration, far from it, he was being mistreated. The respect that Saint-Mars reportedly had for him later in their relationship, especially in the testimony of Monsieur de Palteau, had not appeared yet. At some point either the king made up a story that Dauger had some standing in society that would demand more respect for him or Dauger's quiet behavior and devout practice began to make an impression on Saint-Mars. Louvois used the word "*sieur*" with the last name (*sieur* Logier). Three years before when Louvois was instructing Saint-Mars to treat him severely, he didn't use *sieur*, which, while not an extravagant stylistic gesture, is still slightly formal and respectful. Remember that Louvois had visited Dauger in 1670 so he had a face to put with the name and maybe that produced *sieur*, when in 1669 he called him a *misérable*.

Eustache's prison routine was different from other prisoners. He was kept in bland solitary confinement, the subject of weekly correspondence between his overseers, supervised by only one trusted head jailer, Saint-Mars. The jailer's main task was to look for possible hidden written messages from Eustache, even though in thirty-four years there was never the slightest sign that Eustache wanted to communicate any message to anyone, living or a descendant of the living. We see similarities between his prison life and a life of seclusion that a physically or mentally ill person might lead, arranged by a caring friend or relative. Charles VI of France (1368–1422) comes to mind, a fifteenth-century king whose madness was carefully handled by relatives. Charles VI was kept in safe quarters, given a female nurse late in his life, tended to by doctors, and not menaced with death or harm. The archives show Eustache's jailer, Saint-Mars, increasingly concerned about his illnesses, complimentary of his behavior, and finally, the donor of Eustache's shroud, a new cloth, paid for from Saint-Mars' own funds.[230]

Lauzun (1633–1723)

The marquis de Puyguilhem, Antonin Nompar de Caumont de Lauzun, arrived at Pignerol on 25 November 1671 about a year and a half after Dauger was admitted and six years after Fouquet. Lauzun, Dauger, and Fouquet: a trio that has no equal in Louis XIV's reign. Dumas did not have their stories at his disposal when he wrote his novels, but if he had, his books would have been about them, not about Artagnan, Athos, Porthos, and Aramis.

There is a famous quote by the memoir writer Saint-Simon that describes Lauzun, who came to Paris from Gascony in 1648 as a mere *chevalier*, but

CHAPTER 7. THE PRISONERS

he had introductions to the court from the noble family Grammont, with whom he lived.

> He was a little blond man, of good form, his face showed hauteur and liveliness, but there was no good will there; he was full of ambition, fantastical ideas, jealous of all, always overreaching and overreacting but never content with anything, no schooling, naturally sour, angry, savage, noble in his ways, mean and bad by nature, more by jealousy than out of ambition; still, he was a good friend when he was one, which was rare, a good relative, an easy enemy even to people who didn't matter to him, cruel to a fault, extremely brave and dangerously bold.[231]

After he was released from Pignerol in 1681, although continuing to be vulgar, mean, pugnacious, perhaps deranged, he reconstituted his military career and was so successful in showing the devil his back that he was awarded England's Order of the Garter for helping the English royal family out of a scrappy situation and died at age ninety-one in his bed that he shared with a teenage wife.

About fifty-four years before his death, he lay not on, but under the king's bed in which the king and Madame de Montespan, the royal mistress, were making time for quick sex within the rigid court schedule. He hid himself there in order to find out if the king's mistress would be good to her word that she would promote Lauzun to the king for master of the artillery, however what he overheard instead was Montespan making fun of him for desiring the post. His ears and brain reddened in the dark as he heard her above him, breasts bared perhaps, one leg raised in the sheets as she stretched the other, chuckle that he was an idiot and unworthy of the post, but his Gascon manners and temper were good for laughs and she meant to keep him on a leash. A little while later, after the king and Montespan had rejoined the day's public events and Lauzun had pushed himself out from under the bed when they were gone, Lauzun sidled up to Montespan and politely asked if she had used her influence on the king to get him his position. She got halfway through her assurance that she had done so when he began to repeat word for word what she had said to the king in bed and the king's responses. It would not be the first time nor the last that Lauzun would infuriate the king.

Antonin Nompar de Caumont de Lauzun was born in 1633 at Lauzun in the present-day department of the Lot-et-Garonne[232] to Gabriel Nompar de Caumont, comte de Lauzun and Charlotte de Caumont de La Force, daughter of Henri-Nompar de Caumont, duc de La Force. Antonin had inherited from his father the position of captain of one of the two companies of the

Gentilhommes de Bec-de-Corbin, the prestigious second company of the king's bodyguards (the first company being the Scottish). Members of the company carried a long pole weapon with a curved top that looked like the beak of a crow, therefore the name, Gentlemen of the Crow-Beak.[233] Each body had one hundred men. They marched just behind the king in parades. In 1655 he was captain of the light horse, in 1663, an *aide de camp*. Shortly after, he was made an officer in the newly formed dragoons of the king. At the time he was arrested, he had the high position of captain of the first company of the Guard of the Body of the King and his military rank was lieutenant-general. He fought under marshal Turenne in the Battle of the Dunes in 1658 that liberated Calais from the Spanish and was at the king's side in 1670 in Flanders, but disgrace could come without warning, and on 26 November 1671 Lauzun was no longer a captain but a captive in a procession of a hundred soldiers led by d'Artagnan on the way to Pignerol, where they arrived on the nineteenth of December.[234] Saint-Mars had a nice apartment ready for Lauzun, two rooms situated below the cell of Fouquet. No one knows why Louis XIV ordered him arrested, and not knowing was one of the things that bothered Lauzun most during his ten years of detention.

One possibility is that the king and his mistress, Madame de Montespan, were appalled that the very rich Grande Mademoiselle, Louis XIV's first cousin, Anne-Marie-Louise d'Orléans, duchesse de Montpensier, (1627–1693) had fallen, God help her, stubbornly and deeply in love with the little man and declared to the king she wanted to marry him and give him half the Montpensier wealth that had come from her mother, who died giving birth to her in 1627. It was Louis' place to either accept or deny her request. At first the king gave his consent. But Montespan probably explained to him that this would mean a loss to Louis' direct descendants, including his children by her, of around 22 million *livres* and a great gain to the Orléans (the junior royal line) and it might be better if the marriage didn't take place until the Grande Mademoiselle was no longer of child-bearing age. The duchess was forty-three in 1670 but conception was still possible. Louis' own brother had been born when his mother was thirty-nine. Anne-Marie-Louise d'Orléans was the richest woman in the kingdom and keeping her childless was a way for the heirs of the king, particularly his legitimized children of Madame de Montespan, to get rich. They perhaps thought that the duchess' passion for Lauzun would cool over time, but she didn't lose interest, not even after he was in prison. His imprisonment gave her a challenge: to get him out of prison, and she didn't stop lobbying for it until he was set free. The resolution of the matter resulted in millions of *livres* for Madame de Montespan's children by the king.

Postscript : Not long after Lauzun was released from captivity, he and the Grande Mademoiselle married but the marriage fell completely into the Seine on the north side of the Ile-Saint-Louis, just below the Hôtel de

CHAPTER 7. THE PRISONERS

Lauzun, that still presents a quiet façade overlooking the quay d'Anjou. Lauzun had bought the *hôtel* to be a domicile for himself and his bride. He abused her, and she chased him out of her life like a rat out of a hole, he said, after a couple of years during which they threw things at each other frequently.

For the entire ten years that Lauzun was at Pignerol, he made life difficult for Saint-Mars.

> From Louvois to Saint-Mars
>
> Saint-Germain en Laye 10 December 1671
>
> Monsieur,
>
> Your letter of the 9th of this month told me that after the arrival of sieur Nallot at Pignerol, you have made a lodging for Lauzun below that of Fouquet and that you have made it secure and with bars. His majesty is positive on these but he thinks that more precautions should be made with a *grille de fer* sealed inside the room at the opening of the windows and another in the chimney to keep him from being able to speak with Monsieur Fouquet by the chimney.[235]

Louvois writes to Saint-Mars from Saint-Germain on February 9, 1672 that Saint-Mars should continue to deny Lauzun ink and paper, no matter what he says. He can be given two valets to serve him. And from this letter we learn that Lauzun was making ominous threats to Saint-Mars about what might happen when he was finally released.

> You should not be disturbed by the outbursts that [the comte de Lauzun] directs against you, nor by the accusations he makes; and, as long as you follow to the letter the intentions of the king, you should not be at all worried about the feelings your prisoners might have against you when they are eventually set at liberty.[236]

In March 1672 Lauzun set fire to his floor and this is Louvois' opinion as to why.

> From Louvois to Saint-Mars
>
> Versailles 16 March 1672

When monsieur de Lauzun burned a plank of his floor in his room it was certainly to find out what there was under the floor, and if he does such a thing again, you can speak to him harshly and warn him that he is at risk for being watched by a guard at all times;... you must look often under his bed to see if he has lifted some floor boards to see if he can escape through there.[237]

We have more than one letter that shows that Saint-Mars used physical agility to spy on his prisoners.

From Louvois to Saint-Mars

Versailles 10 November 1675

Monsieur,

I have received your letter of the 30th of the past month. Although you say that your prisoners are always about the same, you must not fail to write me about them. As the leaves are falling now, [the tree you have been climbing up to spy on Lauzun will no longer be useful] to you to see what monsieur de Lauzun is doing in his apartment, and you can now take from him the spyglass that he uses to see signs made to him from the outside, pretending that you have just found it when visiting his apartment.[238]

Louvois writes to Saint-Mars from Montreuil 18 July 1680 in response to a report from Saint-Mars that Lauzun is verbally abusing the staff. Louvois tells Saint-Mars not to be concerned about what Lauzun said and that his officers should not be concerned either. The king wants to know, says Louvois, what the incident entailed involving Lauzun and lieutenants de Blainvilliers and de Villebois. He says to tell Lauzun that these officers are not at Pignerol for being abused and if Lauzun does it again he'll be locked in his room and will not be allowed to take walks anymore.[239]

Dauger Is Valet For Fouquet

To introduce Eustache Dauger as a person placed with Nicolas Fouquet in his prison apartment as his valet, after all the zealous announcements of restrictions placed on both of these men, over and over, for years, death threats to all mankind for any contact with Dauger, constant vigilance to take Fouquet's chicken bones away from him so he could not make them into pens, the onerous, punishing prison regime of lack of communication or news from the outside world, no contact with family, almost no daylight

CHAPTER 7. THE PRISONERS

coming into the windows so that it was perhaps impossible for Dauger and Fouquet to know when a few feet of new snow fell on top of past snowfalls long ago turned to ice—could be said to be, if we did not already know this story is unpredictable, an unwise plotline in a fiction adventure novel.

Nevertheless, here is what happened. When Lauzun arrived at the prison in 1671, Louvois gave permission for Saint-Mars to hire two valets to serve him. It wasn't easy to find servants who were willing to come into a prison and not come out again until their employer was freed or died. Saint-Mars found one valet for Lauzun but after a while he got sick. Lauzun began to act strangely and then violently. He set a fire in the floor of his room, he was for a few weeks suicidal, and then in a constant rage. Saint-Mars must have been desperate to find Lauzun a valet who might calm down the former captain of the king's guards because he wrote to Louvois on February 20, 1672:

> Because it is extremely hard to find valets that are willing to live with my prisoners I am taking the liberty of suggesting that I think that the prisoner that was brought by the major of Dunkirk would make a good valet. He would not tell M. de Lauzun where he comes from after I ordered him not to. I am sure that he would not give him any news and would not quit as do all the other valets I have found. Please favor me with a reply as to the man of the tower.

Louvois's response to this letter is lost. But we know he refused Saint-Mars's request.[240]

Then La Rivière, Fouquet's only valet after Champagne died in 1674, began to be sick quite often, and Fouquet, even though perhaps the most punished person in Louis XIV's reign, still had a high position in the ranks of government "robe" society, and all the king's hatred and all the king's men were no match for the absolute requirement that Fouquet had to have at least one valet to serve him in prison. Fouquet was not expected to stack his own dirty dishes and fasten his own cravat, in fact, if it had been reported to the court, even quietly, that Fouquet was forced to put his clothes on by himself it would have been a huge scandal. As obsolete and frivolous as this rule seems now, it was obligatory then.

Saint-Mars could not find another valet in the town to serve Fouquet. Evidently the family of the prisoner had no more servants to offer, probably because their homes and money had been seized by the king at the time of Fouquet's disgrace and their legal fees for trying to get some of the money back were high, making servants a thing of the past.

So three years later, Saint-Mars again asked Louvois to allow Dauger to be a valet for Fouquet and Lauzun. We don't have Saint-Mars' letter but we have Louvois' reply on January 30, 1675:

> From Louvois to Saint-Mars
>
> Saint-Germain en Laye January 30, 1675
>
> Monsieur,
>
> I received your letter of the 19th of this month and I told the king of your request. His Majesty approves that you give for valet to monsieur Fouquet the prisoner that the sieur de Vauroy brought you; but, no matter what happens, you must never put him with Monsieur de Lauzun nor with anyone else except Monsieur Fouquet.
>
> I am, monsieur,
>
> Your very fond servant,
>
> De Louvois
>
> Postscript: To be clear, you can give the said prisoner to M. Fouquet if his own valet cannot serve him and not otherwise.

A month and a half later Saint-Mars had written for further clarification about Dauger's service as a valet and he received this letter from Louvois that shows some irritation.

> From Louvois to Saint-Mars
>
> Saint-Germain en Laye March 11, 1675
>
> Monsieur,
>
> I received your letter of the 26th of February. If you can find a valet who would be suitable to serve Monsieur de Lauzun, you can hire him; but you must never, for any reason, give the prisoner that the sieur de Vauroy brought to you, who must serve, in case of necessity, only Monsieur Fouquet, just as I already told you.[241]

The first thing that Fouquet would have thought when they put Dauger with him was that he was a spy, therefore their relationship must at first have been strained. Dauger, who had been isolated since he was brought to Pignerol in 1669, might have been uncomfortable and confused about why he was suddenly in Fouquet's comfortable cell with nice furniture, fine dishes and table linen, and perhaps a tapestry or two hung on the walls to

CHAPTER 7. THE PRISONERS   119

lessen the cold and dampness of the stone.[242] He had never served anyone as a valet before, judging by the plaintive phrase of Saint-Mars in his letter to Louvois that he thought Dauger "would make a good valet," which indicates he had no idea if Dauger had ever been a valet before but he was worth a try.[243]

The strict rules that were set at the beginning of the Pignerol saga began to unravel in 1675. It must have been a relief to Dauger, La Rivière, and Fouquet to have a new routine and interesting to have someone new to talk to. Saint-Mars had warned Dauger not to say anything of his past life to his new companions, and Saint-Mars' firm conviction that Dauger would not break that rule was proved correct because for years the relationship between the three men went smoothly.

La Rivière must have taught him what he needed to know about the ratio of wine and water that Fouquet liked,[244] the schedule of waking that Fouquet wanted to keep, how to warm his bed before the night fell, and how many candles could be used in a day according to the allotment that Saint-Mars allowed. Marcel Pagnol, a twentieth-century screenplay writer and temporarily a Mask sleuth, was able to visualize in his mind the apartment of Fouquet with La Rivière and Dauger at his disposal and he doesn't see Dauger cleaning Fouquet's shoes or sweeping the floor. La Rivière was a "professional" at housekeeping so that would fall to him, however Pagnol sees a possible role that Dauger might have played—that of secretary, copyist, or even editor for Fouquet, who was writing a number of devotional works and poetry, including a small book called *The Wisdom of Solomon*,[245] almost certainly not with chicken bones for pens. If Pagnol's suspicion is true, Saint-Mars was violating the king's order that Dauger should not be able to communicate with anyone.

As to why Saint-Mars wanted to use Dauger as a valet for Fouquet, Pagnol thinks that Saint-Mars felt sorry for Dauger, a person who was very much alone but who continued to be respectful and obedient while the jailer was putting up with Fouquet's scams to get letters out and even a jail break was designed by another family servant sent by the family, Honneste. Lauzun's alternating moods and surly threats to Saint-Mars and his staff were unsettling and unrelenting. His visits to the man brought by the captain from Dunkirk must have begun to stand out as a respite from insecure encounters with his other prisoners.

Lauzun Rises

Louvois had pointed out to Saint-Mars the two danger points in Lauzun's room that could be used for escape: the floor and the chimney. A hole in his floor that went down into the space below was how Lauzun exited his room in his near escape in late February 1676. He dug through his floor, got into the vault below, removed bars on the window and used a ladder made of napkins to let himself down into the moat, which he scaled to get up into the court of the citadel. But a sentry saw him and he was taken back to his rooms in the upper tower. Saint-Mars was afraid for his job but Louvois reassured him and told him to do better in the future. He only wanted to know if Lauzun had had communication with Fouquet.

After Lauzun was picked up loose in the citadel and taken back to his rooms, Louvois told Saint-Mars to increase his watch over the ex *Bec-de-Corbin* captain. He put in spyholes above the rooms and bathrooms of the prisoners and bars in the chimneys. Anywhere else a bar could go, it went. Petitfils described these measures and gave the verdict: "None of these precautions helped."[246]

Soon, Lauzun made a similar hole in his ceiling between his apartment and Fouquet's exactly above it, which was the route that led to the end of all of Louis XIV's attempts at removing Dauger's story from history. The exact date is not known. The last time that Fouquet had seen the comte de Lauzun, he was the marquis de Puyguilhem, who boarded in Paris with the Grammont family while trying to rise in the military ranks. Lauzun began to tell Fouquet about his career after Fouquet's arrest (*colonel général des dragons, capitaine des gardes, général d'armée*) and that the Grande Mademoiselle wanted to marry him. Fouquet thought he was a raving madman and didn't believe him. But the rest of the news from the outside was precious to Fouquet, who had known nothing of the politics, deaths, births, mistresses of the king, wars of the king, or the building of the king's huge château southwest of Paris in a flat plain with a small hill town on it that was soon to be the seat of government, Versailles. More news: the death of Anne of Austria in January 1666 of breast cancer, the War of Devolution to acquire land Louis XIV said belonged to his queen despite her having released claim to it at her marriage, the Dutch War, advances on work on the courtyard and the east front of the Louvre, the building of Mazarin's Collège de Quatre Nations, the fall of La Vallière, the ascendence of Montespan—the births of La Vallière's and Montespan's illegitimate children and the deaths of all of the king's legitimate children save one, the Grand Dauphin. The queen Marie-Thérèse was still alive, though, so maybe there would be more children and they would live to adulthood.[247] These conversations were protected by the watchful valets[248] of both men, meanwhile, Saint-Mars sent Louvois reports that his prisoners were safely locked in without any contact with each other or with the outside world.

From 1677 the king began to lessen the restrictions on Fouquet and Lauzun. It was a critical year at court: In 1676 talks had begun to end

CHAPTER 7. THE PRISONERS 121

the Dutch War; Madame de Sévigné wrote to her daughter that a mature widow of quiet and devout disposition, Madame Françoise Scarron, was becoming influential at court; on April 24, 1677 Le Tellier informed Saint-Mars that Lauzun had been named the heir to the deceased duc de La Force making Lauzun a duke, and it also meant that Lauzun would have to be allowed visits from his family members and notaries to carry out the duc de La Force's will, so the prisoners' situation would have to be improved drastically so that witnesses did not go back to Paris or Turin telling horror stories about the restrictive conditions of two high-ranking men. In November 1677 Lauzun's brother and sister came to Pignerol to discuss legalities involved in the inheritance and new freedoms were quickly granted. Fouquet and Lauzun were allowed to walk three times a week on the rampart near their apartments with their valets but Saint-Mars must be with them and they must walk separately, not together. Louvois sent Fouquet a box of tea as a medicine and the two prisoners could play cards, but couldn't game for money.

Fouquet still could have only two letters a year from his wife, could not write letters, could not eat with Lauzun, could not walk in the citadel, could not have newspapers or books, could not talk with officers of the citadel, could not have visitors from the town, could not have family visitors; all those were permitted later. But for a year, Fouquet and Lauzun were walking separately with their valets on the ramparts of the donjon three times a week followed closely by Saint-Mars or one of his lieutenants and a few hours later they gossiped and discussed politics together in Fouquet's room without any supervision whatsoever.

At the end of 1678, either Louvois or the king, perhaps both, became uneasy about the frequent contact of Fouquet, Dauger, and La Rivière. Had they known Lauzun was also a part of the party, they would have been much more than uneasy. They had made it clear to Saint-Mars that Lauzun was never to have any sight of or conversation with Dauger. Only Fouquet could have Dauger in his apartment and then only when his other valet was sick. Lauzun had his valets and Fouquet had his; Fouquet walked with his valets and Lauzun walked with his, no
crossovers permitted. Louvois was pretty sure this rule was being kept.

Some historians have looked for reasons the king and Louvois absolutely forbade Lauzun from seeing Dauger; perhaps Lauzun had seen him in the past and would want to continue the link in the future. The king did not intend to keep Lauzun in prison forever and perhaps when he was released he would talk about the prisoner to others, for instance the Grande Mademoiselle who had invited Lauzun to marry her, and she was unpredictable if she discovered a cause to fight for. Petitfils' theory on the mystery of Dauger's identity was that Dauger had been a valet in Jean-Baptiste Colbert's household and, Lauzun, being in the Colbert circle, would have seen Dauger in the past and would know that he had been an assassin hired to kill Colbert (probably by his rival Louvois) but the plot had been revealed and Dauger was imprisoned. Theories on who might have hired Dauger to kill whom abound in books on the Mask: Louvois hired him to kill Colbert, Colbert hired him to kill Fouquet...no, Colbert hired him to kill Louvois. All implausible. Everything we know about Dauger tells that he did not want to and would never have killed anyone.

The king and Louvois seemed to sense trouble. In the following letter, probably the most important we have from Louvois, this worry was evident because Louvois wrote to Fouquet (directly, Saint-Mars being excluded from the question and the answer) enquiring whether Dauger had told La Rivière anything about himself.

> Louvois to Fouquet
>
> Saint-Germain 23 December 1678
>
> Monsieur
>
> It is with much pleasure that I am carrying out the command of the king to tell you that His Majesty is disposed shortly to make your experience in prison far less onerous; but, beforehand, as he wishes to know if the person named Eustache that has been given to you as a servant has said anything to the other valet that serves you about what he was doing before being at Pignerol [*à quoi il a été employé avant que d'être à Pignerol*], His Majesty has ordered me to ask you about this and to tell you that he wants you to tell me the truth about this without any consideration for the consequences so that he can take measures that he thinks appropriate about that which the said Eustache could have said of his past life to his comrade. The intention of His Majesty is that you will make a response to this letter and seal it before giving it to Monsieur de Saint-Mars and without telling Monsieur de Saint-Mars what it says.[249]
>
> I am, monsieur,
>
> Your very fond servant,
>
> De Louvois

Before the signature, this unusual confirmation of authenticity is written: *"Cecy est l'intention du Roy."*

He says that Fouquet will be given ink, paper, and wax to seal his letter. If the king feels like replying, he will, and then Saint-Mars could give Fouquet as much paper, ink, and wax as he would ask for. On January 18, 1679, only a month later, Louvois says he has received the letter from Fouquet.[250] Note that Louvois was not concerned if Dauger had told Fouquet his story, only if La Rivière knew it. We don't know if that means that Louvois and the king thought that Fouquet knew Dauger's story already, and that is why they had allowed Dauger to spend time with Fouquet. This letter has been interpreted many ways. Some authors have found it useful because they say it gives a hint about Eustache's former life; Louvois says the king wants to know if Dauger had told La Rivière "...what he was doing before he was at Pignerol," which means he was "doing" something. But of course he was doing something. Every living being is doing something even if it is nothing.

Taking Louvois at face value is always a mistake. After many years of thinking about this mystery I have become suspicious of everyone and everything having to do with it; furthermore, if there is any character in the story who merits a look for duplicity, it is Louvois. I think that the phrase "...what he was doing before he was at Pignerol" sounds like *Louvois* wanted to know what he was doing before he was at Pignerol. Louvois may have finally become suspicious about what the king had told him about the prisoner and decided to find out for himself by writing Fouquet a request that would inevitably (he assumed) bring the explanation of Dauger's life.

Discovering secret crimes was of particular interest in that year. The high, secret tribunal charged with investigating and prosecuting poisoners, abortionists, and unholy priests and abbots who were making fortunes saying black masses for their clients, the advertisement being that a black mass could scare off (or bring on) a disaster of one kind or another for a client, was Louvois' main responsibility at that moment, the Dutch War being over and the next war not yet started.

In Louvois' new office at Versailles in 1679, his desk was stacked with folders about *marquises* who were making and selling a lot of poison to a lot of people. The king and his police were overwhelmed. This poison epidemic had crept up on them silently and was suddenly potent and pervasive. Ladies of rank had been found to be visiting houses of black magic and carrying home vials of poison to make peaceful ends with their husbands and room for new lovers. Even the duc de Luxembourg of the house of Montmorency and a captain of great capacity, had gotten caught up in it. One of the king's former lovers, niece of Mazarin, the comtesse de Soissons, had fled to avoid arrest. Louvois was deep in the bowels of dark deeds and dossiers on people who had once seemed perfectly normal but were turning out to be dangerous criminals. His thinking had become tractable and his methods, as they always had been, were sneaky.

His letters to the king at that time were quite often about the interrogations of poisoners who were being questioned at Vincennes and the Bastille. Fathoming and unraveling the Medusa's head of sins and crimes admitted by these busy entrepreneurs who were arranging for murders of respectable people like salesmen might do behind a hardware store counter, was taking up the greater part of Louvois' work day.

CHAPTER 7. THE PRISONERS

> Louvois au Roi
>
> At Paris, 16 September 1679
>
> La Voisin has started to open up about people who have come to her for business. She said yesterday that Mme de Vivonne and Mme de La Motte came to ask how to get rid of their husbands...and Mme de Dreux, wanting the same thing, turned over to her a diamond cross as payment for the service [of the poisoning]... La Dodée, who was arrested and taken to Vincennes at the same time as Trianon, and who had been interrogated only once on minor matters not having to do with poison, cut her throat two nights ago. She had put her dress over the wound and most of her blood was absorbed by it. They found her this morning when they came to bring her breakfast; she was about thirty-five, decent looking... had helped Trianon in her sacrileges. M. de La Reynie[251] thought it best to bury her, which was done tonight.[252]

He considered the situation. The king hadn't released Dauger. Usually prisoners were released eventually, most of the time quite soon after arrest. Dauger was different. He had no family, no friends, or if he did they had never inquired about him or visited him; he did not go mad... if he had, his story would not be interesting because such a typical end would denote a typical prisoner whose story would never be known, so he could be ignored. He could not be ignored. He was devout and perpetually sane and compliant. Like Saint-Mars when he first took in his prisoner brought by sergent Vauroy and needled Louvois for the identity of Dauger ("I get all kinds of questions about my prisoner and people want to know why I am adding so much new security in my prison. I tell them big, fat lies about him and they believe them, which makes me laugh"), Louvois was curious. No one who has learned about this story, not even Louvois, has ever failed to become tantalized by it.

After Louvois received Fouquet's letter about Dauger, the routine for the prisoners was softened again. They could write letters to friends and family, get newspapers, see each other any time, spend all day with each other, eat together, and Saint-Mars could eat with them. Officers of the free company could visit during the day as long as Saint-Mars was present. Finally Fouquet's family was allowed to come to Pignerol to see him. His wife, Marie-Madeleine, their daughter and son, could stay for weeks at a time. Some official business could finally be decided, particularly steps to get some of Marie-Madeleine's own money back from the crown, and what to do about Belle-Ile, that the family had spent a fortune on to create a commercial shipping operation but that the king had taken. A little apartment was made for Fouquet's daughter to live in so she could take care of her father after her mother had to return to Moulins to put into effect some of the decisions and consult with notaries and advisors. Possibly the king had in mind that he would release Fouquet, that the surintendant was now old and frail and poor and would not be a bother if released to a cottage in Brittany with his family. Possibly the royal testosterone-infused fury of a young man of twenty-three had dissipated in the mature man, by then forty-two. We will never know.

The king and Louvois knew Lauzun was theatrical and violent... and smart. They did not know that he had been going into Fouquet's room at night for four years and in consequence, either from Fouquet or from Dauger, he had learned an astounding secret:

> From the comte de Lauzun to the marquis de Louvois
>
> Pignerol January 27, 1680
>
> (...) I declare that I am less impatient to leave prison than to inform you immediately of something you need to know: but it must be told in person and only to you without any other witness. It is in your interest that the message is transmitted in this way (...) only my friend Barrail can be trusted with this task, and it is important for you that it be him, and I plead with you, monsieur, to be kind to me and send him to me, because it is a matter with consequences greater than any you can imagine (...). I cannot explain more in this letter and I anxiously await to hear that you will grant my request which will allow me to tell you the details.[253]

Barrail came to Pignerol on 17 March and left on 25 March, two days after Fouquet died.

8. Pignerol And Exilles

They demonstrated the existence of bismuth, liver of sulphur, and regulus of antimony, the distillation of alcohol, volatilisation of mercury, and preparation of aqua regia, sulphuric and other mineral acids, and the purification of alkalies. They had the scarlet dye for cloth, the secret of which has now been lost and cannot be equalled, and their processes of glass-staining cannot be approached by those employed at the present day.[254]

—The Mystery and Romance of Alchemy and Pharmacy - C.J.S. Thompson

Death Of The *Surintendant*

On April 6, 1680, the Paris *Gazette* announced that Nicolas Fouquet had died of apoplexy (heart attack) on March 23. Louvois and the king learned of this before the public did, because Saint-Mars wrote to Louvois before Fouquet's body was cold that the former *surintendant* was dead and that he had found a hole in Fouquet's room through which Fouquet and Lauzun had been communicating at night and that their valets had been present during these meetings. Louvois had dark skin but he must have blanched when he received this news.

> Louvois to Saint-Mars
>
> Saint-Germain en Laye April 8, 1680
>
> The king has learned from your letter of 23 March the death of monsieur Fouquet and the judgement that you make that monsieur de Lauzun knows most of the important things of which Fouquet knew and that la Rivière knows them too. So the king told me to let you know that, after having patched the hole by which Fouquet and Lauzun communicated, that you should remake the stairs that leave from the room of the dead Fouquet up to his daughter's room.[255] The king wants Lauzun lodged in Fouquet's old room and he is to be visited frequently.
>
> That you persuade Lauzun that Eustache d'Angers [sic] and la Rivière are set free and that you tell the same thing to everyone

who asks you about this; however, you must put these two in a room together where you can assure His Majesty that they will not have any communication with anyone, by speech or writing, and that monsieur de Lauzun cannot know that they are still in the prison.

You should not have let monsieur de Vaux take away the papers and poetry of his father, and you should have locked those documents up to be used as His Majesty might order.[256]

Louvois also sent a letter on April 8 to the comte de Vaux, Fouquet's son, to say the family could have the body of his father. Meanwhile, it was stored at the chapel of the monastery of the Sainte-Claires in the town of Pignerol.

I can imagine that Louvois's first thought when he heard of Fouquet's death was, "If he wanted to die, he certainly could have picked a better time for it." Perhaps Louvois, along with Colbert and the king, still wished for Fouquet's death, nineteen years after he had been arrested in Nantes, but 1680 was bad timing. That was the year that the *Affaire des Poisons* was first announced in the French press, the previous five years of the investigation having been kept secret. The *Chambre Ardente*, the special criminal court set up specifically to find, question, and punish the crowds of poisoners and black mass sayers who had sprouted like mushrooms, small bourgeois rabble who were sellers to upper level society members, had been created by official documents on April 7, 1679 with Louvois its supervisor. The first sitting was April 10 at the Arsenal next to the Bastille, a secure site traditionally used for royal trials.

Fouquet had not been forgotten by his friends or the public. He had been a major news story for a long time and an admired star of the court, so assumptions would be made and questions asked about whether Fouquet had been poisoned. Because of the state trials, poison was a recent topic of breakfast conversations in many Paris households and there may have been some husbands who wondered whether it was safe to eat breakfast anymore. The streets, bars, and shops were filled with informants hired by the Lieutenant-General of Police, Gabriel-Nicolas de la Reynie (1625–1709), and suspects were being brought in for questioning.

Some authorities on the mystery of the Mask have said that Louvois was managing the Mask himself and the king was never interested in the prisoner, however I think in this instance we have proof that the king was active in the decisions made about Dauger. Ordering movements of prisoners to nowhere would be beyond Louvois' powers because if Louvois ordered this himself, the news of it would get back to the king and if Louis XIV had not approved of it, Louvois might very well have been disgraced for overstepping his powers (although he overstepped his reach in other matters continually, so again, we are in a gray area of possibilities, as usual).

Lauzun's confidant Barrail, who was allowed by Louvois, at the pleading of Lauzun, to come to Pignerol to allow Lauzun to pass an important secret to him in person, had left the prison two days after Fouquet died. We assume that Lauzun and Barrail spoke together at Pignerol but we don't know if Barrail gave Lauzun's "matter with consequences greater than any you can imagine" to Louvois once he got to Paris, if it had any bearing on the decision to put Dauger and La Rivière into hiding, or if Barrail's presence at the prison had any connection with Fouquet's death. Barrail retired from court to make his "*salut*" in 1682, two years after his mission to Pignerol.[257] To Barrail's presence in this story we must follow a principle on page one of Louis Battifol's *Vie de Paris sous Louis XIII* in which he states an aspect of his research: "The subject is vast; I had no choice but to make some borders."[258]

Saint-Mars And Louvois Disappear

Saint-Mars did not do anything without an order from Louvois. True or False? We begin to see that Saint-Mars is a more complicated fellow than we thought he was and Louvois had just learned that Saint-Mars might not have been the perfect jailer after all. Despite Saint-Mars' ardent assurances that he followed all orders immediately and exactly, yet Saint-Mars had an independent streak and in the trail of correspondence after Fouquet's death there are signs of it.

Saint-Mars wrote to Louvois on Fouquet's death date, March 23, 1680, that Fouquet had died and that Fouquet, Lauzun, Dauger, and La Rivière had been talking together for an uncertain period of time. All these men had secrets, some of which the king and Louvois knew, some of which they didn't. It is hard to say which secrets they were more afraid had been told to the group, the former or the latter. It probably took five days for the letter to get to Louvois at the chateau of Saint-Germain-en-Laye, a huge castle[259] that was the seat of government west of Paris, maybe six or seven days if snow was still on the Alpine passes. That would be March 28 or 29. In between then and April 8, Louvois and the king talked over this disastrous news. Perhaps for a few days the king put off making a decision because he didn't know quite what to do. Eight or nine days seems like a long time for musing upon this very important crisis, but we know that is how long it took because on April 8 Louvois wrote new instructions to Saint-Mars: he was to announce that Dauger and La Rivière had been released and then to secretly move them together to a cell in another tower and hold them tightly there. He was to spread the story to everyone, especially to Lauzun, that these two former valets of Fouquet were of no importance to the king so that Lauzun would be persuaded that, despite what Fouquet might have told him about these two men, they were insignificant and had gone away. Lauzun had outsmarted them so many times that one would think they would be humble enough to avoid putting anything this important in Lauzun's way and hoping that he wouldn't find out the truth about it, but humble was not a characteristic of either Louis XIV or Louvois. Those instructions to Saint-Mars, assuming a five-day delivery, arrived at Pignerol on April 13.

Between April 8 and May 4 (almost four weeks) there is postal silence from Saint-Mars. Odd. The letter from Saint-Mars that he should have written, past practice being the rule, on April 13 or 14 to tell Louvois that he had received these new instructions and would not fail to carry them out immediately, perhaps was lost. For whatever reason, we don't have a letter that says that. Was Saint-Mars slow in communicating to Paris because he was embarrassed that his very important prisoners had been visiting each other at night through a hole which had entirely escaped regular inspections of the room in which Fouquet lived?

The next letter on record is one that Saint-Mars wrote to Louvois dated 4 May 1680, but the letter was received by Monsieur de Saint-Pouenge,[260] relative by marriage of Louvois, who was temporarily replying to Louvois' mail because Louvois was at Barèges in the Pyrenees mountains taking a water cure for his injured leg that a fall from a horse had caused in 1679. Saint-Pouenge wrote to Saint-Mars and asked that the items found on Fouquet be sent to Paris.

Saint-Mars had been trained to reply only to Louvois and he had no way of knowing whether Saint-Pouenge was a safe correspondent. He perhaps had never heard of Saint-Pouenge. Louvois might have been murdered for all Saint-Mars knew, or overthrown in a coup at court, so until Saint-Mars heard from Louvois himself, he did not feel it was safe to reply and certainly not to mail him the contents of the dead Fouquet's pockets.

On the other hand, one of Fouquet's most recent biographers, Daniel Dessert, points out that Saint-Mars must have been horrified about this debacle and was somewhat frozen in apprehension as to what would happen to him because he had allowed what all jailers fear most: happy secret gatherings of prisoners at night that go unnoticed for a long time. Dessert says Saint-Mars waited to reply to Louvois until Fouquet's body could not be autopsied.

An autopsy enters into this gruesome episode because of the items found on Fouquet's body that were sent, very belatedly, to Louvois. The question of an autopsy was never discussed, that we know of, by Louvois or Saint-Mars, and one was never done on Fouquet's body, but it has been a point on which historians have focused because it was rumored, as Louvois had

CHAPTER 8. PIGNEROL AND EXILLES

feared, that Fouquet was poisoned. Not only rumored, we have a letter from Louvois that seems to suggest that is what occurred.

But returning to May 4: Saint-Mars' letter to Louvois went in the mail on that date and was received by Saint-Pouenge. That letter, whatever else it said, must not have said anything about the contents of Fouquet's pockets. On May 16 (almost two months after Fouquet's death), Saint-Pouenge wrote to Saint-Mars saying that the king wants the contents of Fouquet's pockets. Please send them.

Saint-Mars did not reply to Saint-Pouenge. When a letter together with the items in question did not arrive after a week or so, the king must have interpreted the silence as Saint-Mars' reluctance to reply to anyone but Louvois. Rather than writing to Saint-Mars himself, he sent a messenger to Barèges where Louvois was receiving medical treatment that must have said something like, "Tell Saint-Mars that I want the contents of Fouquet's pockets immediately." Louvois wrote to Saint-Mars from Barèges on May 29 and told Saint-Mars to send the papers and whatever else there had been in the deceased surintendant's pockets to the king without delay. Keep in mind that Barèges is in southwest France in the *Haute-Pyrénées* department[261] at about 4,000 feet (1,250 meters) elevation, three mountain ranges away from Pignerol. It must have taken eight days for the letter to get to Saint-Mars because the jailer responded on 8 June, and must have included a piece of paper but not the possessions of Fouquet because on 22 June Louvois writes to Saint-Mars:

> With regard to the paper that accompanied your letter of the 8th, you were wrong not to tell me what it contained from the first day that you knew of it. In addition, I ask you to send me in a package that which you found in the pockets of M. Fouquet, so that I can present them to his majesty.[262]

Since the correspondents always began their letters with the date of the letter they were responding to we know that Saint-Mars' next mailing was dated July 4. Louvois responded to that missing letter on July 10 with possibly one of the most cryptic statements made in any of the letters between jailer and minister; it's a little postscript about something that Saint-Mars had found in Fouquet's things, which evidently Saint-Mars had finally boxed up and sent to Louvois. At the end of the main part of the letter, in his own handwriting, Louvois wrote, "Tell me how the man named Eustache was able to do what you sent me, and where he was able to get the drugs (*drogues*) he needed to do it. I hardly believe that you provided him with them."[263]

Making Medicines In Prison

Saint-Mars had allowed Fouquet for some time, we don't know how long, to make simple medicines in his room to pass the time, a practice he took up perhaps because his mother, Marie de Maupeou Fouquet, was a practical nurse and home remedy specialist and her son had probably seen her preparations. Even Louvois on 13 June 1678 had asked Saint-Mars if he could ask Fouquet to send him a distillation of *casse-lunette,* a medicine for easing eye pain and improving eyesight made from the herb eye-bright.[264] Fouquet tutored one of the first valets he had in prison, Champagne, in Latin and pharmacy for a while. In the process of investigating the affair of the poisons in Paris it was shown that Fouquet in 1655 or 1656 had funded a trip to Florence by the chemist Christopher Glaser, friend of Sainte-Croix, Madame de Brinvilliers' (the famous poisoner) lover, but we don't know the reason for Glaser's trip; whether it was made to collect an array of medications, specifically poisons, or just information about them. And we don't know if Fouquet had ever made poisons but Fouquet's products while at Pignerol were probably not poisons but health-inducing items like elixirs, plasters, and medicated bandages.

To make even these rudimentary medicines, one had to have herbs, flowers, oils, wines, cloth, dishes, bowls, a mortar and pestle to break down and combine the substances. Certain concoctions had to be heated to high temperatures. Louvois' question is the one that bounces into mind when hearing about this complicated activity in a highly restricted environment: where in the world did these prisoners get the things they needed to make these drugs? Did Saint-Mars provide them? Fouquet obviously was not allowed to make excursions into the mountains around Pignerol to cut swatches of eye-bright off the rocks of the Mont Cenis pass. Nor his valets. Who provided these herbs? Was a member of the *compagnie franche* sent into Turin to buy them? When we look at it from a practical perspective, Louvois' question seems a little less menacing than it did at first. He may have been concerned, not about a poisoning, but Saint-Mars' allowance in Pignerol of an apothecary's corner.

All authors who have written books on the *Masque de fer* have had strong opinions on the "*drogues*" that were found in the package of items that Louvois received. It is clear that Louvois had been told that Dauger was in possession of the substance that he referred to as "drugs," which meant "medicines," because entertainment drugs were not used, unless you call wine an entertainment drug; they had plenty of wine. The historian Maurice Duvivier thought these drugs were poisons; that Dauger, hired by Lauzun, enemy of Fouquet, had poisoned Fouquet, or Colbert had arranged it. John Noone, on the other hand, said that the drugs were invisible ink, something

CHAPTER 8. PIGNEROL AND EXILLES

that Fouquet had been known to make and use in the past, and that the papers found were written by Dauger to communicate to the outside world. Georges Mongrédien thought as I do... these *drogues* were not poison.

In my opinion the drug in Eustache's possession after Fouquet's death was an antidote for poison, because Fouquet, his family, and friends had always feared he would be poisoned in prison. The antidote would be taken at the moment pains from poison would set in. Fouquet at some time in the past had probably told Dauger how to administer it and at his end, when he was dying, Dauger gave it to him, but because Fouquet was dying of a heart attack, the medicine did not help him (nor would it probably have helped him even if he had been poisoned). The substance could have been any of the following or any of numerous other antidotes:

A concoction known as Orvietan, advertised as an antidote for poison, was customized by the preparer using various herbs: garden angelica, healing wolfsbane, birthwort, bistort, sweet flag, carline thistle, gentian, masterwort, black salsif, tormentil, valerian, blessed thistle, dittany of Crete, rue, germander, laurel berries, juniper berries, cinnamon, cloves, viper meat, mixed with white wine and honey. Orvietan was taken in large quantities by the tutor of Madame de Brinvilliers' children to counter the poison he knew she was quite able to dose him with when he was living in her house before she was arrested.[265]

Theriac, an antidote invented by Galen of Pergamon in the second century A.D., was often used in the seventeenth century; it could have dozens of ingredients, but was chiefly snake flesh.

Christopher Glaser's book, *Treatise on Chemistry*, published in 1663, shows that making antimony, another antidote for poison and for treating everything from the pox to indigestion, required a preparation process that makes combining masterwort and black salsif seem easy.

Of Antimony

Antimony is a mineral body, having nearly a metallic nature, composed of two kinds of sulfur; the one very pure and stable, and not far removed from the qualities of solar sulfur, the other combustible like common sulfur. It is also composed of a great deal of sulphurous metallic mercury, and inactive, but drier and more solid than common mercury, and stronger, having a dirty and salty composition.[266]

Once the alchemist found some metal of this description, he or she must make chemical reactions with it to bring it to a medicinal form.

> *Transmutation of Antimony by way of Mars*[267]
>
> *Take a half pound of nails that are used to shoe Horses, put them in a good crucible in the furnace, and cover the crucible with a lid, heat them, and as soon as the tips of the nails are well reddened, add a pound of good-quality Antimony all at once, and cover the crucible with its lid, and place it directly over the coal, so that the the fire is very violent, and that the fusion of the Antimony is done quickly, and that it can act on the iron nails, and reduce it into slags, with which the impure sulphurous part of the Antimony merges, but the mercurial and pure part is separated.*[268]

Fouquet's mother had a recipe for *la poudre Cornachine* that was said to protect against many diseases, made with diaphoretic antimony (antimony that had been put through an oxidizing process that refined the antimony and made it into a usable powder), a sudorific (a substance that causes sweating, such as the bark and root of gum trees), and cream of tartar.[269] Perhaps Marie de Maupeou had made some of this Cornachine powder and her daughter-in-law or her grandchildren had taken it to Fouquet when they were allowed to visit him in prison.

Bezoar stone was believed to be a poison antidote. Lazare Riverius, professor at the University of Montpellier, renown for its medical school, recommended bezoar, a mass found in the intestines of ruminants, or, in a case where such a bezoar was not available, the favoured Montpellier substitute, viper troches.[270] Bezoar was found in a box of precious jewels at Fouquet's Saint-Mandé house and noted in the inventory of Fouquet's possessions:

- A bracelet of eight sections, made from turquoise with eight roses of five diamonds each.
- Another pair of earrings of rubies with eleven diamonds around each.
- A bracelet with large turquoise surrounded by fourteen diamonds.
- A gold-plated watch with a leather case decorated with little gold studs.
- A gold-plated watch showing the movements of the sun, the moon, the days, and the weeks.
- A little paper in which there is bezoar. [271]

From all these descriptions of antidotes to poison and many more in alchemy recipe books, we see the reason for Louvois' sarcastic comment: "Tell me how the man named Eustache was able to do what you sent me, and where he was able to get the drugs he needed to do it. I hardly believe that you provided him with them."

CHAPTER 8. PIGNEROL AND EXILLES

The hesitancy that Saint-Mars had in sending Louvois items he knew were suggestive of lax security at the prison showed worry that Louvois and the king would certainly be very angry and he might lose his job, in which case his career would be ruined. Or, giving Saint-Mars the benefit of the doubt, another innocent set of problems might have intervened in the ability of Saint-Mars to respond immediately to the repeated requests made to him, but regardless of the reasons for Saint-Mars' slow replies, Louvois' surly rhetorical question shows that he was irritated by the entire set of delays and withholdings. The "*drogues*" are a mystery; what they were, how they were made, what they were for...forever unknown. But that is really not pertinent to the identity and life of Eustache Dauger. We are trying to understand—not prison security—but how the people in this mystery related to and thought about each other.

First, Louvois' comment is rather more incredulous and timid than we would expect when referring to a situation where one prisoner has been found with medicines he was not authorized to have. He doesn't threaten punishment. The jailer is dosed with sarcasm, the person holding the medicine is not accused. In other communications, far worse punishments were recommended for other prisoners for far less.

Second, Saint-Mars' reluctance to send Louvois the contents of Fouquet's pockets is a clue to the relationship between Fouquet and Eustache Dauger. Saint-Mars had suggested and pled for using Dauger as a valet for Fouquet, so he was responsible for any trouble that Dauger might have caused. Saint-Mars did not want to admit that Dauger had done anything for Fouquet but help him brew his tea when La Rivière was sick, which was the condition upon which Louvois and the king had allowed personal contact between them. If Dauger was left holding a possession of Fouquet, no matter what it was, it was an indication to Louvois that they had been more than master and sometime servant; they had been friends, maybe accomplices. And that is exactly what the king and Louvois feared most.

His reluctance may also be a clue to the relationship between Saint-Mars and Dauger. Was Saint-Mars only trying to protect himself or was he also concerned about Eustache, because he thought the prisoner would be punished? What had his relationship with Eustache evolved into? Had he already begun to have respect for Eustache, as former guards and governors of prisons said he did in later years?

The mysteries bothered Louvois and so he repeated the eviction of officers that he ordered in 1670 after his inspection of Pignerol, only this time he removed prisoners. La Rivière and Dauger were to be erased. They didn't exist any more. Goodbye, good riddance.

For Louvois, they were not erased. They were like the pieces of purified antimony that were left behind when forcing hot iron nails to draw out slags of impure sulphur, and the king's actions signaled this, or rather inactions. The king did not release the men. The usual practice was to release valets of prisoners as soon as the prisoner had no more need of them. Dauger had been in prison eleven years for no crime that Louvois knew of, La Rivière longer. Instead, the king put the two men into solitary confinement together and ordered total secrecy about their existence. The king's behavior seemed strange to Louvois. Louvois could see, now that Fouquet was dead, that Eustache Dauger certainly had a secret. Previously, one could have thought that Fouquet alive gave Dauger's secret a life, but now that Fouquet was dead, the king was even more afraid of Dauger; Dauger's secret had been set free from Fouquet's secrets but was more potent than before. Louvois had asked Fouquet who Dauger was and Fouquet had replied, but now... could he trust what Fouquet had told him?

It must have been at that time, in the dead of night in his bedroom at Saint-Germain-en-Laye, when the pain in his badly healed leg prevented him from sleeping, when the dry leaves loosed from the gigantic trees in Saint-Germain-en-Laye's forest flew by his window and the Seine caught and held them on the curving contours of the riverbank below him, that Louvois began to think seriously about Dauger, and since the most important thing for any minister of the king to worry about was how the play of a drama could affect himself, he thought about that; about whether he fully understood Dauger's secrets or whether perhaps there were more secrets that he, Louvois, should know about, and not knowing about, could hurt him, his family, and his career.

On April 22, 1681, the comte de Lauzun was freed. After house arrest in Chalon-sur-Saône and Amboise[272] under constant surveillance, he finally was allowed to come back to Paris and his first action was to go to Louvois and have a long conversation with him late at night. Perhaps that is when Louvois got the answers to some of his questions.

Skin Color Of The Crows

On May 13, 1681 Saint-Mars wrote to his friend the abbé d'Estrades that he would soon become governor of Exilles at a higher salary and made a little joke about the skin color of Dauger and La Rivière.

> Yesterday I was informed that I am being appointed to the governorship of Exilles that pays two thousand livres, I will keep my free company and two of my lieutenants, and I will have the guard of two blackbirds that I have had here, that have no other

name but the *Messieurs* of the lower tower. Matthioli will rest here with two other prisoners.[273]

Memoir writers and journalists of the time, in describing a person, male or female, almost always describe his or her complexion in terms of tint, tone, and overall evenness, and without that category in the description, it would be incomplete. Freckles, sunspots, scars, or natural variations were sources of embarrassment.

Professor Vergé-Francesci said that when Saint-Mars speaks of "*deux merles*," literally "two blackbirds," he was telling us that the two men of the tower, Dauger and La Rivière, were dark-skinned. It is certain that in La Rivière's case this was true. He was a native of Cabo Verde and lived with Nicolas Fouquet's mother and father, who were known for taking people into their household who needed lodging.

And we have been told by the doctor who treated Dauger just before he died, Doctor Fresquière, that Dauger's skin was "a little brown. At that time, "a little brown" meant a slightly dark complexion, possibly swarthy or olive, the tint of skin that people with dark hair have. If Dauger had been very dark skinned, Fresquière would have said he was a Moor, the label for a person of Middle Eastern or African descent, or he would have called him "*noir*." The sieur de Blainvilliers said that when he saw Dauger during a clandestine surveillance of him at Sainte-Marguerite, he had a "white" face. "White" is valuable only as a negative... he was not a Moor... he was not that dark... it doesn't tell whether the man was swarthy, distinctly white-faced, or had the normal skin color of a person with dark hair.

In his biography of Queen Marie de' Medici, historian Philippe Delorme quotes Michel de Montaigne's (1533–1592) physical description of her Italian Medici father and his second wife whom he visited at Pratolino, one of the Medici's beautiful country villas. Montaigne was not oblivious to the exotic plants and animals, artificial grottos, labyrinths and fountains in his hosts' garden, but it was his hosts themselves, Francesco I de' Medici (1541–1587), Grand Duke of Tuscany, and his second wife Bianca Cappello (1548–1587) that Montaigne described: "The duchess is pretty according to Italian taste, the face agreeable and imperious, the bosom large and nipples firm. The duke is a large dark man (*homme noir*) with large arms and legs, the face and countenance full of courtesy."[274] It is certain from the historical record and portraits of the duke that he was not of African descent, but his skin tone was certainly olive and his hair was black or nearly black. He looked like others in his Italian Medici family, as did Louis XIII, because Louis XIII had Francesco I de' Medici's skin and hair color; the Medici duke was the French king's grandfather.

I think Saint-Mars was making a play on words; he had one prisoner who was from Cabo Verde, very probably having dark skin, the other prisoner had olive or "slightly brown" skin. Some French dictionaries also give the colloquial phrase "...*c'est un fin merle*," which means "...he is a cunning old thing, a disreputable fellow." So there may be two allusions: the two prisoners are dark-skinned rascals.

Exilles is a small fortress about 36 miles (58 kilometers) northwest of Pignerol on a little mountain in a strategic position in the valley of a stream called the Dora Riparia, a tributary of the Po river. Exilles is today in Italy, but, like Pignerol, was in the hands of the French in 1681. Saint-Mars was ordered to take with him only Dauger and La Rivière and leave behind all the other prisoners at Pignerol including: the Jacobin monk,[275] Dubreuil,[276] Matthioli[277] and Matthioli's valet. But in order to move two prisoners there had to *be* two prisoners and the two secret prisoners, except in the eyes of God, didn't exist so two false prisoners had to be invented. As it happened, the king was about to move troops into nearby Mantua, so Louvois asked the commanding officer of the military expedition, Nicolas de Catinat (1637–1712), to pose as a fake prisoner. He and his valet were introduced to Pignerol as prisoners and lodged in the Angle Tower. After a short time, Catinat left the prison as himself and went on to Mantua.

Between May and October a high security cell was built at Exilles in the *Grosse Tour* of the complex, with the same features that Dauger's cell at Pignerol had, two doors and a cloth that stretched over the inner opening of the cell. This cell had a new feature though; Italian author Ettore Patria stated that the only access to the cell was through the apartment of Saint-Mars,[278] but what Saint-Mars wrote to Louvois was that his own apartment was "joined to" the tower. In the middle of a night late in October 1681 Saint-Mars and his men with the two secret prisoners left for Exilles without informing anyone in the citadel of Pignerol.

Many mountain roads meet in the valley of the Dora, particularly that of the Col des Volettes, coming from the valley of Pragelas and that of the Petit Mont Cenis, passing by the Col de Rouilles. The passes through the Alps were used by Huguenots to flee France, persecuted Protestants who were fearful that King Louis XIV would strengthen the attacks on Protestants' rights and safety which had been more and more reduced since the 1670s. In 1685 the king finally revoked the Edict of Nantes that had allowed Protestants in France to worship in their faith, and from that point they faced violent actions by the army if they did not convert to Catholicism. Many who did not want to do that fled over the Alps to Switzerland, and Saint-Mars and his counterpart in the town of Suse a few miles away, Jean-François Losa, were charged with catching these emigrants and putting them in prison. There were few other activities. Exilles was remote.

CHAPTER 8. PIGNEROL AND EXILLES

There were no paved roads on the passes through the Alps, although we cannot say there was no traffic because Italy was below the southern exits of these passes and Italy was "the accomplice of man's most exquisite imaginings;"[279] it lured humanity to visit, live, work, sell, research, study, and buy. Spain held Milan and some other Italian territories, so their diplomats and couriers were present in large numbers on the passes and government officials from other European states crossed and returned; messengers, soldiers, merchants, priests, bishops, traders, and pilgrims made the trip through the low-lying Alpine valleys (low being a relative term) to get from or to Turin, Florence, Rome, Milan, and Naples or Bari and Brindisi where ships set sail for Greece and Constantinople. These travelers did not stop at Exilles, though, which was a small French military outpost. In the winter, not much came through the fortress except snow and ice under the portcullis. Saint-Mars grew weary of the isolation very soon and began asking for permission to go on short vacations. These were mostly refused.

After the breakdown of communication following Fouquet's death and the sweeping of his two prisoners into a lie of non-existence, one would think that Louvois would feel that a problem had been solved and that the status and security of the two prisoners of Exilles was retired. But soon after the new apartment of Saint-Mars had been built and Dauger and La Rivière had been placed in a new cell next door to it, Louvois was nervous. He asked Saint-Mars to send him reports on his security measures.

Figure 8.1: A 3-D representation of the fort of Exilles as it was a few years after Saint-Mars was governor. "Plan-relief du fort d'Exilles dans son état de 1695." Paris, Musée des Plans-Reliefs. Credit: Martin Leveneur. The fort in the image was destroyed around 1800. The present fort on the site was built from 1818 to 1829.

Saint-Mars reported to Louvois in November 1681:

> In order that the prisoners may not be seen, they will not leave their Chamber when they hear Mass: and in order that they may be kept the more securely, one of my lieutenants will sleep above them, and there will be two sentinels night and day, who will watch the whole round of the tower, without it being possible for them and the prisoners to see and speak to one another, or even to hear anything of one another. They will be soldiers of my company, who will be always the sentinels over the prisoners. There is only a confessor, about whom I have doubts; but if you do not disapprove I will give them the curate of Exilles instead, who is a good man, and very old, whom I will forbid, on the part of His Majesty, to enquire who these prisoners are, or their names, or what they have been, or to speak to them in any way, or to receive from them by word of mouth, or by writing, either communication or notes.[280]

Louvois told Saint-Mars they could have confession once a year, whereas Louvois had told Saint-Mars in 1669 that Dauger could be confessed four times a year. One confession a year is the least that could be offered, and the reason for the reduction is that Louvois wanted a minimum of contact between the prisoners and any other persons whatsoever and probably because he was mad about the whole situation and took it out on the prisoners through reduced access to confession.

Saint-Mars wrote in December, "As there is always one of my prisoners ill, they give me as much occupation as I have ever had with any of those I have hitherto guarded."[281] Louvois replied that the king didn't want them to see anyone other than the same lieutenant that had always seen them.[282]

Once again we find Louvois, on March 2, 1682, writing to instruct Saint-Mars in the safe-keeping of his prisoners.

> As it is important to prevent the prisoners that are at Exilles, who were called "of the Lower Tower" at Pignerol, from having any intercourse, the King has ordered me to command you to have them so strictly guarded and to take such precautions that you can assure His Majesty that they will speak to no one not only from outside but even of the garrison at Exilles; I beg you to report to me from time to time what is happening to them.[283]

Saint-Mars wrote to reassure him.

CHAPTER 8. PIGNEROL AND EXILLES

Saint-Mars to Louvois

March 11, 1682 from Exilles

I have received your letter...that it is important that my two prisoners should have no communication with anyone...I have guarded these two prisoners...as severely and exactly as I formerly did Messieurs Fouquet and Lauzun who could not boast that they had either sent or received any news while they were in confinement. These prisoners can hear the people speak as they pass along the road which is at the bottom of the tower; but they, if they wish it, could not make themselves heard; they can see the persons on the hill which is before their windows, but they cannot themselves be seen on account of the bars which are placed across their room. There are two sentinels of my company always night and day on each side of the tower, at a reasonable distance, who can see the windows of the prisoners obliquely. They are ordered to take care that no one speaks to them, and that they do not cry out from their windows; and to make the passers-by walk on, if they wish to stop in the path, or on the side of the hill. My own room, being joined to the tower, and having no other look out except towards the path, I hear and see everything, even my two sentinels, who are by this means always kept alert.

As for the inside of the tower, I have divided it in such a manner that the priest who says Mass to them cannot see them, on account of the curtain I have made, which covers their double doors. The servants, who bring their food, put whatever is necessary for the prisoners upon a table on the outside, and my lieutenant [Rosarges] takes it and carries it in to them. No one speaks to them except myself, my officer [Rosarges], M. Vigneron [the confessor] and a physician from Pragelas, which is six leagues from hence, who only sees them in my presence. With regard to their linen and other necessities I take the same precautions which I did with my former prisoners.[284]

Letters from Louvois to Saint-Mars continue to arrive regularly asking about the security of the two prisoners in the tower. One is particularly interesting.

Louvois to Saint-Mars

April 16, 1684

It is a long time since you have sent me news of your prisoners. I beg you to inform me how you are managing them and how they are. Tell me also what you know of the birth of the man called La

Rivière and of the circumstances which led to his being placed at the service of the late M. Fouquet.[285]

I interpret this question to mean Louvois wanted to know how Dauger came to be affiliated with Fouquet. Louvois did not care about La Rivière. He suspected that maybe La Rivière and Dauger had come into the circle of Nicolas Fouquet in the same way and wanted a clue, without asking for it, about Dauger's background.

Then on 23 December 1685 Saint-Mars writes to Louvois, "My prisoners are still sick and being treated; other than that, they are very quiet."[286]

A Family

From our seats in the balcony of this mystery, that picture of tranquility that Saint-Mars sent to Louvois about his prisoners two days before Christmas Day in 1685 is a sad presentation: on the left are Saint-Mars, his wife and two young children, on the right the small, private company of soldiers who watch the mountains that withered the small fort into a bunker of humans in a sharp universe of snow and wind, and in the rear the two prisoners, Eustache Dauger and Guillaume La Rivière, living together in an ancient round tower in close proximity to the family. A doctor visited occasionally and a priest from the hamlet of Exilles tottered regularly up the snowy alley to the entrance of the fort (hopefully he rode a donkey?) to say mass for the two prisoners that he could not see, while the meager band of soldiers gathered around the priest, their heads bowed, and Madame Saint-Mars sat somewhat to herself with her two sons at her side. If they did not all feel imprisoned by their isolation then they would have been strange humans indeed; all they had to keep boredom at bay and to entertain themselves was each other. When such a sequestration is forced upon a small group, especially when a woman and children are part of it, character is usually strengthened, morals and rules are either slacked or improved, friendships that would be impossible on the outside of the bunker often occur. No one stays the same, all grow into new characters, and if one of them does not, only an empty shell is left to be buried. People help each other out and all competencies are brought to bear for the entire group. It can also happen that some members of such a group attempt to assert themselves, but that was not the case here, as Saint-Mars' little free company stayed intact and loyal to him, and Madame Saint-Mars did not pack her bags and her sons and move to Grasse. A woman, two children, a few barely trained soldiers, Saint-Mars, possibly a cook, and two prisoners were co-dependant on each other in the fog of the Alps from October 1681 until April 1687.

The members of Saint-Mars' private security company have told us much

CHAPTER 8. PIGNEROL AND EXILLES

of what we know about the Man in the Iron Mask; they had lived with Saint-Mars and his family...and the prisoner...and they reported, as did a few former commandants of prisons where the masked prisoner had lived, that Saint-Mars had great respect for Dauger, that the governor and his men kept their hats off in his presence until he gave permission to put them on; Guillaume-Louis Formanoir de Palteau said that his uncle, one of the soldiers, told him this, and de Chevalier, major of the Bastille in the reign of Louis XV, and Charles de Lamotte-Guérin, Saint-Mars' successor at Saint-Marguerite, remembered that the prisoner was treated well by the governor. This respect on the part of Saint-Mars is one of the greatest mysteries of the mystery.

When careful thought is given to Saint-Mars' evolving respect for the prisoner, it can't be denied that the reports about this from former prison guards and governors are sincere; they were not describing a mechanical deference for a high-ranking member of the hoi-polloi. Saint-Mars knew how to be obsequious, we see that in his letters to Louvois. If Saint-Mars was only superficially flattering to Dauger, the witnesses would not have said anything about the jailer's attitude. All jailers were required to be superficially flattering to high-ranking prisoners and their staff knew if it was genuine or not. Mostly it was not.

In the beginning of their relationship at Pignerol in 1669, Saint-Mars had no feeling for the prisoner at all. His attention was on keeping Fouquet from writing with invisible ink or escaping, and then Lauzun became his responsibility—a nightmare for any jailer who is not comfortable with disorder, for Lauzun was disorder itself. Dauger was an inconsequential addition to his real worries, and Saint-Mars had no time for him. After many years, he urged Louvois to allow Dauger to valet Fouquet, possibly out of pity for Dauger's continual solitary confinement but probably more out of an administrative need to find a valet for Fouquet when his regular valet was sick.

Saint-Mars did not get along with either Lauzun or Fouquet. His letters to Louvois about guarding these two prisoners show only irritation with their eccentricities. While he was aware of Fouquet's former high government rank and knew Lauzun was a member of the nobility, he didn't "respect" them in the sense of admiring them, while the witnesses, all former prison administrators or guards, who presumably would know how rare it was for a jailer to quietly approve of a prisoner and to show that approval by behaving respectfully in his presence, gave their reports of "respect" toward Dauger with confidence.

It was at Exilles in 1681 that the two men began to know each other. At Pignerol, Saint-Mars had had multiple prisoners, some actively engaged in thwarting Saint-Mars' efforts to command them. Having prisoners who were annoying and required guarding defined Saint-Mars' self image as the jailer... as the governor. But at Exilles there was only Dauger and the worn out valet whose master had died at Pignerol. For someone like Saint-Mars, who liked to talk and brag and think of places and people beyond the Alps, he may have begun to visit and talk with his prisoners. We have letters from him to Louvois that tell of his visiting Lauzun and trying to have conversations with him, although Lauzun was half crazy and was using any conversations that Saint-Mars started as daggers and tricks. Saint-Mars had been told to keep the Exilles prisoners safe and without communication to the outside world. But, as we have seen elsewhere, Saint-Mars sometimes followed orders exactly and sometimes he interpreted them according to his own needs and interests. I propose that, because of the setting and the isolation, and because La Rivière and Dauger were the only prisoners at Exilles, making the "guarding" of them very simple and uninteresting, Saint-Mars' sense of his *oeuvre* changed. Saint-Mars had been governor of a prison at Pignerol, but at Exilles, he was almost retired. He was in an isolated place with his wife and two sons and had almost nothing to do, except occasional hunts for Protestants who were traveling over the Alps to escape from anti-Protestant France. But that assignment was a military action; finding would-be exiles in the snow was a catch and capture adventure, not a prison manager job. In his view of his situation, his job as a jailer was insignificant, and so his two quiet, often sick prisoners, living in the same tower as his family, were hard to define as prisoners in the traditional sense. Instead he was supervising a hospice, not a prison. He and his family and his staff were in quarantine with two men that Saint-Mars was more and more suspicious of because of the enormous, expensive, unrelenting, obsessive attention that was being invested in the two strange men. It didn't make sense. And so, as Saint-Mars often did and as people in general often do, he began to make the situation fit what he needed. We saw that when he proposed Dauger as a valet for Fouquet in 1672 he said that he thought Dauger would be a good valet and that he knew that Dauger would not make trouble or try to take advantage of the situation as prisoners usually do when they are given more freedom. Just like Dauger's entrance into Fouquet's day-to-day life, I propose that eventually in this peaceable community, the family, the staff, and the prisoners begin to talk to one another, in the beginning about anondine and practical things. Gradually they respected Dauger because he became a resource.

And what was it that Saint-Mars needed at Exilles, as far his personal and family needs? What was he missing? He had two sons: André Antoine (1672–1693) and Bénigne Antonin (1679–1702). These two boys were nine years old and two years old when they moved to Exilles. Their futures had the same career limitations as most other young boys: they would either be soldiers and officers, as their father and cousins were, or they could try to

CHAPTER 8. PIGNEROL AND EXILLES 145

rise to the lower level of the robe class, public administration; they could become clerks of a court, government inspectors (*intendants*), or tax collectors, among other jobs. They could also end up as merchants or artisans, but that would mean a decline in social status, and Saint-Mars was far too ambitious to have a casual attitude about his sons going down that unseemly path. He wanted his sons to be fine military fighters and leaders, and in order to reach for middle and upper level positions in the military, a little education was necessary. They would need to learn how to shoot, ride a horse, repair their equipment, and know the basics of social rules. For those, Saint-Mars and his *compagnie franche* could be teachers.

A lieutenant or captain must also be able to read, write, and do basic arithmetic. We do not know if their mother could read and write. She grew up in Pignerol, and in small towns, girls might have some teaching by their own mothers and relatives in reading and writing, but they would not get the short periods of tutoring by the local priest that boys would get. Only after 1700 were schools created in villages and hamlets.[287] Saint-Mars could read and write pretty well as we see from his letters to Louvois. That he needed to be able to write and read told him that his sons needed the same skills if they were to rise to a commendable rank in the army and needed them even more if they turned out to be interested in going into public government service. If he and Madame Dauvergne ever gave any thought to their going into religious orders they would certainly need to be literate.

Dauger read books; three witnesses said that. Reading books was one of the ways he occupied himself in prison. If he could read, he could almost certainly write. He was forbidden to write; the worst nightmare of Louvois and the king was Dauger with a pen in his hand. But if he read books, he had an education of some sort, which was rare. Whether he had years behind him of studying the seven liberal arts which were the curriculum in *lycées* for young men of means, grammar, logic, rhetoric, arithmetic, geometry, astronomy, music and medicine, is doubtful. But he was devout, so he knew Bible stories and probably knew the history of the church, the lives of Saint Augustine and Saint Gregory for example. Did he know about historical figures like Charlemagne, Aristotle, Cicero? Unknown. He had enough education to be a tutor for reading, writing, and religious practices to Saint-Mars' sons, and my hunch, which is admittedly influenced by my liking the characters and hoping that they had some hours of the humanities in their solitary confinement, is that Saint-Mars responded to his need for his sons to learn to read and write by asking Dauger if he would be willing to spend some time tutoring them, just like years before when he had to find a valet for Fouquet and was unable to find one so he asked Dauger to step in and help him. In that case he asked Louvois if that would be permissable. This time, he didn't ask.

Dauger, from what we know of him, at least from his willingness to be a valet for Fouquet, likely agreed and was glad to have something to do, in addition to looking after La Rivière, who was getting sicker from heart failure and having trouble breathing. Saint-Mars was, as time went on, grateful for the service Dauger was providing to his sons, the most precious beings in Saint-Mars' life. Dauger was devout, and no doubt taught the boys good moral stories and solid Catholic dogma, and set a good example of a devout, long-suffering person. His qualities earned respect. The two boys may have come to like him.

I hypothesize that this or some similar service by Dauger to Saint-Mars' family was the reason that Saint-Mars gained and kept great respect for Dauger. Dauger's assistance brought a levelling of some kind that both men kept honestly to because if Dauger had not shown himself to be a valuable partner, an *honnête homme*, former guards and jailers who had been close to the relationship would never have reported that Saint-Mars treated Dauger with deference. None of the witnesses who confidently said that Saint-Mars had great respect for Dauger said why he did. If they explained why, and the reason had to do with a transgression of the strict rules for guarding the prisoner, for example if Dauger had been teaching the boys to write, that would have harmed Saint-Mars. Even after Saint-Mars died, prison officials who had worked under him or at his prisons after he had left, would not go into the details of the relationship.

If it wasn't something like this, I have no idea why three reporters, Major Chevalier, de Palteau, and Lamotte-Guérin, some of the most believable witnesses we have on file, said firmly that Saint-Mars was respectful in Dauger's presence.

Vergé-Franceschi also proposed that a close relationship must have grown between the two. "One does not live beside a man for thirty years, being with him each day, without an intimacy developing."[288]

The End Of Exile

Saint-Mars' prisoners may have been quiet but Saint-Mars had made it clear to Louvois that he was uncomfortable at Exilles. Louvois wrote to Saint-Mars on January 8, 1687 that due to the death of comte Guillaume de Pechpeyrou Comminges de Guitaut (1626–1685), the governor of the prison fortress of Sainte-Marguerite[289] on one of the Lerins Islands in the Bay of Cannes on the Mediterranean sea, the king was offering Saint-Mars the position.

On January 4, 1687 La Rivière died of chronic obstructive pulmonary disease, which was called dropsy. He had asked to make a will a few months

CHAPTER 8. PIGNEROL AND EXILLES 147

before, so he knew he was dying. He never saw the Lerins islands or Cannes harbor, where the Phocaeans and the Oxybians mended their fishing nets and repaired their ships that sailed through the Mediterranean and the Adriatic two thousand years before the "Great Century" of Louis XIV, Saint-Mars, and Eustache Dauger.

Another new set of cells would have to be constructed. Saint-Mars made at least one trip from Pignerol to Sainte-Marguerite at the beginning of 1687 to inspect the progress of the third ultra secure cell that Louvois had ordered constructed for Dauger. On that trip, Saint-Mars became sick and remained in Sainte-Marguerite for a month to recover. Perhaps suspicion is not appropriate. It may well be that he had been sick. It also may well be that the frozen zone of Exilles, to which he had to return, could not call him back immediately from the soft temperature, the sea and the shore, the sunlight, or the relaxation of mind that the Provençale coast offers to visitors who come to the Mediterranean sea. Cannes and its offshore islands were wonderful places to recuperate... sick or not. We, with a fervent wish to be able to, even for just an hour, experience the warm light and sand of Cannes, Antibes, or Nice in order to make an informed judgement as to whether this theory might be true, turn back, as Saint-Mars finally had to do, to Exilles, for he had to gather his family, his free company of soldiers, his ancient prisoner, and relocate them to Sainte-Marguerite.

On the way back to Exilles to retrieve his prisoner and his family, Saint-Mars had told the councilmen of Briançon, a mountain stage near Pignerol, that he would come back soon with a large escort. So the city fathers of Briançon were expecting him and his retinue. In mid April, their visitors arrived.

9. Sainte-Marguerite And The Bastille

Six dark cachots with vaults were set along a long, humid corridor. The walls were nearly two meters thick, three enormous gates that the sea air had rusted, heavy doors with metal studs and inverted hinges to discourage any thought of escape. In one of these cells looking out on the bay lived for long years a mysterious recluse. No one could approach him besides his jailers, nor hear him, nor even pronounce his name.

—Jean-Christian Petitfils

Two Nights In Briançon

The following account was given by M. Fernand Carlhian-Ribois, an archivist emeritus of Briançon, at the 1987 colloquium on the Man in the Iron Mask hosted by the town of Cannes and published in the collection of speeches given on the mystery at that conference.[290] It adds to what we know about Saint-Mars and speaks to his relationship with his ancient prisoner.

Cannes is almost directly south of Exilles but the Alps are between, so the journey is not a straight path but follows the zig-zagging series of valleys that are flat enough to travel on, connections of pieces of a topographical puzzle that had been mapped and used for thousands of years by bands of people heading south or traveling north who were perhaps in awe of the nearby peaks but not deterred by them. It was not going to be easy. An unexpected snag in the itinerary came sooner than anyone had thought possible, only one day after leaving Exilles.

Saint-Mars had been told by Louvois that during his trip his movements should be hidden and his prisoner invisible. A few chapters ago it was explained that that goal was not achieved. People saw the troops on horseback, baggage wagons, and the closed litter that Saint-Mars had constructed for Dauger with eight porters to carry it, and their imaginations activated. On the trip to Sainte-Marguerite Dauger was seen wearing a device on his jaw that Voltaire and the bishop Fouquet later said was a device of steel with springs so that he could eat while wearing it.

On April 17, 1687, Saint-Mars, his troops and baggage[291] left Exilles in the morning and stopped the first night at the small hamlet of Oulx. The next day, the 18th, they started for Briançon, a larger town to the southwest, and intentionally arrived after nightfall. The town sent escorts with *flambeaux* to light the street ahead of the soldiers. At the Porte d'Italie, all the vehicles had to halt because in the middle of the main street were a fountain and a drain. The passengers were on foot from that point, and it can be assumed that the baggage had to wait for the owners to come back in the morning. There was no military housing at Briançon, no inn, the old chateau was not safe or comfortable; the troops would have to stay with the inhabitants of the town.

Monsieur Carlhian-Ribois examined the Briançon archives' records stating where the soldiers stayed for the night. A city councilman wrote that Saint-Mars and a captain (his second-in-command) stayed at the house of the *lieutenant du roi* Prat on the ground floor where Saint-Mars had stayed on the previous trip he had made. Lieutenants de La Prade and Boisjoly spent the night at the house of Monsieur Jean Loyseau. Major Dampierre, officers Formanoir and Rosarges were lodged in the houses around the Place des Halles (today the Place d'Armes) and the Maison du Roi (today the Palais de Justice) with the exception of a sergent and three musketeers who were assigned to be at the gates of the town. Each person was settled in for the night (horses too) and the commune gave everyone supper.

Carlhian-Ribois pointed to two problems in the report of the city councilman: he was reservedly jubilant in interpreting the report as proof that the description of the prisoner being guarded on this trip and carried in a closed litter is false because a prisoner with a mask, or any prisoner at all, is not mentioned. It seems obvious that if there was a captive in the group, he would have been commented on.

Saint-Mars may have told the hosts that Eustache was a "captain." Louvois' orders had been to keep the prisoner hidden and prevent any attention from outsiders. For the Briançon stopover, this ruse worked well to meet that requirement; it fooled the archivist Carlhian-Ribois and would fool anyone who did not stop to think that Saint-Mars did not have a "captain" on his staff, at least not one that was ever recorded in all the information we have about his free company. He had lieutenants, officers, and sergents, but never a captain. Saint-Mars would not have let Dauger out of his sight, just as he kept Dauger in his presence at all times at the chateau of Palteau years later when they were traveling to the Bastille. Dauger was a passive person who was not considered a risk to break away from the guards and run across the marketplace of Briançon to head for Switzerland. And if he had, Saint-Mars would certainly have killed him. Dauger knew that. The "captain" and Saint-Mars were never separated and the city councilmen were not concerned about why.

The description of the visit on the 18th of April in the Briançon archives also does not mention litters or porters. So we have to discard (says Carlhian-Ribois) the reports of the *chaise à porteurs*, the *toile cirée*, and the mask because the Briançonnais would have related these things. The man and the mask must have been a hoax. Not necessarily. Two answers to this argument are possible. The litter might have been in the baggage in storage to be taken out when the topography would make it usable. The high, twisting paths from Exilles through the upper valley of Pragelas and that of the Petit Mont Cenis were not safe for the cumbersome litter. Saint-Mars needed that litter for the flatter terrain further south and could not risk it being destroyed in an accident. The porters could have been merged with the troops until the time came for them to be put to work. Or, the porters and the litter might have been waiting for the soldiers and the prisoner at a stop further down the road that was a convenient rendez-vous station.

The councilmen understood that the "captain" was a soldier and soldiers often had wounds that were covered in a variety of ways so if Dauger was wearing a mask when he was at Briançon, the officials would not think it was unusual and would not mention it. Posterity's agitation about the mask has been due to its being on a *prisoner*, which observers interpreted as a device to hide a secret. A wounded veteran, retired from the wars, hiding an old wound with a mask, would not be interesting. Those people were everywhere.

Saint-Mars Grants A Request

Saint-Mars woke up in Briançon on the 19th and was preparing to leave with his men but the lieutenant of the king, Monsieur Prat, was called aside by one of the councilmen to alert him that a few hours after everyone in Briançon had fallen asleep the night before, some advance men for the vice bailiff of the jurisdiction, an important official who had been expected to arrive before Saint-Mars, rode into Briançon, dismounted, and reported that the vice bailiff had finally gotten through the snow-clogged Lauteret pass and would be arriving later that day.

In all Europe, when an official made an entrance into a town, whether Paris, Amsterdam, or Briançon, the custom was that the highest city officials should go out past the city gates toward the advancing visitors and meet them officially with soldiers, flags, and such other shows of color and bravado that they could afford... a bishop or priests were always impressive... and then ride with the visitors back into town, a practice that honored the town as well as the visitors. The Briançonnais normally did not have soldiers, but on this day, they saw their opportunity to have some. When Saint-Mars' hosts came to him, hats in hand, he probably thought they were coming to say goodbye, but instead they had a request.

The lieutenant of the king Prat and the officials asked Saint-Mars to lend them his soldiers for a greeting committee to go up the road a half mile or so and salute the vice bailiff and his aides when they appeared over the hill and then ride with them in an honorific parade into town, and it was understood that the town would be responsible for all the costs for the ceremony and for the extra food and lodging of his group. Could he possibly delay his departure for one day and allow the loan of his soldiers for a welcoming procession?

Saint-Mars agreed to this request.

Here again we see the character of Saint-Mars. He claims to be tough but often is flexible. He praises himself to his superiors as having a zipped mouth but we see that he sometimes enjoys giving mysterious hints about his prisoner. Having his cohort morph into an ostentatious part of a caravan to impress an official of the territory appealed to Saint-Mars' ego. Would Louvois, if he had been there, have consented to delay by a day the transport of the king's most important prisoner to humor some aldermen who wanted to put on a show?

What was worse, the Briançonnais were particularly good record keepers. The chief councilman of Briançon, who, in his official duties, was responsible for paying out of pocket for the expenses for feeding and housing the visitors, and, having no knowledge of the secrecy of the trip, carefully recorded details of the stay in Briançon, attached his notes to his receipts showing payment, and turned them in to the city comptroller for reimbursement.

> At Briançon, the chief city councilman had himself paid all the costs of this lengthened stay and he wrote: "On the 18 April, the company of Saint-Mars having stayed the nights of the 18 and 19 April with 1 captain, 2 lieutenants, 2 sergents, and 43 soldiers, I paid 362 rations for the men and the horses. (Article 83 du compte des consuls de 1687, série EE 156).[292]

The receipts became part of the city's archives and they give information that Louvois would rather we not have. Saint-Mars' character is not that of a hard man with a soft center; nothing so dramatic as that. He is a soldier from a modest family who has dreams of grandeur that fade with each passing day. He makes the best of what opportunities he has, strikes hard bargains with Louvois to get promotions, titles of nobility, higher salary, time off,

CHAPTER 9. SAINTE-MARGUERITE AND THE BASTILLE   153

but he is not at court; he is about as far from court as could be. And he is not on the battlefield, where he says, as a soldier, he most wants to be. He's on the road with a small, unofficial company made up mostly of his relatives and one stranger that he has been told to take care of. He was proud, for a few hours, to be at the head of his company, their arms born bravely, their mission a ceremony for the vice bailiff, who was a day late but was compensated with a welcome he probably never forgot; even if there was not a bishop in the line, the parade of Saint-Mars' *compagnie franche* and his musketeers was as fine a welcome as he was ever likely to receive.

The extra day in Briançon was not a part of Saint-Mars' report to Louvois when the travelers arrived at Sainte-Marguerite, on the contrary, Saint-Mars wrote that he had pushed his team hard to use only twelve days in transporting the prisoner.

> I made the trip in only twelve days because my prisoner was sick; he told me that he could not get enough air. I can assure you, Monseigneur, that no one saw him, and the way in which I guarded him and conducted him during the trip made everyone wonder who my prisoner was. The bed of my prisoner was so old and broken, like all the things he had, table linen and furniture, that it wasn't worth the trouble to transport them and I sold them for thirteen écus. I paid to the porters who brought traveling chairs from Turin for me and my prisoner to carry us here, 203 livres.[293]

Saint-Mars left exile at Exilles behind, joyfully, and he cut ties with the past, including selling his prisoner's furniture to someone in Exilles. Whether the prisoner's furniture and table linens were threadbare and broken or not, Saint-Mars didn't want to load them on a wagon and bring them to the southern hemisphere of his brand new life. He cut his losses with Exilles, cut his prisoner's losses, and set off for Cannes with his family and his *compagnie franche*.

Sainte-Marguerite

When Petitfils wrote his book on the Mask in 1970, he described the Sainte-Marguerite island prison houses as in "ruin." They have since been repaired and are a destination for tourists who want to visit the only extant rooms in which the Mask was imprisoned. A boat from the Cannes harbor will take only a few minutes to sputter across the two miles to reach Sainte-Marguerite, and from there one can look across the water to the Ile Saint-Honorat, which is named for Honorat, a monk in the fourth century, who came many hundreds of years after Ionian Greeks and then Romans had built communities and villas with ocean views. "The Annalist of Lerins states that the Romans built there sumptuous dwellings, fortifications and an arsenal, ruins of which were still to be seen in the 16th century."[294] Around 1073 C.E. abbot Adelbert built a fortified monastery on Sainte-Marguerite.

Louvois told Saint-Mars that he agreed to the cost of the third super secure cell for Dauger for 5,024 *livres* and for building a second story of cells and a house for Saint-Mars north of the other two levels of the prison which would communicate directly with the apartments of the prisoners. Only the lower floor has survived.[295] "I have the honor to tell you the way in which I have lodged my prisoner, who is, as always, extremely well behaved, in one of the two new cells that I had constructed according to your orders."[296]

Saint-Mars' youngest nephew, Joseph de Formanoir, the future sieur de Blainvilliers, visited his uncle at Sainte-Marguerite and began to be interested in "*La Tour*," so much so that he disguised himself as a soldier so he could watch Dauger in secret at night. The hot, high sun, the waves, the never still soft breezes of Sainte-Marguerite were paradise after Exilles, and the whole family, Dauger included, had eleven years of rest there; even the nights of storms banging on the rocks below were restful.

Figure 9.1: Postcard showing the prison of the Masque de fer on the Ile Sainte-Marguerite (on the prominence at the far left of the land mass). The author is grateful to Professor Carole Crumley for the image.

Madame Saint-Mars died after her oldest son was killed in 1693 at the battle of Neerwinden and her younger son also fell in the same fight, badly wounded. After that tragedy, Saint-Mars was much more alone in his governor's house and the comforting riviera must have been less beautiful. Nevertheless when his superior in Paris, Barbezieux, Louvois' son, asked him to take the Bastille governorship in Paris, the highest post in France for a prison governor, he hesitated before his inevitable fate. He was the last of the three musketeers who had arrested and guarded Nicolas Fouquet: d'Artagnan, the chief of the company, Saint-Mars, and Besmaux. D'Artagnan, whose careful, honest guard of Fouquet at Vincennes prison is one of the few honorable chapters in the history of Louis XIV's reign, was buried in 1673 at Maastricht, shot in the jaw during the siege of the city during the Franco-Dutch war of 1672 to 1678; François de Monlezun, sieur de Besmaux, who had been governor of the Bastille for forty years, had died in 1697; Saint-Mars's time had come, the capstone of the trio had to be placed.

The Bastille

Dauger traveled to Paris in an open litter with Saint-Mars. They were escorted by six members of Saint-Mars' company and not many troops because the Bastille already had guards and soldiers: Jacques Rosarges, Saint-Mars' lieutenant and one of a handful of people who could interact with Dauger, came into Saint-Mars' service at Pignerol and would be promoted to major when they got to the Bastille; the sieur Lécuyer, an old soldier of the company of Saint-Mars, was hired in 1670; Guillaume de Formanoir, Saint-Mars' nephew, chief of the guard, who was later called "*seigneur de Palteau et autres lieux*"; the *abbé* Giraut, the almoner, *sommelier* and innkeeper of the Bastille, who had been with Saint-Mars at Sainte-Marguerite; Antoine Ru, who joined Saint-Mars in Provence, jailer in charge of keys; and the surgeon (person who performed medical bleedings), Abraham Reilh, former soldier from Nîmes, who became the almoner at the Bastille.[297]

During the trip to Paris, passing through the Yonne department in Burgundy, they stayed two nights at Saint-Mars' own property, the manor of Palteau, where servants took notice of the tall white-haired man dressed in black with a black mask on who came with their master. Skirting the Morvan mountains, in a few days the soldiers and their prisoner arrived on the eastern outskirts of Paris.

One way to describe the Bastille is to describe its bulk; "...eight towers, their walls ten feet thick and over seventy-eight feet high." Much more interesting than the height of the towers is the height of apprehension the sight of them caused people who approached the fortress... their instincts, their perceptions, and why blood flushed to their necks when they came near. The perception of anyone in the seventeenth century, either resident of Paris or

first-time visitor to the capital, of the Bastille would not be the shock and horror that twenty-first-century visitors
would feel to see such a tall, dark, towered bulk, because people of that time were comfortable with fortresses; they were everywhere in the city and in the provinces. But the reputation of the "chateau," as it was called in charters of its founding, and the rumors about what might have happened inside it, were thoughts that the free company soldiers of Saint-Mars' caravan, like everyone else, had to suppress as they traveled toward the first drawbridge of the property of the king on September 18, 1698.

Approaching the city from Vincennes castle, they traveled beside the Vincennes forest for a while, then the outskirts of the town began to appear on the rue du Faubourg Saint-Antoine, a long suburban highway. They passed the Saint-Antoine-des-Champs abbey for women. Straight ahead of them they could see the walls of Paris and attached to it a monster closed like a fist that, in close proximity, could be seen to have Seine waters slopping against the bottom of its towers. But it was impossible for Saint-Mars' men to move in a straight line to enter Paris because the prison stood right in the middle of the road, so the men took a detour to the right to go through the fortified Saint-Antoine gate (destroyed in 1788). Once the guards of the gate had let them pass into Paris, they rode down the rue Petit-Saint-Antoine, a short diagonal path,[298] which suddenly opened on a little *place*, to the right being the entrance to the rue Saint-Antoine. They turned left and straight ahead of them lay the first entrance to the Bastille complex, which, in addition to the prison, held the house of the governor, his stables, housing for staff, sentinel posts, and various other dependencies that the men and their horses and the litter carriers would see on their way in, including little shops along the sides of the fortification walls that sold items at high prices which went into the pockets of the governors of the Bastille.

Simon Nicolas Henri Linguet (1736–1794), former prisoner of the Bastille, whose book on his twenty-month stay there caused a lot of problems for King Louis XVI (it was one of the writings that produced anti-royal sentiment) described very well the rest of the trip to the inner great courtyard of the prison.

> Above the first gate was a storehouse with different sorts of arms and old armour; next to this gate was a guard station where each night two sentinels were placed to answer calls of those who appeared on the outside wishing entry and to open the gates if the applicants were legitimate. This gate led to a first exterior courtyard in which were the housing of the *Invalides* [retired soldiers who formed part of the guard of the Bastille], the stables and the coach house of the governor. One could also arrive at this court-

CHAPTER 9. SAINTE-MARGUERITE AND THE BASTILLE 157

yard by the Arsenal [located between the Bastille and the Seine to the south]. This first courtyard was separated from a second courtyard by a gate next to which was another guard station, then a moat and a drawbridge. In this second courtyard to the right were the living quarters of the governor. Next to the governor's mansion was an avenue of about fifteen *toises* [90 feet or 27.5 meters]... All of this was constructed on a bridge that lay over the great moat and on which was another drawbridge. On the other side of that was another guard station.[299]

Paris historian Hillairet gives a description of this final security post. "These draw bridges were guarded by a sentinel enclosed in a caged shed; it was formed by a barrier of timbers that had iron braces. This defended the heavy entrance door made of oak braced with iron."[300] Once you passed the last sentinel hut, you saw a great courtyard 144 feet long by 75 feet wide and at the far end of it there was a well.[301]

One reason for the Bastille's menace was its blockade of the rue Saint-Antoine, which was a major thoroughfare, a long and wide street that was used for outdoor festivities and had been designed as such when it was created as a joisting ground for the Hôtel des Tournelles, a royal palace that used to be where the Place des Vosges is now. Nearby was the Place Baudoyer, where market vendors brought full carts of produce and hawkers encouraged the purchase of onions and rabbits. A few blocks north was les Halles, another market place with a huge fountain decorated by the same sculptor that decorated the new west wing of the Louvre for King Henri II, Jean Goujon, having bas-reliefs of maidens pouring stone water over the flowing water coming out of the spigots below. This area was busy, bright, commercial, bourgeois, and multi-colored, despite the convents on either side of it. The Bastille, on the other hand, was a dark shadow over this busy merriment, and the effect on the Parisians was one of the reasons, I think, that the fortress was so hated. Its temper was in stark contrast to everything else around it; in addition it was very much in the way. One had to go around it to get in and out of town. It could not be ignored. It was not sitting to one side of the road. It was *in* the road. It was despotism sitting exactly where people wanted to pass through. It was an imposition on life.

The reason for this inconvenient placement was that the Bastille was planned to be, when the first stones were laid in 1356, a fortified city gate in the wall under construction by King Charles V to protect Paris from invasion by the English, with whom France was at war. The *porte* Saint-Antoine let pedestrians, wood carriers, wagons, monks, and soldiers in and out of the city to the east by the rue Saint-Antoine. There were two towers, the Tour de la Chapelle and the Tour du Trésor, with a portal in between them consisting of a portcullis, its drawbridge, and another stationary bridge.

Charles V, as *dauphin*,[302] in 1358, two years after the gate had been made, was attacked by rebels in his palace on the west end of the city island and two of his marshals were murdered in front of him. In order to save the kingdom in the name of his father, King Jean I the Good, a prisoner in England, Charles had to flee Paris and was able to return only when his supporters raised troops and money to protect him. The old palace didn't seem safe to him after that and he moved to the far east of the city, close to the city wall where the Saint-Antoine gate had been built to stop any attempted English invasion, but the dauphin Charles had agreed to the Treaty of Brétigny in 1360 to release his father from Edward III's English prison in exchange for 600,000 *écus* and the possession of Calais, so the strengthening of the Bastille at that point could be said to be more out of fear of the Parisians than the English. He told his engineers to make a small fort out of this gate and they started on the project in 1370 by raising the height of the towers and building two more towers of similar height on the Paris side that were just like the first two towers, connecting all the towers with a curtain wall. These second towers were later called the Tour de la Liberté and the Tour Bertaudière. Four more towers were eventually added and quarters for the governor in the advance courtyard, and in the 1500s, an elevated bastion, chevron-shaped, that pointed out into the faubourg. Eventually a garden was created on it in which privileged prisoners could walk.

Dauger did not see any of this. He was in his litter with blinds drawn. He got out of the litter with his mask on in the large courtyard and was immediately led—we know from Lieutenant du Junca's journal—to the closest tower, the Basinière. It was to his left as he exited the litter. After nightfall he was taken to the Bertaudière tower to the room he had been assigned on the third floor and which du Junca had prepared in advance with some furniture. Contrary to usual procedure, he had no cellmates. Du Junca was careful to write he was "*seul*" (alone) in the chamber. The most respected prisoners were placed on the second and third floors where it would be almost bearable in summer and barely above freezing in winter, rather than other cells in the highest and lowest levels which were burning hot and freezing cold.

Linguet tells his personal experience with Bastille amenities:

> In the cell were provided two mattresses infested with bugs, a cane chair with a seat in shreds, a folding table, a pitcher for water, two ceramic pots, one for drinking, and two stones to make a fire; that's the inventory, at least it was mine. After many months, one of the *porte-clefs* got me a fireplace shovel and

CHAPTER 9. SAINTE-MARGUERITE AND THE BASTILLE 159

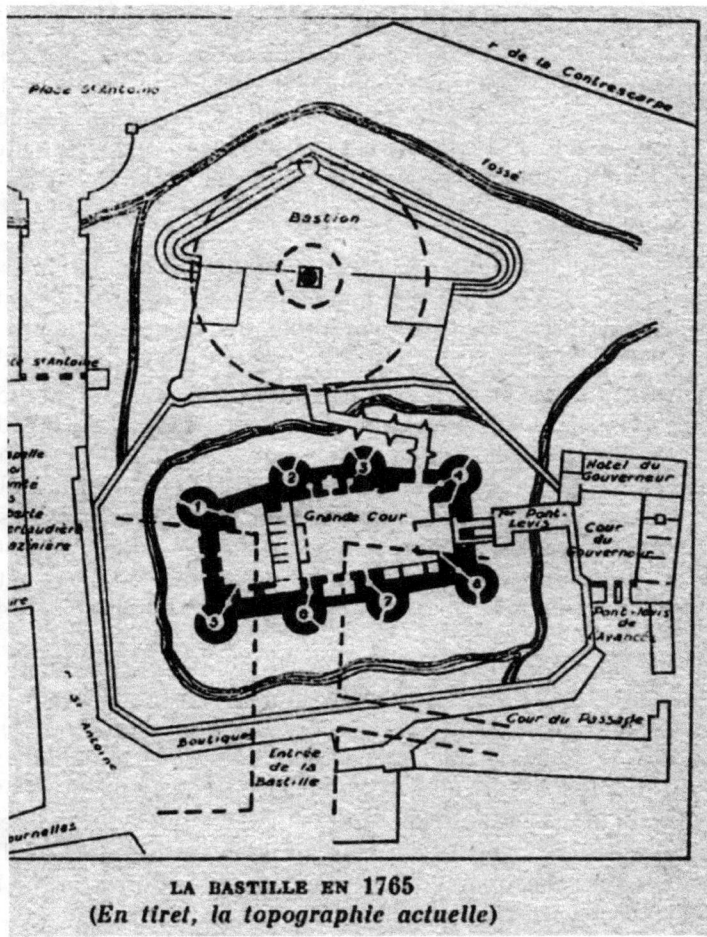

Figure 9.2: Plan of the Bastille in 1765 and its surrounding corridors, dependencies, and the bastion to its east (top of map). From Jacques Hillairet's Evocation du Vieux Paris, Les Editions de Minuit, 1952. The obelisk that was built to memorialize the victims of the 1830 Trois Glorieuses was ordered in 1830 and completed in 1840 stands in the middle of the area of the old bastion.

tongs. It was impossible to obtain andirons; and either because of politics or maybe inhumanity, that which the governor did not want to furnish, neither could the prisoner purchase with his own money. It was only after eight months that I could buy a teapot, twelve months to buy a solid chair, and fifteen months to get ceramic plates to replace the disgusting tin provided by the house.[303]

Dauger, accompanied by Rosarges, second in command to du Junca, waited while du Junca opened a fortified door leading to the stairway of the Bertaudière and the three of them went up to the third floor and waited again until the two heavy doors to Dauger's room were unlocked. Du Junca said in his journal that he had furnished it with all the necessary items; whether they were similar to those that Linguet found in his cell a half century later is unknown.

As there is a record of another prisoner occupying this room in the Bertaudière tower a few years later and Dauger was always housed alone, Dauger must have been moved from his room to another space in the prison. There had been apartments made in the walls of the old portal structure between the Tour de la Chapelle and the Tour du Trésor[304] and perhaps that is where he lived, because he was old by the time he got to the Bastille, and Saint-Mars did not worry anymore that an individual or faction would try to capture him. He had been an exemplary prisoner, quiet and obedient for three decades, so he could have been placed in a room or rooms where the temperature was steady, where perhaps he had a window without bars, where he could see the rue du Faubourg Saint-Antoine and the countryside. Hopefully he did not have to beg for fireplace andirons, tongs, and a shovel.

What were the days like in the Bastille? All the diaries say boredom was one of the worst mental burdens. Many famous prisoners wrote journals, plays, books, and memoirs in the Bastille: Voltaire, Fouquet, the *maréchal* Bassompierre, Madame de Staël. One would require pen and paper for this and those certainly were not allowed to Eustache. One of Nicolas Fouquet's most important aides, his secretary and man of confidence, Paul Pellisson, wrote letters to friends and to the king while he was in the Bastille after Fouquet's fall, and this quaint, poetic tribute to "freedoms" in the Bastille doesn't hide his fear and loathing about being a resident:

> After having assured Your Majesty of my most profound respect and the most perfect veneration that is always due to Your Majesty, I will employ, if Your Majesty will permit me, a style that will be more likely to entertain than to tire. There are here [in the Bastille] a dozen liberties that all together are not worth the twelfth part of entire liberty. They are called: liberty to walk in the courtyard; liberty to walk on the terrace, liberty to walk alone; liberty to use the stairs; liberty to have a window in one's cell, liberty to write letters having to do with one's personal business; liberty to have a visitor with an officer present; liberty to have a visitor with no witness present; liberty to be sick; liberty to be as bored as one likes. The last two are allowed to everyone.[305]

CHAPTER 9. SAINTE-MARGUERITE AND THE BASTILLE

The authorities wanted strict secrecy as to prisoners' identities and how many people they were locking up, one of the reasons that when Dauger arrived he was ushered into the nearest closed space and not taken to his room until after dark. Prisoners had to hide themselves if visitors came into the courtyard so that the outside world could not be informed. Dauger's mask was assumed by witnesses and historians to fit into that tradition; people who have studied the case have assumed he must have resembled a well known public person so his face had to be covered with a mask.

Linguet in his *Mémoires* wrote about the pain of not knowing how many people were imprisoned around him, whether they were suffering from loneliness, as he was, and the impossibility of reaching out to them. Talking through the chimneys was not as easy in the Bastille as it might have been at other prisons but Linguet says that even so, the prisoners had ways of getting information about what was going on around them, one being the sound of thick, iron-braced doors swinging open and closing and the scraping of the massive keys in the locks. If there was another prisoner nearby, you could hear these doors and locks grinding open and you knew there was a fellow inmate where the sound was coming from because his food was being brought to him and his chamber pot changed.[306]

The reputation of the Bastille was that it was fully populated...how could outsiders know how many people were there? There were never very many prisoners there at a time, actually. Louis XIV put more people in the Bastille than anyone else, 2,320 imprisonments (2,016 men and 226 women). Over the previous two centuries there had been probably eight hundred prisoners admitted.[307]

> If we look at the total as a yearly average we see 43 entrances per year on average under the reign of Louis XIV, 52 during the Regency, 33 during the personal reign of Louis XV and 20 under Louis XVI. Six times more men than women, 400 preachers, less than a thousand nobles, 4,000 roturiers coming from the *haute bourgeoisie* and the *petit artisanat*, they were a diverse group of people. Most people were there for political crimes, some for press violations, selling prohibited writings. Also assassins, thieves, counterfeiters, violent people, libelists and false witnesses. The *escrocs* [small-time crooks]...only occasionally, and usually these were transferred quickly to another prison. Madmen, charlatans, false sorcerers and other astrology pushers.[308]

Louis XIV should not have put Dauger in the Bastille because it was a place where staff and prisoners came and went, stayed at their posts a little while and left, stayed in their cells a little while and left, people who observed, remembered, and repeated. The Bastille was a kiln for rumors that solidified, were passed about, and leaked to Voltaire, who talked a lot about the prisoner to a big audience.

Here is the fault in Louis XIV's program for total anonymity—his biggest mistake. Louis XIV did not—could not—foresee or imagine in his wildest nightmares that the era of absolutism would ever be over. He counted on the fact that even if some people commented on the unusual treatment Dauger got, the terrifying power of the king to kill or imprison anyone who dared voice a question about him would eternally be a safeguard. The idea that his great-grandson, Louis XV, would read published books with theories and rumors about the prisoner would have been shocking to Louis XIV. This was Louis XIV's secret, he was in total control of everything that happened in France, or so he thought, and if he demanded the secret be kept forever, it would be. But the unusually soft arrangements for the prisoner combined with the extra stringent security, the fact that he wore a mask, and perhaps the most attention-getting thing of all... that he didn't have a name... made the guards and servants at the Bastille curious.

Louis XIV didn't give his subjects much credit, or posterity either; everyone has a name and if it is ordered that a man has no name the impossibility of that statement casts suspicion on the dictator and immense curiosity on the unnamed. The moral to the Aesop's Fable of "The Fox and the Monkey" is, "A false tale often betrays itself." "No name" was going too far; "no name" was beyond the reasonable shorthand for "important prisoner." "No name" gave a responsibility... to wonder.

Part 3

THE HABSBURGS, THE MEDICI, THE BOURBONS

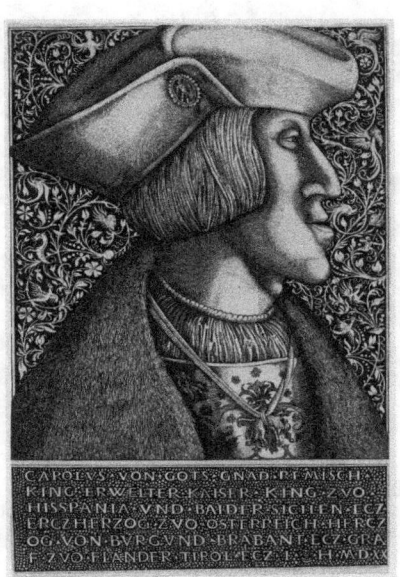

10. Queen Anne Of Austria And Cardinal Jules Mazarin

"[She was] tall, well proportioned, possessing the whitest and most delicate hands that ever made an imperious gesture, perfectly beautiful dark green eyes that often opened wide, a small vermilion mouth like a smiling rose, long and silky hair, of that pleasant reddish blond color which gives, to the face which it falls around, the suavity of a blond and the animation of a brunette: this was the woman that Louis XIII married."

—Alexandre Dumas

La Mort

Anne of Austria's apartments at the Louvre were, as was traditional for queen mothers of the Bourbons, on the ground floor of the new south wing looking over the Seine river on one side and onto the courtyard on the other.[310] In January 1666 in those rooms she lay dying of breast cancer. She had wanted to die at Val-de-Grâce, but officials ordered her to die in the Louvre because she was the Queen Mother of France and the Louvre was her official residence.

The swelling, the stench of dying flesh, the bleeding and boring into the tumor by doctors had overwhelmed her so that she probably didn't know if it was cold outside that January or not, whether there was ice on the river, whether the sounds on the quay below her were shouts of men with bundles of firewood on their backs, or dogs barking at the boats passing downriver, or angels of mercy humming in an increasingly loud cacaphony to give her passing spirit courage. Val-de-Grâce, however, was not an ambiguous presence. Her heart, up until now, figuratively, and in a few hours, literally, was and would be at Val-de-Grâce, an abbey she had founded, funded, and protected most of her life. And it had protected her.

Even in the semi-conscious state of her last hours, she thought clearly of the Saint-Anne oratory at Val-de-Grâce, and perhaps her mind, to tilt her thoughts away from the intense pain in her chest, touched on each piece of her precious treasure trove of sacramental crosses and reliquaries that lay there. She saw the urn containing her no longer beating heart being gently placed in its own aedicule by the reverend superior mother. Next to her urn, she saw a large silver crèche, a precious representation of the Christ child's first bed, standing on jasper legs and supported by two silver angels. The Child himself lay in a bed of gold. Three hundred reliquaries of many different precious materials were on the walls and tables, placed so that those in the chapel would always have one to focus on no matter where their praying lips parted. There were enameled gold figures of Saint John the Baptist and the twelve Apostles, little diamonds applied to their draperies. Six crystal chandeliers provided light in the dark and huge crystal vases with designs etched in gold reflected the candlelight into the ceiling and the floor. On the altar she saw a brittle gold sun, enameled in red, its rays and circumference carrying diamonds. The cross pressed inside it was diamond-studded. An angel, also enameled and dressed in diamonds, floated under the disk as if to help God keep it afloat in the sky.

Val-de-Grâce abbey was across the Seine on the rue Saint-Jacques, the southern leg of the great south to north axis through Paris engineered by the Roman city of Lutèce sixteen hundred and fifty years before Anne's death, although the Parisii Celtic tribe that been the town's administrators for two hundred years before that, probably laid out the roads.

After she died her body would go to the royal necropolis, Saint-Denis abbey, and her heart would be taken in a procession over the Pont Notre-Dame to the Ile de la Cité, across the island, and then over the Petit Pont to the rue Saint-Jacques that led up the hill to Val-de-Grâce. There the procession of bishops, prelates, and pious participants would bend to the left and enter the chapel without a glance to the road's beam-like continuance, south to Orléans.

The church of the convent of Val-de-Grâce was and still is on the rue Saint-Jacques, but the rich instruments of the religious service, the crosses, candelabra, precious linens, canisters of incense for the heavy, swinging censors that fanned the sweet, thick smell of heaven into each corner of each arch, each eyelid of each Madonna, and each inch of each painting and fresco, were stolen or melted down in 1792 when the revolutionaries who had overthrown the royal family decided that religion was a burden they could do without. Anne of Austria's reliquaries were among the first objects to be piled into corners in the foundries waiting for workmen to pull them up and toss them into the burning ovens.

On her last full day of life, January the nineteenth, the future fate of the royal Bourbon family was not on her mind. She had saved the family and the state from almost certain destruction and she assumed, as all the people in France did at that time, that it was saved forever and ever, amen. The

CHAPTER 10. QUEEN ANNE OF AUSTRIA AND CARDINAL JULES...

future of France was for the Virgin and Her Son (and her son) to conserve. It was out of her hands now and she had not thought about it in a long time.

One of Anne's biographers, Claude Dulong, describes the queen's last hours:

> Her doctors gave her opium (they called it *jus de pavot*) which gave her a few hours of relief from pain and some sleep. At the eve of her death, on January 19, 1666, raising her hand that used to be so beautiful, Anne whispered with a little turn of the head, 'My hand is swollen. It is time to depart.' The archbishop of Auch, her *grand aumônier*, said then that it was time to receive the sacraments.
>
> Before taking communion, Anne wanted to speak to each of her sons separately. Then the room filled again when the sacrament came from Saint-Germain-l'Auxerrois, in grand ceremony. The archbishop made a little speech that it was time for her to confess and that even as daughter of so many kings and emperors, aunt and sister of the most powerful princes of the earth, she was now equal to the least creature...
>
> Her emotions aroused, Anne's face flushed, her eyes shone, and for an instant she looked as she had always looked. 'Look at my mother,' said Louis XIV. 'I have never seen her look more beautiful.' Then he began to cry. Anne, without weakening, fixed her eyes on him and pronounced, 'Do what I told you; I'm telling you again with the Holy Sacrament on my lips.'
>
> What was Anne asking of her son? That he would renounce vengeance, that he would stop *'pour l'amour d'elle,'* to persecute so many figures of the old court and even his own house, which had been, sometimes unjustly, wrapped up in the disgrace of Fouquet.
>
> This same January 19, in the evening, Anne, not feeling her pulse, asked for extreme unction. The fervor with which she received the sainted oils had no equal except for the care that she had, in receiving them, not to derange her 'cornettes', her sleeping kerchief, as the Grande Mademoiselle remembered, stupefied at a refusal to have things out of order to the very end.
>
> Around midnight, Anne had let her head fall to the side, Louis XIV thought she was dead and he fainted. They had to take him to an outer room and he stayed there, not having the courage to watch this long agony.
>
> Despite her weakening, that got worse from minute to minute, Anne still had consciousness and prayed constantly. When the

archbishop of Auch asked her to thank God for all the graces that she had received from Him during her life, she turned her eyes to her confessor, the English abbot Walter Montagu, the witness of her past, the confident of Buckingham and Mazarin, to say: 'Monsieur de Montagu, here next to me, knows what I owe to God, the graces that He made to me and the great mercies that I have received from Him.'[311] Those in the room did not understand these words and why they were addressed to Montagu. Only Madame de Motteville, recalling the desperate adoration received in the past by the queen of the English duke of Buckingham and of which the English abbot knew the secret, deducted that he knew what Anne had had the force to resist. Later, Motteville asked Montagu if her interpretation was the right one. Montagu confirmed that it was. He emphasized that he, a priest, an abbot of Saint-Martin, who was often at Pontoise, friends with the mère Jeanne Séguier, *supérieure des carmelites*, did not ever know a heart more pure, intentions more honest than those of the queen and he was happy that she had justice before dying. One remarks all the same the word 'intentions.'

She asked for a crucifix and died with it in her arms at five in the morning.[312]

Infanta

The queen had a temper, which the misogynist historians of the nineteenth century stoutly described as universal in Spanish women. If we list Anne of Austria's ancestors we see a lot of people who were not Spanish. She was the daughter of Philip III of Spain who was descended from Austrians and French, had a mother who was of the Habsburg house of Austria-Styria; she lived in France from age fourteen, married a man whose mother was a blend of Habsburg and Italian Medici and whose father had been a rogue king of Navarre, a province halfway between Spain and France. Her paternal grandmother, Anna of Austria, was Austrian. Her paternal great-grandfather was Emperor Charles V, brought up in Flanders, whose mother was Spanish and whose father was Burgundian, Austrian, and English. Her maternal grandparents were Austrian and Bavarian. With that genetic mixture of Italian, Spanish, German, English, and Austrian blood, Louis XIII's wife was labeled "Spanish."[313]

Born on 22 September 1601 at Benavente palace in Valladolid, christened Ana Maria Mauricia, the eldest child of King Philip III of Spain (1578–1621), she had been a serious girl, pretty, with chestnut hair often seen in the Habsburgs, a somewhat rounded nose, a small, feminine mouth, and the hauteur seen in young royal children; for she was the eldest princess of the Spanish Habsburg house, the *infanta*. She had been brought up to abide strictly by the commandments and schedule of the Catholic church by her extremely pious mother, Margaret of Austria (1584–1611), and when her mother died at age twenty-six when Anne was ten, there were many aunts and governesses to continue her religious instruction. Anne was consequently all her life a very devout woman, having a particular affection for the Virgin Mary and for Mary's mother, Anne. In the royal palace Alcazar in Madrid the silver tables in her mother's rooms, fashioned from American silver that had floated perilously across oceans, and the glint of gold thread on the stiff lace collars of her father and his ministers were visible signs that she and her parents, and eventually her brothers and sisters, were rich children of God, members of the ancient and revered house of Habsburg, rulers of Austria (thus her title, that of her mother and her grandmother), Spain, Flanders, and many other domains in Europe and America.

Although she was the eldest child of Margaret of Austria and Philip III, as a female, Anne had no right to rule Spain unless there were no males in line for the throne; and there was one: her younger brother, Philip, who would eventually be fourth of that name to be sovereign of Spain. Anne and her sister Maria-Anna were well aware that they were morsels to be used in politically arranged marriages with their parents' friend states or maybe an enemy state; young princesses traipsed off to the house of the most dangerous military or strategic threat. The beds of these girl children and other royal girls of European families became the hunting ground for peace, or at least for a breathing space in between wars.

Anne was fourteen years old when she was sent to France, Spain's adversary, in 1615 to marry Louis XIII, also fourteen, son of the assassinated Henri IV. The ceremony took place on 25 November in Bordeaux. From that day many devastating things happened to the queen—accusations of infidelity, of having knowledge of plots to kill King Louis XIII and his prime minister Cardinal Richelieu, the treason of friends, many miscarriages, the infidelity of her husband, his stern abhorrence of her Spanish family, of her sex, often of her mere presence. Richelieu had been her enemy from the time he came into the king's high council in 1624, sometimes posing as a friend, then as a guardian, finally as an inquisitor who placed spies in her staff of chambermaids, her house officers, and her religious entourage, waiting for her to make a mistake that would ruin her and possibly dethrone her. Richelieu did his best to control the king's opinions about any girlfriend, boyfriend, lover, servant, confessor, priest, or layman who got close to his king, a changeable man, given to depressions, who could on a whim strike the cardinal down and take his anti-Habsburg foreign policy down with him.

Characteristics that historians have preferred for her: she was frivolous, obsessed with luxury, ate too much, was lazy, tempermental, shrill, easily angered, conspiratorial, dull, and ruled by the Christian calendar and the Jesuits and suspected of being secretly married to Cardinal Mazarin, her state counselor who lived in the Palais Royal with her and her sons after their father died. Her intense devotion to the Virgin Mary and the constellation of saints of the Church is disdainfully noted but since it would be unseemly to use her piety against her, historians usually just sniff at this part of her, without caring to examine what, in her case, piety meant. Here is an example of the calumny expressed about her by a French historian: "Of indifferent intelligence and weak character, the Queen-Mother, who was entirely taken up with her religious devotions, card-playing, theatricals, and petty Court intrigues, knew nothing of State affairs."[314]

Historians have not protested the invidious offensive that Louis XIII and Richelieu subtly advanced against Anne of Austria that she was unfaithful to her husband, particularly with an Englishman titled the duke of Buckingham, who became obsessed with Anne in 1624 and suddenly forced himself on her in a garden in Amiens where the court was staying. As soon as she realized what was happening, she called out for help and her lady in waiting immediately appeared but the incident was suspected of having been staged and her husband was enraged and thought of her from then as a seductress. In turn, historians agreed with him.

Mother Of *Dieudonné*

The central theme of Anne of Austria's presence at the French royal court, where she was the reigning queen from 1615, was her "sterility," as historians often call it, although having numerous miscarriages is not sterility but a tragic tendency to lose a child before term with the ensuing grief and permanent sense of loss, which they avoided talking about or even acknowledging. She had not produced for France what she had been brought to France to produce, a dauphin who would carry on the Bourbon dynasty, and hopefully, a hero king who would subdue all France's enemies by a glorious mix of political and military prowess blended with extreme devotion to God, the Virgin Mary, and the saints.

In the 1630s France and Europe had given up hope that Louis XIII and Anne of Austria would ever produce an heir. The wise men were divided between two possibilities: either Anne would be divorced, sent back to Spain, and Louis XIII would marry another woman to produce his heir, or the king's brother, Gaston d'Orléans, would become king when the sickly Louis died; Gaston, seven years younger than the king, was emotionally around fifteen years old—a dithering, wayward, mercurial, selfish, secretive, traitorous,

CHAPTER 10. QUEEN ANNE OF AUSTRIA AND CARDINAL JULES... 171

handsome humbug—if he had become king, France would have fallen victim to Gaston's staff of courtiers and religious counselors which would possibly have brought the Spanish Habsburgs to the throne of France.

The comment below of (presumably) a spy reporting on Anne's household to Richelieu shows the state of apprehension and doubt in October 1630[315] about Anne's ability to have children.

> [Richelieu] sent the Abbé de Beaumont two or three times to find out from Madame de Sinency (sic) how the Queen's health was, if she was still of the opinion [that the queen was pregnant], because Monsieur Bouvard [her physician] thought that accidents usually happen to her pregnancies to terminate them too early.[316]

If her physician had this attitude, how was anyone else to be optimistic?

Between 1630 and 1637 Anne's carriage regularly left the courtyard of the Louvre and crossed the Seine to the convent of Val-de-Grâce that stood at the top of the rue Saint-Jacques, where she had a little apartment, and in this privacy and distance from Richelieu's spies, she wrote secret letters to her two brothers, King Philip IV of Spain and the Cardinal-Infante Ferdinand, Governor of the Spanish Netherlands, mostly about small things, because she wasn't permitted in state business so she could not have passed secrets if she'd wanted to. She also wrote to conspirators against the crown who had been thrown out of France because of their conspiratorial actions, most of them in league with her.

The letters were passed to couriers, one being Anne's trusted aide La Porte, and two other men, Craft and Augier,[317] both associated with the English embassy...and Montagu. Some went to Marie de Chevreuse's sister-in-law Odette, abbess at Jouarre, a nunnery east of Paris, who directed the letters to Lorraine; from there they went to Brussels to the inboxes of Chevreuse, Marie de' Medicis, Madame du Fargis, and Mirabel, the former Spanish ambassador to France from Spain.[318]

Richelieu produced to Louis enough secret surveillance on Anne's activities to charge her with treason, and she was brought in for a scary admonishment. On August 17, 1637, the king and Richelieu demanded she sign an agreement that said she would behave herself in the future, would not write to her Spanish relatives or her conspiratorial friends, and would have every letter she wished to send to anyone reviewed by Richelieu's agents. Her little apartment at Val-de-Grâce was entered, searched by Richelieu's deputies, and forbidden her. The contract might as well have said that she was expendable because she hadn't had an heir, and if she should go on writing to the enemy there might be more serious consequences. The two examples of past removal of her female royal ancestors by arrogant husbands only a hundred and fifty years before, the divorce of Spanish Catherine of Aragon (1485–1536), her great-grandfather's aunt, by King Henry VIII of England because Catherine had not been able to produce a male heir, and the declaration of Catherine's sister, Joanna of Castile and Aragon (1479–1555), as crazy with a consequent forced seclusion for life and taking of her power by her father, husband and son, were family traditions she did not want to follow. This was very frightening, without doubt. It must have caused her to privately fume at Louis XIII and Richelieu; she hated them both.

The major result of the attack on Anne's character and loyalty was, after being accused of treason by Louis XIII and Richelieu, three months later Anne managed to entice her reluctant husband into her bed, conceive, carry the pregnancy to term, and deliver at Saint-Germain palace on September 5, 1638, a baby dauphin.

Because there had been twenty-three years between her wedding day and the arrival of the dauphin, assumption of legitimacy was forfeited and adultery was suspected. Nevertheless the baby was welcomed by everyone, people generally wanting twisted satisfaction in disdaining the morals of the woman but accepting the child as a holy gift. Her second son by Louis XIII was Philippe, titled duc d'Anjou and later the heir of Gaston's title and position, duc d'Orléans, born on 21 September 1640.

Anne of Austria had made herself important to France by giving birth to two children, but Louis XIII continued to threaten to take away her children and her only restraining arm on the king was Richelieu, therefore the pre-*dauphin* psychological controls that Richelieu had always used with the king and queen continued; before 1638 he posed as a gatekeeper because she had not had a baby, and after 1638 his power over her was more viscerally felt because she knew if he did not counsel the king to let the children stay with her, she would lose them. Until the cardinal's and the king's deaths in December 1642 and May 1643, her life was still under surveillance and her situation impotent. Her potency has not been recognized by historians since. Her major biographers give her only measured credit.

Anne Richardt, for instance, wrote:

> Was she intelligent? She certainly drew hatred toward herself, was employed in deceptions and arguments, but she met bravely the most perilous situations and showed a tenacity, a "viril" courage before adversity that we have to give her credit for. Her confi-

dence in Mazarin, maintained through winds and seas, led to giving the monarchy a victory purchased at great price.[319]

Her strongest biographer, Claude Dulong, was ambivalent about Anne's interaction with Buckingham and her relationship with Mazarin... whether it was sexual or not... and she, like Richardt, said we have to give her credit for showing some political skills once she was regent, mainly because Mazarin taught her how to lie and manipulated her to act as he wanted. "Have to give her credit"...? These two respected scholars saw Anne as a political force but, as she was a woman, she must be pardoned for showing the strength a man would show. Chantell Grell in her beautiful, illustrated book on Anne of Austria records all the misogynist criticism of Anne by historians but has only in her defense, "Queen and regent, Anne of Austria could not escape the judgment of posterity. Nevertheless, she keeps her secrets."[320]

Mazarin

Anne of Austria had her finest hours after Cardinal Richelieu and her husband died (in December 1642 and May 1643 respectively). She was finally free of the spies that had been following her for decades, of the unending frowns and disapproval of Louis XIII, restrictions on her life activities, and was left to happily (she was very happy to be a mother and spent time with her children, having true affection for them, which was very unusual for royal parents in France at the time) bring up her eldest son to be ruler of France while she acted as regent during his minority. She had only one major political upheaval in the years between 1643 and 1666, the year she died, and that was a serious one, the *Fronde* (1648–1653), a rebellion of the parlement of Paris and some of the nobility who protested that their positions were being undermined and their incomes cut. But... and this came as a surprise to everyone at court... to help her through this crisis Anne turned to another cardinal who appeared at court at the moment that Richelieu died, Cardinal Mazarin, an Italian who spoke her native Spanish language, and he took control of the situation and mastered it very well, bringing himself and the royal family, which he had smoothly joined, out of it in safety.

Mazarin, born Giulio Mazzarino in 1602 and raised in Rome, had traveled in Spain, became a favorite of the Colonna family in Rome, gotten a law degree, became a soldier and a diplomat, and, probably through the influence of one of the nephews of the Barbarini pope, he was made canon of Saint John Lateran and the basilica of Saint Mary Major. He never applied to or was admitted to the priesthood. After spending time in France as papal nuncio between 1634 and 1636, he immigrated to France and was made a cardinal through Richelieu's influence in 1641.

He was an opportunistic state official, a risk taker, both at the card table and in political operating methods, a deceiver, a miser, a thief, and much else, but he was also a master diplomat, and the Peace of the Pyrenees that he negotiated with Spain brought France peace... well, more peace than France had experienced since 1635 when Richelieu and Louis XIII declared war with Spain. He brought the long war to an end by a treaty in 1659 that promised King Louis XIV in marriage to Marie-Thérèse (1638–1683), Anne's niece, daughter of her brother Philip IV, a twenty-one-year-old pious girl whose mission was the same as Anne's had been in 1615: bind Spain and France together so that harmony would always exist between the two countries; and produce Bourbon heirs. Nudging Spain and France toward the desperately needed peace for eighteen years ruined Mazarin's health and contributed to his death on March 9, 1661 at the age of fifty-eight. Mazarin got fantastically rich off the French state but he never turned against it. He died in a bedroom in the governor's house in the *château-fort* of Vincennes, a fourteenth-century bastion where, standing under its huge towers today, one cannot help saying in awe, "This is France."

Mazarin was pitched out of the country a couple of times during the *Fronde*[321] despite and because of his close relationship with Queen Anne, and Colbert sent and received coded messages, often carried by musketeer d'Artagnan, from Mazarin in exile in Germany to her majesty about how to handle the rebellion that had spread from Paris to other parts of the country, especially Bordeaux that followers of the rebel prince de Condé had taken control of, but Bordeaux solved itself; when it came time for the fall grape picking, the Bordelais had a change of heart and turned on Condé, not wanting his faction to reap the precious harvest, agriculture coming before politics in wine-growing regions.

It is hard to know if Richelieu realized that Mazarin and Anne would develop a soft spot for each other and behave for a while as teenage lovers, as some of their letters to each other prove. Some historians say Anne of Austria and Cardinal Mazarin were married but that is not possible. The accusation of secret marriage has become a regular small brutal dig at Mazarin and Anne of Austria in history books that has never been robustly refuted, perhaps because it is an excuse to bring a little titillation into the story at their expense, but it is impossible that they were married for the following reasons.

Mazarin had become a cardinal in the church by befriending Richelieu without ever becoming a priest, as was possible then, and wanted to be pope eventually and he couldn't have been elected pope if he had been married... and Anne of Austria was pleased to be a widow and would not have

CHAPTER 10. QUEEN ANNE OF AUSTRIA AND CARDINAL JULES... 175

traded it for anything. Her sullen royal husband had given her twenty-seven years of sorrow and humiliation, and now both he and Richelieu were in heaven, or in a place where they at least couldn't be in control of her life anymore. She finally had freedom to live life on her own terms, retreat to her apartment and oratory at Val-de-Grâce[322] whenever she wished, and watch her son put on his crown, the young Louis XIV, only four and a half years old at her husband's death in May 1643. But Richelieu almost certainly was aware that his successor and Anne were enjoying their new situation; he had spies in her staff of ladies-in-waiting and chambermaids, but they reported no late night rendezvous, and Richelieu died quickly after Mazarin came back to court so he never had time to find out if their relationship was sexual, and we don't know either, but it is highly unlikely. Anne of Austria was deeply, intensely devoted to the Virgin Mary; her Spanish family and the nuns and priests who controlled her early life had soaked her in the teachings and prescribed actions of the church of the Counter-Reformation, which she followed scrupulously. Everything in her life was adjusted to her Catholic beliefs. Many historians believe she was an adulteress and others believe to the contrary that she would never have committed sin, before her husband died or afterwards, with Mazarin. And she herself told us, through Madame de Motteville, her friend and *dame d'honneur* at court[323] who wrote her impressions and memories of the queen, that Mazarin was not interested in sinning with her; whatever else that means, we cannot say and she did not, but it certainly meant that he was not making sexual love to her.

Most importantly, their marriage was prohibited by the church because Mazarin was Louis XIV's godfather; the church forbade marriage or love affairs between godparents and the birth family of the godchild, especially the parents of the baby. No, Mazarin and Anne of Austria were not married; they had (at first) a happy asexual flirtation.

The Queen's Leadership

Despite Mazarin's slowly unfolding power over the state and over the queen, in her actions, we see that she was was ardently committed to France's future and to the domination of the Catholic religion in Europe. She never diverted from those two aims. Abbot Montagu and other devoted helpers were far more loyal and enduring than favorites of any other character in this period of French history in which allies came and went daily, sometimes twice daily. She must have been the sort of person that inspired perpetual devotion, even in the face of prison or death. But instead of praise for her fearlessness that was so evident that it amounted to leadership, historians are content to remember her for a flirtation initiated by a foreigner (the duke of Buckingham) when she was twenty-three years old... by a man whose flagrant abuse of others was well known in his home country... by a

Figure 10.1: Anne of Austria (1601–1666). Engraving by Claude Mellan. Circa 1662. Courtesy National Gallery of Art, Washington, D.C., USA.

popinjay whose handsome looks he thought gave him permission to attack women... she was a victim and was blamed for the assault against her.

Historians have been guilty of passing along the conventional sleazy insinuations about her... they have barely contradicted them. They easily could have because an exam of her entire life shows a woman who left absolutely no affairs, no adultery, no sin in her wake. Many pious women in the Grand Century met lovers half or twice their age after mass. That was not her piety. Anne of Austria was a devoted Christian who kept her wedding vows. In her mature years, she was smart, able to think politically as well or better than the counselors on Louis XIII's high council, certainly better than the king's brother and the prince de Condé. She gave orders for government actions firmly, for instance, ordering the parlement to go to Montargis when they had started acting against her in the *Fronde* and holding her ground as a descendant of Emperor Charles V of Spain would be expected to do when the *messieurs* of the parlement showed up on her doorstep a few days later on their own initiative to negotiate with her; she said she was surprised to see them there. "I had thought you were at Montargis," which was her sarcastic observation that they were disobedient and she was not pleased. Her actions during one night of January 1649 when she and her family had to flee the Palais-Royal secretly to avoid being under siege by her parlement enemies were those of a cool madam leading her chicks to safety without hesitation or blinking. She spent the evening with her ladies in the Twelfth Night ritual of saluting the person in the room whose piece of cake had a bean in it, finding the bean in her own plate, which made her queen of carnival for the night, and eating her serving with relish while all knew that at two in the morning she and her intimate court would go out the back door and get in carriages to ride fast to Saint-Germain-en-Laye, where they could preside over their next political moves. This is not a passive, lazy, fuzzy-headed Spanish woman, it's a Frenchwoman trying to save the king's crown with brave deception in a deed that could have ended very badly.

She took risks that perhaps were unwise and irrational. But she achieved her aims, she kept her faith, she kept her crown, she was loyal to her husband and to France, she produced and oversaw the education and training of one of France's most powerful kings and she bowed out quietly when he signaled he was ready to rule alone; her risks paid off. Her most extravagant risk, which shall soon be a concluding topic of this book, brought riches and power to France. We are the beneficiaries of her daring crusades to this day.

11. Louis XIV

"I spot in the pasture by my workshop, a cock who is the most insolent cock the world has ever seen [...] the bird is stupifyingly shameless. The sun pours over him, burnishes his paunch, making of him a lighthouse of a Crimson God, a seed of Astrapatte's erection (yes, that's what I meant) [...] How glorious, what a superb creature [...] a king! Versailles! Le Grand Roi! Le Roi Soleil!"
—Seen on display above a tapestry at the Jean Lurçat exposition at les Gobelins, Paris, Saturday, September 10, 2016.

Louis *Dieudonné*

To call Louis XIV a "jailer" of the Man in the Iron Mask, as the marquis de Louvois and the chevalier de Saint-Mars have been labeled in a previous chapter, would have the aspect of *lèse-majesté*, that is, the word is not dignified enough for the magnificence of the king, were it not for the fact that Louis was the chief jailer in this mystery of jails, jailers, and prisoners. If his majesty did not want to be grouped together with his lesser operatives in the matter of Eustache Dauger then he should not have arrested him.

Louis *Dieudonné*, third king of the Bourbon line, a cadet branch of the Capet dynasty, was born at Saint-Germain-en-Laye on September 5, 1638, became king of France at his father's death on May 14, 1643, although France was ruled by his mother, Anne of Austria, until his thirteenth birthday, was crowned the fourteenth Louis of France in Reims cathedral on 7 June 1654, and ruled France until September 1, 1715, when he died. Under Louis XIV's rule France became the most illustrious country in Europe, politically, militarily, and culturally. His wars and the many entrenched weaknesses in the economic system reduced France's treasury to a disreputable state from which it slipped even further in following generations until the French Revolution when the lawyers, the middle class, and some of the nobility of France declared enough in 1789, the monarchy was abolished, and the state was rethought and renovated.

Perhaps Louis XIV's most important contribution to France was as *dauphin*[324] from his birth on September 5, 1638, to the death of his father,

Louis XIII, on May 14, 1643. At the instant that the *dauphin* was born, he assured France that when their sickly king died, which everyone knew would be soon, there would be a continuation of the Bourbon dynasty and the former would-be usurpers of the throne, the Guise family, would be legitimately locked out and prevented from undoing Henri IV's demilitarization of the Catholic versus Protestant religious wars that had bankrupted and broken France; the Retz, Brissac, and La Trémouille families' hopes would be crushed. It was the infant Louis' arrival that was his greatest contribution to France, his genes were his gift; they were a deliverance from uncertainty, a hope for relief from hunger, a possibility of better governance and lower taxes. If he had never become king through some unfortunate circumstance, his birth would still be worthy of mention in textbooks about the history of France. Louis, while he reigned, was officially named and known as the gift of God, *Dieudonné*, to the French and to his Bourbon family and would have deserved that name whether he reigned or not.[325]

The Baby Jesus And *Dieudonné*

The birth of Louis XIV came at a time that was not only necessary for the political safety of the Bourbons, but it was also supportive of a larger religious collective consciousness that had been forming since the Council of Trent ninety or so years previously (1545–1563) that responded to the Protestant Reformation's call for a "reform of the Church in head and members."[326]

Figure 11.1: Medal of Anne of Austria, mother of Louis XIV, founder and benefactor of Val-de-Grâce. J. Warin, 1645, bronze. Hôtel de la Monnaie. Photo by author 2018.

The Reformation had preached a philosophy of the individual's responsibility for his day of judgement, putting the personnel of churches and donations to churches in a secondary role, which brought fear in the Catholic church fathers since the logical outcome of that philosophy was that they would not be needed as much any more and possibly not at all eventually.

Jean Meyer points out that the *dauphin's* birth in 1638 dovetailed with the emerging seventeenth-century cult of the infant Jesus.

> We do not say often enough that he was the vessel carrying an immense hope, almost a myth, forged more or less spontaneously from his birth.[327]
>
> Saint Bernard and Saint Francis of Assisi began the devotion to the birth and infancy of Jesus in the thirteenth century...Saint-Theresa of Avila promoted this cult in the sixteenth century but it was in the early seventeenth century that it became popular in places north of Italy largely because the Bérulliens began to promote it in tandem with 'a new conception of infancy'...The queen promoted this cult. She started a group to encourage it, patronized by some of the great political names of France, the chancellor Séguier, the duchesse de Sully, the president Brûlard and many others.[328]

In devout religious circles Louis XIV was believed to be the messianic king that was expected after the religious upheavals of the sixteenth century and was interpreted as herald of the return of Christ and the Last Judgement.[329] The birth of the *dauphin*, immediately named "Louis *Dieudonné*," because he was seen as a gift from God just like the gift received by the aged Biblical figures Zachariah and his wife Elisabeth, parents of Saint John the Baptist, allowed the French people to feel a release from the stresses they had for so long endured, violence, starvation, war, indignities of body and soul, and to presume an end to these terrors.

Appearance

To look at the person of Louis XIV in his childhood, his adolescence, and his adulthood, one would believe that he was at least as beautiful as God would have been had He decided to come to earth. Louis in his youth had beautiful blond curls, was perfectly made without any deformity, and in addition, he had a stately presence, even as a child. He was the director, the chief, the *patron* from the beginning. His stance, his movements, the tension in his body that was lordly and proud, astonished his family and all who saw him and listened to him. Often the descriptions of Louis XIV by relatives and courtiers emphasized his graceful, restrained, and regal show, and then, in frustration in finding the right words to describe his natural royal appearance, they ended by saying that if he had not been king, he still would have been commander of any scene he stood before.

His first cousin, the Grande Mademoiselle (1627–1693), who was his childhood companion and might have been his wife had she not ruined her chances by becoming a leading *Frondeur*, gave us this description of Louis in his youth:

> The height of the monarch is somewhat taller than others, in birth as well as the way he carries himself. He has a regal, elevated, proud and agreable presentation, something between a sweetness and majestic in his expression, the most beautiful hair for its color and curls. He has beautiful legs and a firm stance; taking all into account, he is the handsomest of his realm and most certainly of all other realms...
>
> He presents himself reservedly, he doesn't say much; but to his familiars he speaks well, correctly, and never says anything awkward, laughs agreeably, has good taste, discerns and analyzes people well, has a natural goodness, is charitable, giving, plays as king and never makes a step in which he is not in the role.[330]

Primi Visconti (Giovan Battista Feliciano Primi Fassola di San Maiolo 1648–1713) came to the French court from Italy in 1673 when Louis XIV was thirty-five years old and in his most bellicose years, those of the Dutch War. Primi, perhaps because he was a man and not as concerned with the king's beauty as the Grande Mademoiselle had been, did not think that the king was handsome:

> The King is not handsome, but his features are regular, his face is marked with smallpox scars; his eyes are majestic, lively, playful, voluptuous, tender and large; finally, he has a presence and, as they say, a truly royal air; if he were only a courtier, he would distinguish himself among the others.

And he also said, "He has the gravity of a king who plays a leading role on stage."[331]

Ezéchiel Spanheim, the ambassador from Brandebourg, whose description of the marquis de Louvois was given earlier, gave masterful and insightful

CHAPTER 11. LOUIS XIV

Figure 11.2: Louis XIV, buste en médallion. Anonymous. Between 1650 and 1700. Marble. Photo by the author 2024 at Musée des Invalides. Louvre.

portraits of Louis XIV. At the beginning of the entry on the king's appearance we find right away the typical mention of his astounding birth:

> Also his extraordinary birth, which brought him the name of *Deodatus* or *Dieudonné*, for having been born after the sterility of a marriage of 23 [sic] years of Louis XIII and the deceased queen his mother, seems already to foretell an interesting future. This birth is matched by his very fine physical presence which has increased with his age and has all that one could wish for in size, bearing, deportment and good appearance—to put it succinctly, he has an exterior full of grandeur and majesty... Also he can express himself well and with dignity. He is careful with his words so as not to say something that might not be correct or that might reveal too much of himself. He can speak with a wonderful combination of grandeur and familiarity in his conversations with people and can conduct himself without either haughtiness or degradation.[332]

The King's Brother, Philippe I D'Orléans

Louis was polite to his brother, just as he was polite to everyone. He might have even loved him, but more than anything, Louis wanted Philippe to know his place, the example of his uncle Gaston, the brother of Louis XIII, having told a cautionary tale against letting the second born get too much authority or attention. Luckily, Philippe was a cross-dresser which made it easy for Louis XIV to take a bemused, authoritarian, and haughty stance with him, to allow him his place at court, the highest in France next to the king, which couldn't be denied him, but to manage his talkative, emotional brother with a steady hand and a watchful eye. Philippe was open about his sexuality; he dressed in women's clothes, did not wear a hat so his wig didn't get messed, had ribbons galore on his outfits, and loved jewelry. At the end of the Dutch War in April 1677 Louis put him in the field under the marshal Luxembourg (1628–1695) with an assignment to take Saint-Omer, which the Dutch sought to take by forcing battle near Cassel. The duke was in the center position of the line with the infantry and artillery. He reorganized and rallied his infantry when they fell back by leading a charge to the enemy, and at the end of the day joined in the victory with Luxembourg who praised the duke for his bravery and smart command. Taking Luxembourg's cue, the press and the public rejoiced for Philippe and called him brave under fire. Louis did not like the accolades that Philippe deserved and got, so the press and the witnesses had to withdraw, and the king never gave him a command again.

Philippe had a natural understanding of good architecture, bought modern Dutch paintings that have stood the test of time far better than the king's French painters, put together a team of financiers who built the Orléans wealth so that it far outstretched his brother's belongings and lasts until the present day.

He was two years younger than the king, born on September 21, 1640, one day before his mother's birthday. He was a small man with a long narrow face and the dark curly hair and coloring of his father that was from Marie de' Medici's father, François de' Medici, oldest son of Archduke Cosimo I of Florence. He had Anne of Austria's mouth, eyes, and hands. He had none of Louis XIV's majesty or bearing.

Character

Hélène Delalex in her book *Louis XIV intime* frets that we cannot know Louis XIV because he was an extremely secretive person.

The human personality of Louis XIV is mostly absent in history

CHAPTER 11. LOUIS XIV

textbooks. Of his reign, the longest in the history of France, one knows about the magnificence of the monarch, the constructor of modern France, the builder whose name appears on the pediments of the great monuments raised to his glory, the war chief enlarging the borders of the kingdom, the patron, great enabler of masterpieces of art and spirit ...But the inner man escapes.[333]

François-Timoléon de Choisy, whose memoirs have a little more spice and individual quotations than some other memoirs of the age, said that Louis had a habit of making replies and comments that had "a bit of salt in them, which made them agreeable and memorable. He was truly the king of oratory and a model of French eloquence. The comments he made extemporaneously were far better than those in studied speeches."[334]

The king can be known as we have said we can know Eustache Dauger—as a stellar black hole: we analyze the steaming debris around him being swallowed into his essence. In many ways, the life of Louis XIV was very normal and known to us in all its important parts. He was the first born son of a mother in her late thirties who spoiled him and loved him very much and a father who died before he was five. His brother was two years younger and very different in personality and appearance. He had a stepfather who was loyal to him, he had a modest education but one very focused on what his future vocation would be, he was a strong-headed child, he was an ardent lover of many women, had a first wife he respected but didn't love, had mistresses that absorbed all his attention for a while and then he finally saw those relationships were shallow; after he was a widower he married a second wife who had conservative values with whom he ran a school for girls, was greatly saddened by the death of almost all his children and a few of his grandchildren but helped one of the latter to become king of Spain, decorated his houses magnificently but had to sell the silver when times got tough, and died in his bed of complications from diabetes. That is a lot to know and it describes a man like many others.

But of course he was not like other men. He was king of France for a very long time, seventy-two years. The not ordinary things he did were starting wars for questionable reasons, getting a lot of people killed because of them, and deciding that the Protestant religion was evil and should be banned from France, no matter what his Protestant grandfather Henri IV had fought and died for. These blisters hardened and infected Europe for centuries.

Jean-Baptiste Colbert (1619–1683) and Michel-François Le Tellier, the marquis de Louvois (1641–1691), Louis XIV's war minister, were a duo of brilliant and ruthless government officials that left each meeting of Louis XIV's high council with briefcases of new orders from the king about matters as diverse as troop movements on the Rhine and plans for additional buildings at Versailles, and it is hard to know which end of the spectrum represented by those two aspects of governance was more important to the king. They carried out Louis XIV's agenda for him and he stirred their jealousies of each other keeping either one from getting to a boiling point. The king purposefully caused them each to be uncomfortable in their posts by making it clear that that were allowed them to have as long as it was his pleasure. Colbert started his career working in the war office and was passed to Cardinal Mazarin to clean up his financial books, in which position he soon discovered Mazarin's unpredictable character and his deficiency of scruples about money.

The King's First Wife

Marie-Thérèse was Anne of Austria's niece and the first cousin of Louis XIV. She and Louis XIV married in summer of 1660 and had six children, only one of whom lived past young childhood. The surviving son, Louis, called the Grand Dauphin, is a mystery in some ways because he was so in awe of and afraid of his father that we do not know if this fear caused him to be a non-entity who only wanted to hunt wolves or whether, if he had ever become king, he would have woken up. Queen Marie-Thérèse was a Habsburg princess. Although her father, Philip IV of Spain, had a jaw affected by manibular prognathism, a Habsburg genetic trait, to an almost hideous degree, Marie-Thérèse had no outward indication of the deformity.

When Queen Marie-Thérèse died in the summer of 1683 of an infection, Louis XIV is reported to have said that her dying was the only trouble she had ever caused him. At least once, though, she angered the king severely, wrote Primi, when in late November 1662 she objected to the presence at court of his first mistress, Louise, and the king refused to see or speak to her for weeks. The queen mother had to step in to reconcile her son to his humiliated wife. By 1683, he had probably forgotten that incident.

In the evenings from eight, the queen played cards up to the hour of ten when the king came to take her for dinner. While she played at cards, the princesses and duchesses made a circle around her to watch and behind were *dames* and *seigneurs* who stood. It was first-come first-serve to get the best viewing space next to the princes of the blood and the ministers. The queen liked the game *l'hombre* best but she always lost.[335]

The King's Second Wife

Madame de Maintenon (1635–1719), formerly Françoise d'Aubigné, then Madame Françoise Scarron, and eventually Louis XIV's second wife, was a careful conductor of her affairs and she crafted her history artfully. Her memoirs and letters muse on her long journey to the altar with the king as a perpetual devotion to duty and to prayer, encouraged and counseled by her confessor. Her mission: to deliver the greatest king on earth from the sinful double adultery he was happily committing with Madame de Montespan, his mistress, into a comfortable armchair next to the fire across from Queen Marie-Thérèse, his wife.

She was born November 24, 1635, in the *conciergerie* of the prison in Niort where her father was in jail for unpaid debts. She was a Protestant and was poor most of her life. After her father was released from jail she and her family sailed from La Rochelle in early summer 1644 on the ship *Isabelle de La Tremblade* for Marie-Galante, the Antilles island in the Americas that is south of Guadeloupe and north of Dominica, where her preposterous father had been offered the governorship, which, like everything else in Constant d'Aubigné's life, fell through after they got there.

Her father deserted the family and they returned to France. Françoise and her two brothers lived with Arthémise de Villette, their Calvinist aunt, who lived in the *château-fort* of Mursay, ten kilometers north of Niort,[336] the family home of the d'Aubigné. Françoise fed farm animals and swept floors at Mursay. The governor of Niort's wife, an ardent Catholic, felt it her duty to intervene in the Calvinist upbringing that Françoise was being exposed to at Mursay and took her in to be a servant. Strong-arm efforts to turn her to Catholicism followed, including a stay at an Ursulines convent in Niort which was painful for her, although she received an excellent education with the nuns, her beautifully written letters to friends being evidence.[337] Eventually she was put into a squeeze between being a Protestant in a Catholic convent or converting to Catholicism and becoming the wife of a severely crippled arthritic in Paris, for whom she would be an emotional companion and nurse. This gentleman was Monsieur Paul Scarron (1610–1660), a burlesque poet and playwright whom she married on April 4, 1652 when she was sixteen and Scarron was forty-two. After he died she was given a small pension by Queen Anne of Austria but when Anne of Austria died in 1666, Françoise's pension was cancelled and poverty loomed again. Her friends felt sorry for her... she was such a gracious, soft-spoken, and self-effacing woman, pious and of irreproachable conduct.

She met Madame de Montespan at the salon of the Hôtel d'Albret and was hired as governess for the children of the king, charged with keeping their existence a secret so that Montespan's husband would not take them away, which he had every legal right to do.

Over many years, until 1679 when the swell of her favor was finally evident at court, she kept Louis XIV at a distance emotionally, while approaching him familiarly about his children's health and education, which made her a confidant but not a sexual one. He began to want to be more than a father of his children to her. They married secretly just after the queen died in 1683. They had no children.

Secrets

Ironically, as tenaciously as Louis XIV wanted to be thought glorious by acts of war and by the sparkle of his court, at the same time he wanted to shadow his thoughts, his intentions, his inner personal life. He had a public face for his public life, and many historians describe this mask as theatrical, because it was so hardened and never broken. "When one contemplates Louis XIV in his majesty, he whom the brush of Hyacinthe Rigaud gave us so perfect a painting, one sees an actor who plays his role on the stage of a theater that he doesn't have the liberty to abandon, a role accepted, a role assumed, a role borne."[338]

Christophe Levantal says that all the memoir writers and biographers of Louis XIV wrote that his major characteristic was "a great art of concealment supported by perfect self-control."[339] As Levantal said, there are many testimonies to Louis XIV's secretive nature; Primi gives a typical one in his memoirs:

> He wants to know everything: ministers, state affairs, presidents, parliaments, judges, the smallest things, favorite ladies, gallantries; in short, in each day there are few events of which he is not informed, and there are few persons whose name and habits he does not know. He is insightful, knows everyone's secrets, and once he has seen a man or heard of him, he always remembers him.[340]

Not only do other courtiers describe the king this way, but the documents of his administration show us this secretive nature, which is why I believe Louis XIV was the executor and decision-maker about all aspects of Eustache Dauger's life; some writers have guessed that Louis' subordinates, for their own personal reasons, controlled this incarceration and perhaps told Louis XIV very little about it, but that is counter to many statements of contemporaries of the king that he was a consumer of rumors and gossip about the people around him and spent time carefully going over police and undercover agent reports on Paris criminals and royal court figures. Insignificant as some of these reports were, the king was very interested in them. To give a very small example, in 1701, after Monsieur d'Argenson, the lieutenant general of police, had turned in his September report of odd news that his spies had heard on the streets, in bars, in private homes, in parlementary debates, d'Argenson was asked by the Secretary of State to look into one of these in particular.

> 28 September 1701
>
> Comte de Pontchartrain, Secretary of State, to M. d'Argenson
>
> You mentioned to me a Dutch lemonade seller who has a little store at the door of the *Comédie* [theater] where many foreigners gather. The king is curious to know if this woman has naturalisation papers and under what authority she has this shop, and why you have not closed her down, seeing as there is bad behaviour there.[341][342]

The memoirist Saint-Simon was old enough to be at court only after Louis XIV was what we would call "an old man," even though the king was only sixty-two in 1700 when Saint-Simon appeared at court. Of all Saint-Simon's precise and insightful comments on the king, this is the one that may be the most chilling.

> He was jealous and suspicious of those who were sensitive, respectful, well educated, well meaning, and eventually as he grew older the suspicion about such people grew into hate. This aversion extended to his generals and his ministers that he divided by preference for those who needed him the most. His jealousy on this point was so strong that it became a weakness.[343]

Louis XIV was not one person, he was many, and as the multiple personalities grew older he became more tightly compressed within himself, as a fist clenches more and more over time, regressing to the infantile state when an open fist is impossible. He was either an enigma, which most people would call him who try to know him from books and manuscripts, or he was not an enigma but a man persecuted by fears that historians have not yet understood.

De Choisy, a contemporary of Saint-Simon, has, in his descriptions of the king, much the same sly honesty as Saint-Simon.

> Spattered with the same illusions of grandeur as Caesar and Alexander, he had weaknesses as they did, and sometimes the hero faded and the man appeared.[344]

Louis XIV, Author

Louis XIV was the author of two books: *Manière de montrer les jardins de Versailles* and *Mémoires pour l'instruction du Dauphin*. He had generous editing help but he seems to have been the originator of the ideas in the books and had personal control over the final products.

Death

Louis' horoscope that was drawn at his birth had predicted that, "...there will be misery in the end." There was.

The king and his brother, Philippe d'Orléans, had a rare and heated argument on 8 June 1701 over Louis' refusal to give Philippe's son, the duc de Chartres, a position in military affairs, which he merited by his previous salutory military actions and by his position at court. Philippe went back to Saint-Cloud that evening, suddenly collapsed in the arms of Chartres and died the next day.

Louis XIV lost nearly his entire family between 1701 and 1712. His only surviving legitimate son by Queen Marie-Thérèse, the *Grand Dauphin*, died in 1711 of smallpox. The medical journal that his doctors had kept said Louis XIV left his son's deathbed so quickly that he arrived at the chateau of Marly in the middle of the night and found it deserted, no servants and no lights. Sitting in the dark, ruminating on his sadness, he fell victim '...to extreme shaking and an attack of vapors caused by the violent seizure of the heart,' had convulsions, and was in an 'unnatural' state."[345] There were no more journal entries on the king's health after 1711.

The *Grand Dauphin* had had three sons with his legitimate wife, the dauphine, the second oldest of whom, the duc d'Anjou, had gone to Spain to be king, because the last of the Habsburg Spanish kings, Charles II, died without children and chose to leave the throne to Marie-Thérèse's grandson. The *Grand Dauphin's* third son, the duc de Berry, died as a result of an injury in spring 1714. The eldest son of the *Grand Dauphin*, second in line for the throne of France, the duc de Bourgogne (1682–1712), and his wife, Marie-Adelaïde de Savoie (1685–1712), died six days apart in February 1712 of measles. Their oldest son, the little duc de Bretagne, died of the same illness in March. His brother, five years old, lived through the winter months of 1712 only because his governess protected him from the doctors and their "remedies," and would reign as Louis XV (1710–1774).

Of the king's last days, we have two complete descriptions by contemporary journal writers that are expertly collated by Alexandre Maral in his book *Les Derniers Jours de Louis XIV*: that of the duc de Saint-Simon, whose *Journal* is fascinating in its detail but also its commentary on the issues and personalities responsible for the detail, and Philippe de Courcillon marquis de Dangeau (1635–1716), one of the few people who, at the end of Louis' life, could be called a personal friend; he and his wife had an apartment in the palace of Versailles and often spent evenings with the king and Madame de Maintenon conversing and listening to private musical performances. He was the same age as the king and had been a courtier in the suite of the *Grand Dauphin*'s wife.

There are also letters that were sent to the Spanish court from 17 June 1715 to 11 March 1716 nearly every day giving information on the king's deathwatch written by the *abbé* Mascara, originally from Bergamo, Italy. He was one of many people in Paris who scrounged for the details of the king's illness, but only he was secretly sending the information each night by courrier to Spain's Secretary of State Grimaldo. Petitfils calls him "agent of the court of Madrid."[346] Mascara knew that an eyewitness to the king's death chamber came back to Paris each night so he made a point to visit the *hôtel* of the marquis Louis d'Auger de Cavoye, the *Grand Maréchal des Logis*, each evening of the deathwatch. Cavoye, who had said goodbye to the king on August 26 and returned to Paris on the 28th, had been allowed to place one of his most trusted valets at Versailles in the antechamber of the bedroom where the king was dying; this servant returned each evening to Paris to tell Cavoye what had transpired and how the king was.

Saint Simon had noticed in May 1715 that the king was visibly weakening, losing weight and his appetite. But he kept a nearly normal schedule until August, going hunting, doing government business, greeting dignitaries, even viewing from Marly, the king's small palace not far from Versailles, with the court on May 3, an eclipse of the sun.

It is tempting, three hundred years later, to make the comparison of the astronomical eclipse and the gradual covering of Louis XIV's *soleil* at the end of the summer of 1715. The process did not take long. On August 12 Dangeau said in his *Journal* that the king had pain in his left leg and thigh. He was present for the *coucher* (the public formal bedtime ritual) of the king that night at midnight and recalled that when the king was undressed he looked like a dead man. At the end of August 13 the doctors examined the affected leg and found only a small red mark on the middle of the calf. Maral says they probably still didn't know that gangrene was beginning. Dangeau pointed to Wednesday August 14 as the day that the king began to be visibly ill. For a time on the 15th the king seemed to revive a little and have a little appetite. He worked with his ministers Voysin, Desmarets, and Pontchartrain. On the 16th he awoke bathed in sweat and unable to move. His mattress had to be changed. Up to August 18, he continued to eat his ceremonial meal in public and meet with his ministers on government business.

By August 19 he was sicker and in more pain and the doctors sent for water from Bourbonne. They judged he had no fever. But when that night they went to change the dressing on his leg they found the leg swollen and some small black marks on his foot. The doctors knew what these marks meant: gangrene. They didn't state this fact to the king and Madame de Maintenon, who was in an armchair by his bed constantly, or put the case that an amputation of the leg was called for to prevent the gangrene from spreading because they feared to tell the king and his family that he was dying. Instead, they courageously, on the 20th, proposed an aromatic bath of herbs in Burgundy wine. He was very thirsty and his pulse weakened.

The *Gazette* published an article on the 24th to let the public know the monarch was indisposed. The editor said he had gout and sciatica, meanwhile Saint-Simon, who was with onlookers at the *petit couvert* (the informal public supper) that same day said he noticed that the king could only take liquid. Now the doctors said he had probably had an "internal fever" since Pentecost (the fiftieth day after Easter) and said gangrene was the reason, not being able to deny it anymore since the infection had taken his foot.

His majesty's senior staff came to formally salute the king and give him courage. He also called Pontchartrain to his bedside, who was the Secretary of State of the *Maison du Roi* and of Paris. He said when he was dead for him to take his heart to the *Maison Professe des Jésuites*,[347] where his father's heart was, and no other expense was to be made. It went without saying that his body would go to the royal necropolis at the Saint-Denis abbey north of Paris.

On the 27th the abbé Mascara wrote to the marquis de Grimaldo in Spain:

> At 4 a.m. the king was very sick. He had lost consciousness and was failing minute by minute...at 5 a.m. the king took a little broth. At 6 a.m. Mareschal [his surgeon] changed the bandage on the king's leg, which was held stable by the man who had come with the valet of Cavoye. The leg was as black as carbon. The foot and the calf up to the knee were without feeling and lost. Above the knee the flesh was more viable but the infection was gaining ground. His mind was fine, his eye was clear, the chest and stomach in very good condition, as if the king was only thirty years old. In the bedroom of the king were Madame de Maintenon and Mademoiselle d'Aumale, her secretary...the valet of Cavoye was in the antichamber with the princesse de Conti, the prince de Rohan, the chancellor and few others. When

the doctor came out of the bedroom he reported that the pulse of the king was "abominable," a little raised and intermittent, irregular.[348]

On the 27th the monarch and his wife, Mme de Maintenon, burned the paper contents of some boxes.

On the 28th, an opportunist, perhaps well meaning, came to the gates of Versailles to say he had a remedy that might cure the king, a potion, and with Madame de Maintenon's permission and a growl of warning from Dr. Fagon, the king's chief doctor, it was given to him at noon and it roused him a little but he soon was half unconscious again. At 6 p.m. that night Louis told Madame de Maintenon she could leave and two hours later she left for her boarding school at Saint Cyr, where she had perhaps been desiring to retreat for some time. Dangeau said the royal pulse continued bad but the gangrene had not progressed. On the 29th Louis heard his last mass, although what he heard might have sounded as if it were from a distant world because at 10 p.m. the gangrene had gained the thigh. Madame de Maintenon returned to Versailles on the 29th because the king had forgotten that he dismissed her and asked for her. She stayed all that day in his room, but late on the 30th the king became unconscious and she left again for Saint-Cyr, having given her carriages, horses, and almost all her belongings to her friends and servants, and never returned to Versailles. That night the *abbé* Mascara had been received at the *hôtel* of the marquis de Cavoye and had heard the report that the king's leg was gone and with it his life would soon follow.

The dying man's confessor and spiritual advisor, *père* le Tellier, and the king's friend de Villeroy[349] were with him until he died. On the 31st the king was not conscious. Late at night priests performed the *Litany of the Dying* with chanted music. The *Final Anointment* had already been given on the 25th. He died on September 1 in the morning at 8:23 a.m. His doctors undressed him, put him in clean clothes, cleaned his bed linen and put him back in bed. His two *garçons de la chambre*, Tartillière and Lagamie, closed his eyes and mouth. A crucifix was put in his hands and for twenty-four hours visitors could view his body. A military guard had already been readied to take the *dauphin* and his baggage to Vincennes on the order of the regent, the duc d'Orléans, who was immediately firmly in charge, and the little boy was at Vincennes before dark fell on September 1.

Monsieur's son, Philippe II duc d'Orléans, was to be, until the dauphin came of age, the ruler of France.

12. Louis XIII: A Medical Examination

It must be said that, in the state of physical and moral disrepair in which he found himself, the idea of dying without leaving an heir to the crown, which so needed one, was very cruel. To have worked so much, suffered so much and caused so much suffering to abandon France to his brother!...

—Claude Dulong

Essay on King Louis XIII by Théophraste Renaudot, editor of *Recueil des Gazettes de l'année 1631*. Paris: *Au Bureau d'Addresse, au grand Coq, ruë de la Calandre, sortant au marché neuf, près le Palais à Paris.*

From Monceaux on 28 August 1631

If the king (as I wrote you recently about his ministers) had been spending his time at leisure and did not want the public to know, and I therefore refused to tell you anything about his activities, you would rebuke me. Pray God that you are also at leisure. But that being said, I will satisfy your curiosity about the king and his activities.

You should know that the rare illnesses, which have been present here lately, are greatly lessened, thanks to God. His Majesty knows that exercising is the best way to prevent sickness. He is almost every day at the hunt, where there is not his equal in the world. He also has a good state of health; he does in perfection all the exercises of body and spirit, and these are poor in so many others who suffer from illness.

Judge the king's superior ability to recall names. He can recall the names of 4,000 people, and he has only to see a person once to know his name forever. His spirit and judgement are evident in the choice of his Ministers and in his management of his business. His conduct puts all the Political figures that have allied with the institution of the Princes to shame, and they are not honest about what they say. The king is an excellent horseman. A good musician. His expertise in making furniture, cannon, and arquebuse and other arms, rise to a miraculous level. His deep piety is interpreted by all his subjects as proof that he is the finest man of his Kingdom. The Queen being of this nature also, it must be said that none of their subjects have a better marriage than the king and queen have together.[350]

Figure 12.1: King Louis XIII of France. Jean Morin after Philippe de Champaigne. Circa 1639. Etching. Ailsa Bruce Mellon Fund of the USA National Gallery, Washington, D.C., USA.

Louis XIII

In the last chapter Louis XIV came to us as a clouded, proud, careful, ultra polite programmer of many European wars in the seventeenth century, but he was not a captain...not a warrior. He watched military sieges he had ordered placed from a distance and his horse's hooves did not get wet at the famous crossing of the Rhine in 1672. His father, Louis XIII on the other hand, was a leader of his men, unfeeling to cold or heat, always on horseback going to somewhere that he had recently left a few days or weeks ago. Louis XIII is the man accused by Voltaire and Dumas[351] as being either the cuckolded husband of the devious, adulterous Anne of Austria, mother of the Mask, or himself the devious, adulterous sire of the Mask with an unknown lady. Being a central figure in the mystery, his life and personality are of interest.

CHAPTER 12. LOUIS XIII: A MEDICAL EXAMINATION

Louis XIII was born at the chateau of Fontainebleau on September 27, 1601, and he died at the chateau of Saint-Germain-en-Laye on May 14, 1643. His father was Henri IV, king of France and Navarre, former chief of the Protestant military forces in the last phase of the wars between Catholics and Protestants in France in the late 1500s, and his mother was Marie de' Medici (1575–1642), a daughter of a Habsburg archduchess and a Medici grand duke of Florence. Queen Marie was regent for Louis XIII until he was old enough to rule, and, to his great distress, refused to give up power until forced. Louis XIII and his wife Anne of Austria, the daughter of the Spanish king Philip III, had two children, both boys, one born in September 1638, who would be Louis XIV, and one born in September 1640, Philippe, who would be the duc d'Orléans.

The above newspaper article signed by *Gazette* editor Théophraste Renaudot (1586–1653) in 1631 about King Louis XIII may have been written by Cardinal Richelieu, chief minister of state. Renaudot, a doctor, had been encouraged by Cardinal Richelieu and Louis XIII to start the *Gazette* for which both men wrote anonymous articles to put their version of political events on the street and to humor the population with comforting descriptions of how fine everything was going at court and on the battlefield. In 1638 Renaudot received the direction of another newspaper already in print, the *Mercure français*, and in 1652 he was appointed historian of the king.[352]

Louis XIII faced the challenges he was given (father assassinated, dysfunctional family, royal responsibilities that, because he stuttered and lisped, made him embarrassed and angry, Catholic versus Protestant quarrels that the Edict of Nantes had not prevented, the descendants of the Habsburg emperor Charles V maneuvering to use France's domestic turmoils to their advantage, and much else) bravely and was able to find, listen to, and support a person who was capable of shouldering the difficult international and domestic problems of the time, Cardinal Armand-Jean du Plessis de Richelieu (1585–1642). Tuberculosis probably was the ultimate cause of Louis XIII's death at age forty-two but his intestinal problems, exacerbated by the medical treatments of the time, forced purging and anal evacuation, were able to torture him quite thoroughly while the tuberculosis progressed.

Lloyd Moote in his book *Louis XIII, the Just* said that there was a sadistic side to the king. His curiosity on the battlefield about agonizing and dead soldiers was noted by memoir writers, who say when he came upon a contorted dead face, he, from his war horse, imitated the ghoulish expression. Some sort of fascination there for pain and for memorizing it. Moote's book and others about Louis XIII explain that he was an exacting man in his personal affairs, especially when he felt he had been badly used. Not an unusual attitude for an absolutist king, but rather than ordering the offender to prison or to exile, he had a liking for contracts to be written, notifying his victim in print of his or her risky behavior, something Henry VIII of England or Sulieman the Magnificent would not have taken two seconds' interest in. Louis was born in a time when horoscopes were taken very seriously and there was usually a specialist present at the birth of heirs to the throne ready to pounce on the exact moment of delivery and from there cut the black sky up into the astrological sections that were relevant to the birth and then write an analysis of the temperment of the future ruler. His birth sign was the Balance, so he was immediately known to be *"le Juste"* (the one who gives justice) and this sobriquet remained attached to his Christian name.

I believe that *"le Juste"* may not have as much to do with his application of justice as one would think at the first hearing of it, but it certainly describes his neurotic need for control in his personal relationships, and when there were errors in these he insisted on specifing on paper his opinions and corrective actions. "Just"... as in just so; or just do as I say; or be aware that I have concentrated on your inadequacy for a lengthy period, have dissected it completely, have examined the alternatives for my actions with great intensity. He would, when worked up into a storm of angst, order Richelieu to delay his regular work—such as consulting ambassadors and spies, directing the king's council, planning military advances or retreats aimed at keeping France out of range of fire of the Spanish and Austrian Habsburgs—to be a paralegal editor of Louis' little contracts. The liking for writing contracts came early to Louis. At age nine, not long after his father died, according to his doctor, to amuse himself on a Saturday afternoon (June 26, 1610), he contrived a little game whereby he "married" his dwarf Dumont to Marine, a dwarf of Queen Mother Marie de' Medici; he asked for paper and wrote the contract for it.[353] "Just," as a nickname for Louis XIII, in my opinion, has to do with an obsessive need for precision, especially for precision in matters of the heart where precision is impossible. The heart beats with a rhythm, blood flows in spurts, love is alternating, there is no precision in interpersonal relationships.

Louis got along well with men and had platonic and sexual boyfriends; two young lovers in particular fell into the latter category and he had to face the tragedy of finding that both of them were conspiring against him. The important relationship of the boy with his father was both loving and provoking. Henri IV and Louis were both stubborn characters with tempers; Henri, one of whose nicknames was *"le vert galant,"* meaning "always ready for love," was passionately fond of many mistresses and the babies they delivered for him, and he wanted them all raised in the same nursery at the château of Saint-Germain-en-Laye with his legitimate children from Marie de' Medici thinking, perhaps, that they would all be happy together? Henri II (1519–1559) also had blended his legitimate and illegitimate children at Saint-Germain,[354] it was the way things were traditionally done, and *holà* to

CHAPTER 12. LOUIS XIII: A MEDICAL EXAMINATION   199

anyone who sneered at it as improper, which many people did, especially the dauphin himself. Louis, the legitimate heir to the throne, hated his half brothers and sisters and openly despised the mistresses who slept with his father. Henri, who was not coy about his impurity, joked with his son about sex and penises and set the tone for the crude sensuality that ruled the life of the court. Perhaps that was the reason Louis was such a prude. Henri IV, as we said early in this book, was violently assassinated in Paris on May 14, 1610 while in his carriage that was stopped in a traffic jam. The nine-year-old Louis was witness to the carriage barrelling back into the *Cour Carrée* of the Louvre, his guards and courtiers lowering the bleeding king into a chair in the corner of the courtyard where there was a spiral stair to take him to his rooms. They gave his lips some wine but his body never felt the drops. He was dead before his supporters reached the first tread.[355] The scene must have been on Louis' mind often.

His relationships with women were more complicated. He showed love, in his own way, for a number of women, including his mother, Marie de' Medici, who gave him reason not to love her. His ability to forgive her repetitive gross acts of selfishness and treason are admirable but overly patient. It is a sign of his sanity that he finally exiled her. Some people can unwind a kingdom faster than others and she was one of a number of those that Louis XIII had to contend with in his lifetime. He was fond of his dead father's divorced first wife, Marguerite de Valois (called sometimes Queen Margot), one of Catherine de' Medici's children, and she was affectionate to him. She had no children and willed him her valuable *hôtel* and gardens along the river opposite the Louvre in Paris but she was so in debt when she died that it all had to be sold to pay the creditors.[356]

Louis XIII was a gifted artist and craftsman, as *Monsieur le docteur* Renaudot told his curious readers in 1631. He made miniature weapons and model forts, and presented his firstborn son with a small *arquebuse* he had forged himself. He was a painter and music writer, a guitar player; he enjoyed cooking omlettes and desserts for his friends. Roland Mousnier says, "On the third floor [of the pavilion of the king at the Louvre there were] large and lovely rooms, vast and well lit where Louis XIII had his forge, his carpentry workshop, his printing press, his painting easel, and the desk where he wrote articles for the *Gazette de France* and the *Mercure français*, first worker and first journalist of the kingdom."[357] He learned from a German expert carpenter to use special tools to produce furniture pieces that had curved legs and backs in the new style. His artistic talents were inherited from his mother, who could draw and paint well and attracted to France Italian and Dutch artists and architects, including Rubens and Giambologna. He wore simple clothes in brown or black and avoided ceremony whenever he could.[358] Above all he loved hunting and being on task with his soldiers, both of which involved horses, that he rode very well, and his dogs, which were at Louis' side in large numbers all his life. He could make and repair his own bridles, reins, and leads. His friends noticed that he could hunt day and night, seeming never to tire and never sweating. He also rarely blew his nose.[359] His body did not conduct his inner waters very well, it seems.

Biographers of Louis XIII, after presenting plenty of sad and worrisome personal traits, usually sum up his character in tones as laudatory as Doctor Renaudot's. Victor Lucien Tapié in his 1967 book on Louis XIII and Richelieu, in writing about a serious illness of the king in 1630 that the doctors thought would take his life, described the people's chagrin over their king's possible demise: "Despite his personal failings, his stern character, his stiff and intimidating dignity, he illicited the respect of all and the affection of some who benefited by his courage, by his devotion, not to himself, but to a salient, grand task."[360]

Louis XIII Was Married To Anne Of Austria

However, when Anne of Austria's biographers analyze her husband, often the opinion is just as strong that the king was an unfeeling, spoiled cad whose addiction to his own somber hauteur ruined his life and would have been the downfall of France had it not been for Richelieu who knew how to simultaneously manage foreign threats and quiet the king when he had fits of melancholy and paranoia. The following exchange between the king and Mademoiselle de Hautefort (1616–1691), his focus of nervous attention at the time of his wife's pregnancy, during the queen's labor in giving birth to the future Louis XIV obviously gave Anne's biographer Claude Dulong the chills:

> In the night of the 4 to 5 September, at last, the pains of the queen started. The labor was so hard for a little while that they feared for her life. Mlle de Hautefort, in the alcove of a window, was found crying by the king. The king told her there was no reason to be sad. Surprised, shocked, the young lady attendant and friend of Anne could not stop herself from reproaching the king for his insensibility. 'I will be satisfied if they can save the child,' he said, 'and I'll leave it to you to grieve for the mother.'

Some historians have been so disgusted by this nasty comment that they have refused to believe it. But, says Dulong, it is just the sort of thing Louis XIII would say... it fits his character. "What an incomprehensible person, really, and how we recoil at such a man!"[361]

CHAPTER 12. LOUIS XIII: A MEDICAL EXAMINATION 201

His tangles with the Habsburgs, the Savoyards, the Mantuans, his Protestant minority in their own fortified enclaves, and his personal heartaches with his family paled in comparison to his greatest dilemma, the lack of an heir to his throne, and this could not be solved by his justice alone. As kings and emperors throughout history have found frequently, solving political problems could be much helped or even solved by an heir, and a legitimate heir was not always easy to come by. The solution to that problem depended on an amicable relationship with his wife, Anne of Austria, and their marriage remained what it had been in 1601 when Anne and Louis were born days apart and both sets of parents, one in Spain and one in France, began negotiating a political pairing, formalized in 1615 when man and wife were fourteen years old, that decayed a little more each year, especially after Anne's miscarriages began. Louis himself was largely responsible for the roadblocks. His rigid expectations of her, a person very different from him, made for strains in many aspects of their lives, and Richelieu, motivated to obstruct their union to maintain his influence over the king as well as other personal desires, subtly manipulated their marriage.

By 1622 the couple had had three years of conjugal relations, at least one miscarriage in 1619, during a time in the king and queen's marriage that they had been fond of each other, and no births of live children. On March 14, 1622, the pregnant queen fell on the steps of the *Tribunal*,[362] a little stage at the south end of the salle des Caryatides where kings would sit on a throne to watch their courtiers who danced and frolicked during ceremonies and parties under a little salient balcony on the north end of the room where musicians played.[363] A miscarriage of a male fetus resulted from the fall.[364]

The most aggravating thing about this miscarriage from Louis' point of view was that its cause was frivolity. Louis XIII hated frivolity. He hated play, he hated fun for fun's sake, he hated jokes, he hated aimless chatter, he hated carelessness. After midnight, Anne, returning from a party given by the princesse de Conti[365] with two friends, found herself forcibly encircled in their arms and being skipped across the stone tile floor as a stunt. The king never forgave her and even after two live births in 1638 and 1640, Louis was semi-estranged from Anne until he died in 1643,[366] a viciously narrow, obsessive, destructive attitude which nearly resulted in the end of Bourbon rule in France, not to mention the pain it caused his wife.

Indeed it would be wishful thinking (or propaganda) to say, with Monsieur Renaudot, that no French subjects had "a better marriage than the king and queen have together." During the three years before March of 1622 their marriage had been at least friendly, but after that fall on the throne steps Louis had no affection for his wife. He had decided that an unnecessary, scatterbrained act of a few moments, even though others had instigated it, defined his wife and that was her permanent caricature...just so. From that point their relationship was a mixture of required public joint appearances and synchronized, all business meetings in bed that resulted in miscarriages.

Doctor Jean Héroard

The reason we know more about the youth of Louis XIII than any other king in history is that his doctor, Jean Héroard (1551–1628), kept a daily journal that described almost every minute of the boy's life from his birth to age twenty-seven. Héroard was appointed by King Henri IV to be doctor to his son the dauphin. Doctor Héroard was, as all good doctors should be but as few were in the seventeenth century, very attentive to details and believed that taking care of a patient, at least this particular royal patient, meant keeping a meticulous journal. This he did so ably and thoroughly and for so long that we have from the good doctor a journal of Louis XIII's state of health from the moment he was born on September 27, 1601 to 1628, when the doctor died, leaving Louis at twenty-seven years of age without his constant companion and healer. Héroard was ahead of his time in his medical practice in connecting physical health with mental health because he also wrote in the journal Louis' day-to-day activities, the hour he woke, what he ate, what time of day he went to see his mother in her rooms, how many times he had sex with his wife, when he went to mass, and when he practiced dancing and drawing. Héroard told us of the infant's first hours, the toddler's first tantrums, the arguments with his father, examples of the giddy adventures that the young boy had, such as the one on a drive with his guards and a pet monkey in his carriage (22 August 1612).[367] When the monkey took fright after Louis ordered fireworks to be shot off, he defecated all over the dauphin and the carriage. His aides had to take the boy to the river to wash him off. Such things we know only because of Doctor Héroard.

Inheritance

As complete as Doctor Héroard's multi-volume notes are on the day-to-day existence of Louis XIII, there are certain physical characteristics of the king that are not explained as fully (or at all) as would be in a medical report today, particularly some that are inherited deficiencies and craniofacial differences.

In the seventeenth century marks and scars from wounds received in battle, nutritional deficits, consequences of syphilis, and inherited defects, among many other evils were common and often not hidden from public view. There were no surgical repairs for them, so handicaps were accepted and family and friends were indifferent, unless the deformity was massive, in

CHAPTER 12. LOUIS XIII: A MEDICAL EXAMINATION

which case the person would be put away in a lodging of the family, of a servant, or in a convent and sequestered, or if the person was poor, he would become homeless and wouldn't live long. Therefore the following aspects of Louis XIII's body were probably not considered of any importance, certainly not to his ability to supervise council meetings, hunt animals, fight in battle, get on and off a horse, or sire heirs, which were essential duties of a king. Whether for that or some other reason, Doctor Héroard didn't write much about his master's physical challenges.

Baron Edward Herbert of Cherbury (1582–1648) was an ambassador from the English court to the court of Louis XIII from 1622 to 1624. He was also a philosopher, courtier, author of a book on Henry VIII, and author of comments on Louis XIII's physical appearance, that being a category of information that all ambassadors commonly transmitted to their handlers at home, since everything that was noticed was possibly useful.

Lord Herbert of Cherbury wrote in his diary on the day that he was first introduced to the king of France:

> ...this being done, I presented to the king a letter of credence from the king my master: the king assured me of a reciprocal affection to the king my master, and of my particular welcome to his court: his words were never many, as being so extream [sic] a stutterer that he wou'd sometimes hold his tongue out of his mouth a good while before he cou'd speak so much as one word; he had besides a double row of teeth, and was observed seldom or never to spit or blow his nose, or to sweat much, 'tho he were very laborious, and almost indefatigible in his excercises of hunting and hawking, to which he was much addicted: neither did it hinder him, 'tho he was burst in his body, as we call it, or herniosus; for he was noted in those sports, 'tho often times on foot, to tire not only his courtiers, but even his lackies, being equally insensible, as was thought, either of heat or cold: his understanding and natural parts were as good as cou'd be expected in one that was brought up in such ignorance, which was on purpose so done that he might be the better governed, howbeit, he acquired in time a great knowledge in affairs, as conversing for the most part with wise and active persons.[368]

The ambassador says, in brief, that Louis XIII stuttered, held his mouth open for long moments before he could form words, had extra teeth in his mouth, rarely spit or blew his nose, and although he was prone to "ruptures" in his body (herniosus), nevertheless he indulged in extreme exercise in all weathers. These are blunt revelations that repel the vision of a "king": a velvet cloaked, well formed man on a beautiful horse urging his captains forward with eloquent, authoritarian directives. The ambassador was not writing propaganda to the king of England, propaganda and subtlety being for newspaper editors; he wanted his master at home to know that Louis XIII had some physical abnormalities and a speech defect.

Claude Dulong in her book on Anne of Austria also told of Louis' stuttering and deficiency of fluid drainage. She says that it was thought that perhaps Louis XIII had epilepsy because he had seizures from time to time, but these never included incontinence or tongue biting, which frequently happen with epileptic seizures.[369] Dulong also said that Louis was slightly "hydrocephalic,"[370] which means having fluid in the brain, but there is no evidence that excess fluid in the brain was one of Louis' many medical problems. I think her comment is a misnomer for the marked length of his face, which makes his head look overly large. He had a short forehead, below which was a long, narrow face and an extended, pointed chin. Anne of Austria's biographer suggests Louis had hypertrophy of adenoids and tonsils that resulted in the paucity of nasal secretions, but since the problem was evident in other parts of his body (sweat glands), she doesn't commit to this diagnosis.[371]

A Cold Case

For a long time this mystery has been what law enforcement detectives call "a cold case," an old crime that was never solved because proof, or even reputable evidence, was never found. Cold cases of long standing are, beginning only a few years ago, being deciphered and even solved by the use of data which has been developed by the study of the human genome. Bits of a suspect's DNA can be put into a massive database of DNA from thousands of people and results can be exculpatory for the crime or the opposite. About five years into my study about the mystery, I followed up on some descriptions of Louis XIII's odd physical characteristics, or traits, as gene scientists call them. I had not expected to find anything in particular about the mystery, only about the king, who intrigued me. I soon saw I would need to learn enough about genes and how they behave to understand the king's odd craniofacial traits. I learned that those traits might have had a relationship with his severe chronic intestinal problems... and with cleft palate, even though his genes for cleft palate had not produced the trait... he did not have cleft lip/palate but was liable to have children with cleft lip and or palate.

Predictions

Louis XIII's extra teeth, lack of ability to keep his mouth fully closed when he desired it to be closed, and insufficiency of sweat and mucus are physical manifestations of genetic markers in human chromosomes for cleft lip and palate.

Geneticists have concluded that those who have one or more of the above and certain other physical anomalies have an increased probability, compared to the general population, *of having siblings and/or offspring who have fully presenting cleft lip and/or palate.* A person with the genes for cleft lip/palate who does *not* have a cleft, often, nevertheless, has a structural insufficiency in the maxillofacial bones, muscles, and dental ridge that gene mappers have discovered comes from genes associated with clefts. The insufficiency may or may not show itself on the face.

Craniofacial specialists can now decide if there is a probability that a couple's unborn child may have a cleft lip/palate by examining the teeth, jaws, mouth muscles, and palates of the parents and asking about any craniofacial abnormalities that their parents or close relatives had. Overt cleft palate history in a parent would certainly be a predictor of cleft lip/palate in an offspring, but, after finding other mutations on the gene locations[372] where cleft lip/palate is found, geneticists have concluded there is a predictive value in anomalies that do not present as overt cleft.

Double Row Of Teeth

Dental surgeons call the eruption of a tooth or teeth in an abnormal position an ectopic eruption. Lord Herbert of Cherbury may have been told by someone about Louis's extra teeth because it isn't likely that Louis showed them off to people, but in any event he either saw the extra teeth in the upper jaw of the king's mouth or knew absolutely they were there. A memoir by a member of the Burgundian parlement, Monsieur Philibert de La Mare (1615–1687), published between 1670 and 1682, also mentions a double row of upper teeth. "Louis XIII had a double row of top teeth and this is what caused him difficulty in speaking, which in turn made him angry and unsociable."[373]

Whether there was a "double row" of teeth or simply extra teeth that appeared to be a double row we can't know but if he had a syndrome (a group of symptoms that form a predictable core) associated with double rows of teeth, like Gardner's syndrome, he could well have had an entire duplicate row.[374] Gardner's syndrome also presents with tumors and cysts in the intestines (colorectal polyposis and Desmoid tumors) and since we know that

Louis XIII had chronic intestinal problems and almost died of an infected cyst in his intestines in 1630, it is possible he had Gardner's syndrome. It is impossible to diagnose a syndrome without advanced medical tests, which it isn't likely we will ever have on Louis XIII unless DNA could be found that could be tested.

Dental abnormalities—such as supernumerary (extra) teeth, microdontia, tooth agenesis, impaction (teeth that form but do not descend), pulp stones, ectopic teeth, and a variety of abnormalities of the roots and pulp of the teeth that have to do with size, position, and the ratio of parts of the teeth above the gum line with parts of the teeth below the gum line—of teeth in a relative (parent, brother, sister, grandparent) who does not have cleft lip/palate contend for cleft lip/palate in offspring that have the genes of any of these relatives.[375] We have seen above that Louis XIII had some of these teeth abnormalities, i.e. supernumerary teeth.

Orbicularis Oris Deficiency

Madeleine Foisil, an historian of Louis XIII's childhood, separates her readers even further from the glorified *topos* of "king." She wrote, "[His] right eye was fragile and teared chronically.[376] His mouth was not fully closed, exposing his tongue that he chewed especially when he was angry."[377]

The lack of muscle strength to keep one's mouth fully closed is a deficiency of the band of orbicularis oris muscles that encircles the mouth, attaches to the upper jaw, the lower jaw, and the lips, and is used to close the mouth. Gaston, Louis XIII's brother, also had difficulty closing his mouth.[378]

There can be subtle although noticeable signs of mouth muscle weakness in a family member without cleft lip/palate that may be genetically linked to obviously presenting cleft lip/palate in another family member. Some relatives of individuals with overt cleft lip/palate have been found in medical studies to have a significantly increased frequency of orbicularis oris defects compared with controls with no family history of cleft lip/palate.[379] One study that reached this conclusion found that orbicularis oris muscle discontinuities were found in 10.3 percent of the non-cleft relatives, a statistical significance of ($P=0.04$). Male "unaffected" relatives had a significantly higher rate of discontinuities than male controls (12.0% vs. 3.2%; $P=0.01$).[380]

The insufficiency of mouth muscles can also be connected to what is called "Long face syndrome," and portraits of Louis XIII in childhood and adulthood show that his face was long and narrow with a long triangle-shaped chin. The term "Long face" used in dental, craniofacial, and orthodontic medical practice means excessive vertical growth of the upper jaw.

The primary distinguishing characteristic of the long face pattern is a large total anterior facial height that manifests almost entirely in the elongation of the lower third of the face, leading to disproportions on the facial height and width indices. A major component of the problem nearly always is an inferior rotation of the posterior maxilla. As face height increases and the maxillary palatal plane and posterior teeth are more inferior, the mandible tends to rotate downward and backward. For this reason, the vertical disproportion also affects antero-posterior jaw relationships.[381]

Joanna of Austria's (maternal grandmother of Louis XIII) portraits show maxillary deficiency and a long face, which was scientifically established by a study of her cranium and skeleton by archeologists and dentoskeletal specialists in 2005 using state-of-the-art radiology. The archduchess was the first wife of Francesco de' Medici and was buried in the Medici chapel in Florence, safe from the French revolutionaries' thorough ditching of all the French royal burials from the Saint-Denis necropolis near Paris between 12 and 25 October, 1793.

The remains had been thrown in the pits without care or organization. Those who came to take them out on January 18, 1817, placed them in five great coffins, four with bones from the Valois and a fifth with bones of the Bourbon. They took these in procession to the chapel of the church. The next day they went to the crypt.[382]

This unusual growth of the upper jaw and the lower jaw in tandem with a mouth muscle defect illustrates that all face parts make way for each other for better or worse, in terms of aesthetics and function.

Body Cavities

We heard Lord Herbert of Cherbury, ambassador to France from England, say of Louis XIII, "...*he was observed seldom or never to spit or blow his nose, or to sweat much.*" Louis XIII's sweating difficulty is called hypohidrosis, which is an abnormal deficiency of sweat in response to heat. It may seem illogical that sweat and sinus glands are related to teeth, but in chromosomes, they are.

Marvellous is the process of generation that takes place in a baby not yet born. Future body parts with cavities are created simultaneously in the fetus, but the cavities are not all destined to be in the same place in the child's body. They are spread out over the organism and are for different purposes and will be different sizes in the finished human child. Once again, gene mapping gives an answer to one of the small puzzles about Louis XIII's health:

> Hair, teeth, sweat glands and...breasts, organs seemingly so various in their purpose and plan, are intimately connected. They are all places where skin has swollen or cavitated to make something new. The simple tube that is a hair follicle, the robust anvil of dentine and enamel that is a tooth, and the bulging burden of ducts that is a breast, are all variations on a constructional theme. A genetic disorder—there are more than a hundred—that affects one of these organs will often affect another. These organs do not merely share an origin in skin; they are also made in much the same way. Even as hair follicles are forming throughout the foetal epidermis, other epidermal cells are clumping and cavitating to form teeth or mammary glands. Like the hair follicle, each of these skin organs is a chimera: part ectoderm, part mesoderm."[383]

Hypohidrosis and cleft lip/palate can occur together because the errors in these two seemingly disparate body attributes—sweat glands and the roof of the mouth—have the same genetic origin.

Stuttering

As to Louis XIII's stuttering: the behavior has a tendency to run in families but gene mappers have not found the genes for stuttering. The third son of Henri IV's brother, François I de Bourbon, prince de Conti (1558–1614), stuttered.

Sometimes when we find that a hero is flawed, we are disappointed, and Louis XIII had some faults that were on a continuum from serious personality disorders to unpleasant medical conditions. He was certainly depressed, obsessive-compulsive, ornery, stubborn, sadistic, and unpredictable. Some of his dangerous and irritable personality traits might have been caused by his physical disorders, especially his stuttering, which, for anyone whose main purpose in life is to be a smooth public figure, would be embarrassing and disorienting. But on the other hand, the king managed his challenges with courage in an era when there were no medical interventions to help him keep his mouth closed, no speech therapy lessons, no craniofacial specialists. He had many military successes and brought France to the entrance of its greatest period of absolutism while pursuing personal artistic

CHAPTER 12. LOUIS XIII: A MEDICAL EXAMINATION

aims in which he achieved great competence; he was satisfied, from time to time, with great loves, and, though he didn't believe it, he was married to a woman who loved him and who bore him successful children who were faithful to his memory and political vision.

Philosophy is the knowledge of what things are, of the essence of things. Voltaire, captain in our travel through the subject of the Man in the Iron Mask, was a philosopher *par excellence*. His very name comes to mind when one says "philosopher." Voltaire was asked by the editors of the *Encyclopédie*, which the editors claimed to be the collection of all knowledge, to write an article on the certainty of history; his axiom was, "All certainty that does not consist of mathematical demonstration is nothing more than the highest probability. There is no other historical certainty."[384]

Agreed. Without DNA analysis, we cannot know if Louis XIII had hypohidrosis, carried genes for cleft palate, or had Gardner's syndrome. Only an analysis of his DNA could explain the reasons for the king's traits and physical processes that were described by witnesses.

"Miserable Anecdotes, Without Truth Or Likelihood"

"The interest of this work is to understand why," said Mask author Jean-Denis Bergasse, "history is not ranked among the exact sciences because the historian has to either look directly at the truth, although is ultimately unable to prove this truth, or fall victim to the temptation of making history as he would like it to be."[385] There is a word in the dictionary for this temptation: pareidolia, the perception of a pattern or meaning where it does not exist, which historians should always avoid; however it is hard to avoid in this story because there are so many events, people, and testimonies that show, not a pattern but a map of disparate elements that bump into each other from time to time. One has to actively resist the temptation to make more of coincidentals than should be made. It is true that it has always been easy for those who want to take personal advantage of the story of these royal characters to blend them in such a way that an exciting *denouement* results. A secretary of the duc de Richelieu[386] named Jean-Louis Soulavie (1752–1813) wrote a supposedly historical account of a story that he claimed the duc de Richelieu told him—a romantic account about the Mask being a brother of Louis XIV. One author read another author and produced variations on the theme and this is the way that some clever explanations of the Mask's royal parentage and supposed sibling came into the popular novels of Dumas and spread from there to movie theaters.

It is usually Voltaire who gets blamed for pareidolia in the mystery of the Mask. Recall that Bergasse called Voltaire "*magicien et charmeur de l'Europe*," because he suggested the Mask was a twin or half brother of the King Louis XIV. Father Joseph Delort could have been speaking to a penitent in his confessional, so strained and strict was his condemnation of the story that Soulavie told. "The *Mémoires* of the duc de Richelieu told us that he was a twin of Louis XIV who was supressed. These *Mémoires* are a heap of dirty, ignorant, miserable anecdotes, without truth or likelihood."[387]

One of the first scholars to examine the case, Marius Topin (1838–1895), was a little calmer in his criticism of the Louis XIV brother theory than Delort but he was also adamant:

> Between us, the most porous theory of the identity of the Mask, but also the most dazzling, is the one that makes the *Masque de fer* a brother of Louis XIV. Montesquieu once said 'There are things that people say just because they once heard them said.' That is true, above all things that are extraordinary or marvellous. That is why when the *Masque de fer* is mentioned, most people immediately connect him with a brother of Louis XIV. Whether he was born from a love affair between Anne of Austria and Buckingham, or that, a legitimate son of Louis XIII, he was the twin brother of Louis XIV, doesn't matter to the average person. Those theories are variations in a solution that is profoundly rooted in the public mind, and that it would be preferable to totally eliminate, because it still has numerous believers, and it touches on the rights to the Bourbons to the throne of France.
>
> Who came up with this much published theory and who revived it in our day? What proof, or at least what probabilities can be produced? On what memories, on what writing is this supposition based? Are there official documents that support this? Does this solution comport with the character of Anne of Austria and Louis XIII? Is it reasonable? I spoke in the past tense because in supposing (which we hope to show was impossible) that the *Masque de fer* was an older brother of Louis XIV, it remains that he did not leave posterity, so the crown would have legitimately come to Louis XIV.[388]

Mask author Jean Markale was yet more reserved about the brother/twin story: "But when one comes across wormholes in History, it is tempting to explore them."[389]

13. Secondary Plan Of Nature

Many times it happeneth that a portion or part of the bone of the pallat, being broken with the shot of a gun, or corroded by the virulency of the Lues venerea, falls away, which makes the patients to whom this happeneth, that they cannot pronounce their words distinctly, but obscurely and snuffling: therefore I have thought it a thing worthy the labour to shew the meanes how it may be helped by art.

—Ambroise Paré, 1575

Singular

When I began studying the Man in the Iron Mask, I thought that he possibly had Down syndrome. In my professional life as a journalist, I interviewed many experts for articles about complex subjects, and so I felt comfortable contacting the Clinical Center for the Study of Development and Learning at the University of North Carolina at Chapel Hill, located about a mile away from my house, where, I guessed, there would be an expert on Down syndrome who could confirm my analysis of the problem of the Man in the Iron Mask. I look back on my naïve confidence of that day and cringe. Such bravado.

I was forwarded to Professor Stephen Hooper, an expert in child neuropsychology and then (in 2009) director of the center. He is, at the time of this writing, associate dean and chair of the Department of Allied Health Sciences in the UNC-CH School of Medicine, professor of psychiatry, and has many prestigious posts at the development and learning center.

I made a list in preparation for my meeting with Professor Hooper of the few certain descriptions we have from eyewitnesses about Eustache Dauger, mostly from jailers who worked at the prisons where Eustache lived. With this sparse list of reliable descriptions, I thought the professor would be able to make a judgement about whether the Mask had a developmental disability, such as Down syndrome. Here is the list I made and showed to Professor Hooper:

- Saint-Mars, the Mask's supervisor in prison, and his staff respected

him;
- Eustache never complained about any aspect of his prison life or asked to leave it;
- He was given anything that he asked for that was customarily allowed a prisoner;
- He wore a mask over his upper face when he went out of his cell, at least at the end of his life;
- He was "interesting" by virtue of the "singular tone" of his voice;
- Observers could see his lips and teeth even when he had his mask on;
- He kept a pair of polished tweezers with him;
- His skin was light brown or olive;
- His hair was prematurely grey, perhaps even white;
- He was threatened by his jailers with instant death if he said his name or anything about himself;
- He was tall (whatever that meant at that time—people were shorter then than now—so we cannot know whether this means tall in our modern conception, which might be six feet or taller, or tall for that era, which could be five feet, eight inches or even less);
- He had a normal body, presumably in the sense that he didn't lack a leg or an arm or have a limp or a misformed body;
- A witness at Sainte-Marguerite prison said he had thicker than average lower legs;
- His clothing was often brown or black;
- The staff procured for him fine linen and books;
- The Governor and his staff remained standing and respectfully abstained from wearing their hats when in his presence;
- The Governor and his staff went often to eat with him;
- He was known among the staff as "La Tour."

I explained to Professor Hooper the object of my visit: solving the mystery of the Man in the Iron Mask. Professor Hooper is a scholar of neuropsychology; his research and that of many other senior researchers in the field whose work he administers are respected specialists on the development of the human brain. He might have thought, after I got through with my introduction, that he was facing yet another person with a developmental problem, one whose resistance to impulse was so weak that she couldn't stop herself from interrupting the morning of a major university clinical center with questions about French history. But he was polite enough not to pull his chair back from the table in the conference room where we were, knit his brows together, and look for the intercom button. On the contrary, he listened patiently to my list of Eustache Dauger's qualities, for which I am profoundly grateful, because his calm answers to my questions have made all the difference. Maybe he was intrigued by being presented with an odd problem that seemed to be harmless—a distraction from the other arduous

CHAPTER 13. SECONDARY PLAN OF NATURE

and consequential queries he had to worry about that morning.

After listening to my reading of the list, he, without any delay, said the prisoner did not have Down syndrome. He said that the prisoner was obeying orders and being patient and that Down syndrome people do not always do that. Professor Hooper said it sounded like this man had more "cognitive reserve" than a person with Down syndrome would have had, indicated by the fact that the masked prisoner understood the rules and could follow them. The Mask also did not seem to show perseveration, which is doing the same thing over and over again even if it doesn't get the results wanted; he was not missing cues from other people. In short, he showed flexibility and competence in interpreting the cues from his surroundings and the people in charge of him. Men and women with Down syndrome tend to have perseveration and cannot always accurately interpret ambiguous messages coming from other people.

That took the wind out of me. I was disappointed that my planned, easy slide to illumination had been so quickly blocked. It had taken only five minutes. After I opened my mouth again I heard myself asking him what he thought about the Mask's constellation of characteristics. Any ideas? He offered me this suggestion: the reason for the mask might have been to hide a cleft lip and palate. People with unrepaired cleft lip and palate, he said, are embarrassed about the deformity of their nose and mouth and tend to put something over them when they are in public. Cleft palate patients also have a singular tone to their voices, a whistling, irregular nasality.

He had put together the wearing of a mask and the "singular tone" of Eustache's voice. Hooper's professional opinion was that the masked man had a cleft lip and palate and wore the mask in public to cover the birth defect. He didn't have any comments about the other items on my list, as dressing in brown clothes and the rest of the descriptions were now obviously put off to a future, less important set of questions, not for him but for me. We both calmly accepted the answer to the main problem.

Suddenly, I saw Eustache Dauger's prison. He had been trapped by a facial birth defect long before being trapped by Louis XIV. I immediately admired him for enduring so patiently and honorably a tremendously difficult existence. Such a person deserves the attention that has been given to him for three hundred years by scholars and distinguished writers and by ordinary people all over the world who have casually picked up a paperback about him and not been able to put it down until late Sunday night with a sense of restlessness when the last page did not solve the mystery. I awoke to the fact that Eustache richly deserved all the previous dedication to explaining his story by Petitfils, Montgrédien, Vergé-Franceschi, Voltaire, Iung, Delort, Duvivier, Sonnino, Noone, Tiollas, Mast, and many others. I thought that if Eustache had had the courage to live as he did, I could at least have the courage to enter the reading rooms that these brave scholars had entered. I would not leave him until I had tested the hypothesis and, if it proved substantial, to propose this solution to the mystery.

All well and good to have an insight into a possible clinical secret of the Man in the Iron Mask, but none of the books I had read on the Mask considered the possibility that Eustache Dauger had a facial birth defect. I was to be a pioneer guided only by the small set of descriptions about the Mask's physical attributes that were given by witnesses. While these descriptions have been presented in each book, article, and play about the Mask, some of them have had too little attention. They have not been researched as medical clues, and in most cases, they have been mentioned, then dropped by the wayside like used wrapping paper while opening the same boxes over and over again only to find the same questions, the same suspects, and the same empty answers.

The discussion of the physical and social difficulties that come with cleft lip and palate, especially in a patient whose lip and palate has not been repaired, is given here not only to show connections between descriptions of Dauger and symptoms of cleft lip and palate to help detect whether Dauger had cleft lip and palate but also to show the personal challenges he faced and how he spent part of his time during his life, as the genetic birth defect of cleft lip and palate requires regular personal care and can be accompanied by illness and pain, which Saint-Mars would have helped him manage.

Three Clues That Indicate Cleft Lip/Palate

In the descriptions of Dauger by eyewitnesses, there are three that are more revealing than the others. The first one, the mask, has been extensively reported, discussed, and analyzed, and the most popular theory among writers has been that the mask was worn to hide a facial likeness to another person outside the prison. The other two indicators of his appearance have had almost no attention at all: that the servants of Palteau saw his "lips and teeth" when looking at his masked face; and the unusual tone of his voice.

The Mask

There have been many pages written about Eustache Dauger's mask; so many that the words "Eustache Dauger" and "Mask" are interchangeable. Dauger wore a cloth mask over his upper face, including his nose, when he went out of his cell, at least during his years at the Sainte-Marguerite prison (1687–1698) and at the Bastille (1698–1703). That fact is based on numerous eyewitness reports, not the least of which is du Junca's Bastille journal entry

CHAPTER 13. SECONDARY PLAN OF NATURE   215

on the masked prisoner's death on November 19, 1703 (see chapter 2). The only people who saw Dauger without the mask were Governor Saint-Mars, Lieutenant Rosarges, Ru the turnkey, and Saint-Mars' nephew Joseph Formanoir while watching him secretly at night from a distance. Doctors who entered his cell to treat his illnesses and the priests who said mass for him only saw him with his mask on.

Lieutenant of the Bastille on 18 September 1698—the day of Dauger's arrival at the Bastille—Etienne du Junca was a conscientious man who had just met his new boss, Saint-Mars, Lieutenant Rosarges, and the members of Saint-Mars' personal military company that had traveled from Sainte-Marguerite who were from that hour his co-workers. Also with them was one prisoner. Consistent with his self-assigned task of keeping a journal entry on each prisoner, he made a report of the new arrival and of what Rosarges had told him about the history of the prisoner. Du Junca did not say the prisoner wore an iron mask (nor did anyone else, except the people who supposedly saw a metal device on his face while he was being transported to Sainte-Marguerite in April 1687). Du Junca wrote the man was "always masked."

Most writers about the mystery have said the mask was:

- To hide wounds on his face received in battle or in an attempted murder, in which he had either been the victim or the aggressor;
- To hide his resemblance to a familiar public face;
- To give him privacy.

To hide wounds on his face:

Distinguished French Mask scholar Michel Vergé-Franceschi, professor at the Université François-Rabelais in Tours, France, author of an extensive book on the Mask that was published in 2009, said the mask was worn to hide a badly wounded face.

Vergé-Franceschi says the Mask was sick and disfigured:

> If the mask was worn to hide a resemblance to some important well-known figure, as Voltaire guessed, the resemblance existed in 1669. If the prisoner did not have a mask on in 1669 it was because he arrived at Pignerol on 21 August with a face so mutiliated with fresh wounds that his skin could not stand being covered. Was his face striped with knife slashes? If so, when was the damage done and why? We can see that the prisoner arrived covered with medical dressings.[390]

To hide his resemblance to another person:

Hiding identity was the most frequent use of a face mask at that time so it makes sense that Voltaire and many others thought he was masked because he resembled the king, the king's brother or father, perhaps one of the king's cousins, or a high-ranking member of the Paris Parlement, and to keep people from knowing who he was related to, his jailers forced him to wear a mask. If Voltaire had known that the cloth mask was worn by the prisoner only when he was a mature adult and an old man, his instinct to think logically would have brought him to the following rebuttal of his resemblance theory. With age, the nose lengthens and thickens, the chin sags, wrinkles emerge, and the eyes become more hidden by folds of skin. If the jailers had forced the prisoner to wear a mask because he looked like someone else, then it would have made sense for him to have worn the mask when he was younger and not to have needed it as he grew older. Whereas the pattern we see is that he did not wear a mask when younger but reliable testimonies say that he did as an older person.

To give him privacy:

If Dauger had a facial disfigurement, the mask provided privacy and warned people off who might have unwelcome questions for him.

> When the stigmatized person's failing can be perceived by our merely directing attention (typically, visual) to him—when, in short, he is a discredited, not discreditable, person—he is likely to feel that to be present among normals nakedly exposes him to invasions of privacy, experienced most pointedly perhaps when children simply stare at him. This displeasure in being exposed can be increased by the conversations strangers may feel free to strike up with him, conversations in which they express what he takes to be morbid curiosity about his condition or in which they proffer help that he does not need or want.[391]

Covering a facial deformity (the term dentofacial disharmony is currently in use by professionals) is common among people who have had facial injuries or genetic defects that cannot be repaired to avoid uncomfortable stares from other people. During the time that I questioned social workers and speech therapists who see cleft lip/palate patients in clinical settings, I pressed them to consider that the mask that Dauger wore was for a reason other than embarrassment; perhaps it was to prevent getting sick? But they were certain that he was hiding his deformity from others out of a need to ward off stares, laughter, and taunting.

CHAPTER 13. SECONDARY PLAN OF NATURE   217

It is ironic that, while for him, the mask was a comfort, for former inmates and guards, the mask caused attention. He drew and draws attention from historians and from almost everyone who hears his story, *because of* his mask.

Two other pieces of evidence show more specifically that Dauger had cleft lip and palate, and they have not received any attention by past researchers.

Singular Tone Of Voice

Voltaire in 1751 said that a doctor who treated Dauger said that *the tone of the prisoner's voice was "singular."*

People with unrepaired cleft palate have a marked hyponasality and difficulty making certain voice sounds. This characteristic came to Voltaire third hand. It could therefore be suspect. But it has the ring of truth because it is odd enough that it is not likely to have been invented. And paired with the wearing of a mask, it balloons into a very credible clue.

In a previous chapter a quote from Voltaire's *Siècle de Louis XIV* contained the description of Eustache's unusual tone of voice. Here is that description again:

> An old doctor who treated patients at the Bastille, who had often given medical help to this singular man when he was sick, said he had never seen his face, even though he had often examined his tongue and the rest of his body. He had an admirable physique, said this doctor: his skin color was a little brunette; he was interesting by virtue of the singular tone of his voice; he never complained of his situation and never gave any hint of who he was.[392]

Researchers on the Mask have barely noticed the report by Doctor Fresquière[393] that Dauger had an unusual tone of voice. The attribute must have been quite distinct for Doctor Fresquière to have remembered so clearly that his patient had interesting speech, and his son-in-law Marsolan, who reported this to the duc de Richelieu, must have also thought this was worth repeating. The sound of someone's speech is not usually included in a description of a person unless it's very clearly out of the ordinary. One reason the doctor may have kept this memory was that he had little else to go on. He couldn't see his eyes, his skin, his nose, and not much of his mouth. He looked inside his mouth (at least he looked at his tongue), but without the bright lights that doctors have today that light up quite thoroughly our teeth, palates, cheeks, tongues, and other parts of the interior of our mouths, there was probably little the doctor could have noted there. Without a sight of the man's eyes, nose, lips, and forehead, the tone of his voice took up, by default, a central place in his assessment of the prisoner.

The doctor says Dauger was interesting due to the tone of his voice, but not only "tone" but *"le seul ton,"* which means "the singular tone."[394] "Singular" is an adjective that has the synonyms "unusual," "distinctive," "out-of-the-ordinary." Sound and tone may mean the same thing but can also mean two different things, and since the doctor did not say "sound" but "tone," then we have to think he really meant tone or he would have said "sound." Tone has to do with how the vocal chords and the nose and mouth produce the sound, how the production of air through the mouth and nose of the person affects the *tone* of the voice we hear.

An unrepaired cleft lip, even if the palate is not cleft, will cause difficulties in pronunciation because the lips are used to form many of the sounds we make for speech. Depending on how much the lip cleft has altered the ability of the muscles around the mouth to move, there may be difficulties in forming words for which strength in the lips is critical, "m" sounds and "p" sounds, for example. The most difficult pronunciations are those that involve the upper lip, which, being in two parts rather than just one, cannot be positioned properly for some sounds.

But an unrepaired cleft *palate* meddles much more severely with speech. To speak, we sculpt air that we bring up from our lungs into many hums, hisses, vibrations, brakes, and accelerations using our lips, nose, jaws, teeth, and their attached muscles. In the soft palate there are muscles that aid speech. If the palate has an opening in it, the muscles are compromised and cannot make certain speech sounds that need the full function of the muscles, especially the ability of the soft palate and the uvula, the little mass of flesh that hangs from the back of the soft palate, to touch the back of the throat making a block that stops the flow of air for certain sounds. If the air we push up from our lungs for speech does not find this congestion, it will continue on its way through the nose, and the sound of the speech will be noisy, slightly vibrating, and formed by the open nasal cavities rather than by a neat, firm stop at the back of the throat. There are a number of other "stops" in other locations in the interior of the mouth that we make when we speak, and an opening in the palate, the lips, or the dental ridge makes those stops either impossible or difficult. The speech comes to the listener as either condensed (hypernasal) or muffled (hyponasal). If the mouth parts and muscles and the bones of the jaws are not aligned so that the sounds that the patient hears can be formed, the cleft lip/palate speaker makes a phonetic approximation of a sound, or he or she may borrow a place in the mouth to make an adaptation. The person's spoken words are distorted and the voice, in addition to being "singular" is alternately weak with strong intermittent emphasis by the speaker to compensate for his difficulties.[395]

Lips And Teeth

Observers could see his lips and teeth even when he had his mask on. Guillaume-Louis Formanoir de Palteau (b. 1712) when he was a little boy heard this comment from the manor staff who were present in 1698 in his own courtyard[396] on the day Eustache Dauger arrived in a litter followed by Saint-Mars's litter and his free company on horseback.

Guillaume-Louis was told that he (or she?) could see the mysterious man's "lips and teeth" even though he wore a face mask. Through that evidence we are given information that the mask was one that covered the top of his face and was not as long as his chin. We assume it covered his nose, since the peasants did not say they saw his nose, but only his lips and teeth. The peasants saw him from some distance away and they did not speak to him, nor he to them, so we must say that this sounds as if his mouth was open or at least one tooth was visible even when he was not talking.

The servants' observation about Dauger's teeth is indicative of cleft lip/palate because patients with the birth defect have lots of teeth problems, some of them very serious. The dental ridge in the top jaw where teeth grow is affected to one degree or another in cleft palate and this affects the genesis of teeth; anomalies of both top and bottom teeth often occur.

What Are Cleft Lip And Cleft Palate?

The human body is a marvelous single organism, its design based on duality: the brain has two halves, the nose has two halves. There are many pairs of physical features and organs in the body: two ears, two arms, two legs, two lungs, for instance. These pairs are set by nature, most of the time, symmetrically, one on either side of a midline which naturally formed in each of us at the very beginning of our existence in the womb.

A cleft lip is a lip whose two sides did not completely meet each other in the process just described. The two parts of the lip are separated by an open space, sometimes with the teeth, gums, or other parts of the interior mouth revealed through the opening, depending on the size and shape of the cleft. Cleft lip can occur by itself or the aperture can be large enough to include some part or parts of the structures behind the lip and in the interior upper part of the mouth, in which case the condition is called cleft lip with a cleft palate. Palates can be cleft even if the lip and dental ridge are completely formed.

Further, because all parts of the face are in one symphonic design,[397] nature seems to lose control of the process of making face parts symmetrical when there is an incomplete closure of even one small part of the total, and so some other face features besides the divided lip and palate, such as the nose, gums, teeth, bones, and the muscles around the mouth, are irregularly placed and sometimes distorted and/or weakened.

Since there is a pathway in cleft palate patients from the mouth to the nose, liquids, including saliva, must be prevented from going into the nose. Fear of suffocation can occur for a cleft palate patient since breathing through both the nose and mouth can be stifled through accident or mistaken action, so swallowing food and liquid must be done slowly and carefully and the patient has to be ready to pull out a bolus of food if it begins to block the opening in the palate that leads to the nasal passages, using an instrument if necessary.

Studies agree, with some small differences, on the rate of occurrence of cleft lip and palate. One study in 2015 said, "In a population-based study of approximately 8 million births, the prevalence of CL/P was 9.9 per 10,000 births. This estimate was consistent with the prevalence of 10.2 per 10,000 births as reported in the United States."[398] The incidence of cleft lip and palate for male infants is twice that of females.[399] More girls than boys in Caucasians have cleft palate without cleft lip, the occurrence being about 1 in 2000 full term births.[400]

Teeth And Nose

A cleft palate causes other traits of the face to alter. Cleft lip/palate patients usually have teeth problems. They are very likely to have teeth abnormalities of location as well as angle of growth, size and shape. Infection of impacted teeth is a possibility for these patients as it is for impacted teeth in non-cleft patients, but infection can have more consequences if the teeth next to the impacted teeth are in disarray. Severe crowding of teeth is also a possible result of cleft palate, which can cause inflammation and infection. Extra (supernumerary) teeth in the mouth often appear and can be almost anywhere, including behind or in front of other teeth, through the palate, inside the cleft, or even through the lip or inside the nose. Their shape may be distorted and they may be present at birth.

The nose of a person with cleft lip/palate is affected by the deficiency of tissue and bone that usually support the nose at its base. "Unilateral clefting, both complete and incomplete, results in a nasal deformity that may be caused by three major factors: imbalance of the facial musculature, hypoplasia (underdevelopment or incomplete development of a tissue or organ) of the skeletal base, and asymmetry of the skeletal base."[401]

A Social Pathology

Children with cleft lip and palate are bullied and objectified by their peers. A recent study on the social torture that cleft lip/palate children endure states that cleft lip/palate is a "social pathology" because it impacts the child's social life. (Keep in mind that the children in the study had surgical repair of their birth defect; an unrepaired cleft would make taunting much worse.) Questionnaires asking if their classmates made fun of them were filled out by fifty-five school-age children with cleft lip/palate in multiple schools.

> Sixty-nine percent of the children reported having suffered from taunting and peer victimization in school. In eighty-four percent of the cases, taunting was linked to the CLP defect itself. The teasing started in primary school to reach a peak of aggressiveness in middle school. Forty-two percent of patients reported that bullying occurred at least once a day. Regarding the psychological impact of taunting, fifty percent of patients reported sadness, thirty-one percent depression and 26.3% were marked for life. At one time or another twenty-nine percent of patients did not want to attend school because of the teasing.[402]

The study followed up on six of the students who had entered the workplace and two were still being made fun of.[403]

History Of Repair

Since the beginning of the twentieth century, medical facilities and personnel being available, surgical repair of cleft lips are typically done when babies are at least three months old and at a mean age of four and a half months,[404] and doctors and parents rarely wait longer than that to repair the defect. Most cleft palates are repaired when the child is ten to fourteen months old at a mean age of eleven and a half months[405] and clefts of the alveolar ridge are fixed at around age nine years. Dr. David Zajac, director of Speech Language Pathology in the University of North Carolina at Chapel Hill Craniofacial Center adds that, "In addition, many will need a final major surgery at skeletal maturity called maxillary advancement—usually in the late teens. We see many cases where a teenager has had ten to fifteen surgeries if the cleft is severe." (Information from Dr. David Zajac,

Director of Speech Language Pathology, Division of Craniofacial and Surgical Care, Craniofacial Center, Adams School of Dentistry, the University of North Carolina at Chapel Hill, June 30, 2017.)

However, in parts of the world where the surgery is hard to come by, children may have to wait a long time, even into adulthood, before getting surgery on their cleft lip and/or palate. Meanwhile, they live every day with a jumbled erroneous formation of gums, teeth, and lips. In some parts of the world, even in the early twenty-first century, a medieval attitude is still shown to those who have this affliction: the person is thought to have engaged in a devilish practice or had an atrocious disdain for pious mores. Often it is the person's mother who is accused of sexual transgressions, and her punishment is said to be carried out on the child.

Eustache Dauger lived before the surgical operation to fix cleft palate had been worked out. Cleft lip, though, could sometimes be repaired. The first two doctors to publish surgical procedures for cleft lip were Ambroise Paré (1510–1590), and his pupil, Pierre Franco (1505–1578). Franco published in 1556 an account of the operation for cleft lip as it was practiced then and was the first doctor to theorize that cleft lip and palate were inherited.[406]

Ambroise Paré was a surgeon for four French kings[407] and a battlefield specialist because he accompanied his royal superiors on military campaigns. Paré described in 1568[408] the bandage technique that he had developed for sewing up a cleft lip, which looks, in the engravings in his book and by subsequent authors who passed along this knowledge,[409] something like an enormous figure-eight moustache made of thread, for after the cleft lip edges were given fresh sides (a nonchalant term that surgeons then and now use to describe what must have been a painful ordeal without anesthesia[410]— it entails burning or slicing open and neatly sculpting the two sides of the cleft lip in order to make the scar as straight as possible and to make the two sides adhere to each other), he pierced two semicircular needles though the two edges, then slowly wrapped the string progressively tighter around the needles and the edges of the lips would grow together over time.

One of Paré's students, Jacques Guillemeau (1549–1613), published in 1594 an important work that followed Paré's techniques and designs, which has illustrations of the suturing for cleft lip.[411]

There was no surgical cleft palate repair for Eustache Dauger or anyone else until Carl Ferdinand von Grafe (1787–1840) performed the first surgical palate repair in 1816 during the time that he was professor of surgery in Berlin from 1810 to 1840.[412] One reason for that might be that doctors facing a patient with a cleft palate might think the cleft was due to the necrosis of

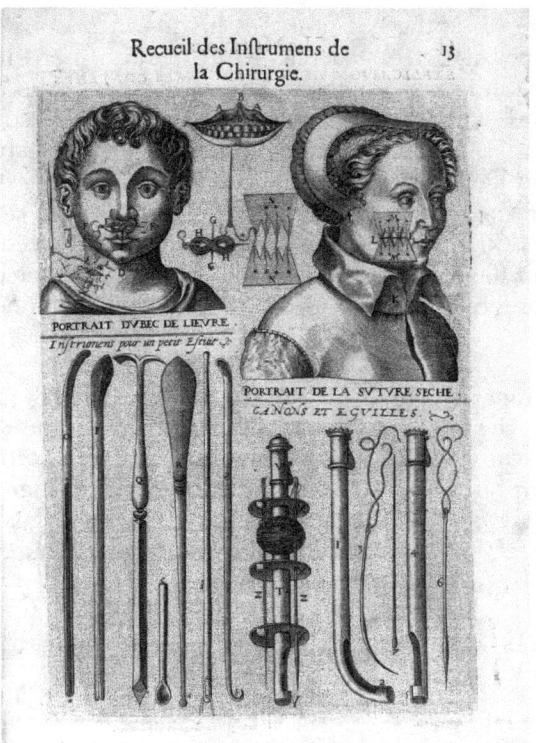

Figure 13.1: Illustration from an electronic copy of Guillemeau's book located on the BIU Santé website, p. 13. The chapter that begins on page 12, is titled: "Le Magazin, ou explication des charactères en la figure pourtraicte du Bec de lieure, etc." The title of the image is "Collection of surgical instruments." Jacques Guillemeau. *La chirurgie françoise, recueillie des Anciens Médecins et Chirurgiens avec plusieurs figures des Instrumens necesseres pour l'opération. Manuelle par Jacques Guillemeau D'Orléans, Chirurgien du Roy et Juré à Paris.* Paris: Nicolas Gilles, 1594. Exemplaire numérisé: BIU Santé (Paris). Adresse permanente: http://www.biusante.parisdescartes.fr/histmed/medica/cote?00252

the palate due to venereal disease so they did not investigate cleft palates too closely for fear of possible "presence of active or temporarily dormant syphilis, or by pathologic changes secondary to severe dental and alveolar decay, scurvy, scrofula, or tuberculosis."[413]

Prosthetics

A difficult problem in the Man in the Iron Mask mystery is the presence of a cloth mask on Dauger in public at all times in his later life but no mention of a mask at the beginning of his life in prison. My suggestion is that he, as a young person, used a prosthetic nose, many images of which are in sixteenth- and seventeenth-century medical manuals, especially those that address war wounds and surgeries. Above we referred to the books of surgeons Ambroise Paré and Jacques Guillemeau that illustrated prosthetic eyes, noses, and teeth that they designed to repair or at least cover wounds on a soldier's face. Thomas Johnson (1595–1644), English translator of Ambroise Paré's book, quoted Paré in a summation of the need for prosthetics for people who have had damage to the face. "Such persons must be so trimmed and ordered, that they may come in seemely manner into the company of others."[414]

The reason Dauger changed his approach to hiding his cleft mouth and palate, was, I believe, caused by facial growth over time that craniofacial specialists say can complicate treatment of their long-term patients: "Finally, one may philosophize that nothing about the human morphology is stationary. Aging is a well-documented process of change. Lifetime dentitional adjustment and changing dental relationships are known to all, even in otherwise healthy persons."[415]

Paré's medical book shows two prosthetic noses, one with a moustache to hide the upper lip.

Figure 13.2: Illustration of false noses from the Ambroise Paré edition of 1575, page 717. Ambroise Paré. *Les Œuvres de M. Ambroise Paré, Conseiller, et Premier Chirurgien du Roy. Avec les figures & portraicts tant de l'Anatomie que des instruments de Chirurgie, & de plusieurs Monstres.* Paris: Gabriel Buon, 1575. The label on the image says: "Pictures of noses."

The clinical term "dentofacial dysplasia," meaning the overall unwelcome contraction and/or expansion of parts of the face when unrepaired cleft lip/palate is present, indicates the intimate connection between facial and dental growth. As Dauger aged, because of worsening or new facial dysplasia, onset of dental infections or growths, ugly remainders from tooth extractions he might have had, he might have more often worn a mask which was a complete protection from stares.

The only remedy available for teeth, cysts, or tumors that were infected or in the wrong place was extraction. Eustache may have had teeth pulled that were causing him pain, teeth that were either supernumerary or only partially developed that had become an annoyance. When dental patients today have teeth pulled, the dentist can offer replacement implants, dentures, or crowns, and we can see in Paré's section of *Œuvres* on prostethics an image of false teeth, proving that the idea was not entirely unknown to doctors.

Figure 13.3: Illustration of false teeth from the Ambroise Paré edition of 1575, page 718. Ambroise Paré. *Les Œuvres de M. Ambroise Paré,... : avec les figures & portraicts tant de l'anatomie que des instruments de chirurgie, & de plusieurs monstres.* Paris: Gabriel Buon, 1575. The label on the image says: "Treatment book; Pictures of artificial teeth."

Obturators And Tweezers

In the same section of Paré's book in which he illustrated false noses and teeth he had a page on, "Of filling the hollownesse of the Pallat," where he drew his idea for palatal obturators, a word he invented from the Latin word *obturo*, meaning "to plug."

> Many times it happeneth that a portion or part of the bone of the pallat, being broken with the shot of a gun, or corroded by the virulency of the Lues venerea, falls away, which makes the patients to whom this happeneth, that they cannot pronounce their words distinctly, but obscurely and snuffling: therefore I have

thought it a thing worthy the labour to shew the meanes how it may be helped by art. It must be done by filling the cavity of the pallat with a plate of gold or silver a little bigger than the cavity its selfe is. But it must bee as thick as a French Crowne, and made like unto a dish in figure, and on the upper side, which shall be towards the braine, a little spunge must bee fastened, which, when it is moistened with the moysture distilling from the brain, will become more swolne and puffed up, so that it will fill the concavity of the pallat, that the artificiall pallat cannot fall down, but stand fast and firme, as if it stood of it selfe. This is the true figure of those instruments, whose certain use I have observed not by once or twice, but by manifold triall in the battels fought beyond the Alpes[416].

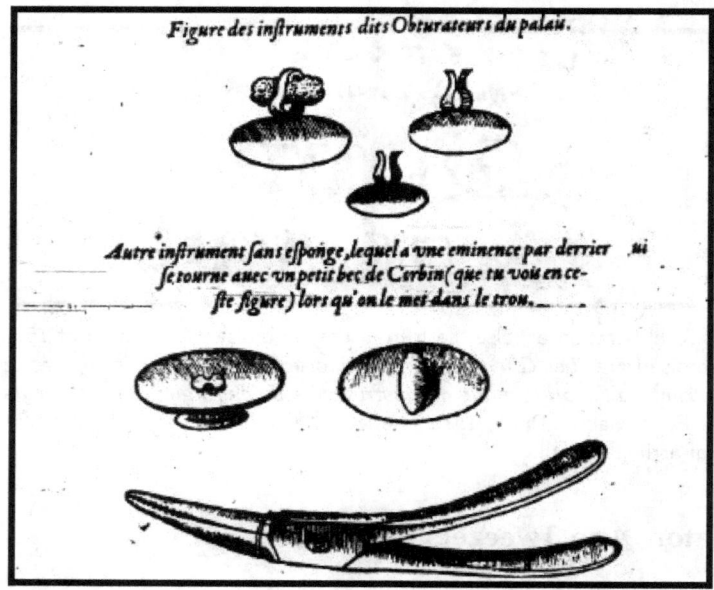

Figure 13.4: Illustration of obturators and tweezers used to put them in and out of a cleft palate is from the Ambroise Paré edition of 1575, page 718. Ambroise Paré. *Les Œuvres de M. Ambroise Paré,... : avec les figures & portraicts tant de l'anatomie que des instruments de chirurgie, & de plusieurs monstres*. Paris: Gabriel Buon, 1575. The label on the top image says: "Figure of instruments called obturators for the palate." The bottom label says "Other instrument without sponge, which has a protrusion in the back which turns by use of a little crow's beak (that you can see in this image) when the patient puts it in the hole." Johnson's images of obturators are very similar.

Ambroise Paré illustrated obturators with the tweezers that he used to remove them in his book *Œuvres*, saying he had seen similar ones used in

Italy. Early obturators were of gum, wax, cotton, sponge, silver, or gold.[417] The caution above about not letting food into the breathing passages is doubly underlined for not allowing the obturator, if there is one, to get into the nose or be swallowed. This is no longer a concern because today's obturators are custom made to fit securely. But in former times obturator users had to remain cautious. From a surgeon in a 1937 treatise on cleft palate:

> Many curious forms of obturator... are employed to remedy congenital defects. Sercombe mentions a case in which destruction of the entire palate was successfully relieved by mechanical means. In some instances among the lower classes these obturators are simple pieces of wood, so fashioned as to fit into the palatine cleft, and not infrequently the obturator has been swallowed, causing obstruction of the air-passages or occluding the esophagus.[418]

Obturators today help people with insufficiency of the palate to manage speech, eating, drinking, and breathing if the timetable of surgeries to completely fix the palate is long, or if the problem, after surgery has offered all it can, requires occasional use of an obturator. Today these dental prostheses are made of plastic, silicone, or other synthetic polymers.[419]

Another indication that Eustache Dauger had cleft lip and palate is suggested by an item he regularly used that is associated with using an obturator: his tweezers. The fact that Dauger kept tweezers near at hand and frequently used them puzzled me when I first fell prey to this fascinating mystery. I interviewed doctors and surgeons who had cleft palate patients and at the end of our conversation I always asked, "Does the presence of tweezers in the life of my protagonist mean anything to you...Tweezers?" And I got the same blank stare from dentists, social workers, surgeons, periodontists, and orthodontists. They had no suggestions. Until at the end of an email to a speech therapist I asked this question and a short reply came back that when giving speech lessons to people with a hole in the palate, he often puts a block into the hole—gum perhaps—so that the person can feel what it's like to properly make the sound, and then uses tweezers to get the blockage out.[420] My persistance in continuing to ask "Why tweezers?" finally was justified. Craniofacial surgeons use sophisticated clamps and sharps to do their work, and know nothing of tweezers; orthodontists know wires and braces, but they don't use tweezers. As interdisciplinary as craniofacial centers are, there are some things that only one doctor knows. Tweezers would be used to reach into the mouth, up to the obturator, and pull on the little crow's beak extension to remove the prosthesis.

The "Iron Mask"

The "iron mask" was not a mask, it was a wire apparatus with springs that Dauger wore at the chin area while traveling between Exilles in the Alps and Saint-Marguerite on the Provencal coast in April 1687. It was never alluded to before or after.

Since this "iron mask" is so critical to the attention that Eustache Dauger has gotten for a few hundred years, it is worth repeating what Louis Fouquet said in a letter about the prisoner having a "steel mask" on his face during the trip. The letter, written on 4 September 1687, four months after Saint-Mars' group reached Sainte-Marguerite prison, says:

> M. de Cinq Mars (*sic*) brought, by order of the king, a state prisoner from Pignerol[421] to the Iles Sainte-Marguerite. No one knows who he is, it is forbidden to say his name and if the name is said, the speaker will be killed. The prisoner was enclosed in a sedan chair and had a steel[422] mask on his face and all that one could learn from Saint-Mars was that the prisoner had been for a long time at Pignerol and that perhaps some people who are thought to be dead... are not.[423]

Louis Fouquet's testimony was written in September 1687; Voltaire gave almost the same story in 1751. In one detail only are the statements exactly alike; they both say the mask was made of steel. Otherwise they are different. Fouquet said he was a "state" prisoner arrested by the king; Voltaire said he was transported in extreme secrecy. Fouquet said saying his name was forbidden and would be punished with death; Voltaire said if he took his mask off he would be killed. Fouquet says he was enclosed in a sedan chair; Voltaire does not say how he was transported. Only Voltaire gives a reason for the chin device—it enabled the prisoner to eat while wearing it.

Three Questions

How did Louis Fouquet know the particulars of Dauger's trip and how did Voltaire learn them? The accuracy of the reports means that the leaker must have been someone with information known only to Saint-Mars, Rosarges, Rû, or one of the Formanoir nephews.

If Dauger was not forced to use the metal mask, then he used it voluntarily on the trip to Sainte-Marguerite, but why was the "steel mask" used only on the trip to Sainte-Marguerite and not ever again? There must have been something that was unique about the trip through the valleys of the Alps

CHAPTER 13. SECONDARY PLAN OF NATURE

to the Mediterranean Sea that would require the use of a chin device with springs either because Dauger wanted it or because Saint-Mars wanted it.

Exilles and Sainte-Marguerite are on a north-south axis with each other but the Alps are between so it took Saint-Mars twelve days to make the trip with his soldiers, baggage, and Dauger in the litter that Saint-Mars had constructed for him with eight porters to carry it. A cross-country trip means packing bags and getting necessary items in the car for use while riding. Dauger was facing being closed up all day in his sealed car so perhaps Saint-Mars made sure that he had a water canteen and some food inside the closed shell he was riding in so he could drink and eat whenever he was thirsty or hungry. Saint-Mars wanted to get to his destination fast and didn't want to constantly stop to look under the waxed tarp to see if Dauger wanted water or food. This method of carrying an important person and providing for his needs inside the covered litter has precedents. Travelers who were rich enough to afford a litter carried by porters would do so instead of enduring a bumpy ride in carriages with primitive axle systems and insufficient or no suspensions. At the end of his life Cardinal Richelieu's body was so wracked with pain that he could no longer travel by carriage; his litter, carried by twelve porters, six working at a time, was something like Dauger's but much more elegant. "Inside, he had everything he needed, he could read, write, if his arm was not too painful (he had a bone inflammation in his arm). He had nothing to fear. The only time he would be bothered by others was when his retinue stopped overnight to eat and sleep."[424]

Every day of his life Dauger had difficulty breathing, drinking, eating, salivating, swallowing, sneezing, and talking because he had a hole in his palate that allowed air and liquids to escape upward through his nose. All people with a cleft palate have to make sure they pilot food, air, and saliva to the escophagus and prevent it going anywhere else. Obturators ensure this unidirectional passage. In a closed vehicle in the latter part of April in Provence, when it can be very warm, he would be unseen by bystanders, as Louvois had ordered and Saint-Mars had promised, therefore unseen by anyone who might have to help him if he was choking, fainting, or ill. Eustache needed an obturator in place while he was traveling and the "mask" held the obturator securely during the time he was in the hot box that he probably could not get out of all day. The archival record of the stay in Briançon showed that they arrived in Briançon intentionally after nightfall. They may have tried to time all their arrivals at overnight stops after dark. That would make very long days in the vehicle.

But the need for an obturator that stayed in place all day was also to ensure Dauger could breathe through his nose to alleviate the near suffocation that was certain to occur both because of the closed litter and because of the travel to a low altitude after spending eighteen years at almost 3,000 feet in the Alps. Saint-Mars, in a letter he wrote to Louvois just after he got to Sainte-Marguerite with his prisoner, told Louvois what the problem was; he said that Dauger had trouble *breathing* during the trip.

When a person travels in a short period of time from a high altitude to a low one, and if they have been at high altitude for a long time, he or she can experience reverse altitude sickness caused by the thinning of blood and lack of oxygen in the body. A study of a very small number of people returning to low altitude from high altitude showed that in the first day or so after return, the subjects felt really well with good appetite and a sense of well-being, but after a day or so they began to show symptoms which worsened over days: fatigue, headache, dizziness, sleepiness, insomnia, unresponsiveness, memory loss, agitation, sore throat, coughing, expectoration, chest tightness, increased appetite, reduced appetite, abdominal distension, diarrhea, and unexplained joint pain.[425] Exilles' altitude is 2,854 feet above sea level (870 meters) and Sainte-Marguerite's altitude is 151–229 feet (46–70 meters). That is a descent of approximately 2,600 feet in twelve days, which is what Saint-Mars told Louvois it took to make the journey (April 18 to April 30, 1687).

Saint-Mars had made the trip from Exilles to Sainte-Marguerite at the beginning of 1687 to inspect Dauger's new ultra secure cell and his own new living accommodations that were being built at the prison and after he got there he told Louvois that he was sick and had to recuperate for a while at the island before he started back to Exilles. He may have experienced reverse altitude sickness himself and could see that his men and Dauger on the trip south would have the same shortness of breath, fatigue, and illness that he had. He knew Dauger already had regular shortness of breath. Attaching Dauger's obturator firmly in his palate so he could eat, breathe and drink safely while being carried in the sealed chair would insure comfort to Dauger and keep Saint-Mars from worry that his passenger would have a health crisis during the trip.

Silver, Gold, Steel?

How was this obturator made? Early obturators were more complicated than Paré's button obturators. They were made of metal and had little wings on them that were gently forced from the palate up onto the nasal floor and tightened in place with tiny screws.

Here are the substances used for making obturators up to 1823 that are in old medical texts. The device Dauger wore must have been made of one of them or a combination:

Hollerius, 1552: Wax; sponge Alexander Petronius, 1566 : Wax; gold; cotton Ambroise Paré, 1575: Gold; silver Amatus Lusitanus, 1653: Gold R. Wiseman, 1676: Resinous alloy Fabricii Hieronimi, 1723: Sponge; lint; silver Lorenz Heister, 1739: Gold; silver Jean Astruc, 1754: Gold; silver Doctor Lefebvre, 1823: Silver; gilded silver; gold; platinum

The most often mentioned material in this list is gold. Steel is not on the list but both Fouquet and Voltaire say they understood the material was *"acier"* (steel).

Saint-Mars may have called on someone in Turin or other Italian town—a doctor, clock maker, artisan, jewelry maker, or a mechanic—who could create a device that would securely close Dauger's cleft. The history of obturator manufacture suggests that the seal that fitted into the opening had wings attached to a band that went around the head and springs were added to the design so the patient could breathe, eat, and drink. This was what both Saint-Mars and Dauger needed for Dauger's long hours enclosed in Saint-Mars' grandiose, fully closed box carried by porters for twelve days.

Wire masks with chin and forehead bands to correct retrognathic maxilla defects in patients are frequently used today by orthondontists and craniofacial facial specialists. The patient is fitted with metal pins set into the jaw that attach to the chin band, and the pressure thereby created by the pressure of the head band and the pull of the chin band pulls the maxilla forward, correcting the retruded center of the face. They are called maxillary protraction appliances. Dauger had a device similar to this but the action needed was to keep a palate appliance in place, nevertheless, the orthodontic mission was approached as orthodontists in our day treat their patients.

Verbatim

The mask and what it was made of and why Dauger wore it on the trip to Sainte-Marguerite have been turned around and around by every Mask sleuth for three hundred years. The challenge to solve the mystery of the Mask is like a snow globe: turned over, the excitement starts, then the pieces start falling but not into place. For now, this author is convinced, in the context of the theory that a long trip required an unusual medical device, that the mask was exactly what Bishop Louis Fouquet and Voltaire said it was: a device, probably of steel, to hold securely a palatal obturator, so it wouldn't fall out and be lost in the bottom of the traveling chair, attached around the head at the jaw area with springs so he could eat and drink without having to take it off. He needed this special help to breathe, eat, and drink only during the route through lower Provence, when the land was flatter than in the Alps and therefore the travelers and the traveling litter would be more exposed to view so the tarp could not be taken off during the day making it necessary to provide for all contingencies. He never needed it before the trip to Sainte-Marguerite or after it, so it was never seen at any other time.

Both Voltaire's hubris and our own hubris are responsible for letting our imagination develop a whimsical, even punitive, scenario, which served our purposes for entertainment, instead of listening to a clear, factual statement. Voltaire violated his own espoused desire for existential knowledge and encouraged posterity to follow him. It was not Voltaire the *Philosophe*, but Voltaire the playwright, the tragedian, who advertised the *Masque de fer*.

14. The Case For The White Blackbird

A "*merle blanc*" (a white blackbird) is an idiom for a person or thing that does not exist or cannot be found.

During the three-hundred-year search for the Man in the Iron Mask, readers and researchers have assiduously sought a description of the prisoner and what he spent his time doing, where he came from, why he wore a mask, what sort of person he was, and why he was put in prison by Louis XIV. He was allowed books, medical care, "everything that could be given to a prisoner," but was subjugated to the most strict, secret security measures ever used in the *Ancien Régime* brought to (semi-) perfection by Saint-Mars, lifetime jailer of the Mask, with his private company of guards, many of whom were his cousins and nephews, a fastidious but incomplete watchman, hindered sometimes by his natural humanity.

One way to describe him is that he was and still is a "*merle blanc*," a white blackbird, a human being that cannot possibly have existed, a person so unusual that he did not have a name we can trust, did not have a birth certificate, and would not have had a shroud unless Saint-Mars had donated one. He did not have a face that could be seen during his lifetime and didn't have a face that could be seen after his death because it was purposefully ruined by acid when he was buried.

He did have an arrest warrant, a death certificate and Lieutenant de Junca's journal entries from the Bastille, and those confirm that he was a real person. This means, and we repeat, that looking for Dauger is a detective process and that theories that grow out of a few verifiable, archival facts must be built; theories that follow on other theories, and until we have DNA or testimony from a qualified source that has been lost, all we can do is theorize.

Who Was Eustache Dauger?

Voltaire said he was a brother of Louis XIV, perhaps a half-brother. Nineteenth-century archivists said he was a poisoner or an Italian count. Jules Lair, Nicolas Fouquet's early biographer, said:

> Who was this person and why was he arrested? He was French, Catholic, a valet by profession. It is reasonable to think that his name was really Eustache Dauger. He had been employed for a certain action, which was never revealed. In all likelihood he was one of these men that one assigns a repugnant mission, stealing something or kidnapping people... or worse... and who, once the job is done, is silenced by killing him or putting him in prison.[426]

Twentieth-century professors agreed with Lair; he was a valet whose disintegration came about from completing a malicious project of Louvois or Colbert and he deserved what he got.

Historians of the *Masque de fer* backed away early in the nineteenth century from agreeing with Voltaire and, having peppered jolly criticisms at his guesses that the masked prisoner was a member of the Bourbon/Habsburg royal family, they refused to ever reconsider the proposition. Remember that author Pierre Roux-Fazillac warned his readers against "irrational thinking" about the Mask.[427] Did they think following that line of research would bring them ridicule, as it had for Voltaire? Or were they afraid of the burden of trying out this theory (the family member theory) because, if it led to a question about Louis XIV's legitimacy, it would necessitate a lengthy and perhaps painful reappraisal of Louis XIV's reign?

Avoiding facile conclusions has been the advertised goal of almost all Mask researchers, but that goal has gradually changed into resistance to considering Voltaire's theory because there is too much at risk, too much chance of embarrassment in front of peers, too many dark paths, and too much research that might have to be done after a decision to settle on an outsized solution. A *New York Times* opinion writer's words in a recent essay about whether to believe conspiracy theories shored up my confidence in my extreme explanation of the mystery of the Man in the Iron Mask, which is similar to those that have been slandered by some of the most esteemed scholars of French history. The op-ed writer cautioned that one cannot dismiss a precarious theory, refuse to confront it, because it appears, at first reading, to be fantastical.

> [D]ismissiveness can itself become an intellectual mistake, a way to sneer at speculation while ignoring an underlying reality that deserves attention or investigation. Instead, you have to be able to reject outlandish theories *and* acknowledge a pattern of government lies and secrecy around a weird, persistent, *unexplained feature* of human experience... the wild theories are false; even so, the secrets and mysteries are real.[428]

An investigator has to carefully consider all the data, even data others have decided are weak. It may lead to truth or it may not, but fear of the data is not an option. It may be that the "wild theories" are not completely false.

Three hundred years ago an unusual person with an unusual set of life events prompted intense interest by all who came into contact with him or heard of him, and all attempts up to now of posing him as a commoner have failed to get a solution that fits the testimonies, decisions by his jailers, extreme security, and Dauger's character. This is not a story about the periphery, it's a story about the center. It is about one completely unknown man in the clutches of one of history's most famous kings, and they must have had something in common or else the king would not have kept Dauger until his death without reason or trial, without accusation.

After years of research on a wide sweep of history and personalities, genetics and gene mapping, facial recognition, social rules, child abandonment, medical childbirth practices, surgical repair of wounds in the seventeenth century, twin studies, military history and warfare, alchemy, and craniofacial birth defects, I am convinced that this prisoner was a legitimate child of Louis XIII and Anne of Austria, a brother of Louis XIV and Philippe d'Orléans, born in the fall of 1643, after his father Louis XIII had died, with cleft lip and palate, thus a legitimate heir in line, after Philippe d'Orléans. Plural indicators show that this theory, a return to the very first theories about the Mask, is worth studying further, not only in the present work, but for researchers and scientists in the future.

The Case For A Royal Third Son

Cardinal Richelieu died on December 4, 1642. Louis XIII died one hundred and sixty-one days later on May 14, 1643. There were five months in between.

In the previous chapter Louis XIII's severe intestinal problems were described as lifelong but intermittent. He had both short and long durations of intestinal pain with accompanying fever and weakness and a few near death crises. During his reign, his doctors, the press, foreign ambassadors, and Richelieu, his first minister, reported him to be sometimes sick but for the most part he was active, doing state business, on his feet and his horse, traipsing from Saint-Germain-en-Laye to his new small hunting lodge in the tiny hamlet of Versailles and back, performing duties of state, and participating in religious ceremonies.

Here are excerpts from the king's schedule from the *Gazette* newspaper in early 1643:

From Paris January 3, 1643

The king left Saint-Germain on the 29th of last month [December 1642] and went to Versailles, returned to Saint-Germain on the 31st; the next day, New Year's Day, His Majesty, after his devotions, touched a great number of sick people.[429]

From Saint-Germain January 9, 1643

The king left here for Versailles, returned to this town on the seventh.[430]

From Paris January 24, 1643

On the 19th of this month the king ordered the Marshals de Vitry and Bassompierre released from the Bastille.[431]

From Paris January 24, 1643

On the 20th of January was held the burial service for the Cardinal Duc de Richelieu.[432]

From Saint-Germain January 31, 1643

On the 29th his majesty came back from Versailles where he had gone on the 24th.[433]

From Saint-Germain February 13, 1643

Cardinal Bichi arrived at Saint-Germain on the 27th of the past month and went the next day to see the king at Versailles and was well received just like he was the other times he visited the king. He also received and gave visits to all the court.

From the festival of the Purification, that the king passed here in his ordinary devotion and all the court at his example: his majesty did not take any time away from the great business of his council and state and did not leave here [Saint-Germain] until the 9th of this month when he went to sleep at Versailles, from where he returned on the 11th.[434]

From Saint-Germain February 20, 1643

The king stayed at Versailles from the 8th to the 11th of this month and returned here the 18th in good health, thanks to God: The king had dinner on last Sunday, the 15th, for Monsieur his brother and also present were the bishop of Metz, the Marshal de Schomberg, and other seigneurs. The Tuesday preceding his majesty had Cardinal Mazarin to dinner and the bishop of Metz, the Marshal de Guiche, the sieur de Chavigni [sic], secretary of state, and four other seigneurs.[435]

From Paris February 28, 1643

CHAPTER 14. THE CASE FOR THE WHITE BLACKBIRD

> The king is at Saint-Germain: he is feeling better after a light indisposition that he had for a few days previous.[436]
>
> From Saint-Germain March 20, 1643
>
> The king is in good health.[437]

In summer 1642 Louis XIII and Richelieu were campaigning separately in the Roussillon[438] and, after eighteen years of a tumultuous relationship, were finally losing whatever respect for each other they had left. Richelieu exposed the king's boyfriend, Cinq Mars, as a conspirator with Spain and executed him, the king having lost enough love for his pretty boy that he didn't object. Louis went back to Saint-Germain-en-Laye in mid August where his wife had stayed with her children, Richelieu went to his country house at Rueil, never to advance again, and the royal couple were comforted by the physical and political presence of Mazarin, the Italian deal maker who held their hands and promised that all would be well. After Richelieu died in early December Louis kept a schedule of council meetings where business of state was conducted with Mazarin at his side.[439] The honeymoon could only last a few short months because it was Louis' time to die.

Louis XIII was not bedridden before the end of March 1643. From his bed in his last weeks, April and the beginning of May, Louis XIII concluded his affairs. He let out of prison the high-ranking state, military, and religious leaders that Cardinal Richelieu had incarcerated, de Vitry, Bassompierre, and the religious philosopher Saint-Cyran, among many others. The princes of Vendôme, illegitimate son and grandsons of Henri IV, were called back from exile. He wrote his will and patented his orders for how the kingdom was to be led until his four and a half year old son was old enough to be crowned.

From the beginning of April to the fourteenth day of May, he died slowly. His wife sat by his bed until the end and was overwhelmed with tears when it came. Madame de Motteville said the queen's ladies had to help her leave the room and that the queen told her she felt that her heart had been ripped open. She had been married to Louis XIII for twenty-eight stormy years, there had been a few years when they had been truly man and wife, and their sexual life, although complicated, had brought two sons. She was relieved that she would not have to parry his distrust and disdain anymore, but she now felt alone for the first time in her life. She had her son, *Dieudonné*, sent from God to rule France, and she believed she was responsible to God to protect his throne until he was of age. All these emotions overwhelmed her.

The next day, May 15, 1643, she proceeded to Paris with her two sons and all the courtiers and their crews, a file of ants in the process of making a new nest with a new queen. Motteville says the queen was praised in the streets by crowds of people as she approached Paris and she showed her son Louis to them from the window of the carriage, "as the present from the heavens that they had wished for."[440]

Just before the king's death, the dukes and bishops who were expecting Anne's regency to better their station in life began to jostle each other for the front seat in affairs: the deceased king's brother Gaston d'Orléans, the duc de Mercœur, the duc de Beaufort, the bishop of Beauvais, and the duc d'Enghien, who would soon be the prince de Condé. Behind broad smiles were teeth. After Louis XIII's death their scheming and importunities increased to the point where Anne judged the best thing to do was to throw money at them. Motteville's memoirs describe Anne's dilemma:

> She was uncertain about how to rule, which caused those who wanted favors to press her for decisions. There were so many people eager to talk to her that often she kept to her room so that she would get some relief from this crowd. As she was not accustomed to reign, she did not know how to refuse the *Importants*, nor acquiesce to those who deserved reward. This skill is difficult and would merit all the strength of a Queen less energetic than ours... *Monsieur le cardinal* [Mazarin] saw these people trying to take advantage of the queen and he thought it was horrible they would do that and he told the queen he would take care of it all. This offer of help came from a very capable person, who was able to assist the regent in a way that flattered her and shifted most of the burden of governing to the cardinal.[441]

If anyone was going to throw money and it was to be caught, Mazarin instinctively put his hand out. The new cardinal got his red slipper through the door just before Richelieu and Louis XIII died because he had impressed them with his respectful, mannered personality and his record of skillfully solving diplomatic crises. They thought he would be the ideal person to end the long war with Spain.

> Giulio Mazarini was a cardinal, as were many others, but no one could imagine him in the place of Richelieu. He was neither minister nor lay minister, Italian by birth, half Spanish by the years he spent in Spain, he quickly became a half king and would stay that up until his death. Never did a drifter so magnificently inherit his destiny.[442]

CHAPTER 14. THE CASE FOR THE WHITE BLACKBIRD

Louis XIII's will had given orders for a group rule of the country after his death that, while it ordered that his wife be named regent, gave her status only as a titular member of the high council, supervised by career government officials, but the day after his death, the lady, in mourning veils, the new king and his three-year-old brother at her side, at a special session of parlement in the *Palais de Justice* in Paris, made her case to the high nobility and judicial officials that she should be regent with ministers to serve *under* her on her council, a complete overturning of Louis XIII's instructions. Cardinal Mazarin was made room for in the council beside existing council members, none of whom were prepared for Queen Anne appointing Mazarin the chief minister. In January the potentates of the state, archbishops, and a long line of robed parlementarians had carried Richelieu's casket to the chapel in the Sorbonne college that he had built, glad to be rid of a hated chief of state, who, although a cardinal, had been accused by the powerful Catholic political faction of being anti-Catholic because he believed Spain was a threat to France and joined with Protestants to deter Habsburg invasion, and also because his tactics in anything he did or tried to do were often cruel and deceptive.

Motteville, in between showering the queen with praise, often abruptly put wise... almost cynically wise... judgements into her journal as she did when she succinctly summed up the problem Mazarin posed and predicted its effects on the state:

> France could have avoided much trouble if the court had been composed of men wise enough to know that it is impossible to find a perfect man; and if, preferring peace over their ambition, they could have patiently followed the wishes of the Queen, because they were going to be governed, in the end, by a minister in chief of one sort or another. This particular man [Mazarin], being a foreigner, having no previous debts to anyone at court, being clever and not a tyrant; he was preferable to many others. But damage was done because the Queen let him have too much authority, and this excess of power was disliked and those who had wanted his post undercut his reputation and criticized him violently.[443]

In these crucial months, when making harsh political judgements was the order of the day and poker playing for favors and jobs was intense, I think Anne of Austria delivered a baby that she and her husband had conceived before Louis XIII's final illness began. We know that the inclinations of Anne and Louis towards their marital bed are impenetrable, but one thing is certain: a peacefulness came over the couple that was new to them when Richelieu died. His death lifted a shadow they had lived under for a long time and a sexual encounter might have been one fruit of the new order. Since 1615 they had had intercourse many times, often when they were in a bad humor with each other, that did not result in live births; then late in their marriage they conceived two children who lived beyond infancy, so it would not be out of the ordinary for them to continue as they had before, but now with a lighter heart because Richelieu was no longer the operational authority; they finally had their own authority and they could do as they liked, in bed, anyway.

In the first days of October 1643, Louis XIII's widow and her two sons were living in the Palais-Royal on the corner of the rue de Richelieu and the rue Saint-Honoré that Cardinal Richelieu had built in a new subdivision north of the Louvre and willed to the king. Louis XIII had not been interested in the house but Anne was happy to move into such a beautiful new city mansion with lovely gardens that her children could play in. Otherwise very healthy all her life except for her reproductive problems, she was away from the public for about two weeks with "jaundice" right after she moved into the palace, reports Jacques Roujon in his book on Louis XIV and Louvois. "The doctors said it came from being under too much pressure and heartache."[444] In those two weeks it is possible that Anne was coping with the last days of a pregnancy and a delivery. A delivery at the beginning of October 1643 would be the result of an impregnation in December 1642 or January 1643... when Louis XIII was doing state business, travelling, and entertaining. If he was giving dinner parties at Versailles for diplomats and bishops, he could have had sexual relations with his wife sometime between December and March. It is uncomfortable to think of a dead man having sex, even though we know the man was alive when he was in bed with his partner. It is in the shadow of Louis XIII's death that we view a possible pregnancy of the queen, making it seem surreal. Babies are born, in an idyllic world, only when the husband is alive, and if he dies, the baby, in the eyes of onlookers, seems erased too. But that happens only when the mother dies. Husbands and wives conceive together and sadly some husbands do not live until the birth.

Anne was forty-two years old in 1643. As her husband's decline intensified in April, she must have gradually become aware that she was pregnant, because she had been pregnant many times before, but this was a surprise to her. Her attention was focused on the beginning of her regency. She may have thought herself too old to become pregnant. She had lost many of her previous pregnancies and she may have been quite ambivalent about whether she wanted this one to come to term or not because her husband, the king, father of the baby, was dying and in a short time would be dead. If she had announced a pregnancy suddenly, those who wanted power could say, this woman was an adulteress in her youth and evidently, now that our king is mortally ill, she has reverted to type; she has been hav-

CHAPTER 14. THE CASE FOR THE WHITE BLACKBIRD 241

ing sex with strangers while our king was dying! The old rumors about her supposed "affair" with *milord* Buckingham in her twenties would upset the tenuous situation she faced in becoming regent for her son Louis XIV. Mazarin's comfortable relationship with the queen had made his competitors very angry and they were searching for the reason that this Spanish-speaking Italian had broken into the government of France and what they could do to topple him. She and Cardinal Mazarin had asked Parlement to break Louis XIII's will that had limited her powers after his death; Parlement had allowed the will to be set aside, but a baby on the way might have tilted the politics against her because it might be suspected that the child was Mazarin's. Not paranoia. This is exactly what was theorized by French historians in the nineteenth century who went to great lengths to make Mazarin the father of both the Mask and Louis XIV. François-Vincent Raspail (1794–1878) accused pope Urban VIII of annulling Anne's marriage to the king in 1632, allowing Mazarin to marry her, and fathering children with her. Victor Cousin (1792–1867) was kind enough to allow Louis XIII to die before he allowed Queen Anne in Mazarin's bed. Mazarin-the-father is a modern accusation too. Here is what Vergé-Franceschi said in 2009:

> In arranging the story to have the Mask born in 1643, Voltaire wanted to make him a full brother of Louis XIV (born on 5 September 1638) and the duc d'Orléans (born on 21 September 1640)! Anne d'Autriche became a widow of Louis XIII, who died 14 May 1643; if this is the proposed year of the birth of the Mask, there are some interesting questions that are useful to examine. Did the regent queen console herself a little too soon in the arms of Mazarin, who arrived at power on 5 December 1642, just after Richelieu had died?[445]

This accusation, which she would not have been able to substantially refute, there being no DNA tests to discover the father, would have wrecked Mazarin's, Louis XIV's, and her own political career and sent France back into civil war. At least it is reasonable to think that those were her concerns at the time. It was a critical crossroads for France when no mistakes were allowed. Historians of the Man in the Iron Mask, when searching for a moment at which the queen might have had a third baby by her husband, never did the gestational arithmetic to see that a child could have been fathered by Louis XIII just before his death. The historians who have laughed at Voltaire for wondering if the Mask might have been a child of the king and queen might have been too hasty to pick a fight with the *Philosophe* and not willing to be open minded. We see that the eighteenth-century's "faithful disciple of the French skeptical tradition of Montaigne, Saint-Evremond, and Bayle, and the energetic propagandist of British empiricism"[446] perhaps should not have been so quickly and rudely dismissed.

Her husband's increasing weakness and the planning that she and her supporters were undoubtedly doing in her private chambers to prepare for the time when the king would be dead and her regency would start took up all her energy and she put the signs that she was pregnant out of her mind. This is not uncommon for women who are faced with blended consequences of a possible pregnancy. Louise Bourgeois (1563–1636), a noted and professionally trained midwife in the early 1600s in France, Marie de' Medici's midwife, wrote a book about midwifery called *Instructions to her Daughter* (*Instructions on the Practice of Midwifery*). She said that sometimes women are not able to tell whether they are pregnant or not, even if they have experienced pregnancies before.

> There are some things more difficult to judge than others. That is why, if a woman doubts she is pregnant, she should keep quiet for a while so as not to unduly alarm anyone and not to risk the reputation of the *sage-femme*. The reputation of the *sage-femme* should not rest on the mistaken ideas of a patient. The midwife must steer clear of these ruses and must put her energy only into safely delivering babies.
>
> There are some women, especially those who have pale skin, and not yet well recovered [from a pregnancy], who have a blockage in their womb, which is tightly closed... even though they have their periods as usual; but what they think is a period is only bloody mucus. They assure the midwife that they have not had a period for some time; the midwife examines her and finds the blockage and tells the woman she is not pregnant. Even women who have experienced other pregnancies can be mistaken about her pregnancy for a few months.
>
> Anyone who really wants to, can deceive herself and others a long time [about a pregnancy]... With those women who are honest [about their symptoms] it is easy [for the *sage-femme*] to know the truth, but sometimes women will lie about things you would never believe.[447]

The opposite delusion, rarely, but under certain circumstances, can make a woman who is dimly aware that she is pregnant to fail to attend to the pregnancy and she "continues to think, feel, and behave as though she were not pregnant."[448] Studies that have been done on denial of pregnancy find that at least up to twenty weeks of the pregnancy, denial is not rare. At twenty weeks of gestation, 1 in 475 women do not have knowledge or are supressing knowledge that they are carrying a child. As the pregnancy goes on, this statistic changes gradually; only 1 out of 2,500 women are unaware they are pregnant when they give birth.[449]

The time of pregnancy can bring fears and, "...on occasion, these fears are so overwhelming that women are driven to deny their pregnancy. This inappropriate defence mechanism may be so powerful, that the woman is genuinely unaware of her condition. It seems that external stresses and psychological conflicts about pregnancy may lead to denial in otherwise well-adjusted women."[450]

Another study on denied pregnancies began with the assumption that women who denied pregnancy would be schizophrenic, delusionary, or habitual liars. The authors of the study did not find this was true. No definitive description of a pregnancy denier could be found. Social isolation, low intelligence, low socio-economic status, immaturity, younger age, premarital conception, unmarried status, or naiveté about bodily function were not causative. The study did find three risk factors. "Summarising the sociodemographic analyses, *there is a higher risk for denied pregnancy in very young or relatively late reproductive age, i.e. for women who do not expect (yet or anymore) a pregnancy... Further risk factors are an unstable relationship and a critical social situation.*" The authors' general conclusion was that no general description of a woman who denies her pregnancy can be made. "Rather, the impression emerged of a manifestly heterogeneous group."[451] It is undeniable that Queen Anne had three risk factors however: a *"relatively late reproductive age," "an unstable relationship,"* and *"a critical social situation."*

Pregnancy And Delivery

Anne of Austria would have gained some weight if she was pregnant but she was already full figured and her recent widowhood would require black voluminous clothing and black veils over her head and upper body. She would have been tired more than usual, but, as the doctors said publicly, she had just been through great sadness and family troubles and her health had been affected. If a married woman is young and in good health, people think perhaps a baby is on the way if there is weight gain and flowing clothing. If a woman is forty-two, a new widow, and a pious, devout queen regent with formidable political power she had just skillfully pulled out from underneath the deceased king's brother and cousins, pregnancy is not the first thing that comes to mind if she has gained weight and wears modest clothing.

Whatever her plans for her third baby had been, those were changed by the child's appearance when it was delivered. Once more, her womb had failed to bring forth a viable baby. She was familiar with this outcome, as it had happened many times before, her pregnancies from 1622 to 1631 all ending in miscarriage, as far as we know.

The Mother's Fault

I believe the baby who would eventually become known as the Man in the Iron Mask had a congenital cleft lip and palate, a diagnosis I based in the previous chapter on testimonies from people who guarded and doctored him.[452] The defect made the baby aesthetically unfit for presentation to the world, and would also have been interpreted by the French people, courtiers, politicians, and foreigners as a sign of his mother's immoral character. Mothers' unwise or illicit actions before and during pregnancy were thought to cause visible signs of deformity in a newborn. Such a child would certainly call into question her fitness to reign as regent, and she might have been separated from her two previous children, sent away from court, and Gaston d'Orléans, the king's brother, appointed as her replacement.

> Unhallowed behaviour engendered an unnatural fruit. The couple was punished, through their child, for the transgression of some taboo... It was said that the parents had sinned, had had sex when it was forbidden or had sex with someone they weren't supposed to... later, the chastisement was levelled somewhat and evolved into believing the cause of a deformity was the mother's depraved imagination.[453]

Malformations might be seen as a sign of the devil or of adultery: "...a blemish, cleft palate, a clubfoot, extra fingers or toes... many newborns with anomalies were considered changelings, offspring of fairies substituted for a stolen child."[454] In some cases, the child was considered to have special powers or to be a message to the parents and their community, which came with its own set of prejudices.

Ambroise Paré (1510–1590), battlefield surgeon and author of many medical books, including *Monstres et Prodiges* (*Monsters and Prodigies*), published in 1573, gave thirteen causes of birth defects; all but one were superstitious. [Note: the word *"monstres,"* from the verb *"montrer"* meaning to show, refers to people with all manner of deformations from the extreme to the hardly visible].

> There are many causes of monsters. The first is the glory of God.

The second is His anger. The third, too much semen. The fourth, too little semen. The fifth, the imagination. The sixth, the narrowness of the womb. The seventh, the indecent posture of the mother, having stayed too long with her legs crossed or held against the stomach. The eighth, by a fall or a blow to the mother during pregnancy. The ninth, by hereditary or accidental illness. The tenth, by corruption of the sperm. The eleventh, by a mixing of the sperm. The twelfth, by the presence of lice. The thirteenth, by Demons or Devils.[455]

He references Damascene, "a serious author," who saw a baby girl that was "as hairy as a bear" because the mother had stared at a portrait of Saint John the Baptist [in his animal skin coat] while she was in bed with her husband.[456] It was forbidden to have sex on Sunday, Lent, during menstruation, or lactation. A child born with a birth defect would be considered a sad example of a mother who had sinned or been negligent to her unborn child.

These slurs might not have been made against a queen whose reputation had been as pure as bleached silk, but her reputation had been impugned in 1625 by Cardinal Richelieu and her husband for political and personal reasons and some still believed that she had been unfaithful, and her enemies would have been quick to accuse her of immorality. The birth of a son with a birth defect was a tragedy for her, but she was determined that it would not topple her; she was at the point of achieving her lifelong goal: to place her treasure, Louis *Dieudonné*, on stage, a God-given, fair-haired boy who would rule the world with the mark of the Holy Spirit and his mother next to him, modeling Mother Mary's wise and protective cloak.

Nowhere

Eustache Dauger never had any public identity at all. He was never a part of the court, the streets, the salons, the villages, the markets, or even of a family. He was always hidden—in hiding—a person who was not seen by anyone except an extremely small and quiet set of people who were engaged to take care of him. That is why no one has ever been able to find him. His paradox, and this has a lot to do with why we are perennially interested in the man, is that he is simultaneously totally unknown and very well known. He came from a nowhere place that we have no information about to a nowhere place that is amply documented (his prisons), but we are still lost between two nowheres.

If, as seems to be the case, Eustache Dauger came out of nowhere, where was nowhere in that time and place? What solution did people have in the seventeenth century if they wanted to put a troublesome, embarrassing, or sick person into nowhere? Unfortunately for thousands of men, women, and children, putting people into nowhere was quite common in France in the seventeenth century, and in most of Europe. Families regularly locked away wayward wives, overly active children, and unhinged brothers and uncles in monasteries, convents, and hospitals, either state governed or privately owned. *Lettres de cachet*, orders for arrests on a whim, were issued by authorities upon casual requests from family members or disgruntled acquaintances.

> 17 juin 1728, Vanneroux
>
> The sieur Bellavoine against whom this complaint is made is a very bad influence on law-abiding people; the salacious relationship with the demoiselle Loison is obvious; their illicit living is known and is a scandal. The dame Rivou, a fruit seller, knows this situation well, and she assured me that the demoiselle Loison was a loose woman, and that her father who is secretary for the intendant of Perpignan was about to ask for her to be locked up in a convent... The widow Bellavoine and her family ask that Louis Bellavoine be remanded to the château of Guise and his family will pay his pension and his transportation there according to the instructions of His Excellence.[457]

Nowhere Has Been In Plain Sight For Millennia

The cultural tradition that I propose to explain the mystery of the Man in the Iron Mask is not arcane, it is one of many dissertation topics and career specialities of professional academics in the field of French seventeenth-century history—treatment of children in the medieval and modern age, including: child abandonment, the taking of newborns by parents to drop-off zones where they would become the problem of an orphanage; to paid substitutes to be nursed and raised in a location distant from the family until they were weaned, could walk and talk; and in the case of babies with birth defects, their removal to a distant location where they might or might not be placed with people who would care for them. There are many names for these practices but they all amount to temporary or permanent child abandonment.

Babies born to wealthy parents who did not want them were given to a trusted friend or a high-ranking member of their paid staff who took the child to be raised, at least in the infancy and young childhood of its life, to a caretaker, preferably at a decent distance from the parents' home. The future duc du Maine (1670–1736), illegitimate son of Louis XIV with Madame de

CHAPTER 14. THE CASE FOR THE WHITE BLACKBIRD 247

Montespan (all of Louis XIV's illegitimate children were later legitimized), just after he was separated from his mother's birthing bed was given to the comte de Lauzun, the king's chief of guards at that time (later prisoner at Pignerol), and Lauzun took the baby through the park of Saint-Germain-en-Laye to a waiting carriage where Madame Scarron (later Louis XIV's second wife) secretly took charge of him, hired nurses, and raised him until he was old enough to be given to a governor.

The memoir writer Saint-Simon said that Louis XIV's *valet de chambre* Bontemps took a dark-skinned female baby that Queen Marie-Thérèse had given birth to, who would be known as the Mooress of Moret, to a nunnery at Pont-Loué not far from Moret-sur-Loing.[458] The father's identity has always been a mystery, but since the scientific discussion at the time about a baby born with differently colored skin from either the mother or father concluded that the cause of the disaster was that the mother had looked at or thought about a person, an animal, or an event that confounded the normal process of forming the child and left marks of discoloration or ruination, the assumption by the king and the court was that the child had been sired by the king but his wife's household had a Black servant and looking at the Black man made her baby Black. The infant was declared dead and then spent her entire life in the nunnery of Moret.

These examples of babies born to parents of high rank handed off just after birth or in early childhood to an intermediary who would then take the baby to an unrelated family living an obscure life but known to the parents or to a nunnery or monastery show that the porters that would be entrusted with the baby at the first move to ignominity were high-ranking members of the household hierarchy (Lauzun, chief of the king's personal guards; Colbert, government director for finances and the king's house; Bontemps, trusted valet of high rank in Louis XIV's household).

Sending children into the countryside, often to religious houses where silence was part of the operational construct, was the cultural response in France in the seventeenth century. Both rich and poor followed this path when faced with unwanted and unpresentable children; for the poor, anonymous abandonment was the solution, and for the rich, a pension paid to a monastery was the lifelong consequence.

Monasteries And Nunneries

Children who were lucky and whose parents or guardians had the means to pay a pension would be sent to an institution, almost always a religious house. The nuns and monks, in addition to strictly following religious teaching and the rules of their order, took in and cared for marginalized

Figure 14.1: The Mooress of Moret. Louise Marie-Thérèse (1664-1732). Anonymous. Circa 1680. Oil on Canvas. Bibliothèque Sainte-Geneviève, Paris, France. Photo by the author 2024.

people of society usually for a fee.

"Historians have recently come to speak of the 'permeable' nature of convents, and this is a very useful way of understanding their structure."[459] Nunneries and monasteries provided lodging to people who were homeless or marginalized for a variety of reasons, including as a result of a *lettre de cachet* such as the one above. These lodgers were not professed nuns or monks, although they could eventually take orders if the institution would accept them; they lived sequestered inside the gated community and were taken care of or, in the case where a *lettre de cachet* had been issued, held prisoner by the religious. A monthly pension was paid by someone, perhaps a family member or a friend, or by the individual resident, if he or she had self-admitted.[460] The unseen multitudes of residents in religious houses were of many types: some were old and infirm, some were sick, some were dying; some were daughters for whom there was no room in the family budget and who were not thought to be marriageable because they were ugly or had a physical deformity; some were mentally ill; some were alcoholics and homosexuals; some had a defect, physical or mental, that made the person a difficulty for his or her family, an embarrassment, a dishonor, a problem that had to be put away.

La Couche And Abandoned Babies

The *couche* is the name of the practice of sending babies into the countryside to be nursed by hired country women who made money this way. "The mortality rates were appallingly high."[461]

The children in the house had to be handled with various methods to keep the caretakers comfortable, especially if there were a lot of pensioners: tight swaddling was done with all babies to keep their limbs straight and to keep the children from crawling, which was considered animalistic and therefore abhorred. The swaddled children could be hung on hooks above reach of animals that might wander into the house, and they could sleep or cry without being watched and were not at risk for falling into the hot soup on the fire. As the seventeenth century went on, alcohol, opium, and morphine were available for sale in doses for children.[462]

Eustache Dauger Was Not Dropped On Church Steps

When I started this study, I thought Dauger was abandoned as an infant to incompetent or at least ill trained people, maybe dropped into a cavity designed for this purpose in the wall of a convent or church late at night. But then I realized that if he had cleft lip/palate and survived, it means he had, in the first year of his life at least, caregivers who succeeded in giving him life and milk in very difficult circumstances, because without a nurse who had the patience and perseverance to overcome the trouble a cleft lip/palate infant has drinking milk, a child with this birth defect would usually die of starvation not too long after birth. It is unlikely the overworked religious members of the institutions who took in abandoned children or the countrywomen who earned their living by setting up cots in their houses for babies and toddlers that were a burden for their parents would have bothered to take time to manage this extra challenge. Dauger would have been left in a corner to die.

But he didn't die, which means someone took good care of him.

15. The Clue Of The Missing Apostrophe

"Baptize this child!"

—Anonymous

His Name, The Forbidden Clue

In the winter of 1678 Louvois got curious enough about Dauger to write to Fouquet at the Pignerol prison to ask him what he knew about Dauger and dictated a strategy for the answer which would exclude Saint-Mars:

> [The king] desires to be informed... if the man named Eustache, given to you as a servant, has not spoken in front of your other valet of how he was employed before coming to Pignerol. His Majesty has commanded me to raise that question with you and to tell you that he is waiting for you to notify me of the truth of the matter without qualification so that he might take appropriate measures regarding what Eustache may have said of his past life to his colleague.

Louvois wanted to know what we all want to know: where was Dauger before July 1669, where was he living, what was he doing?

Many years ago in Paris I went to the Baccarat museum on the rue de Paradis[463] and I discovered, while passing one shop window after another, that the rue de Paradis was where the best French china and glassware were sold, and you could buy a Baccarat ten-inch tall glass water pitcher and a Lalique elephant to triumph over your centerpiece. The rue de Paradis was famous for its stores stacked with china, glass, and breakables of all sorts. In one shop, sleeping, was a cat in the front window...actually its paws were pressed against the front window and the beautiful array of glass red cordial glasses, lidded soup tureens, and streamlined Lalique ladies, heads to the sky, were enclosing the cat like diamond trees in a forest. He had, at some point during the day, wandered through the vessels and platters without a misstep. That there could *be* a cat in such a store, let alone a cat allowed to make its way through fabulously expensive breakable merchandise, was a warning: don't analyze the capabilities of an animal or a person until you know much more than the framed image. There must have been certain things that happened...a certain history of adventure or lack thereof, in order for the cat to get to the front of the window...and more, to settle itself comfortably prone for passers-by to see, and not to have broken anything. The cat was there but how did it get there? It wasn't lost. It was at home. In a china shop. What path did it use to get there and was that path usual, remembered, or random? The imagined perilous journey of the cat through the Baccarat wine glasses is similar to imagining Eustache Dauger's path from his baptism to Captain de Vauroy's arrest warrant. What in Dauger's story could be used to find any sliver of his life before prison without breaking anything? Historians and amateurs have sought this sliver for three hundred years. For the last fifteen years so have I. The following is the strategy I chose to make some sort of sensible theory about this subject. In the king's arrest warrant, there is one handle on Dauger's life before prison and it is dependable and repeated a few times: his name. I decided to try to find the prisoner's pre-prison home using his name, Eustache Dauger. Since his name was such a source of worry to Louis XIV, maybe it had something to do with his origins.

The prisoner didn't have a name, said the king. That is ridiculous. Of course he had a name: Eustache Dauger.[464] He was named at his baptism. All children had to be baptized; even abandoned children, by law, had to be baptized by the people that found them, and quickly. The delay between birth and baptism that sometimes occurred for children in stable households was not an option for a foundling, and at the baptism the child would be given a name.

Names

Names, both forenames and surnames, relate to baptism and godparents...to a family; the custom for naming orphans was that the name assigned would be for the place where he lived, or perhaps a name that commemorated his discovery might be used. How Dauger got his name might indicate something about his godparents or his parish, because he certainly had godparents, if only strangers who were appropriated for the baptismal ceremony, and that ceremony took place in a parish; every hectare of French soil belonged to a parish. How were names decided upon, especially those of abandoned babies, "dropt" children as one English report called them, and was there a difference in naming practices for abandoned children as opposed to children whose parents wanted to keep them? That is important to finding a hint about Eustache Dauger's past because, judging from his lack of known family, he was a "dropt" child.

The Church's Preference

From the first to the sixth centuries in Europe, the Romans and their successors, Germanic invaders from the east and north that conquered large parts of France, Germany, and Italy, kept to a limited window of days after birth to name their newborns (Romans—eight days for girls and nine days for boys; Franks—ninth night for both), and they baptized them only at Easter and Pentecost.[465] But high infant mortality required a new tradition of baptizing a baby just after birth, so that if it died in infancy, it would have been baptized, a requirement for burial in consecrated ground. Naming and baptizing began to be done together, and the church, having firm control over the sacrament of baptism, tried also to have control over the first names of children and wanted those to be saints' names and not those chosen from relatives' names or names of people with social advantages for the child. The names of historical characters that had been popular, like Alexandre, Olivier, Roland, Lancelot, Saladin, Foulques, Rostaing, Isnard, Amiel, Marquis, and Palamède for boys, and Anglo-Saxon and Germanic names for women like Ermentrude, Hildegard, Audrey, Godiva, and Adela were strongly discouraged.[466]

> More than ever, the [directors of Christian conscience] wanted the name to reflect a personal imitative relationship between the new child and the saint for whom he or she was named... The Church wanted its faithful to consider the godparent affiliation as superior, because it was linked to the sacred, and the flesh parents should take second place.[467]

Families acknowledged the preferences of the church and then mostly continued to name their children according to their own preferences and family traditions. Jean-Claude Sangoï, in research on naming children in southwest France, found that before the eighteenth century, families named their children for godparents and grandparents, so that, by his or her forename, the child joined two families' social groups and became part of a genealogical chain. "The custom that led to a homonymy (the same name) between godparents and godchildren appeared in the sixteenth century in France. This practice did not correspond to the view of the Church, but the Church did not contest it."[468]

After the Council of Trent (1545–1563) the church doubled its effort to instruct parents that they should give their children the names of saints whose life story appealed to the family as worthy of spiritual imitation. The church also wanted the name to be preferably, not that of a local saint, but a saint of the church at large like Pierre, Jean, or Jacques (Peter, John, or James); Marie and Anne were favored for girls. In England and Italy as well as France this became the rule with some alteration according to the country.[469]

Named For A Godfather, Godmother, Or Grandparent

I found many examples of famous people who were named after a godfather, godmother, or grandfather. André Le Nôtre, born 12 March 1613, the seventeenth-century's most famous and successful landscape designer who designed the gardens of Versailles for King Louis XIV, was baptized on his birthday at Saint-Roch church on the rue Saint-Honoré in Paris. His godfather was André Berard, sieur de Maisoncelles, controller general of the gardens of the king, and his godmother was the wife of Claude Mollet.[470] The first baby born to Madame de Beauvais, Anne of Austria's servant and long-time friend and confidante, had Anne of Austria and Gaston Jean-Baptiste de Bourbon, Louis XIII's brother, for godparents and she was named Anne-Jeanne-Baptiste. Her fourth child, perhaps not her husband's, was given the name Etienne, for Etienne La Farge, the *"bon pauvre"* who was a fixture of the port Saint-Paul and probably chosen at the last minute to be godfather.[471] Saint-Mars married the daughter of a man named *Antonin* Collet, Marie-*Antoinette*. She and Saint-Mars named their sons André *Antoine* and Bénigne *Antonin* to continue the tradition of having *Antoine* in family names. Even a town could be a godparent: Madame de Longueville, a noblewoman and leader of the Fronde who could not have timed the birth of her child at a worse moment, went into labor after she fled into the Paris Hôtel-de-Ville with other anti-royalists to escape arrest at one of the flash points of the Fronde and named the child Charles-Paris, making the city of Paris the boy's godmother.

Named For Place Of Origin And Property Owned

People were often named for the place they had lived a long time or where they were born, whether they were poor or rich. The musketeer d'Artagnan's name given at baptism was Charles Ogier de Batz de Castlemore but he called himself after a property of his mother's, Artagnan. Or a birthplace could be the basis for the name. Pierre Contant d'Ivry (1698–1777), an architect and decorator, was born at Ivry-sur-Seine in 1698.

Name Of Parish Saint

Godfathers and grandfathers would often be named after the saint to which their parish church was dedicated, so a son would be baptized with the name of the saint under whose roof he was receiving baptism but his father, godfather, and grandfather might all have that name too, so in that case, the baby is named after all of them, including the parish saint. Eustache le Sueur (1616–1655), a Paris painter and draftsman, was baptized in Saint-Eustache, his parish church. A copy of his baptismal record exists, which states that his parents lived in the rue de la Grande Truanderie at the time he was born.[472] His godfather was Eustache Le Conte.[473] Perhaps Le Sueur's godfather was also a member of the parish of Saint-Eustache, this being the reason for his own name.

Name Of The Saint Whose Festival Fell On The Birthday Or The Baptismal Day

Children were often named for the saint on whose festival day they were born. In Romania, certain parts of Russia, and Spain, it was very common to use this rule for the name of the last child born to the family, as it was thought this would protect the child from witchcraft.[474] One of Anne of Austria's middle names was Mauricia because she was born on Saint-Maurice's feast day, 22 September.

Name Of A Major Holiday Of The Church

Naming a child Noël if it was born on Christmas Day would be one of the name choices, on Easter the name might be Pascal (from Pâque), or Toussaint if the birth was on All Saints Day.[475]

Named For A Mythical Or Historical Ancestor

Some regions were very proud of a mythical or historical ancestor and many children who were born within the geographical aura of the hero were named for him or her.

The forename Eustache was a six-hundred-year-old venerable name in the neighborhood of Calais where Dauger was arrested because the illustrious Eustache III, count of Boulogne (1056–1125), with his brothers Godefroy [Godfrey] (1060–1100) and Baudouin [Baldwin] (circa 1065–1118), sons of Eustache II, count of Boulogne (1015–1087)[476] and Ida of Lorraine (circa 1040–1113), stormed the walls of Jerusalem in the first crusade in June 1099, and took the city from the Fatimid caliphate. The names Godefroy and Baudouin are found frequently in families in the Boulonnais, but the name Eustache appears even more frequently because, unlike his brothers, who remained in the Holy Land to stabilize and maintain the Christians' grip on the lands they had seized, Eustache III returned home and inherited the important county of Boulogne from his father, Eustache II. Whether the third Eustache regretted leaving his brothers in the Holy Land we do not know, but his dividend by returning home was the rule of one of the most important counties of Flanders, that later was annexed by France in the fifteenth century. Eustache IV (circa 1130–1153), joined the house of Blois through his wife, wrangled with the house of Plantagenet for control of England and lost it to them. Two-hundred years later, when the English king Edward III took Calais in 1347, the king, because he was angry at Calais' fierce and steady resistance, asked for six rich city officials to appear before him to give reason why he should not kill all six on the spot. Led by Eustache de Saint-Pierre, six esteemed citizens with nooses around their necks offered themselves in place of any other bloodshed the English might desire, and were pardoned because Edward's wife Philippine de Hainaut begged her husband not to kill them.

The name Eustache with its feminized version, Eustachie, was often chosen by rich, devout families of the Boulonnais and Picardy who founded and administered monasteries and nunneries from the first crusade to the English fourteenth-century victories and beyond.

Abandoned Children

Abandoned children, when there was no way to determine the original name or if the prickly situation that led to the abandonment disallowed the use of the birth family name, were given names formed by one of the formulas above or were given names that had something to do with where or how they were found, combined perhaps with the name of one of the godparents that had been asked to stand at the baptismal font with the priest.

A nineteenth-century example from the civil records of the Pas-de-Calais department:

> Registre d'état civil du Transloy, 1856... placed in the middle of a haystack of wheat, we found a child wearing a calico shirt, marked with the letter H, a white and gray stripe skirt, backless dress, brown background, in Indian with small squares and dots, of a three-piece bonnet colored Indian violet, with black and white stripes and white dots. After inspecting the child, we recognized that it was female, that she looked four months old.

CHAPTER 15. THE CLUE OF THE MISSING APOSTROPHE

> She wore on her neck, suspended by a cord or a silk gimp, a copper medal having on one side these words "God in Me, heart of Jesus" and on the other "Me (erasure) in God, heart of Mary."[477] We did not see anything that could help us discover who abandoned her. Right away we gave the child the name of Henriette-Marie *Deschamps* [of the fields] and ordered that she be admitted into the hospice of Marie-Madeleine-Anne-Barbe Chatelain, wife of Hippolyte Fessier, of this commune.[478]

This second example also shows the custom of naming an orphaned child using a signal of its discovery.

> In 1784 on Monday, 2 August, was baptized by me, the undersigned priest, Augustine-Josephe who appears to have been born fifteen days ago at least and was found on this day at two o'clock in the morning in the house of Jean-Baptiste Potel, a master shoemaker in this place, who, when he opened his front door holding a candle, saw a person quickly enter his house and place the child in a chair and ran out of the house with the words, "Baptise this child." The godfather was Henry Theodore Caudron, lay cleric in this parish and the godmother was Josephe Binaut, wife of Potel who signed with the same Potel. The name of *La Chaise* (chair) was given to the child.
>
> [Signed] Roussel, parish priest,
>
> Potel, H. Th. Caudron, Josephe Binaut

The child's first name was for the month (August) she was found and Josephe for her godmother. The surname was La Chaise because she was dropped into a chair by the person who abandoned her.[479]

The most likely choices for the origin of the prisoner's forename (*prénom*) are these:

- Saint Eustache's festival day is September 20. If the child was given on September 20 to the person who named him, or if September 20 was the day he was baptised or the day he was born, then the name Eustache would have been an appropriate choice for this homeless boy.

- He might have been named for the saint to which his parish church was dedicated. If he was born in a parish devoted to Saint Eustache his forename might have devolved from that sacrality. In Paris that parish church would have been Saint Eustache located on the north perimeter of Paris' Les Halles central market. It was the parish church for the Palais Royal.

- If the person who acted as godfather or godmother in the baptismal ceremony was named Eustache or Eustachie, he could have been blessed with the same forename.

The Surname "Dauger"

Eustache Dauger was the name of the prisoner, according to his arrest warrant. The king ordered that his name not be spoken by anyone, by Dauger or by anyone in his service, neither in his presence nor in any document. This stands out to me as an aberration from the rule that should have applied to a non-noble, unknown, presumably unimportant prisoner, which would have been that he would have been given a permanent nickname or that his name would not be a cause for any rules whatsoever, let alone a rule that called for death if it was transgressed. The testimonies we have about the abolition of his name (du Junca specifically noted in his journal that, "his name was never known," the duchesse d'Orléans said he was forbidden to say his name, the letter by Louis Fouquet said he was forbidden to say his name), are so frequent that I wondered if his name was a reference to his past life. In this following series of paragraphs, I explain why I decided to theorize that his name contained the place name of one of his past domiciles: Auger.

The Apostrophe

I am proposing that the prisoner once lived in a community that had a name starting with "Auger." I wonder if the *D* at the beginning of his name is a relic of a preposition that got elided into the rest of the name. Possibly someone, hearing "d'Auger," spelled it without an apostrophe. As has been said before, spelling of family names was often approximated and what was heard by the ear would often be written by the hand in a manipulated or broken set of letters that might be the spelling of a similar name that the listener had seen in the past, for instance the bishop Louis Fouquet wrote "Cinq Mars" for "Saint-Mars" in his letter about the sighting of the prisoner in Provence.

Searching for Dauger's origins using the spelling of his last name requires an understanding of the French use of the apostrophe in conjunction with the preposition *de*. The English translations of *de* and its elided form *d'* are

CHAPTER 15. THE CLUE OF THE MISSING APOSTROPHE   259

"from" or "of." In English there is no difference in the spelling of the prepositions "from" or "of" when they come in front of a vowel or a consonant; an English speaker says, "He is from Orléans," and "He is of the Touraine." The grammatical rule in French for placing the prepositions *from* (*de*) or *of* (*de*) in front of a place name is, if the place name begins with a consonant, the preposition is written *de,* for example, *de* Montpellier, and if the place name starts with a vowel, the preposition is elided to *d* + *apostrophe,* for example *d'*Artagnan or *d'*Orléans. In this grammatical context an apostrophe is used to signify that a letter has been omitted.

De Indicates Noble Status (Most Of The Time)

Usually surnames in French that have a *de* or a *d'* before the name signify that the person owns land or has seigneurial title to a parcel of land, but there can be surnames that have a *de* or a *d'* in front of the name that do not indicate nobility. The preposition is used without social signals but in a literal way, uniquely to show the connection to a place.

The surname that is at the center of this mystery is "Dauger." In the name "Dauger" there is no apostrophe that would indicate that the person owns land in or is affiliated with a place called Auger. Possibly an apostrophe was dropped in the day-to-day business of work and need for simplicity. A "dropped" child was more likely to have a dropped apostrophe in his name, because of a lack of social standing or to avoid interest, if public interest was unwanted. Or simply from carelessness.

However in various documents written in Dauger's lifetime, his name is spelled d'Auger." Do we have reason to believe that the man was from Auger, if such a place were to exist, or that his father had a connection or owned land in Auger? Was the *D* at the beginning of Dauger an incomplete elision of the article *de*? Or is the name Dauger totally unconnected to the name of a place, just like Joan of Arc's father who was named Darc but was not from Arc.

The main actors in the Mask mystery and the scholars who have written about it have occasionally played loose and lively with the Mask's surname and that has not been helpful to anyone at all. In the writing of Dauger's name there has been a storm of prepositions (*de* and *d'*; *De* and *D'*) with and without apostrophes, various spellings of the rest of the name, leading to contradictory insinuations of social status, in which the king, Louvois, and Saint-Mars all roll around in the orthographic confusion, with some people (maybe the king) writing the name "d'Auger" (because he has friends who have that name), Saint-Mars writing it "d'Auger" in his August 21, 1669 letter to Louvois,[480] Louvois writing it "Dauger" in his letter to Saint-Mars on

July 19, 1669, and "d'Angers" in his April 18, 1680 letter, and even "Logier" on November 27, 1672.

The confusion in the spelling of "Dauger" has been a detective's nightmare. Writers on the Mask often say that Louvois and the king purposefully obfuscated the details of the arrest and incarceration so that anyone who got curious would never find clues. Although that's true, some of the problems have come from the lax spelling practices of the time. The *sieur* X would know that the *sieur* YY spelled his name on letters, "YY," but *sieur* X might write "Y" if he was referring to YY, either not caring or not remembering that his friend spelled his name "YY." It was all acceptable, and no one had to pay a price for a name spelled variably over dozens of documents as long as the general meaning came through and the person being named was understood among all parties.

But when it comes to parsing finite bits of clues to a mystery, the spelling *does* matter.

If the Man in the Iron Mask's name had started with letters *other than D + a vowel*, like Fontaine or Masson or Collet, the task of tracing him would be very difficult or impossible. As it is, we have a chance of finding him if first, we acknowledge that one path to thinking about Dauger's location before he was arrested is to wonder if the name of his former home is located in his surname; Dauger with a *D* and no apostrophe in his name *could* mean that he was *from* Auger but not a landowner and without rank in society.

Mapping Dauger

I spent a lot of time with ancient and modern maps looking for places in France, The Netherlands, Belgium, and Canada with Auger in the name, as well as Dauger, Ogier, d'Auger, Auge, Dauge, Daugé and other variations. Almost all the candidates were in France, one or two in Canada, some on the border with Belgium. I looked at maps and satellite images without knowing what I was looking for, names of villages, mountains, roads, icons for churches, lakes, abbeys. There are far too many places with Auge in the name to list. Normandy has twenty-six towns named Auge because they have a historical territory named the Pays d'Auge in the department of Calvados. A few: Barou-en-Auge, Castillon-en-Auge, Les-Moutiers-en-Auge, Saint-Pierre-en-Auge. People who live in the *pays* are called *Augerons* or *Augeronnes*.

In addition to the concretion of towns in the Calvados department, there are many towns all over France with Auge in their names or a variation of Auge.

CHAPTER 15. THE CLUE OF THE MISSING APOSTROPHE

- Auge, department of Ardennes, region of Grand-Est
- Auge, department of Charente, region of Nouvelle-Aquitaine
- Auge, department of Creuse, region of Nouvelle-Aquitaine
- Auge, department of Jura, region of Bourgogne-Franche-Comté
- Augé, department of Deux-Sèvres, region of Nouvelle-Aquitaine
- Auge-Saint-Médard, department of Charente, region Nouvelle-Aquitaine, merged with Auge and La Bréchoire into commune of Val-d'Auge
- Augea, department of Jura, region of Bourgogne-Franche-Comté
- Augeat, department of Jura, region of Bourgogne-Franche-Comté
- Auger-Saint-Vincent, department of Oise, region of Hauts-de-France
- Auger-Saint-Mard, department of Oise, region of Hauts-de-France
- Augerans, department of Jura, region of Bourgogne-Franche-Comté
- Augers-en-Brie, department of Seine-et-Marne, region of Ile-de-France
- Augerville-la-Rivière, department of Loiret, region of Centre-Val-de-Loire
- Augès (now Mallefougasse-Augès), department of Alpes-de-Haute-Provence, region of Provence-Alpes-Côte d'Azur
- Augeville (now Pautaines-Augeville), department of Haute-Marne, region of Grand Est
- Augeville, department of Seine-Maritime, region of Normandy, merged into Bosc-le-Hard in 1813

I found a fishing pond named Saint Ogier in Lorraine, department of the Vosges, and the village of L'Isle Auger, near Loches in the Indre-et-Loire department. I thought I was onto something when I found the town of Croix in the Nord department of the Hauts-de-France region because it is not only near Calais, it has a street, a park, and a sports stadium named Ogier.

I looked for seventeenth-century people who had a connection of any sort with the name Auger and found one whose surname was Auger, his name originating with a body of water. Father Edmond Auger (1530–1591) was the Jesuit confessor of King Henri III and was a noted preacher, scholar, and writer, trained by Saint Xavier (1506–1552). His family name came from the name of a stream called les Auges, a tributary of the small river called the Grand Morin that runs through the Marne and Seine-et-Marne departments in the historical region of Champagne. In the thirteenth century monks harnessed the stream using wooden troughs to bring water into Sézanne, a town near his birthplace. In French, "trough" translates to "*auger*."[481] The origin of this name serves as a warning on the path of assuming that a person's family name is always the name of a place. Although the little stream known as "les Auges" is a place, the algorithm that time, family preferences, and geography create to designate names does not have rules and differs from region to region.

I looked over the list of towns, and decided that the likeliest candidates would be those that had the exact formation of letters that is in the name Dauger, which stripped down the list considerably; all that remained were the villages L'Ile Auger in the Loire Valley, Auger-Saint-Vincent, and Auger-Saint-Mard in the Valois, the latter two being a half mile from each other and combined in modern times to one village.

The name of L'Ile Auger did not begin with Auger, so I started to focus on Auger-Saint-Vincent, a town in the Oise department in the historical region of Picardy and found half the history of France in a miniature portrait: Childebert, Charlemagne, Eleanore of Aquitaine, Madame de Sévigné, the Bastard of Dunois, and Joan of Arc... victorious and imprisoned.

16. Oger The Dane

> The emperor goes underneath a pine
> and calls his barons up to give him counsel:
> Archbishop Turpin and the duke Oger,
> Richard the Old and his descendant Henry
> from Gascony, the bold count Acelin,
> Milon, Thibaud of Reims, his cousin
> Gerin and Gerier were also there —
> Together with the others came Count Roland
> and valorous, well-born Olivier —
> More than a thousand Franks from France were there.
> And Ganelon the traitor came there, too.
> The council that gave rise to grief now starts.
> The Song of Roland, 12, 170

A Short History Of The Valois

Shakespeare said in his tragedy *Macbeth*, "The land has bubbles as the water does." During my years of research on the Man in the Iron Mask I have uncovered many bubbles in the documents of the case that have suggested to me that Dauger might have lived in the Valois, an historical district in the region formerly known as Picardy, for some part of his life before he was arrested by Louis XIV in July 1669. My discoveries are the first hints of where the prisoner might have been before he was a prisoner. Since historians and their followers have fervently wanted to know even a good guess about this, in this chapter I have expanded my theory and described the land he may have known. Here is a short portrait of the Valois and the area around Auger-Saint-Vincent, a village in the center of it.

One of France's richest territories for forests and planted plains, Picardy is in northern France to the west of Belgium and Germany. In World War I and World War II it absorbed a lot of blood; before the armies in 1914 marched across Flanders Fields they marched across Picardy fields. Picardy[482] is known to have many underground communal refuges because the land has been so often invaded by soldiers trying to get somewhere else; farmers and their families reached permanent homemade underground bunkers and waited for the invading soldiers above to burn their homes and slaughter any sheep or goats the residents had not been able to drag down into the tunnel with their children. Picardy farmers have often had to wait for soldiers' heels to march away before they could emerge into the daylight and survey the wreckage.

Julius Caesar (100 B.C.E.–44 C.E.) at the beginning of the first millennium calculated that he could rule Rome by conquering the Celtic tribes in Gaul. The glory, he thought, would bring him an empire. The Aeduii, the Belgii, the Arverni, and other Gallic tribes fought Julius Caesar valiantly but by 51 B.C.E. he was master. He saw that their forests, so precious to them for their mystery and economic possibilities, were one of the most valuable parts of his new territory, and he continued the long tradition of taking care of them because they provided green wood for building and fencing, dead wood for heat, undergrowth for pigs to graze on, and wild game to eat: birds, rabbits, deer, and boars. Augustus Caesar and Agrippa, his engineer, built straight roads across Gaul to connect these forests and to travel through them, often labeled in much later times *Chaussées Brunehaut*.[483]

German tribes invaded from the east through Picardy and overcame Roman France, and they also valued the forests and created forestry administrations to regulate usage. In the sixteenth century *capitaineries* were created by the king, administered by royal salaried captains, who were often *seigneurs* in royal favor, who limited some forests to royal use, scheduled the annual cutting, mowing, selling, prohibited transgression of rules, and punished criminal behavior. One of these captaincies was headquartered at Villers-Cotterêts, very near Auger-Saint-Vincent, and it controlled the large forest named the Halatte, formerly commanded by the Celtic Sylvanectes tribe, extending from Paris north to Laon.

> In the distant past, the forest of Halatte was part of the forest of Cuise (*Cotia Sylva*), which united under its name the great hills of Retz (*Retia Silva*), of Compiègne, des Ageux (*Haya or Laya*), of Halatte (*Ilaya Lata*), the woods of Chantilly and of Hérivaux.[484]

A map of the Valois shown on the Auger-Saint-Vincent webpage shows the Valois to be bound by the forest of Compiègne at the north, Villers-Cotterêts forest on the east, the city of Senlis and the forest of Ermenonville at the southwest, and the town of Le Plessis-Belleville to the south.[485] The Automne River flows through the departments of Aisne and Oise and merges into the Oise river just above Verberie on the northwest of the *pays*.

CHAPTER 16. OGER THE DANE

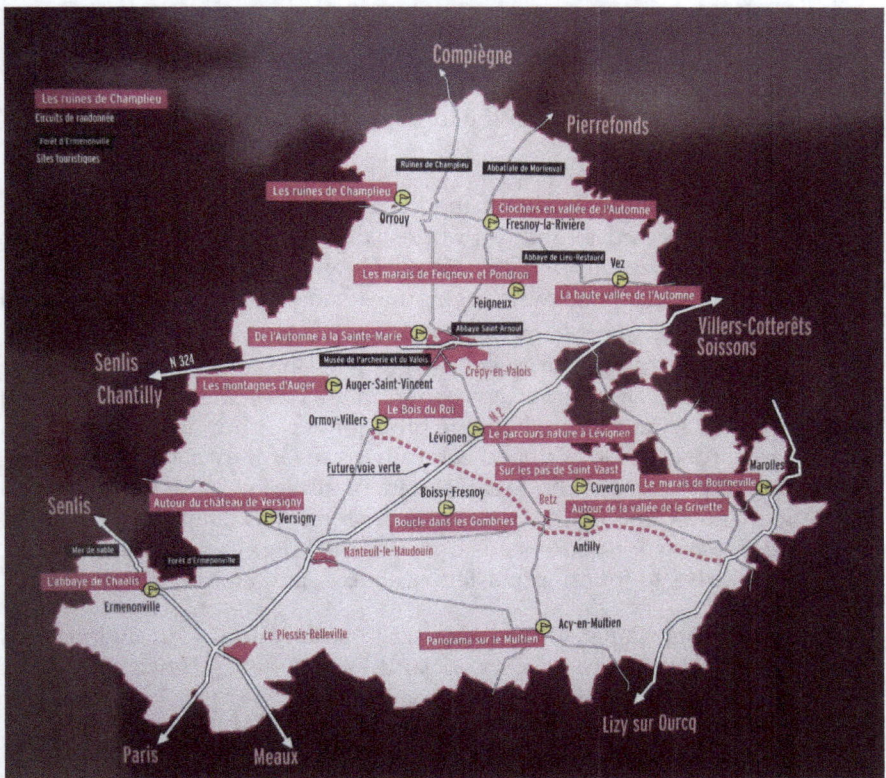

Figure 16.1: Map posted at the Auger-Saint-Vincent city hall showing the territory of the Valois. Photo by the author 2015.

The Valois Was A Royal Domain

Hugh Capet (circa 940–996), duke of the Franks, took advantage of the weakness of the reigning Carolingian king and was proclaimed king of the Franks in 987 by an assembly of leaders held in Senlis, a Valois city founded by the Romans in which the Merovingian and Carolingian kings and queens often held court. That is how the third race of French royalty, the Capets, came to power, and the Valois was a royal domain during all three races' tenure. The duchy's name comes from the Latin name for the fortified residence of the Merovingian and Carolingian counts that controlled the county before the year 1000: *Vadum*.

King Philippe-Auguste (1165–1223) appropriated the Valois in 1185. The counts of Valois had had their capital at Vez, between the towns of Crépy-en-Valois and Villers-Cotterêts, but Philippe-Auguste moved the capital to

Crépy-en-Valois and gave Vez to Raoul d'Estrées as a gift for his help in winning the battle of Bouvines. In 1284 King Philippe-le-Hardi (1245–1285) made the Valois into a duchy that he ordered would be under the control of the second son of all kings in the future and at each duke's death would return to the king.

A nineteenth-century historian of the Valois asked, "How was it that this *forêt d'Halatte* attracted so many Priories, Communities and Abbeys that were grouped as bees around the hive? How did it become a royal forest in which so many kings with their suites had passed in the shade of its trees?"[486] The irony often found in the rules that kings set for their realms is seen here: while a king or queen wages war and spends lots of money to reach a pinnacle, above and separate from all, he or she at the same time cannot separate from those who have brought her or him to power and so must be rewarded... and watched carefully to see if they show signs of interest in another master. The royal leaders of all three races, Merovingian, Carolingian, and Capetian, gave parts of the forest of Halatte to those loyal to them as presents for good deeds done for the king. In turn, many recipients used the gifts to found monasteries, abbeys, and churches.

The queen of Hugh Capet, Queen of the Franks Adélaïde of Aquitaine (circa 950–1004), founded the monastery of Saint-Frambourg in Senlis in 990 and her gift was imitated by queens, dukes, and counts to show their affiliation with the Frankish royal family and to thank God that the world had not ended in the year 1000, as many had thought it would. Another monastery in Senlis established in 1062 by Anne of Kiev (circa 1027–1075), queen and widow of Henri I (1008–1060), was dedicated to Saint-Vincent of Saragossa (d. circa 304).[487] The abbey of Chaalis founded by Louis VI (1081–1137) in memory of his brother Charles, the abbey of Sainte-Victoire built by Philippe-Auguste (1165–1223) to give thanks for his victory over the English, the emperor, and the Flemish at Bouvines (July 27, 1214), and the abbey of Royaumont, the recipient of King Louis IX's (1214–1270) riches, protection, and personal visits, were royal houses of God that formed "...a magistrature of peace in an area where the battles each day made life violent."[488]

Auger-Saint-Vincent

At the beginning of the twenty-first century there were approximately 51,000 people living in the Valois and in 2020 the Auger-Saint-Vincent town administration estimated that 500 of them lived in Auger-Saint-Vincent.[489]

The town's center is dominated by a church dedicated to Saint Caprais[490] of Agen (d. circa 303), a hermit and bishop martyred under Emperor Diocletian (244–311). Its second patron is Saint-Vincent of Saragossa. A structure for worship was probably on the place in the eleventh century but the tower and the existing early Gothic shelter for worshipers were completed in the twelfth century and many additions have taken place over a thousand years. Old flaking blue paint is still on a few of the engaged columns painted by a decorator's hand in the far past.

There are four places in the vicinity of Auger-Saint-Vincent that drew my attention when I studied old and new maps of the town and the surrounding countryside.

Mont Cornon, Fortress Of Oger The Dane

At Verberie near Senlis, Emperor Charlemagne (748–814) had a summer residence where he kept company with his knights, one of whom was Oger the Dane (Ogier, Hoger, and Hogier are alternate spellings), who was, according to one legend, a former heir to the crown of Denmark who preferred to serve Charlemagne and was rewarded with land in the neighborhood of Verberie 2.3 miles (3.7 kilometers) north of Oger-(Auger)-Saint-Vincent at a crossing of the great road to Flanders, the *Chaussée Brunehaut*, at the hamlet of Chavercy. The abbot Claude Carlier, an eighteenth-century historian of the Valois, wrote that at Chavercy there was:

> ...a hillock a quarter of a league long (.75 miles), about three hundred feet wide. It is surrounded on all sides by slopes, like a mound: its surface is flat. Oger, who had decided to build a chateau, chose this mound to place it on. He found, towards the middle of one of the lengths of this hill, a crescent-shaped depression and he resolved to build there.[491]

Also in Charlemagne's donation to his knight were the villages of Oger-Saint-Mard and Oger-Saint-Vincent, Reuilly, Chamicy, Verrines, Leplessy-Cornefroy, and Trumilly.[492] Oger[493] built a *château-fort* on the top of the "hillock" which came to be known as Mont Cornon.[494] It had a large tower, two other smaller towers, and a chapel in between. In 1690 one could still see parts of the wall of the chapel, and in 1749 the iron gate of the fortress was still in the ruins on the hill.[495] After Oger died around 811 his lands returned to the crown and at the beginning of the tenth century they were given to the counts of Valois. (Martigny Daniel, twenty-first century historian of the Oise department, says he thinks this name comes from a former landowner of the hill and is probably older than the eighteenth-century maps that show it. By email to the author from Martigny Daniel, October 15, 2023.)

Oger the Dane's name drifted into the names of places and people in the Valois, who desired to appropriate some of Oger's glory and to emphasize Charlemagne's affection for their homeland.[496] The historian Carlier said that in charters and acts of notaries of the twelfth and thirteenth centuries he found many people named Oger, and a twenty-first-century historian and Mask author, Paul Sonnino, found in the archives of the Oise department that the name of Oger in its various spellings—Ogier, Auger, and Augier—continually appear.[497] Oger's name appeared on playing cards; famous knights and queens were objects of affection and emulation for children and adult players, who threw down cards on the table that had colorful pictures of historical kings, queens, and jacks (jacks are called *valets* in French), their names written next to their faces, and Oger the Dane was usually on the *valet* of spades card. The first part of the name Auger-Saint-Vincent honors the knight who lived in their neighborhood once upon a time, and even if Oger the Dane and some of his story are debatable, the attachment to Oger by communities in the Valois cannot be questioned.[498] Myth becomes stronger than fact over time; a place where your ancestors lived becomes hallowed, and their glory is borrowed and enjoyed by decision makers of descending eras. Claude Carlier wrote, "In the end, there is no fable that doesn't have some truth, a fact in its foundation. Fables do not erase truth. They mix with truth in the mists without doing any damage to either. Dissipate the mists with the flame of critical thinking, and the truth will shine through."[499]

Parc Aux Dames

Only one mile (1.9 km) from Auger-Saint-Vincent is a property called Parc aux Dames,[500] where, four hundred years after Charlemagne's death, a noble woman named Eléonore of Vermandois (circa 1149–1213) founded an abbey for women in 1205. It is a vast privately owned park now, with a small lake.

The ever helpful *abbé* Claude Carlier said that Eléonore had not been able to have children with her husband, Matthew, count of Beaumont. She saw that the best way to leave a legacy was to begin giving money and land to religious establishments and to perhaps start a monastery. Her opportunity to do that came when her sister Elisabeth died. Her brother-in-law, the count of Flanders, Philippe d'Alsace, inherited his wife Elisabeth's (d. 1183) property, including the Valois, and they had no heirs. The way in which Elisabeth's sister Eléonore was able to control the land of Parc aux Dames is not clear in the historical accounts but in reading Carlier it looks as if Eléonore got the land away from Philippe d'Alsace by the intervention of Philippe-Auguste, the king, Eléonore's cousin, and he gave permission to

Eléonore in a charter in 1194 to donate the lands to support the religious life of the Valois, and the Parc aux Dames was her largest and most permanent gift.[501] In short, the king took the land and then allowed Eléonore to dispose of it.

Eléonore's parents, Raoul (d. 1151) and Pétronille (1125– ?) the sister of Eléonore of Aquitaine (1122–1204), count and countess of Vermandois and Valois, were major donors to the abbey of Longpont,[502] also in the Valois, founded seventy-three years before, a Cistercian monastery, as was her own Parc aux Dames. She set about building her abbey according to Longpont's example.

The monastery had among its first donors Philippe I de Nanteuil, the son of the countess of Dammartin, Nicolas de Chavercy, the Chevalier Simon, mayor of Acy-en-Multien, Marguerite countess of Blois, King Saint Louis (Louis IX 1214–1270), his mother Blanche of Castile (1188–1252), and Isabelle de France, Louis' sister. Nanteuil, Dammartin, Chavercy, and Acy-en-Multien are names of Valois towns near Parc aux Dames, so these *seigneurs* and countesses were local donors to the new abbey.

The first abbess of the monastery of Parc aux Dames was named Elisabeth (d. 1224?). She had been replaced before the year 1224 by the second abbess named Catherine, who herself was followed by five abbesses, Eustache I, Richilde, Marie de Voisins, Marguerite la Rigaude, and Catherine II.[503] The third abbess, the seventh, and the ninth abbess were all named Eustache, which can be the name of a female as well as a male, although sometimes the name was feminized to Eustachie.[504]

The abbey was almost destroyed during the Hundred Years' War between England and France. The English burned the church, the belltower, the gateway, and the refectory. Then famine came to the region. Only one nun survived.[505] The abbey was destroyed after the French Revolution, completely, down to the soil; only some dependencies remain and a small section of the chapel.

The Fouquets At Parc Aux Dames

Even in the heart of the Valois, the Paris branch of the Fouquet family was active. They were known, this family, as an interdependent, close clan whose resources were both financial and strategic, and they also were, Nicolas Fouquet in particular, problem solvers. They were productive and successful. They rose to the top of their chosen professions and this was true for the female members of the family as well as the male.

Three women in the family were abbesses of Parc aux Dames. Suzanne Morély was a relative of Marie de Maupeou Fouquet, possibly a maternal aunt, and she was the thirty-third abbess. Marie's sister Marguerite (d. 1652) was the thirty-fourth abbess beginning in 1647,[506] and one of her daughters, sister to Nicolas, Marie-Elisabeth (d. 1683), was the thirty-fifth abbess of Parc aux Dames from 1652 to 1683.[507] Nicolas used his powerful position as chief lawyer for the king in parlement and his wealth to help his sister Elisabeth to repair and upgrade Parc aux Dames, where the church vaults were crumbling, the cloister was half finished, and a new altar was needed, which Nicolas provided. It bore the following inscription:

> Nicolas Fouquet, vicount of Melun, having the highest position in the Senate, procurer general, donated this altar during the time that his sister, Elisabeth, was abbess of the Monastery in the year 1658.[508]

L'Arbre De Beaulieu

In the winter of 2015 I had been seduced by the lore of Charlemagne and his court, particularly the honorable knight Oger, and had carefully studied old and new maps of the Valois, all in preparation for a personal visit to the formerly royal domain. I had been pouring over the Cassini maps[509] of the historical Valois, particularly the area around Auger-Saint-Vincent. I was not looking for anything particular; I was just trying to get an idea of where the major towns were in relation to one another... measuring distances... enjoying the rhythm and poetry of the place names. My husband, an archaeologist who specializes in interpreting old maps, taught me how to use France's IGN webpage to bring forward maps of France of different time periods and I had happily been exploring not only the immediate vicinity of Auger-Saint-Vincent but had dawdled in the little hatched ridges of other parts of the southern Valois, the Seine-et-Marne department to the south, the lands east of Senlis, large woods and little *bois*, little hills with icons for "*justice*," indicating a place of trial and punishment, scribbled blocks of buildings with crosses on top (a church or chapel), and bigger deposits of blocks with bigger crosses for abbeys. Near Senlis[510] are the lands that belonged to the rich and influential house of Orgemont and then the Montmorency until the last duke of that faithful house committed a grave act of treason against Louis XIII and the king took the lands and gave them to his cousins, the Condé.

I went to the Auger-Saint-Vincent website and found a treasure of facts, place names, and people of the ancient Valois, and I was especially grateful to the village officials who had taken great care to give a detailed history of their town and an explanation of the two parts of the town's name,

CHAPTER 16. OGER THE DANE

Auger and *Saint-Vincent*. But it was when I returned to the Cassini map that I noticed, very near Auger-Saint-Vincent, a tiny icon of a single tree and it intrigued me. It was labeled the "*Arbre de Beaulieu*"... the "Tree of Beaulieu." It was next to another icon for a minor religious establishment labeled "Beaulieu."

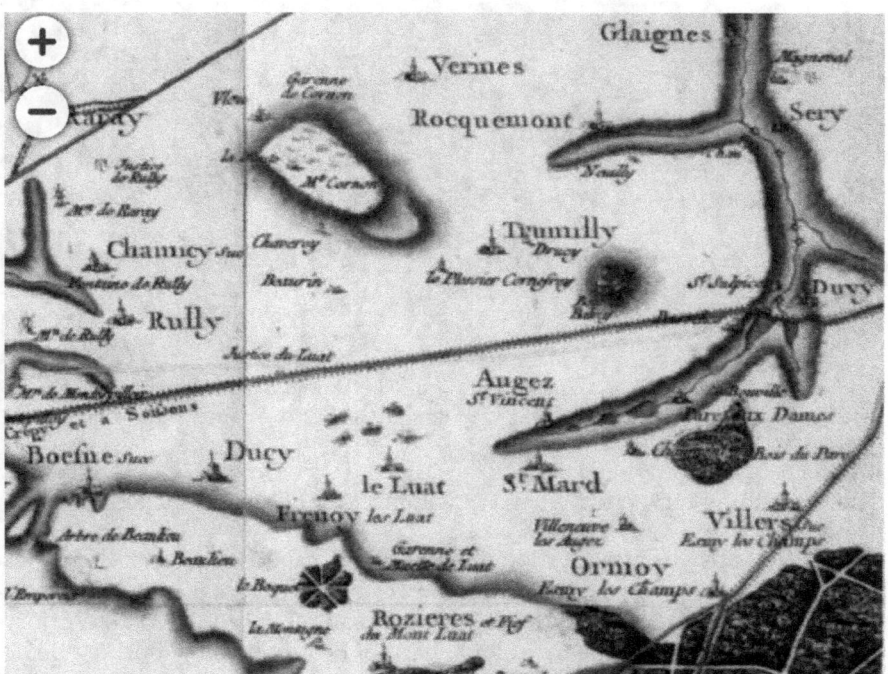

Figure 16.2: The icon for the Tree of Beaulieu is at the left of this Cassini map dated 1756...a very small tree in the shape of a L under the label "*Arbre de Beaulieu*." You can also see Parc aux Dames to the east of Auger-Saint-Vincent. Cassini map courtesy of The United States Library of Congress.

When my husband and I drove to the Valois in May 2015, we went first to Auger-Saint-Vincent, parked the car, and saw the outside of the church Saint-Caprais (the inside was locked) and looked at the west façade that had recently been restored; we read some public postings about the history of the area at the town hall. There was no one on the streets, no one at city hall... only some pigeons on the church tower, and they were not impressed with us.

Then we drove to Parc aux Dames, only a few minutes away, which we found by asking directions a number of times and finally taking a jostling drive down a narrow gravel pathway but there was a large iron gate across the entrance to the park, so we couldn't go further. It is a private property.

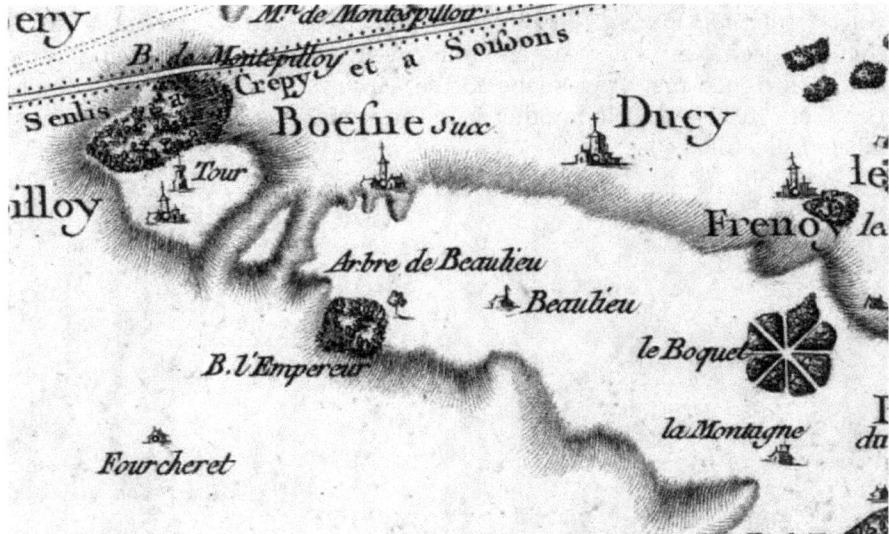

Figure 16.3: Detail of Cassini map courtesy of The United States Library of Congress. The icon for the "Arbre de Beaulieu" appears just under the name of the landmark.

The same thing happened when we went to Mont Cornon: locked fence.

I wanted to answer my question about what Beaulieu was and if there was a tree there, so we stopped where some people were repairing a barn and I asked a man where Beaulieu was. The man said, "Oh, you mean the priory of Beaulieu!" That was the first I had heard of Beaulieu being a priory. So he gave us directions and we found Beaulieu, a privately owned farm, standing alone on a bald hill with a 360-degree view over the countryside.[511] There was another set of buildings across the highway that looked much newer that I later learned was the "new" Beaulieu. We drove up to the walled farm and got out. We rang the bell at the gate and asked the person who responded if the owner was there but she said no. We looked around for a tree but didn't see one. I walked down the gravel and sand lane where one of the old barns was and my husband took my photo with the farm behind me. He also noticed some white places on a flat area of grass just in front of the entrance gate. He photographed them. We were due to be somewhere else and were tired after a full day so we went back to our hotel.

When I got home I discovered the existence of a group in France that preserves data about historical trees in France. It is aptly named A.R.B.R.E.S. I wrote to them for help on discovering what the Tree of Beaulieu might have been. I had seen on the Cassini map an icon in the shape of a tree marked as "*Arbre de Beaulieu*" just south of the Valois communes of Ducy and Fresnoy-le-Luat. Next to it was another marker for a place named Beaulieu. I said I had just returned from France and had visited the place where this icon is and that I was directed to Beaulieu by a person I had stopped on the road for directions who said it was a priory. I said I didn't see a tree there but on the modern IGN map I had bought of the area there were many places named "*L'Orme de ....*" et "*Le Buisson Pouilleux*" et "*Le Poirier de la Crosse*," so I could tell it was customary in that area to name places after trees. I was curious that there was not a tree at the old priory that could be significant enough to be marked on a Cassini map but that there must have been one in the past and could the association help me learn what it was.

The president of A.R.B.R.E.S., Georges Feterman, wrote back that it often happens that a place has the name of a tree that is no longer living but the name has remained. Another member of the association, Frédéric Cousseran, also wrote to me and sent some information on the old *Arbre de Beaulieu*, which he said was now dead. He referred me to a document registering the "*Vieille Orme de Beaulieu*" on France's *Base Mérimée* that shows a photo of the top of the hill in front of the door to the farm enclosure with the old tree with scaffolding all around it, no leaves and almost no branches, probably already dead and being held up by the scaffolding as a last effort to keep the famous tree standing. The note says "Marked on old maps, [the tree] stands where it did when Joan of Arc's troops passed on their return from Reims where Charles VII was crowned and when Joan was taken prisoner in 1430 and put in the jail at the chateau of Beaulieu-les-Fontaines nearby. The tree was known at the time of Henri IV. The owners of the property have tried to conserve the tree." The department archivist of the Oise, Madame Romet, told me that the farms of *Beaulieu-le-Vieux* and *Beaulieu-le-Neuf* are today in the commune of Baron. The archivist said that the farm of Beaulieu was bought in 1775 by Jean-Baptiste Chartier from Antoine Lhoste, *maître ordinaire de la chambre des comptes* (*acte de vente du 12 avril 1775 passé devant Me Boursier, notaire à Paris*). She also said Beaulieu had likely been a seigneurial farm that was owned by a religious establishment. In 1840 the property was divided into two making the "old" farm and the "new" farm. (Email to the author from Clotilde Romet, Directrice des archives départementales de l'Oise, July 30, 2015).

If the person who gave me directions to Beaulieu, who identified the farm as a "*prieuré*" was speaking from historical knowledge of the farm, then it must at one time have been a "...country house of a church administrator" according to a definition of French country manor houses in one scholar's study.[512] The *Base Mérimée* and the Oise archives do not have a record of this, however, so it may be that the characterization of the farm as a "priory" is a local tradition.

The *Base Mérimée* entry gives the name of the farm as *Manoir de Beaulieu-le-Vieux* and says it was a "*grange dimière*," that is, a farm that stored the produce that the farmers in the *seigneurie* owed to the *seigneur* that owned the land. Taxes were paid, not in coin, but in wheat, sheep, hogs, and other products of the farmers' work and a tenth of what was produced was owed in tax, thus the name "*dimière*," "tenth." Beaulieu was declared a protected cultural asset by the government of France in 1982. The government's documentation notes that the original "*pediluve*," a footbath to wash horses' hooves when they come back from the fields, is still in the inner courtyard. The house and barns date to the sixteenth century with restorations in the seventeenth and eighteenth centuries. The formation of the house and two barns makes a U-shape with the courtyard in the center. The wall around the courtyard with the house and commons is of the eighteenth century and there is a continuation of the wall around the rest of the farm. There are two simple small houses at the far end of the enclosure.

Whoever wrote the *Base Mérimée's* description of the setting of the farm accurately defined its beauty in this sentence: "The manor is... a large ensemble isolated in the middle of the fields and visible from afar."[513] The *Arbre de Beaulieu* that can be seen in old photos before the dead tree had to be removed, was huge... a single, giant marker over the flat plain of living crops on either side of the highway between Paris and Compiègne. On the sunny day in May that I was there, the crisp sound of the wind flowed over the silence of a grand vanilla vista; I looked for the tree and didn't see it, not yet understanding that a tree which was young when Joan of Arc and Etienne de Vignolles passed by on their way to the battle of Montépilloy and in its glory when Eustache Dauger and Madame de Sévigné were alive, would most certainly be gone by 2015. I understood that inevitability later when we got home and my husband, after looking carefully at his photos of the ground at the front gate of Beaulieu, said that the white marks in the ground outside the old house were not stones but the rocky dead remains of the famous tree. In French government photos taken over the last fifty years the tree declines from a skeleton with scaffolding, then round slices of the trunk posed on its grave, to finally the dusty marks of its soul that we saw when we drove up the hill to find the Tree of Beaulieu.

Figure 16.4: Image courtesy of L'Association A.R.B.R.E.S. pour les amoureux de la nature. https://www.arbres.org

17. Madame De Sévigné's Clues

I can say in advance that both these courses lead to the same conclusion — that the uncanny is that species of the frightening that goes back to what was once well known and had long been familiar.

—Sigmund Freud

Marie De Rabutin-Chantal, Marquise De Sévigné

The first *rapporteur* of French history I ever heard of was Madame de Sévigné. In 1963, my father, after a day of research in the Bibliothèque Nationale, told me that his day at the library had been exciting and eventful. One could, he said, respectfully ask to see letters of Madame de Sévigné and the librarian would bring you a folder of them...the original letters! I asked who this lady was and he told me she wrote letters to people about Louis XIV's court. In retrospect, I wish I had asked which of her letters he had requested to see because he was studying Danton and Robespierre, leaders of the French Revolution who lived a hundred years after the marquise de Sévigné. It shows that to appreciate any period of France except for the earliest days of the Franks and the Merovingians, one must read Sévigné. She speaks the universal French experience...and with brio!

In two of Madame de Sévigné's many famous letters,[514] she said that she saw "Auger" when he was a boy. She wrote to her daughter on October 18, 1671: "This Auger is a boy that I have seen and to whom I would speak, and who told me all that very naively. I am positive about it."[515] Her reputation with historians is that, in addition to being a brilliant writer, she knew things that no one else knew, but how she knew them is not always clear. In the following interpretation of her mysterious letter, which has never been deciphered by Sévigné scholars, it seems she may have known that at one time, Dauger was at Beaulieu.

Never has a mother's love for her child given history such flavor and steam as the love of Madame de Sévigné (1626–1696) for her daughter Françoise, the comtesse de Grignan (1646–1705). Madame de Sévigné was a French widow who pined permanently for her displaced adult daughter, who had moved away from Paris to live with her husband in Provence. She is arguably history's most important lady of letters, literally, because her letters to her daughter Françoise over more than twenty years and also to friends and relatives gave precious, bevelled insights into the society of Paris and Versailles in the seventeenth century. On Madame's stationery, Françoise went with her to the wedding on 29 November 1679 of the daughter of the powerful minister of war, the marquis de Louvois, at his chateau of Meudon near Paris that Louvois had bought only a month before the wedding. Madame knew that Françoise was familiar with the setting; the chateau of Meudon sat above Paris with a view over the city and the upriver banks of the Seine.

> What should I tell you? Magnificence, fireworks. All of France clothed in gorgeous costumes threaded with gold, precious stones, braziers of fire and flowers, traffic jam of carriages, shouts in the streets, flambeaux on fire, retreat of the crowd and exhaustion, then the swirl of confusion, fatigue, requests unanswered, compliments without credit, civility to strangers, aching feet in long lines.[516]

Philippe Coulanges (1562–1636), Madame de Sévigné's maternal grandfather, a civil servant who got very rich from the purchase and resale of the right to collect taxes, bought a collection of small properties at Sucy-en-Brie that he merged into one and built a large house.[517] Madame, born Marie de Rabutin-Chantal, was an orphan by age seven and Philippe Coulanges was her guardian so she spent many summers of her childhood in the country, free to wander by herself in the daytime, to survey fields and small huddles of trees overlooking the Marne river. Her unsupervised adventures gave her a love for nature, and many of her famous letters take the reader to gardens, trees, and clearings. In the winter, she lived at her grandfather's Paris *hôtel* on the Place Royale, now the Place des Vosges, a huge square of multi-storied brick and stone contiguous town homes built on the ruins of an old royal palace called Les Tournelles across the street from the Saint-Paul church and its cemetery.

Her children, Françoise and Charles (1648–1713), were fathered by the marquis Henri de Sévigné (d. 1651), a *Breton* nobleman, and it is through him that Madame acquired Les Rochers, a country chateau in northern Brittany. She had married the marquis in Saint-Gervais church in 1644 not far from the couple's Paris home on the rue des Lions-Saint-Paul. He didn't stay home much, though, just as most military men did not, either because they were away fighting for the king's agenda or because they were dueling at dawn in the open lawns of the Place Royale or the Pré-aux-Clercs, a narrow piece of unoccupied land on the Left Bank that belonged to the University

CHAPTER 17. MADAME DE SÉVIGNÉ'S CLUES 279

of Paris. But Henri de Sévigné was not killed on either of those two properties; he was shot by the chevalier d'Albret, brother of the future marshal, a "very pretty boy who killed all his world,"[518] behind Picpus[519] on February 4, 1651, and died two days later. Pistols had been drawn by the two men over the honor or lack thereof of Charlotte Bigot, known to her admirers as "La Belle Lolo." The only thing that remains of Charlotte Bigot's memory is that her reputation was the reason we have the remarkable Sévigné letters, which might not have been written had her husband lived. Madame de Sévigné had many suitors after her husband died, but she decided to remain single, a decidedly unusual decision for a widow... almost unheard of. She lived modestly but comfortably with an aunt just after her husband's death, and the two ladies brought up Françoise and Charles and four of her aunt's children. She never remarried, and aside from her occasional sojourns at Les Rochers,[520] she always lived in the Marais, never much farther than a half mile from the Place Royale where she had been born.

Madame, despite being a Paris townhouse dweller, knew the newest hairstyles at court, the magnificence of Madame de Montespan's gowns, and had been a neighbor of Madame de Montespan's usurper, the governess of the king's children, Françoise Scarron. At the end of each of her letters there was more passed to the reader than ringlets and bows; steel strings of recognition of the shadows of a society under the sway of devout, aristocratic, and royal families who showed themselves to be both ridiculous and dangerous at the same time. She repeated the stories she heard at dinner parties and from her correspondents like Ninon de l'Enclos, a courtesan, and from confidences from literati and military captains like the great marshal Turenne, a neighbor and suitor after her husband's death... and Nicolas Fouquet. She scattered her insights, always finding the comedic side of the social scene and always cautious not to reveal anything that would compromise anyone, in letters to her friends, to her cousin, Roger de Rabutin comte de Bussy (1618–1693), also a writer, and most importantly, to her daughter, Françoise, who married a nobleman, François Adhémar comte de Grignan (1632–1714), and moved with him to his chateau in Grignan in Provence[521] where he was lieutenant governor, the highest-ranking official of the province. Madame de Sévigné was so crushed by the departure from Paris of her daughter that she spent days in tears and lack of sleep after Françoise left in May 1671 in her traveling coach to make her way to Lyon, then over the Rhône, and finally to the Adhémar family's estate.

To console herself she wrote frequent letters to her daughter that are full of news from Paris and the court. Some of her letters are journalistic descriptions of political events that add human sentiments and wit to supplement dry official histories: a description of Nicolas Fouquet's trial for treason; the scene of Madame de Brinvilliers' execution by beheading and burning for poisoning her father, two brothers, and a number of other people. The stories of what the marquise de Sévigné saw and heard in Paris and in the neighborhood of Les Rochers in Brittany turn posterity's gaze from Louis XIV's ordered image of his court and wave her readers into an antechamber of gossip, things a mother would write to a daughter to keep her *au courant* with Paris' and the court's vicissitudes and foolishness.

Letter From Madame De Sévigné To Her Daughter Françoise, Comtesse De Grignan, From Les Rochers, October 18, 1671

Madame lived in Paris and near the rural coast of Brittany but her heart was with her daughter in Provence and her letters often show a struggle to blend all the scenery of her life and her daughter's life into the same moment, and that is the case of the letter in which she says she has seen Dauger in the past. The first paragraphs of the October 18, 1671 letter are pointed criticisms made directly to the comte de Grignan for making her daughter pregnant again because pregnancy strains her health. Then she says she longs to see Madame de Grignan's first child, a little girl, that had been born in Paris the previous year. "Alas!" she writes, "I would need the black man to create a highway in the air to you because the roads here below are so flooded that we are besieged."[522]

Then she quickly changes the subject from her grandchild and lamentations about the heavy rain she has had recently at Les Rochers and begins to respond to a story that her daughter has written to her about a man named Auger. Madame was careful not to give the mail censors any details.

> ...But I come back to your story. I made fun of La Mousse's[523] story but I don't mock yours at all. You told it very well, so well that I shivered when I read it; my heart beat hard. In truth, it is the strangest thing in the world. This Auger is a boy that I have seen and to whom I would speak, and who told me all that very naively. I am positive about it. It is a sylphe surely. After the promise you made, I don't doubt that those who bring you here [sylphes] will do it quickly. The recompense can be disputed, and if I don't see you coming, I will think that it is the result of a little war among them as to who should have the delight [to transport you]. It is well they should vie for the honor, and if sylphes could die, they could not choose a better battle for it. Finally, my dear daughter, thank you a thousand times for having so well told me this unusual story; this is the first of this kind that I would like to respond to.[524]

CHAPTER 17. MADAME DE SÉVIGNÉ'S CLUES

Figure 17.1: Les Rochers, Madame de Sévigné's Breton home. Photo by the author 2012.

Interpretation

Roger Duchêne, editor of Madame de Sévigné's letters, in his commentary about this letter struggled to explain the mysterious set of statements by judging she had mixed a Breton myth about the Korrigans, who were little beings that could transport people from one place to another with the speed of light in the mists (foam) of *La Mousse*, the fog and white rain that fall upon the Breton coasts frequently, with a story told by a servant of the comte de Grignan's household named Auger about a hermit named *frère* Nicolas who lived in Salon in Provence, and Duchêne cannot stop himself from adding that she is also showing her interest in the controversial Jansenist philosophy of the nuns at Port-Royal.[525] In Duchêne's theory, Auger is merely a conduit to the hermit.

The Black man...

The first mysterious reference she gives in her letter is "the black man" ("*homme noir*"). Without quite being finished with her preliminary remarks about fantastical travel, Madame says she could ask "the black man" to make a road for her that leads to Provence. But Madame de Grignan is not unprepared for the Black man; Françoise had just written to her mother about Auger's Black man and the mother is replying and adding thoughts and experiences of her own.

The sylphes...

The fantasies about sylphes and their habits are typical folkloric joy rides in praise of her daughter. Madame de Sévigné calls Auger a sylphe, a genie of the air according to Celtic romantic legend, because she has seen him in a certain place in the past, yet her daughter's letter poses him in an entirely different location, whether at Grignan or somewhere else. Sylphes, being air sprites, can move very fast between places and take travelers with them, and so to call Auger a sylphe means he has been in two very different places and she has seen him and talked to him in one place and is astonished to hear from her daughter that he is in another place. This overlapping of two different places is a common operation in the marquise's letters and usually it is to express her obsession to travel to her daughter, as it is here: Auger is a sylphe, and she needs a sylphe to conquer the muddy roads from Brittany to Provence to land in a second at her daughter's door. It is typical in Sévigné letters to see the topic change fast and jump from one cryptic pronouncement that is tied to a literary or mythical origin to another one that is based on a new theme. Her writing is sylphe-like. It moves fast.

La Mousse, the Hermit, and Port-Royal...

The reference to "La Mousse" is definitely a *double entendre* structured with her friend La Mousse and a Breton weather folktale about mists (mousse),[526] but La Mousse doesn't add to the underlying message and neither do the hermit or Port-Royal, a monastery in Paris. I suppose that Françoise de Grignan might have spent a lot of time and effort writing to her mother a story about a local hermit, but Madame's emotional response is out of line with that scenario. Madame is startled, shaken, unnerved, by what her daughter has written to her. Unless *frère* Nicolas was preaching heretical doctrine in the streets of Salon, there is nothing about him that would cause Madame's heart to beat violently.

The man named Auger who lived in the Grignan household...

Professor Michel Vergé-Franceschi, who had pointed me to Madame de Sévigné's knowledge of Dauger in his book on the Mask, was excited about this connection but I draw very different conclusions from Madame's comments than he did:

CHAPTER 17. MADAME DE SÉVIGNÉ'S CLUES 283

> The comte de Grignan... had at his house a person named Auger in 1669–1671... who himself had a black servant that Madame de Sévigné calls the 'black man of Auger' in five letters to her daughter in which she associates this black man with the English Order of the Garter! There is the heart of the history of the *Masque de fer*![527]

It is true that the Grignans had a person in their household named Auger and he may have had a Black servant. It might help solve the mystery if more about Auger's identity were known and exactly what his relationship was to the Grignans. But I think that Eustache Dauger and Grignans' Auger are two different people and probably do not have anything in common other than the similarity in their last names. The Grignan's Auger, said Vergé-Franceschi, was living in the comtesse's chateau in 1671 and Eustache Dauger had been arrested two years previously so they cannot be the same person. If Auger was Eustache Dauger, or his cousin, brother, or father, then, after all the searching that has been done for two hundred years by careful, professional researchers, it would seem such a simple link would have been made.

Madame de Sévigné's emotional response to what her daughter wrote her is evidence that the story is unusual and weird. To be strictly fair, maybe there were two Augers in France at that moment whose existence was frightening. It is possible. The name Auger in its many spellings was not a common name but was not an alien surname at the time either; it shows up infrequently here and there in newspaper reports about military events and policy creation, in charters and notarized documents.

A boy to whom I would speak...

The most revealing sentence Madame wrote is this one: "This Auger is a boy that I have seen and to whom I would speak, and who told me all that very naively." Not only does she say she has seen him but she says under what circumstances; that she "would" speak to him, which indicates she saw him a few times or possibly regularly, and would say hello to him and stop to have a conversation sometimes, or at least once when, "...he told [her] all that very naively," "that" being what her daughter had written to her about Dauger. She calls Dauger a "boy," so we know that when she saw him he was a boy. If his birth year was 1643 that means he was twenty-eight years old in 1671 when she wrote to her daughter that she had seen him in the past. If she saw him when he was still a "*garçon*" he must have been around twelve years old because she says he was very able to tell her his story. If he was twelve when they met, that would mean she had seen him in the years close to 1655. At that time she and her children were living in a house in the rue du Temple[528] with her aunt, Henriette, marquise de La Trousse and her aunt's four children. She moved there in 1651 when her husband died and lived there until 1669 when she moved to #8 rue de Thorigny. We can't know exactly where she saw Dauger, but we can learn from her use of the word "would," an auxiliary verb that here conveys a habitual past practice, that he was living where he could be accessed by a member of the public, not in seclusion, but in a household or institution of some sort where she visited occasionally.

It is allowed to guess: where "would" she regularly or infrequently see Dauger? In Paris on the rue du Temple at the Saint-Martin-des-Champs priory near her home? At the Saint-Louis-des-Jésuites church on the rue Saint-Antoine where she often went to hear Bourdaloue[529] preach? Was he a street beggar? Unlikely because ladies like the marquise would not stop to have interesting conversations with beggars. She attended literary salons at this time, including the exclusive salon of Marie-Madeleine Fouquet,[530] wife of Nicolas Fouquet, which met at the Fouquet's townhouse in Paris on the rue Croix-des-Petits-Champs. At the church of Notre-Dame-des-Anges on the rue Saint-Antoine, the chapel of the
religious order of the Visitation that her paternal grandmother[531] had founded? She had hundreds of friends in Paris, including some in the robe nobility and could have seen him at any of their houses: Guillaume de Lamoignon, chief president of the Paris parlement and godfather to Guillaume La Rivière, one of the Fouquets' foreign *emigré* adoptees who was Fouquet's valet at Pignerol; Simon, marquis de Pomponne; the cardinal de Retz; François, duc de La Rochefoucauld, author of the famous *Maximes*.

At the end of the paragraph she firmly says that the story is "unusual" and she described her reaction to it as physically stressful... that she shivered when she read about Auger and her heart beat very fast. Reading the story was a shock to the marquise, and whatever sort of person Françoise described to her, he was at least an "unusual" boy who had a unique set of circumstances or a history that he willingly, "naively," explained to Madame de Sévigné.

Her mother sent another letter to Françoise three days later on the same subject with a paragraph that was far more mysterious. It was her promised *réponse*.

Letter From Madame De Sévigné To Her Daughter Françoise, Comtesse De Grignan, From Les Rochers, October 21, 1671

Sévigné scholars have struggled to describe the 21 October letter that is a continuation of her comments in the 18 October letter without showing

CHAPTER 17. MADAME DE SÉVIGNÉ'S CLUES

much confidence in their own creativity. One called it "a wolf hunt that led to devilish deeds and Chinese shadows."[532] It is strange, disjointed, and seems to have a purpose but not a beginning or an end.

I read the letter and it was so incomprehensible that I realized that I would have to refresh my knowledge of Madame de Sévigné so I went to the library to read some journal articles about her writing, hoping to find an explanation of the text, but Sévigné scholars have never been able to understand this letter. What the professional scholars *did* know was that she, as did other *précieuses*, prided herself on playing games with her words and phrases, and in this social contest of witticisms a favorite game was the *jeu des portraits*, describing a place or a person using alterations of letters, allusions, similes, metaphors, and other word athletics to drop hints about the place's or person's identity that the reader was challenged to decipher.

First she gives her daughter news of the court: she writes about the upcoming second marriage of Monsieur (the brother of the king) to Elisabeth-Charlotte of the Palatinate. Then she vaults into a story about a walk she took recently in her Breton woods at midnight.

> ...There are wolves in my woods. I have two or three guards who follow me in the evenings, guns on their shoulders; Beaulieu is the captain. We have honored the moonlight with our presence these last two days, between eleven o'clock until midnight. We saw first a black man; I thought of the one of Auger and prepared to refuse the garter. He approached, and it turned out it was La Mousse. A little further on we saw a white body, fully extended. We approached courageously to that; it was a tree that I had cut down last week.
>
> How is that for extraordinary adventures; I fear that in hearing them you will be light headed because of the state you are in. Drink a glass of water, my precious. If we had sylphes at our command, we could tell you a story that would hold all your attention, but it's only you who can see such devilish deeds without doubting it. As for talking about Auger, I must talk to you in person for that. This tale has taken all my attention; I have sent a copy to my aunt, thinking that you would not have the courage to write it so exactly twice. God knows that I am entertained by such stories far more than those of the Renaudots[533] who wave their pens in the air at my expense. There are certain things that one would very much like to know! But as to those, not a word.

In order to understand the unlocking of the word game, the original French text is necessary.

French original text

> ... Il y a des loups dans mon bois [aux Rochers]. J'ai deux ou trois gardes qui me suivent les soirs, le fusil sur l'épaule; Beaulieu est le capitaine. Nous avons honoré depuis deux jours le clair de la lune de notre présence, entre onze heures et minuit. Nous vîmes d'abord un homme noir; je songeai à celui d'Auger et me préparais déjà à refuser la jarretière. Il s'approcha, et il se trouva que c'était La Mousse. Un peu plus loin nous vîmes un corps blanc tout étendu. Nous approchâmes assez hardiment de celui-là; c'était un arbre que j'avais fait abattre la semaine passée.
>
> Voilà des aventures bien extraordinaires; je crains que vous n'en soyez effrayée en l'état où vous êtes. Buvez un verre d'eau, ma bonne. Si nous avions des sylphes à notre commandement, nous pourrions vous conter quelque histoire digne de vous divertir, mais il n'appartient qu'à vous de voir une pareille diablerie sans en pouvoir douter. Quand ce ne serait que pour parler à Auger, il faut que j'aille en Provence. Cette histoire m'a bien occupée et bien divertie; j'en ai envoyé la copie à ma tante, dans la pensée que vous n'auriez pas eu le courage de l'écrire deux fois si bien et si exactement. Dieu sait quel goût je trouve à ces sortes de choses en comparaison des *Renaudots*, qui égayent leurs plumes à mes dépens. Il y a de certaines choses qu'on aimerait tant à savoir! Mais de celles-là, pas un mot.[534]

At Madame de Sévigné's Brittany estate Les Rochers today, visitors climb a wooded, curving, long driveway to reach the clearing on which the small chateau and its detached chapel sit side by side with restored gardens on the side and back which do not have Versailles' or Chantilly's grandiosity; Madame's gardens were her botanical friends, she named the paths through them for her loved ones.

Two general themes are immediately apparent in the letter. The first is the aura of fright; she whispers about the frightening things that arise in one's imagination when natural features of the dark woods seem other than what they are: a "white body, fully extended," is only, when one comes closer, a tree that has been cut. The second is her intensity; she finds the story very interesting and important, so important that she warns her daughter not to speak about this any more until they are together, and that, "There are certain things that one would very much like to know! But as to those, not a word." Madame facetiously warns her daughter to calm herself after hearing the wolf tale since Françoise is pregnant, but still leaves the hint that being unnerved by the story might be perfectly understandable. She advises her to "drink a glass of water" as a remedy and this is a quote from Molière's play *L'Avare*.

Madame considered strict secrecy to be necessary when speaking of this story because the king's agents spied on the mail therefore her nervous reticence indicates that someone or some group of people might get in trouble if the authorities came to know of it and quite possibly that Madame de Sévigné and her daughter's family might be at risk for trouble if they were revealed to be connected, even ever so slightly, with Auger.

Interpretation

The overall emotion conveyed, then, is fear and intensity, but now the game gets more complex, because tracking the wolves in her woods is, in fact, a word game, and a good place to start unraveling it is to start with the simplest play on words, the garter, the *jarretière*.

Refusal of the garter...

The English royal Order of the Garter's (*Ordre de la Jarretière*) motto is, "Shame on him who thinks ill of it" ("*Honi soit qui mal y pense*"), a phrase which supposedly came from the lips of England's King Edward III when, at a court dance, the lovely Countess of Salisbury's garter fell to the floor and he rushed to lift it up and give it to her with this little sermon to onlookers: he was touching the lady's leggings but anyone who thought that this act was ominous should be ashamed. Those special few admitted into the distinguished English Order of the Garter, founded in 1349, are bound by this optimistic and cautionary rule. If Madame de Sévigné was thinking ill of a possible encounter with a fearful thing in the dark woods, which is antithetical to the motto of the Order of the Garter, she would have to refuse an offer of the *jarretière*; a sophisticated joke that Madame de Grignan probably had no trouble understanding. Twisting the pledge of the Order of the Garter into her own irrational fears in the dark is so refined and subtle that we are warned that we are at the mercy of a skillful *Précieuse*.

"The Black man..."

"We saw first a black man; I thought of the one of Auger..." She is referring to the Black man she spoke of in the 18 October letter, but she isn't expecting him to pave a road for her this time. At this point the flow of the story and the tone of foreboding that Madame is stirring up rules out

Auger, the visitor at the Grignan's chateau, and implies that she is now referring to the *garçon* Auger. Her Auger seems to have had a valet or friend with him who was Black. The word she uses is not "*brun*" as in the description given about Dauger's skin; this is a Black man (*noir*) of African, Indian, or Middle Eastern descent. A small population of Blacks were in Europe at that time, acting usually as servants; they are often seen in court portraits with their mistresses, in the role of pets, as objects of affection but also amusement.[535] However it was unusual to see a Black man in an uncontrolled setting within arm's length in one's own personal space. If she had seen such a man with Auger, Madame de Sévigné might well have felt some fear.

Eleven o'clock to midnight...

Solving the *jarretière* reference was pleasant and gave me confidence so I looked for other jokes in the story. At first I thought that there was a secret message in "*onze heures à minuit*" and I looked through Molière's plays to find it and even wrote to French friends to ask if they could interpret this but: no. At last I considered that it may be a repetition of an element in a story that Madame de Sévigné's friend the comtesse de Lafayette (1634–1693) wrote in a description of the last hours of the life of Henriette-Anne of England, the first wife of the king's brother, who died on 30 June 1670 within a few hours of a late walk she took in her garden at Saint-Cloud: "She ate supper as usual and she went to walk in the light of the moon until midnight."[536] The comtesse de La Fayette's book about Henriette-Anne's life and death was not published until 1720 but she and Madame de Sévigné were very good friends because the comtesse's mother had married an uncle of Madame de Sévigné, and since they were both writers, they were in close contact. La Fayette had surely told her friend the details of the death of Henriette-Anne because all of Paris and most of France were fascinated and horrified by the nightmarish, painful, night of descent into death that came before morning and La Fayette had been an eyewitness. Henriette-Anne had nothing to do with wolves, though, so I was once more unsteady. The letter was written on 21 October, close to All Hallows' Eve (31 October), and people often get obsessed with the moon and midnight around that time, although Madame's letters have plentiful references to the moon and midnight at all times of the year. Perhaps there is nothing playful at all in the phrase; no need to invent, Madame has invented enough to satisfy.

I sent a copy to my aunt...

Since Madame says she has copied Françoise's letter and sent it to her aunt, which must be Henriette de Coulanges, marquise de La Trousse, whom she and her children lived with on the rue du Temple, that is a clue that the interaction with the *garçon* Auger was in a place that her aunt also frequented... that her aunt would also have seen the boy or known something about him and would be interested in hearing Françoise's news.

Beaulieu is the captain...

Right away the name of the man who guarded her with a gun on his shoulder on her walk in the woods, "Beaulieu," caught my attention because I had been looking at the farm of Beaulieu, approximately 3.54 miles (5.70 kilometers) from Auger-Saint-Vincent, in old maps of the Oise and had been there myself in search of the famous Tree of Beaulieu. Michel Lasnier, nicknamed Beaulieu (d. 1690), was Madame's *maître d'hôtel* and almost a family friend because of his long service with her mother's family, the Coulanges; a solid, factual reference to a man who worked for her.[537] So "Beaulieu" was a red herring.

There are wolves in my woods...

Wolves were in the woods everywhere in France and Europe in 1671. Would not that be a good reason to stay inside her ancient but fortified manor at midnight? A fifty-something lady of means out in the woods at midnight wandering around her property when there might be wolves waiting? I didn't know what to do with "wolves" any more than "eleven o'clock to midnight."

When I was going through some of the photos I took when I was in Auger-Saint-Vincent I noticed that one of the signs on town history posted on the town hall said, "The seigneurie of Fresnoy-le-Luat is cited from the twelfth century. The community of Luat was attached to it in 1825." The sign said the origin of the name was from the Latin *lupus saltus* meaning "the leaping wolf." The French word loup in English is wolf. From Fresnoy-le-Luat to Beaulieu is 1.6 miles (2.57 kilometers).

Then I went back to the last sentence of the tale, that seems to be a flourish at the end of the wolf walk, that contains the word "tree" ("*C'était un arbre* [tree] *que j'avais fait abattre la semaine passée*"). In the story, then, are the words *Auger, Beaulieu, Luat*, which is from the Latin for wolf, *Loup*, and *arbre*. All four words can be found on the Cassini map and other old maps in the neighborhood of Auger-Saint-Vincent. When I did a search for villages very near Auger-Saint-Vincent and compared them to the paragraph, more similarities appeared, and then I began to search for less obvious references to town names in the area.

Un corps blanc tout étendu...

The play with letters in the name of the hamlet of Fontaine-lès-Corps-Nus can be seen in Madame's phrase *"un corps blanc tout étendu"* ("a white body fully extended"). It is important to keep in mind that *jeux des portraits* for town names are harder to decipher than names of people because town names were variously spelled on maps, few people had maps or used them, and also because there were not signs in towns showing the name... one heard the name and decided for oneself how to spell it. In a word game structured on the fanciful placement of letters, variations in spelling can trip up the player both in the seventeenth century and in the twenty-first century. For instance the spellings of the villages Fresnoy-le-Luat and Fontaine-les-Corps-Nus vary greatly on old maps:

- In the eighteenth-century Cassini map the names are spelled "Frenoy les Luat" and "Fontaine les cornus."

- In a 1615 map by Damien de Templeux the towns are "Frenoy Leluat" and "Fontaine Les Corps nuz."

- A map of the Duchy of the Valois judged by *Gallica*[538] to be from the 1720s gives "Frenoy" and "Fontaine" (no hyphenations on either one).

- In 1641 a cartographer in Amsterdam spelled them "Freney Leluat" and "Fontaine les Corps nuz," as did another Dutch cartographer in 1663.

- In 1732, a map of the courses of the rivers Oise, Aisne, and Marne spells the names "Fresnoy," "Louats," and "Fontaine les Cornuds."

- A map of the pays d'élection of Crépy of 1698 has these spellings: "Fresnoy Le Lua." (Fontaine-les-Cornus is not on the map.)

- The modern map posted in Auger-Saint-Vincent on the town hall spells the towns "Fresnoy-le-Luat" and did not show "Fontaine-les-Cornus."

Two place names in the near vicinity of Auger-Saint-Vincent preciously float through the sentence about the white extended body:

Corps b l a **n** c t o u t é t e n d **u** = [Fontaine les] **corps nu**.

Or

Cor p s b l a **n** c t o u t é t e **n** d u = **Cornon**. Mont Cornon, Oger the Dane's former *châteaufort*, is 2.1 miles (3.38 kilometers) from Auger-Saint-Vincent.

CHAPTER 17. MADAME DE SÉVIGNÉ'S CLUES

Gun on the shoulder...

I began to understand why the *Précieuses* loved finding hidden words in innocent texts. A *jeu des portraits* is like a crossword puzzle or the board game of *Scrabble*. The names of towns I found were not that hard to see because the letters in the names were in the same order as the coded words. Anagrams, where the order of the letters is mixed up and where all letters have to be used, would be much harder. There could be anagrams in the text and I have not been smart enough to see them.

I couldn't make "*fusil sur l'épaule*" work with any of the town names on the map. I looked up the phrase and found that it is an idiom since the nineteenth century: to change your "*fusil sur l'épaule*" means to change your mind. That didn't seem to fit anything but I no longer trusted any of the phrases in the story to be innocent, so I believed there was a message there and in frustration I began researching seventeenth-century weapons and military history. I found a quote from a book by historian André Castelot which described the arms and order of ranks in processions.[539] He said the *Gentilshommes à Bec de Corbin*, members of the personal guard of the king since Louis XI, who carried long pole arms with a beak-like iron crooks on them,[540] were allowed to carry their long arms on their shoulders in parade whereas soldiers with swords and muskets carried them at their side or over the saddle. They were the second company of the king's personal guards (the first company was the Scottish[541]) and they marched next to the king in procession and were impressive due to the bristle of their long, beaked weapons.

> Two hundred gentlemen *à bec recourbé*, called *de corbin*, their weapons on their shoulders, a privilege of their post, marched two by two and opened the procession. Then the royal guard, formed by heralds of arms, the foot archers of the Porte and the Provost, the archers on horseback, the twenty-four personal archers of the king dressed in their ceremonial vests of silver and gold, the Hundred Swiss armed with their halberds.[542]

If the "*fusil sur l'épaule*" is a reference to *bec de corbin*, perhaps it is a reference to the comte de Lauzun, who before his arrest in November 1671 was one of the captains of the *Gentilshommes à Bec de Corbin*. Madame knew who the comte de Lauzun was but could not know he would be arrested a few weeks later and sent to Pignerol where Eustache Dauger was a prisoner. It could also be a reference to a "*bec*"...a nose. In another chapter I proposed a theory that Eustache had a prosthetic nose when he was young and later wore a mask because in adulthood an unrepaired facial cleft is unpleasingly altered by late-stage growth of teeth, and jaw growth can exacerbate physical asymmetries as the patient ages. Either of these veiled references could have been meant. If Madame saw Dauger when he was young, he might have been wearing a false nose.

Un arbre...

Maybe "Beaulieu" was not a red herring after all. The last sentence in the game is "a tree I cut down last week." When I realized she had finished her soliloquy with "tree" I felt a little of the same shock that Madame de Sévigné said she had when she saw a white, stretched out body at midnight in the dark woods. I had started to play the game innocently with a garter and a quaint fourteenth-century English quasi-fable, then appeared some warnings of my prize, and finally came the confirmation that, with the appearance of "tree" in the same paragraph as "Beaulieu" and in the context of a confidence about the boy Auger, I was looking at a suggestion that the marquise, who said she had at least once seen this boy, was hinting in her word game about Beaulieu and the villages around Auger-Saint-Vincent.

The Game Continues – The Captain And His Friends

The *comtesse* had arrived at her husband's estate at Grignan in the southeast of France in the spring of 1671 and wrote to her mother a few months later about a person named Auger. It sounds as if Françoise, the *comtesse*, did not know that her mother had ever seen the subject of her interesting story but her mother immediately made her aware that she was "positive" she had seen Auger in a different setting than the one Françoise described him in. How did Françoise, countess of Grignan, hear the story?

Her husband was much older than she, his third wife, and he was the highest ranking royal official in Provence so he was in touch with military and royal staff and would have access to secret information that would affect decisions about the army and marine, as Provence has the Mediterranean sea for a border, although the major maritime centers of activity were west of Grignan. His family, the Adhémar, was old nobility of the sword in Provence. From any of these resources the count of Grignan could have learned about an arrest in Calais two years before in 1669... and casually told the story to his wife, because the prisoner was more interesting than the usual miscreant. When the count's and countess' friendships and family connections are considered, one person surfaces whom we know: Captain Vauroy.

The possibility that Captain Vauroy, who arrested Eustache Dauger, was the source of the story that Madame de Sévigné, the count's mother-in-law, gave to posterity, is seen through a set of people who were both active in

CHAPTER 17. MADAME DE SÉVIGNÉ'S CLUES

Dunkirk and in Provence.

Captain Vauroy, who before taking his position as captain of the hunt for Bergues, Dunkirk, and Furnes in October 1667 and his post as sergent-major of the town and citadel of Dunkirk in December 1662, had been in the army with the rank of captain. In Dunkirk he worked directly for Godefroy d'Estrades, the governor of Dunkirk, who had formerly been one of Nicolas Fouquet's closest colleagues, had become suspect at the time of Fouquet's disgrace but had rehabilitated himself with the king and Colbert by negotiating the sale of Dunkirk from England to France in 1662; Godefroy d'Estrades was the man Louis XIV ordered Vauroy to lie to about his mission to arrest Dauger, who was friends with Vauban and who had hosted Vauban and Louvois in Dunkirk just before Dauger was arrested in 1669. Louis d'Estrades, son of Godefroy, named on April 21, 1669 governor of Bergues and Furnes, was a friend of Vauroy.

The count of Grignan had a cousin by marriage, Antoine Escalin Adhémar, marquis de La Garde (1623–1713),[543] who had been governor of Furnes near Calais and Dunkirk from 1668 to 1669, the year of Dauger's arrest. La Garde (is there another connection to the wolf word game here, "J'ai deux ou trois *gardes* qui me suivent les soirs") was not only a relative, he was also a very good friend of the count Grignan, proved by the fact that he was best man at the count's wedding to Françoise de Sévigné on January 27, 1669. La Garde had a friend who was in service for the king at the same time and place in the *chastellanies* of Bergues, Dunkirk, and Furnes, Captain Alexandre de Vauroy.

The governor of the citadel of Dunkirk, the fortified center within the city of Dunkirk, was in 1669 Monsieur du Fresnoy, married to the sister of Madame de Saint-Mars. Monsieur du Fresnoy's wife was in a serious affair with the marquis de Louvois, du Fresnoy's superior...and none of this was a secret to anyone. Du Fresnoy was happy; it was a very good thing for one's wife to be sleeping with Louvois: good connections and lots of financial advantages. Vauroy had two bosses, du Fresnoy and Godefroy d'Estrades and they all reported to Louvois. All these officials were soldiers, friends, and administrators in Dunkirk and the nearby towns of Bergues and Furnes, all very near Calais, between 1662 and 1669.

A complicated collection of friends, relatives, and business associates; not unusual. In the 1100s or the 1300s there might have been fewer links between people, fewer friendships. The plagues had killed so many people in the 1300s that no one could find workers to plant the crops. By the seventeenth century, though, the arcades of power were filling with people, many from the same families. The desire of the middle class low-level parliamentary administrators to rise to noble status so they did not have to pay taxes brought nobles of the "sword" and of the "robe" into familial relationships, because the old nobles were often poor, the social climbers were rich, and so the blood and money was mixed and the bones of one became the flesh of the other. When this blanket of cousins, sisters-in-law, brothers, mothers, lovers, and memorialists, their servants, members of the royal house, their mistresses, and those who showed up for duels at the royal square early each morning...and even the people who ran the rumor mill whose memoirs help us know this seventeenth-century world...is lifted, there lie relations by marriage, by underpetticoat permissions, by genes, by neighborhood, by political handshake, by subterfuge, or any number of ways. There was one clique. They all knew each other, cheated on each other, criticized each other, killed each other. Some behaved honorably some of the time, some feigned madness, some were mad. I discovered a house of Babel, a tower of many rooms with the same people in and out of all of them. Not one was a stranger to the other.

Is the word in Madame de Sévigné's wolf tale "Captain," as in "*Beaulieu est le capitaine*" a reference to the seasoned former infantry officer Captain Vauroy, who might not have been able to keep himself from telling a good friend and colleague, La Garde, about the night he was ordered by the king to use a personally signed warrant for arrest for a man with an unusual set of circumstances? And did La Garde then pass the story along to his cousin and close friend the comte de Grignan? I used to resent Vauroy's silence. He knew the things we want to know. Why could he not have written a memoir or a page of memories of the event and chosen a trusted person to keep it for him so that we might eventually see it?

Perhaps he did.

18. Beaulieu And The Lhoste

"Racine lost his mother at age three months, his father when he was three years old. But that often happened, consequently it was not all that traumatizing. And afterwards he lived with a caretaker."
—Jean Rohou. Histoire de la littérature française du XVIIe siècle

The Fouquet Connection Strengthens

In the previous chapter Madame de Sévigné said she had seen "a boy ... Auger" in the past. Her cryptic letters of October 18 and 21 of the year 1671 hinted, through a *jeu de portraits* that she associated "Auger" with the place in the Valois that we came to *via* another path, the path of the D + apostrophe: the farm and the famous tree of Beaulieu near Auger Saint-Vincent.

Madame de Sévigné was a good friend of Nicolas Fouquet. She was horrified and saddened when he was arrested by the king for treason in 1661. Her description of seeing Fouquet coming out of his cell at the time of his trial with his guards (the famous d'Artagnan in charge) to face his judges is as close to a video of the event as we can have. She and Fouquet were connected, and in chapter 16 Nicolas Fouquet's maternal family were shown to have been connected to the abbey of Parc aux Dames, in that his aunt and his sister were consecutive superior administrators of Parc aux Dames; Fouquet helped his sister refurbish and repair the convent and the chapel.

Most authorities on the mystery have noticed that Louvois in his letters to Saint-Mars never was disturbed that Fouquet and Dauger were spending time together at Pignerol; Louvois only broke out in a sweat when there was a risk of Lauzun or La Rivière being in his presence. Louvois had made clear that Dauger was only allowed to be with Fouquet as his valet in Pignerol when La Rivière was sick, was absent from Fouquet's room. Dauger was not allowed to be with Lauzun under any circumstances. The reason all four of these prisoners had a comfortable, clandestine relationship for about four years was because Saint-Mars had been outwitted by Lauzun and Fouquet and had not found the hole in Fouquet's floor that had been used as a communal access for all of them until the day Fouquet died. But Louvois didn't mind that Dauger was with Fouquet and didn't object or care that Dauger was also present to Fouquet's family when they were finally allowed to visit Fouquet in the last year of his confinement. A guess about this social puzzle is that Fouquet and his family knew Dauger already or knew about him. Or at least Fouquet knew his story.

Did Fouquet also have a connection to Beaulieu that we have visited in person, on maps, and through letters of Madame to her daughter in October 1671?

Yes.

I found the link in the documentation of Nicolas Fouquet's trial when Olivier Lefèvre d'Ormesson (1616–1686), a good friend of Madame de Sévigné and the *rapporteur* (the parlement member responsible for keeping records of the legal process and reporting it to the king) for the Fouquet trial for treason and theft, said that the names of the two lawyers that were hired by his mother and his wife to defend him were Barthélemy Auzanet (b. 1592) and Jean-Marie Lhoste (d. 1672).[544]

Permission for Fouquet to have a lawyer had been granted by the king and Colbert only in December 1662, more than a year after he had been arrested and many months after questioning of Fouquet had begun and after months of maneuvers by his mother and wife, Marie de Maupeou Fouquet and Marie-Madeleine de Castille Fouquet, including setting up a secret printing press to print the record of the trial while it was happening and distributing it.

Here is Jules Lair's description of the lawyers:

> A person who knew Barthélemy Auzanet described him as a careful man, good education, unequalled honesty of judgement. Honest in his recording of facts, he was more interested in saying directly what his argument was than in flowery language. The qualities of his soul were not less esteemed. He was a man of the old school of morals, he had candor and dignified simplicity of "*l'innocence des premiers siècles.*" He was tall and thin with a slightly sheepish expression, and his eyes veiled beneath long eyelashes. The whole of his appearance was of a studied calm. Although of an advanced age, 70 years, his intelligence was as sharp as ever. Lhoste, who came from Montargis, had been President of the Bar. He was, just like Auzanet, talented and of honest character.[545]

There is a problem with understanding where Jean-Marie Lhoste was from

CHAPTER 18. BEAULIEU AND THE LHOSTE

because d'Ormesson said he was "from Montargis" but other references say he was from Paris and lived with his wife on the rue de l'Hôtel des Ursins.[546] D'Ormesson either wrongly thought that Jean-Marie was from Montargis, a proposition I find unlikely because d'Ormesson's memoirs, position, and behavior do not show him to be sloppy with his facts, or Jean-Marie Lhoste was a part of the Montargis Lhoste family by way of a yet unknown genealogical path. Lair probably assumed Ormesson was correct in his statement that Jean-Marie Lhoste was from Montargis and wrote that in his biography of Fouquet.[547]

Marie de Maupeou Fouquet probably hired Jean-Marie Lhoste to be one of her son's lawyers not only based on his excellent record of litigation but also because he was a fellow activist of the *dévot* community, a colleague of Madame Fouquet and of Vincent de Paul. A book on the history of the *dévots* in Europe mentions Jean-Marie Lhoste in connection with the foundation of the school to train missionaries for overseas missions.

> The great charitable works took place in these institutions: the general hospital, the hospital of the Incurables, the outreach to prisoners. Also in the work of Saint Vincent de Paul, which took the form of missions in the countryside, a formation of secular clergy and *enfants trouvés*... The foreign missions had also many fine *sodales*. Antoine Barillon, Laurent de Brisacier, Jean-Marie Lhoste were those who prepared the foundation for the seminary on the rue du Bac.[548]

Jean-Marie Lhoste's relationship with Vincent de Paul comes up in a letter of de Paul to his co-executive Louise de Marillac written in 1636:

> What shall I say to you about that good young woman who is with M[onsieur] Lhoste, except that it is a fine act of charity. However, we must be careful not to make a practice of it. Would it not be better, since you are bound to it, to put Jeanne there along with that poor Suzanne? Two would live better together and perhaps it will do them no harm.[549]

The editors of the *Correspondence* added a footnote for this quote: "Perhaps [this refers to] Jean-Marie Lhoste, who, after having been a lawyer in the parlement, became administrator of the Hôtel-Dieu and the Hospital of the Incurables, as well as of the general hospital and Saint-Jacques aux Pèlerins. He died February 17, 1672."

Jean-Marie Lhoste Had A Brother

To associate ourselves again with the farm of Beaulieu, here is a repetition of the words of the Oise departmental archivist about the sale of the property in 1775:

> Madame: By a letter dating 5 July 2015 you informed me of your research on a priory called "Beaulieu" which is on a Cassini map near Ducy and Fresnoy-le-Luat. The farm of Beaulieu was bought in 1775 by Jean-Baptiste Chartier from Antoine Lhoste, master ordinary of the chamber of accounts (act of sale was April 12, 1775 by the notary Monsieur Boursier, at Paris).[550]

Antoine-Léonor Lhoste, *maître des comptes* in the Court of Auditors, the owner of Beaulieu in 1775, sold the "*domaine de Beaulieu, écart de Baron en plein coeur du Valois, à plus de trente kilomètres au nord-est d'Aunay*" in 1775 to Jean-Baptiste Chartier.[551] The seller of Beaulieu was a descendant of Antoine-Léonor Lhoste (d. 1700), brother of Jean-Marie Lhoste.

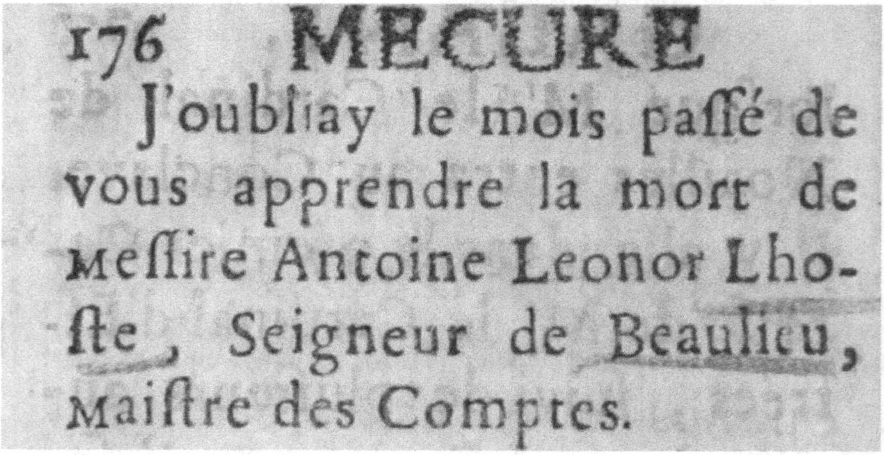

> 176 **MECURE**
> J'oubliay le mois paſſé de vous apprendre la mort de Meſſire Antoine Leonor Lhoſte, Seigneur de Beaulieu, Maiſtre des Comptes.

Figure 18.1: Seigneur de Beaulieu Antoine-Léonor Lhoste's death notice in *Le Mercure de France*, December 1700.[552] "I forgot last month to tell you of the death of Monsieur Antoine Leonor Lhoste, Seigneur de Beaulieu, Master of Accounts."

Antoine Léonor Lhoste's Paris home was #16 rue des Bourdonnais, owned by a succession of Lhoste de Beaulieu families from 1683 to 1722, two masters of accounts and one member of the Grand Council [of the king].[553]

Here is a notice stating that that Jean-Marie Lhoste, one of Fouquet's lawyers, was the brother of Antoine Léonor Lhoste, *sieur de Beaulieu*. The notice shows a judicial record of the Paris parlement 18 March 1652 in which notaries made changes to the passage of property from Antoine Léonor's deceased wife, Marguerite Varet, to Jean-Marie Lhoste, "*avocat en la cour*," Antoine Léonor's brother.

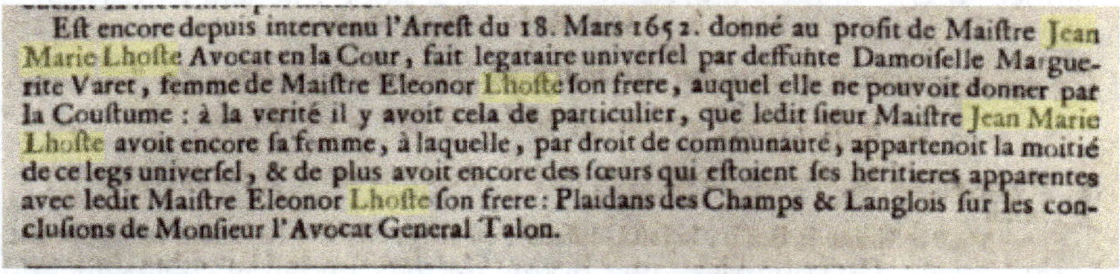

> Eſt encore depuis intervenu l'Arreſt du 18. Mars 1652. donné au profit de Maiſtre Jean Marie Lhoſte Avocat en la Cour, fait legataire univerſel par deffunte Damoiſelle Marguerite Varet, femme de Maiſtre Eleonor Lhoſte ſon frere, auquel elle ne pouvoit donner par la Couſtume : à la verité il y avoit cela de particulier, que ledit ſieur Maiſtre Jean Marie Lhoſte avoit encore ſa femme, à laquelle, par droit de communauté, appartenoit la moitié de ce legs univerſel, & de plus avoit encore des ſœurs qui eſtoient ſes heritieres apparentes avec ledit Maiſtre Eleonor Lhoſte ſon frere : Plaidans des Champs & Langlois ſur les concluſions de Monſieur l'Avocat General Talon.

Figure 18.2: "Is again since arrived the Order of 18 March 1652, for Master Jean-Marie Lhoste, Lawyer at Court, to be the universal legatory by the deceased Demoiselle Marguerite Varet, wife of Master Eleonor Lhoste his brother, to whom she cannot give according to Custom: to be sure there was this in particular, that the said Master Jean-Marie Lhoste had a wife, to whom, by right of their community, belonged half of this universal legation, &, what is more, had sisters who were the apparent heirs with the said Master Eleanor Lhoste his brother: Pleadings of Champs & Langlois on the conclusions of Monsieur the Advocate General Talon." Jean Du Fresne, *Journal des principales audiences du Parlement, avec les arrêts qui y ont été rendus. Nouvelle edition, revûë, corrigée et augmentée de plusieurs questions & reglemens placez selon l'ordre du temps depuis l'année 1622 jusqu'en 1661*. Vol. 1. Paris: Rollin fils, 1733, 215.

There is evidence that shows that Antoine Léonor had the same missionary zeal and dedication to the establishment and administration of hospitals as his brother. In an accounting charter of 1684 listing acquisition and payment of debts and annuities, the name of Antoine Léonor Lhoste is present in connection with two of the hospitals for which his brother Jean-Marie was administrator: the Hôtel-Dieu and the Hospital of the Incurables.[554] It can be posited that the brothers' inclinations to be aware of and solve problems of people who entered the hospitals in Paris, many of whom were abandoned children, were presumably the same.

Saint Vincent De Paul

There have been plenty of rogues and sinners in this story up to now, and if you are looking for a saint to balance the account, you have him in Saint Vincent de Paul, who, as we have said before, was the creator of the Ladies and Daughters of Charity, of whom Marie de Maupeou was a founding and active member.

The plight of abandoned, orphaned, and abused children had been dreadful long before the seventeenth century, but, as was noted above, it had also been long accepted by society. Around 1600 appeared in Paris from the countryside a man who could not and would not accept it. Vincent de Paul was a priest whose devotion to the poor, the sick, those misaligned with society, abandoned children, and galley slaves, received the grace of being beatified in 1729 and canonized in 1737 under Pope Clement XIII. What is more remarkable is that he deserved to be officially named a saint because he really was one. Vincent de Paul had no illusions about the terrible state that the world was in, but he set out to fix what he could, rather than retreat into mysticism, rhetoric, philosophy, or a bishopric. Amazingly, he *did* fix some things and his charitable foundations, the *Dames de Charité* and *Filles de Charité*, are today still serving the poor and the marginalized in 1,516 communities in 96 countries, their dominant mission being sheltering and caring for abandoned children.[555]

De Paul began his mission outreach in January 1617 when he created the Congregation of the Mission, a group of lay men who, in groups, traveled to towns and stayed for short times, always with the permission of the town administrators and the community members, treated the sick, preached, heard confessions, performed baptisms, and acted as mediators for problems in the community. In August of 1617, de Paul created the Ladies and Daughters of Charity pursuant to his realization that it was senseless to evangelize the poor unless they were also fed, nurtured, nursed, and helped out of poverty.

He worked closely from then on with a widow named Louise de Marillac (1591–1660), who was a smart, efficient, practical, tireless person, whose Christian devotion, equal to de Paul's, was directed to looking after the bottom line, handling personnel issues with aplomb and a steady hand, and raising funds from rich families around France who looked on with approbation but wanted clean hands. She was an executive through and through.

Louis XIII and Anne of Austria turned over to de Paul in 1631 the Saint-Lazare monastery to use as a headquarters on the north of Paris, on the rue du Faubourg Saint-Denis,[556] a former leper hospital, which became a locked dormitory for sons who did not accommodate themselves to the mores and rules of their families. In other words, a prison for bad children of all ages.

L'Œuvre Des Enfants Trouvés

In 1638 de Paul and Louise de Marillac visited the Paris *couche* and were horrified that almost all the children sent there died in a short time after arrival. They began their *Œuvre des Enfants Trouvés* to save abandoned infants and children, first taking a small number from the Port-Saint-Landry abandoned childrens' quarters to Marillac's house and then renting a house

CHAPTER 18. BEAULIEU AND THE LHOSTE

Figure 18.3: Vincent de Paul (1581–1660). Photo of a poster at the offices of the Saint Vincent de Paul charity in Tours, France, by the author, 2012.

that the *Dames* found money for and the *Filles* supervised on the rue du Boulangers[557] in the Paris fifth arrondissement. From 1638 to 1643 they assisted 1200 children.[558]

Marie De Maupeou Fouquet

When de Paul and de Marillac advertised their goal of sending nurses and food into poor people's homes, they attracted a number of activists, women of means in Paris who dedicated themselves to de Paul and his solutions: the *Dames de la Charité*. One of the first of these was Marie de Maupeou, mother of the *surintendant des finances*, the most powerful man in France next to Mazarin, Nicolas Fouquet. She was, in addition to Louise de Marillac and a few other women, a pillar of the work. Some of the *Dames'* first meetings were held at her house. She was one of many of Paris' *dévot* women, all of whom were dedicated to the overall goals of the Counter-Reformation, the extirpation of Protestantism and the cleansing of morals, but some were more reasonable than others, and Marie de Maupeou Fouquet was one of those. In fact it would be hard to be otherwise in de Paul's projects because he and de Marillac were both practical executors of charitable works who stayed away from notoriety so as to protect their work and their determination to put the consoling love of Jesus into the homes of the sick and poor in a defined, tangible way. One of de Paul's biographers, Luigi Mezzadri, said his method was to do things in a small, unobtrusive way (*de se faire petit*).[559] Ladies who wanted public affection therefore would not have been happy in the group, because the *Dames* were serious about their business and didn't have time for sloppy or self-serving behavior. Marie de Maupeou was the author of a medical encyclopedia[560] of home remedies telling how the poor could make them without having to go to an expensive apothecary.

In Concert

Anne of Austria had known Vincent de Paul before she invited him to comfort her dying husband in May 1643 to help both her and her husband endure the hardship of weeks at his deathbed, because Louis XIII was as suspicious about dying as he had been about everything else in his life, and de Paul had been advising her, with other men she had asked to be on her new Council of Conscious. He was an everyday presence in her house in the role of spiritual advisor, both during and after her husband's passing.

What is the advice that Vincent de Paul would have given to Anne of Austria in 1643 if she had confessed to him that she had secretly given birth to her husband's last child that had been born with an insurmountable physical problem? Vincent de Paul would not have thought the problem was insurmountable because he did not think any problem was insurmountable.

Here is what he told his friend and supporter Marie de Maupeou Fouquet when she requested advice from her spiritual advisor Vincent de Paul about her worry for her adult son Nicolas, whom she feared would be damned for his worldly activities. De Paul reportedly said to her, "Give the mother and child to God," and this advice is still given today by spiritual directors to worried parents; to trust God to take care of the child, but further, that the worried mother should also relax in the arms of the ultimate Caregiver and give up the burden of worry about the child. This is the counsel that he gave to Fouquet *mère* and so Saint Vincent de Paul may have counseled Anne of

Austria to think of her third son as a gift to her and to God. The child's predicament would be his salvation. De Paul would have said, give the child to God, and you must every day pray for him and about the significance of this child in your life and ask God to give him work to do in the world that will bring him and you, with all the rest of your family, closer to the Father, the Son, and to the Virgin Mary and to be a vehicle for your confession, forgiveness, and salvation.

De Paul's position as spiritual and worldly purveyor of asylum for abandoned children in Paris made him the best person to go to about a problem with a child who could not fit into the family he had been born in; even if he had not been at court in the summer of 1643 she might have had to call him to her. However, he *was* at court, perhaps, she might have thought, as a sign of God's arrangements for her; de Paul was already counseling Anne of Austria, the new regent, about many things... personnel in the new government, her sorrow and other mixed feelings about her husband's death, her worry about her new responsibilities... and Father Vincent would have been seen as the ideal helper she needed, a sign that the Virgin Mary was next to her in her sorrows, knowing them intimately, because Mary had also been a mother of a child with a stigma; both mother and child had been ordained by God to not only suffer but to accept that suffering peaceably as a gift to a tormented world.

I think Anne of Austria took Vincent de Paul's advice and the counsel of her own conscience and gave the child to God.

Oblation Of Her Son

There is another category of "exclusion," to use Michel Foucault's term, that was not exactly abandonment, not a *couche*; it was called oblation, a gift by parents to the church of a son or daughter. Oblates were lay persons given by their parents at a young age to a religious order which would henceforth be the only family the oblate would have, a permanent gift of a young child to the service of the church and the monastery he or she was given to.

The word "oblation" originated in the Latin word "*oblatio*" (an offering). This practice was manifested in the fifty-ninth chapter of the Rule of Saint Benedict of Nursia, and the Benedictines accepted this consignment of very young children more than other orders, taking oblates as young as five. Saint Thomas Aquinas, born in 1225, was given to Monte Cassino in 1230 at age five. Abbot Suger of Saint Denis was given to be an oblate of Saint Denis at age nine. William the Conqueror and his wife Mathilda gave their daughter Cecilia to the Church of the Holy Trinity in Caen.[561]

Oblation was an early option for parents who wanted to make one of their children a permanent gift to God. It was an extreme donation, sometimes made by the parents as a confession of a great sin they may have committed. Usually the family had wholesome reasons for giving up their child; ardent Christian devotion that followed the custom that at least one child in the family should be consecrated to the church. The drawback for the oblate was that opting out of taking vows once old enough to make a decision for oneself was problematic. Early church fathers were vigilant to assure that a child that had been obligated by parents before the age of consent had permission without fault to reject the monastic life if they did not wish to take vows, but eventually the vow the parent made was considered a vow *of* the child and later if he or she did not want to take vows, excommunication was the result. Giving a child to the glory of God in a permanent, official contract was a valuable gift that only the most devout parents would consider giving, although it can be argued that oblation was another way to divest the family of a mouth to feed. Whether the act was considered abandonment or not depended on the family's tendencies, history, and financial security.

Assuming the theory of this book as the starting point—and with emphasis on "theory"— oblation for a third son was an obvious solution for Anne of Austria; if she had a baby that had not been announced and had a birth defect (as postulated from witness testimonies in chapter 13), she had the option to do what other women (who could afford to) did with such an infant; she arranged for the baby to be cared for until weaned and then to be placed within a monastery for life, where he could grow up in the Catholic faith, where he would be educated, fed, would have a place out of the weather to sleep, could choose a vocation within the monastic community, such as being a scribe, caring for animals, growing food, making the community's bread, wine and oil, and perhaps eventually taking orders and having rank in the order. His birth defect wouldn't make any difference to his brothers in the monastery, some of them possibly living there for a similar reason, therefore he would not be bullied or physically attacked. Giving her son to be an oblate would not make him a priest or a monk. The oblate was a lay person until he or she, according to his or her own wishes studied for holy orders and took vows.

Whatever the calamities of life that Anne of Austria experienced through child bearing— and she suffered many from a young age—her many miscarriages are well documented in the manuscript department of the Bibliothèque Nationale—it is a fact that children with birth defects were often candidates for oblation. "There is... evidence in the literature of the rejection and neglect of handicapped offspring. In prosperous families, they were the first to be put out to nurse and then sent to monasteries."[562]

A Son For The Church

There was another part of societal accepted practice in the seventeenth century that may have affected the future of Eustache Dauger; it was fundamental in wealthy families, even obligatory, that at least one child dedicate him or herself to the church. In 1643 Anne of Austria already had two sons, she didn't need a third one, at her side at least. She had her *Dieudonné*, her child king on whom she and Mazarin doted and spent long hours and long letters describing and worrying about; she had Philippe, a small active boy with black curls and a petunia mouth, so different from his blond self-contained brother; Philippe was a backup, to be used only in case of the first son's death. The second son in most families went into religious orders or into some part of church administration whether he took vows or not. Philippe couldn't be a priest or a cardinal, because he had to be kept in reserve as a layman, and that was all his mother and Mazarin thought he was good for. He was scatterbrained and talkative. The queen and Mazarin did not mind that his natural femininity intensified openly; they made sure he was subservient to his brother, and otherwise ignored him.

What Anne needed and wanted was a son to give to the church. The pattern that had been typical for centuries in upper class and royal French families was that the first son got the title, the land, and the wealth, and some of the following sons and daughters were expected to hold positions in the church. Her family members and supporters that she admired and whose respect she wanted had all followed this rule.

It is documented that Anne of Austria's entire life's work, her troubled marriage to Louis XIII, her actions to ruin Richelieu, her crystallized devotion to the Catholic church modeled for her by her beloved mother and father, the religious prescriptions she had lived by for forty-two years—these were the offerings the queen had given for fulfillment of her duty to God and the Virgin Mary, to whom she had made a vow early in her marriage, when she first began having miscarriages, that if Mary gave her a son, which She did, *Dieudonné*, the dutiful queen, named for the Virgin's mother, would serve the Queen of Heaven for the rest of her life, would build Her one of the most beautiful abbeys in France, which she did, Val-de-Grâce in Paris, and perhaps silently Anne vowed to give another very precious gift to Mary, one of her younger sons, as was the custom in devout families.

For Anne, this strange, unexpected son was a *"merle blanc,"* a white blackbird, a thing that does not exist. And he remained a white blackbird all his life. Anne of Austria prayed for her secret son, she sent money for his expenses (there are many references to large sums of money that she received "for her charities" and Nicolas Fouquet was a source of funds).

The queen must have remembered and mourned for each of the babies that had miscarried from her body, and this last child was also mourned, but his fate was more pure and symbolic than her other lost babies. He would have a special place in a house of religion. She may not have seen the irony of having what she had prayed for made a solemn secret rather than an advertised holy truth, but no matter. She had borne a son for the church and that was more important to her than we can imagine.

A Safe Home

I theorize that Nicolas Fouquet and his family, particularly his mother, his aunt, and one of his sisters, and Saint-Vincent de Paul helped Anne of Austria find a home for Eustache Dauger immediately after he was born.

Anne of Austria, Vincent de Paul, the Lhoste family, and the Fouquets, each in their own way, had a special interest in children: de Paul was the seventeenth century's greatest champion of harboring and feeding homeless children; Anne of Austria had spent most of her adult life begging God for a child and when God gave her two of them, she loved them, spoiled them, and spent time with them, which queens generally did not do; Marie de Maupeou took orphaned children, both white and of color, into her home where she cared for them. Michel Vergé-Franceschi, in his book on the Mask, said that because François Fouquet was invested in overseas companies doing business in the Antilles, Africa, and Canada, the Fouquets had "an impressive, exotic household of Blacks, Moors, and Indians."[563] Jean-Marie Lhoste was "administrator of the Hôtel-Dieu and the Hospital of the Incurables, as well as of the general hospital and Saint-Jacques aux Pèlerins" and a supporter of Vincent de Paul's work to find homes for abandoned children.

These people, I theorize, tied by charitable, familial, and ideological links, came together to manage a difficult, unforeseen problem in 1643: the queen confided in de Paul, de Paul called on Marie de Maupeou, who took in the child and sent it to the nunnery of Parc aux Dames in the Valois where her sister Marguerite, Mother Superior, and Marie's daughter, Marie-Elisabeth, Nicolas' sister, who would succeed Marguerite, would see to his feeding and care.

At some point, Marie de Maupeou and the ladies of the Parc might have asked Antoine Lhoste of Beaulieu, a neighbor of the abbey and brother of Jean-Marie Lhoste, their lawyer and colleague in rescuing abandoned children, to let Eustache live next door at the Beaulieu farm once he was old enough to learn skills to occupy himself and make a contribution to the community and the church. That was routine for children without parents: as

CHAPTER 18. BEAULIEU AND THE LHOSTE

soon as the social workers, nuns, or other caretakers had taught the children to read and write and decided they were able to work, they were apprenticed, and it was the best part of the awful series of events that had occurred in the first six or seven years of their lives. They were at last out of childhood and abject dependency. They were "from" somewhere. They began to have rights as contributing members of society.

In any event, Madame de Sévigné knew that the "boy" she had seen and talked to and the countryside around the farm of Beaulieu and the village of Auger-Saint-Vincent had something in common; if they did, it is not surprising that "Eustache Dauger" was the name on his arrest warrant.

Dauger was given a name that was the product of current naming conventions by the people who took care of him and he consumed the simple lifestyle they modeled for him and depended on the promises they offered him, as any faithful son is bound to do. He was brought up a member of a devout community, he affiliated with them, he worked and prayed with them, and he rose and slept on the hills and fields of France. When he became an adult ward of Louis XIV's state, he kept the devout lifestyle in which he had spent his childhood and youth that had no pomposity to it. He did not want a rich lifestyle, which he would have been very uncomfortable with. His facial disfigurement had long before marked his character with a priority for keeping out of sight. This is a typical emotional construct for people with cleft lip and palate, even when it is surgically fixed, which his was not.

As I have researched and started to write this story, I find that, although Louis XIV strained to keep knowledge of Eustache to zero and succeeded pretty well, there are clues that, even in his own time, slipped up and out of the darkness that Louis created for us, as crickets that insisted on chirping despite the royal demand for silence of any and all cricket noise. A version of truth contradictory to Louis' version constantly bubbles up in this story, and I think that Louis realized this and was mystified and horrified at it. He was king but not ruler over the persistent small intrusions that indicated that someone or something more powerful than he was chewing on this story behind the walls and that this force was a match for him.

What has never been addressed in books on the Mask was *why* Dauger was so tightly controlled, imprisoned, and never released. Why would Louis XIV have cared if anyone knew about Dauger? If Dauger was his younger brother who needed a sequestered life and was not a threat to the king's rule or role, why the enormous secrecy? Why should he be threatened with death if he said his name or anything about himself? Death was assured if his identity was disclosed but his murder was never considered. The paradox "You will be immediately killed if you speak your story but we will spend thousands of *livres* to keep you alive and maintain infinite security procedures to keep you hidden for thirty-four years" is stark. One would think that a prisoner considered such a dangerous liability to his majesty would have been eliminated. Why was he allowed to stare at prison walls for almost thirty-four years? Why was he carefully nursed and medicated to treat illnesses that might have resulted in death if left untreated? Why was he allowed to live until his natural death?

I do not think that Dauger was Louis XIV's younger brother. I think he was Philippe d'Orléans younger brother. I think he was the second son of Louis XIII and Anne of Austria.

Now *is* the time to think about *why*.

Part 4

IT WILL BE BY THE LADY, NO DOGS WILL BARK

19. A Footed Bowl

> XCIII
> Vn serpent veu proche du lict royal,
> Sera par dame, nuict chiens n'abayeront:
> Lors naistra en Frâce vn prince tât royal,
> Du ciel venu tous les princes verront.

Figure 19.1: A serpent seen near the royal bed, It will be by the lady, no dogs will bark: Then to be born in France a Prince so royal, All the Princes will say he comes from heaven. — Nostradamus, *Les Premères Centuries ou Prophéties*, Century IV (prediction) # 93[564]

> Voltaire was the first to connect the identity of this man to that of the Roi-Soleil. At first the guess was that it was Vermandois but Voltaire said a few years later that he was the half brother of Louis XIV born of Anne of Austria and a lover. It is thus that Voltaire constructed a myth, which, as the Revolution developed, took on more and more "*ampleur.*" Coming closer to the [king], the Masque de fer ended even by being mixed with him. In was in 1790 that was made for the first time the idea that the prisoner was the twin of Louis XIV, condemned for his resemblance to the king.
>
> —Mathieu Da Vinha, Alexandre Maral, Nicolas Milovanovic in
> *Louis XIV, l'image et le mythe*

The surname of the masked prisoner, Eustache Dauger, was very similar to the name of the d'Auger de Cavoye family, small nobles from Picardy whose male members were professional soldiers in Louis XIV's army, one brother even having the same forename name of the prisoner, Eustache d'Auger de Cavoye. Another brother, Louis d'Auger de Cavoye, was a lifelong, close companion of the king who looked just like him.

The Eustache Dauger mystery is like a footed bowl. The large cup of the mystery of the Man in the Iron Mask rests on a foot. The theory that we make here, that Louis XIV was brought into the royal family via the womb of a surrogate in a plot authored by Anne of Austria which she saw as the only solution which would defend her from divorce, possibly prison, possibly death, and would keep the Bourbon family in power and avoid the revival of the sixteenth-century wars of religion is a remarkable proposal.

There are reasons in the historical record that suggest that a harder, harsher look at Louis XIV's birth is warranted. Let us say the theory of surrogacy is our *lettre de cachet*, our written reason for arrest, as Louis XIV once gave to Captain Vauroy as a request for the arrest of Eustache Dauger. We are *"malsatisfait"*..."not satisfied," which was the wording that often appeared in *lettres de cachet*, with the conduct of Louis XIV and his mother Anne of Austria, and we are recommending that an investigation and a trial be made. Just as with the *lettres de cachet* of the Old Regime, the charge may be false or unverifiable, but no law prevents the issuing of the question.

Never before has it been proposed that neither the king nor the queen were donors of life to the future Louis XIV, but that another set of parents, not related to the king or the queen, were the father and mother of the baby given to France on September 5, 1638, the birthday of Louis XIV. Why would that have anything to do with Eustache Dauger?

The king had to keep Dauger in total secret confinement because 1) Dauger was a son of his mother and Louis XIII and he couldn't be allowed to procreate (that child might not have had a craniofacial birth defect and could have come into the hands of people who might have discovered he was a royal son and used it against Louis XIV's own progeny) and 2) Dauger was handicapped and needed a place to live outside society. I think his mother had asked Louis XIV on her deathbed in January 1666 to take care of him, although the way Louis took care of him wasn't what she had in mind. Remember her words to Louis XIV on her deathbed: "Anne, without weakening, fixed her eyes on him and pronounced, 'Do what I told you; I'm telling you again with the Holy Sacrament on my lips.'" He couldn't kill Dauger because he was a member of the royal family so his murder would be illegal and horrific.

Eustache Dauger shared a surname with François and Marie d'Auger de Cavoye and their sons. Although Dauger and the d'Auger de Cavoye family had the same surname they did not know each other or ever interact. We showed in the last chapter that Dauger's name might have been that of the place where he was a child or was baptized, the geographical area near the village of Auger Saint-Vincent in the Valois region of Picardy. The d'Auger de Cavoye family was from the same region of Picardy as the prisoner...the same region that venerated the famous local hero of the Valois, Oger the Dane.[565] The king did not want any comparisons between the prisoner and the brothers in the Cavoye family. Comparisons of his face to the faces of the brothers were already bad enough. Other than a general notice of this at court, no serious questions had ever been raised about why that was. Louis

XIV wanted to keep it that way.

Eustache d'Auger de Cavoye (born 1637, died 1680 in prison), one of François and Marie d'Auger de Cavoye's sons, was known at court because he murdered a page at Saint-Germain-en-Laye; he was involved in a shabby sex scandal that involved a nephew of Mazarin, and his family had incarcerated him. Louis d'Auger de Cavoye (born 1639, according to conjecture...his birth certificate has never been found, died February 1716), a younger brother of the latter, was even more well known for being a war hero, officer of the king's house, Louis XIV's lookalike, and the king's close friend, who had been at his side or very nearby since the king's birth in 1638. Armand d'Auger de Cavoye (born 1638, died 1667), another brother, was also said to look like the king. He was a lieutenant in the gardes françaises at the time of his death at the siege of Lille.

1638

The previous chapters were about Eustache Dauger, whom we have theorized was a baby of Anne of Austria and Louis XIII, born a few months after Louis XIII had died in 1643, with cleft lip and palate, and, according to custom in France at that time, was divided from its parents and given to assigned caretakers because the birth defect eliminated chances for living in public.

Now we look at another birth. This one happened in 1638. The year in which Anne of Austria became pregnant with Louis XIV was 1637, the year that the queen of France's twenty-two year history of repeated miscarriages and no live births had become a threat to dynasty and civil order. It is the thesis of this chapter that there was a deception about Louis XIV's birth in 1637–1638 that Eustache Dauger's existence threatened to reveal. Louis XIV could not afford that revelation; he would have lost his position and perhaps his life, so the events of Eustache Dauger's life took the course they did in order to keep the 1637–1638 deception a secret.

"Il Court De Mauvais Bruits Sur Le Soleil."

The North American twentieth-century poet Maya Angelou advised, "When someone tells you who they are, believe them the first time." The first thing anyone heard about Louis XIV was that he was Louis *Dieudonné*, meaning Louis *given by God*, a name inspired by the gratitude that the royal family and the people of France had for a prince planned for and prayed for over twenty-three years, who came after his parents' spring of fertility had stopped flowing. Under this nickname has always trickled a stream of constant, quiet interrogatories: "Given by Anne and Louis or given by some other power?"

Historian Emile Bourgeois said succinctly that there have always been suspicions about the legitimacy of Louis XIV.

> His birth in 1638, unexpected, at first caused a lot of gossip at court and in the public. It is told that Louis XIII, in love with Mademoiselle de Lafayette, and visiting her at the convent where she had retired from public life, was one evening forced to stop over at Paris and to sleep at the Louvre. This one-night stay in the Queen's bedroom due to a quasi infidelity was a bit of a joke. When Louis XIV was born, France thought no more about it. God had given a dauphin to France by a miracle. France thanked God and proceeded from there to follow with keen interest the progress of Louis *Dieudonné*.[566]

Anne of Austria was accused of committing adultery to conceive Louis XIV. It is as if the two items, Louis XIV's suspected illegitimacy and his suspected holy miracle persona must be brought together like an equation, one belongs to the other, but it always seems as if historians write about the event this way just in case one day Anne's rumored adultery gets a hat and coat and leaves the hall to wander the streets. One has to have covered all the possibilities, just in case. If historians had the firm belief that there had been nothing amiss with Louis XIV's birth, they would not have written, every one of them, that there may have been a slight chance that the bed that husband and wife slept in that night was cold and not hot, or even warm. A proposal of adultery has been facile; it is what male historians have chosen for an explanation of what has always been a weak point in the timeline of Louis XIV. A theory of the king's illegitimacy on both sides of his parentage has been too troublesome to contemplate, too eerie, too contrary to conventional scholarship.

Strange that this proposed pairing of a sinful act and a numinous act, an illegitimate child glorifies France, is a rough approximation of the Christian story of Christ's birth; His human father did not cause the pregnancy and His Holy Father guided him to save humanity. This simile would not seem at all strange to Anne of Austria, and I think she often considered her place in France's history as the link in the equation, or one might say, a personification of it, a surrogate for the Virgin Mary, whose purity provided a solution to mankind's trials and deleted sinful sexual relations from the product, making "a miracle." The night in the queen's apartment was near December 8, the Catholic feast of the Virgin's Conception. Anne of Austria was pleased with comparisons to herself of Biblical elderly couples who conceived children after everyone had given up on a conception and birth, like everyone had given up on her before she triumphed over her age, her husband, and her detractors in bringing a baby to French Christendom.[567] The theme of the "*Sainte Enfance du Christ*" being increasingly popular, it was not difficult for her and those around her—her confessor, her almoner, the nuns in the convents that she visited and others—to place the *crèche* of Jesus within the *dauphin's* cradle.

The image of the royal mother and her son as the incarnation of the Virgin Mary and Jesus was invoked frequently in print and pictures. It crept into the royal family's life and the life of the state with very little nuance. Anne believed it, Louis XIV believed it, and his subjects believed it. Even card games and school lessons were in thrall to the linkage between the *dauphin's* birth and the baby Jesus' birth. In a didactic card game created for Louis XIV's use when he was six years old, the authors of the game, Jean Desmarests de Saint-Sorlin and Stefano della Bella, dedicated it to Anne of Austria, calling her a saint because "...God heard her prayers and gave her a son after twenty-two years of sterility."[568] Mazarin, a clever card player (who cheated) might have thought that Anne held a good hand... a straight... Jack, Queen, King, and an Ace.

Alignment?

The following are historical truths. Not theories.

One: The publicized story of the conception of Louis XIV sounds strained and orchestrated.

Louis XIII was manipulated by a few people to go to the Louvre and the queen in early December, nine months before Louis XIV's birthday: Louise de Lafayette, François Guitaut, and Anne herself, who wanted very badly to get pregnant.

The circumstances of the night on which the conception supposedly took place are described in every book about Louis XIV; the story of a rainy night in December 1637 when Louis XIII stayed a long time visiting his recent heartthrob, Louise de Lafayette, who had entered the convent of the Visitandines in Paris on the rue Saint Antoine, and she pleaded with him, for the safety of France and to lessen the power of Richelieu and his anti-Habsburg politics, to have a baby with his wife. François de Guitaut (1580–1663),[569] the king's chief of guards, waiting for his king for hours outside the convent, used the late hour and a heavy downpour of rain as an excuse for not proceeding to their original destination and insisted that he spend the night in the apartments of the queen in the Louvre. The king said he would wait for the storm to subside but it kept raining, so he agreed to go down

Figure 19.2: Anne of Austria. Claude Mellan. France, not later than 1643. Paper, black chalk. Courtesy of The State Hermitage Museum, Saint Petersburg, Russia.

the rue Saint-Antoine, across the Place Baudoyer near the Saint-Gervais church, through the *place* in front of the Hôtel de Ville, then onto the rue Saint-Jacques-de-la-Boucherie on the north side of the Châtelet, around the Saint-Germain l'Auxerrois church, and from there to the east entrance of the Louvre. He and his men crossed an advance bridge to get to the wooden drawbridge and then entered the gate between the two huge towers built by King Philippe-Auguste in 1190, the same vaulted entrance in which the *signore* Concini, agent of Louis' mother, had been assassinated on Louis' command in April 1617, six feet (two meters) wide by thirty-six feet (twelve meters) long.[570] In the dark and the rain, crossing that medieval six-foot-wide bridge must have seemed to Louis that he was going to his doom and not to his wife, because he often conflated the two things. But he had been told (perhaps not believed, but he had given up protesting) that she had the only furniture in Paris that was fit for him. As he entered the courtyard her rooms were to his left in the modern residential wing on the first floor above ground level. He entered the building either using the staircase on the left of the Queen's wing or the *petit dégré*, the stairwell at the opposite end of the wing that led to the king's rooms with a little corridor to the queen's bedroom. She had been alerted that he was coming.

One of Anne of Austria's biographers, Ruth Kleinman, went to the archived newspaper reports that gave the schedule of the king and queen.

> According to the *Gazette's* report, the king and queen were at Saint-Germain-en-Laye from 9 November until 1 December, when both went to Paris. On 2 December, Louis left Paris for Crône...and from Crône went on to Versailles on 5 December while the queen still remained in Paris. Louis may well have stopped in Paris on his way from Crône to Versailles, and his rooms at the Louvre may have been cleared of furniture since his departure three days earlier." She adds that Louis' doctor, Bouvard, thought the pregnancy could date from late November.[571]

The actions of Guitaut, Anne, Louise de Lafayette, and the nuns in convents all over Paris who that night communicated requests for prayer for the conception of a dauphin seem mechanized, construed, arranged. Many Louis XIV scholars have said the same and have gasped at the miraculous events that led to the dauphin's birth. By "miraculous" they come close to meaning "too good to be true."

Royal Births Under A Tent

Two: Substitutiion was possible because the measures traditionally taken to prevent substitution could easily have been circumvented.

A substitution during a royal birth had not seemed impossible to French royal families for hundreds of years, because rigorous preventive measures were permanently in place to prevent a substitution; why have those if a substitution was not a possibility? Members of the royal family were present at royal births in order to prevent substitutions. The longstanding custom appeared to be a major difficulty for a substitution thesis. If the king's brother and the invited princes and duchesses could see the actual birth in the delivery room a substitution would not be possible. Here is a description by Gustave Witkowski, a nineteenth-century medical historian, of the staging of a typical French royal delivery room:

> When the queen would approach her term, they prepared, near her bedroom, another room where the delivery would take place. In this second room they put the relics of Sainte-Marguerite[572] and they put up two tents: one, larger, was to hold the witnesses gathered for the birth of the *enfants de France*, and, in general, all the assistants; the other, smaller, inside the first one, was for the queen, the king, the *sage-femme* and her aides.[573]

The observers were under the larger tent in the room but were not witnesses to what was happening inside the small tent. I was surprised to find this. The vaunted, often advertised practice of having witnesses "present" at a royal birth seemed in reality to have been that there were witnesses in the room under a tent, but that the need in a prudish society to keep the mother's reproductive organs hidden and for the midwife's need to be able to concentrate on her patient's care, no one but the midwife and her assistants saw the birth. The witnesses could hear the events in the inner tent but could not see them.

Dieudonné's Delivery

Three: The birth event on September 5, 1638, had many convenient events that often do not happen at deliveries of a first-time, old mother.

The invited observers, high-ranking family members, arrived at the end of August 1638 to watch the birth and ensure against substitution. The queen gave birth in the presence of Monsieur [Louis XIII's brother], the princesse de Condé, the comtesse de Soissons, the duchesse de Boüillon-la Mark,[574] the duchesse de Vendôme, the wife of the connétable de Montmorency, Mesdames de Senecey, de Hautefort, de La Flotte, *dames d'honneur*, and many other dames of the court. They were all lodged in the "new" Saint-Germain palace; it was August so it was hot, they were nervous, expecting every day to be called into the queen's room to witness... what? The death of the mother, who was old and whose reproductive history consisted solely of miscarriages, and/or the infant were possible. What would occur if that happened? Or would they be witnesses to the most moving, most joyous birth of a healthy dauphin since Louis XIII's birth in September 1601? Playing cards, walking in the old terraced Italian garden by the Seine, where the machines that once made the waters play in the grottoes that Henri IV had dug into the hillside to amuse his children were rusted solid from long disuse, watching the river flow by, and planning for the possibilities.

CHAPTER 19. A FOOTED BOWL 319

At the end of August the queen was overdue. Louis XIII wrote on 2 September: "The queen is feeling so well that I think we may wait another four days. She is two days into the tenth month."[575] Jean-Baptiste Morin de Villefranche had been asked by the king and queen to be close to the delivery room to record the moment of birth so that he could accurately write the baby's horoscope. Dame Peronne,[576] the midwife, came a few days before the birth and was perhaps more composed than the *princesses et princes du sang* because she was a professional midwife from a family of Parisian midwives, giving her, from experience, a better idea of the best and worst scenarios than the observers had. She was ready to cope with whatever came.

Because Henri IV, Marie de' Medici's husband, in 1601 had been hands-on with every sort of problem or action that others would shrink from, a raw man of earthy wit and determination to father a dauphin, he was at the head of his laboring wife's bed when Louis XIII was born. No possibility of an irregularity there. But his adult son, a father with a quite different temperament, Louis XIII, was at lunch in another part of the Saint-Germain-en-Laye palace at the time of Anne of Austria's delivery.

There was some confusion about the medical personnel in this case. Given the extreme importance of this international event, it is hard to see how that could have happened. First of all, doctors (all doctors were male) did not examine pregnant women or delivering women. It was against moral rules in both the Catholic and Protestant religions.

> Throughout the obstetrical literature, one senses an unwillingness to perform an autopsy when a woman died in the early stages of the pregnancy, and one also senses that vaginal examinations were rare, at least before the onset of labor. The few illustrations showing the exterior female anatomy expressly refer to the 'shameful parts.'[577]

The queen's physician, Pierre Séguin, was ill. Jean Meyer says that Séguin's nephew, also a physician, was asked for.

> Anne asked the king for Séguin's nephew to be there. But the king referred the decision to the cardinal who deigned to acquiesce; the important thing being, the maintenance of the good health of the child and his mother. The nephew had a good medical reputation. The trouble was that the queen-king-cardinal circuit was so slow that ...Louis XIV was born before the permission arrived at Saint-Germain. It is therefore possible that

neither the first surgeon nor his nephew attended the birth. To tell the truth, we are almost totally without information, and we can only think that Dame Peronne took care of everything.[578]

The bishop of Lisieux came to the queen's room to say mass at four in the morning. Then the bishop of Meaux also did a mass. The king was present for part of the morning and he prayed for a happy delivery but he wasn't in good health, having had a *fièvre tierce* for some weeks. At eleven-thirty the king went to lunch and just as he began eating someone suddenly told him the baby was coming and he rushed to the delivery room and was presented the baby by the midwife.[579] The baby weighed nine pounds and had two natal teeth. Louis XIII was overjoyed but he did not approach his wife and had to be urged in her direction.[580] Immediately there was a short procession over the 400-foot (120-meter) distance (a little over the length of a soccer field) from the very open and relaxed arrangement of Henri IV's sprawling "New Chateau" to the narrow, Renaissance "Old Chateau" by the town, and inside the thirteenth-century chapel in the courtyard the baby was consecrated to God by the bishop of Meaux in a brief baptismal ceremony that would serve until a formal baptism could be done later.[581]

In Chantal Grell's magnificently illustrated and penetrating 2010 collection of essays on Anne of Austria, one of the editor's own chapters, "Anne of Austria and Her Judges," quotes Dr. Jean Hartemann, at that time honorary professor of the obstetrical clinic of the Faculty of Medicine of Nancy, who described the delivery of Louis XIV as having many aspects that were unusual for a delivery of a thirty-seven-year-old woman with a history of gynecological and obstetrical problems:

> As to the delivery, managed by a midwife, 'dame Pérone,' [*sic*] under a closed tent, it was, for the final moments of delivery, stunningly brief for a first birth late in the mother's life, happening during a brief absence of the king from the room when he left to get something to eat. The just delivered baby was very vigorous, had many teeth, and the reporters of the time said he had the appearance of a three-month-old... today, we have seen the case presented for the queen's need to have a child and her husband's inability to give her one. The question of the illegitimacy of Louis XIV should be researched.[582]

Louis XIV Looked Exactly Like Louis D'Auger De Cavoye

Four: A lady of honor of the queen, Marie de Lort de Sérignan, wife of François d'Auger de Cavoye, Cardinal Richelieu's chief of Musketeers, had three sons who looked very much like Louis XIV, especially Louis d'Auger de Cavoye, her youngest son. The similarity of Louis XIV's and Cavoye's face, body measurements, and bearing was reported by the memoirist Saint-Simon and repeated in Cavoye's biography. Also said to look very like the king were Eustache d'Auger de Cavoye and Armand d'Auger de Cavoye, two other sons of Marie de Lort de Sérignan.

Theories Drawn From The Above Historical Data

Our *lettre de cachet* dares to consider whether Anne of Austria managed to conceive a baby that she and France desperately needed through the womb of Marie de Lort de Sérignan, a fertile, daring, unassailable woman with a measured sense of humor who in 1637 had already had eight children with her husband. Because of the striking similarity in portraits of the faces of Louis XIV and the de Cavoye's youngest son, Louis d'Auger de Cavoye, at least three previous authors have suggested that Marie or François had a part in Louis XIV's birth; in 1954, Rupert Furneaux (*Man Behind the Mask*) theorized that, based on the extreme likeness of Cavoye to the king, Louis XIV was the child of Louis XIII and Madame de Cavoye. In 1974 historian Marie-Madeleine Mast (*Le Masque de fer, une solution révolutionnaire*) saw a reproduction of the painting of Louis de Cavoye and concluded that François d'Auger de Cavoye and Anne of Austria were the parents of Louis XIV. In 2006 Henri Lamendin (*Petites histoires de l'art dentaire d'hier et d'aujourd'hui*) seconded this latter opinion.

But our opinion is that when you pair a man with a woman who is not his wife, or a woman with a man who is not her husband, you don't produce a child that looks exactly like sons already made by the original pair; you get a similarity, but not a likeness that was so extreme that they could pass for twins. Yet Louis XIV looked exactly like Louis d'Auger de Cavoye, the only minor difference between the two being the presence of a small mustache on the king, which, it goes without saying, is an artificial, cosmetic feature, not a genetic one.

Comparison of the faces in the portraits:

Louis XIV's face shape is square, aesthetically wide at eye level, his chin is square and slightly broad and rounded at the base with a faint dimple. He has aesthetically pleasing lengths of nose to lip and lip to chin, a slightly curved long nose with a pointed tip, the sides of which are shown to be

Figure 19.3: Louis d'Auger (1639-1716), marquis de Cavoye, Grand Maréchal du Logis du Roi. French School. Date unknown. 17th Century. Both of these images, on the left in black and white and on the right in color, are of the same portrait.

slightly concave, a trait which is mentioned by contemporaries but often is not shown in portraits because it was considered a flaw. In a comparison with the portrait above of Louis d'Auger de Cavoye, both men have identical size, position, and length of nostril openings, they have identically shaped and sized lips, they both have shallowly set eyes of similar shape with a very narrow lower eyelid and a thin but prominent upper eyelid, neither seem to have noticeable eyelashes, their chins are identical and their lower vermilions are separated from the protrusion of the chin in the same measurement. There is a noticeable crease at the oral commissures. Louis de Cavoye's eyebrows seem less dense than the king's but their arch is identical. Their columellas' (the part of the nose between the tip and the base that separates the nostrils) length looks identical. The portraits both show nasolabial creases, faint for both. Both show rami (the ascending posterior portions of the mandible) that have very sharp differences in angle (i.e. a square jaw) and both have flat cheek bones and flat cheeks. Louis XIV wears a mustache and Louis de Cavoye doesn't have one. Both men wear curly wigs. Both men have short foreheads with a sharp angle from the brow toward the hairline. The brow ridge is moderately prominent and is well above the eye sockets. Both men have a proud air, as if confident of their superiority.[583]

CHAPTER 19. A FOOTED BOWL

Figure 19.4: Louis XIV. P. van Schuppen. Engraving. 1666. After a painting by Charles Le Brun. Courtesy Bibliothèque Nationale de France.

More History

One: I think the comparison of portraits and the contemporary descriptions that we have of Louis XIV's facial characteristics give evidence that Louis XIV was not related to the families he is officially joined to. In portraits and sculptures, the *Roi Soleil* does not look like any of his close or distant official relatives: his paternal grandfather, Henri IV; Henri's Navarre Bourbon family; his paternal grandmother Marie de' Medici; Marie's paternal Italian or maternal Austrian Habsburg family; either of his parents, father Louis XIII and mother Anne of Austria, both of whom had direct and indirect Habsburg genes; or his brother Philippe d'Orléans.

It rarely happens that a person does not look like, generally or in specific traits, anyone in the family lineage. In a large family with many siblings in each generation, likenesses are there. DNA makes this so...we each have DNA of both parents in most of the cells in our bodies. Likeness in body or face to at least one family member, either a near relative or a distant ancestor, is inescapable, and yet Louis XIV escaped.

Chantal Grell in her book on Anne of Austria quoted the doctor Augustin Cabanès (1862–1928), who gave his judgement on the dissimilarity in the faces and bodies of Louis XIII and Louis XIV:

> In the bearing, the size, the physiognomy, the cut of the figure and the proportions of the lines of the face of Louis XIII, I recognize the face of Henri IV: Louis XIII is Henri IV, sick and degenerating. In all the features of Louis XIV, I find nothing of Louis XIII.

and

> In any of his life stages, there is never the slightest lineament of resemblance between the pretended father and the pretended son. Nothing in the jaw, nothing in the face, nothing in the proportions of the features, nothing in the complexion, nothing in the hair, nothing in the expression...[584]

Louis XIV's face was studied intently by the genius Italian sculptor Gian Lorenzo Bernini (1598–1680), who came to Paris in 1665 to design the east facade of the Louvre, a design he finished but it was not ever seriously considered for the entrance facade of the palace, and while he was in Paris he made a stunning bust of Louis XIV in white marble that is today at the palace of Versailles. The formal sittings were in August and September in Paris at the Palais Mazarin,[585] where Bernini was staying, and Bernini observed the king in council meetings, playing tennis, and in conversation so that he could sketch the king's expressions during activities.

One of Bernini's comments about working on the bust shows the necessity to be wary of artists' images in the matter of accuracy. He said that it was very difficult to suggest in sculpture the king's long eyelashes.[586] On many portraits of Louis XIV his eyelashes are almost invisible and in most of the images studied for this book, no matter the person, eyelashes are almost invisible. A memoir of the portrait sittings says that Bernini tried, in the marble, to improve what he saw in the flesh. He said that the king's eyes "were a little dead, that he never opened them fully and that his mouth changed frequently."[587] When, in commenting on the progress of the bust, the king saw a feature he did not like, he pointed it out to Bernini ("Is my nose really on one side?"[588]) and Bernini changed it.

Rudolf Wittkower, art historian, in a lecture in 1950 told his audience that Bernini said, "His [Louis XIV's] eye-sockets were big, whereas the eyes themselves were small." Wittkower agrees.

> The eyes of the King were, in fact, extremely small. This is clearly borne out by other portraits, such as the rather uninspired pastel in profile by Lebrun of slightly later date. And the faithful engravings by Nanteuil show the King with narrow and almost oriental-looking eyes which have a drooping and rather shifty look about them.[589]

Two: A grave life-threatening menace made a drastic solution necessary. A crisis of the future of nations had come in 1637 which threatened France with being overrun by the Spanish Habsburgs. This crisis has been described elsewhere in this book and many others.

Three: A scientific truth of genetics will help to understand the thesis. Louis XIV's family tree shows a heavy loading of Habsburg genes. Louis XIV's paternal great-grandmother was the daughter of Habsburg Emperor Ferdinand I; Anne of Austria's family tree was dominated on both sides by Habsburg members in multiple generations in both the Spanish and Austrian branches of the family. But the Habsburg signature genetic craniofacial overgrowth did not appear on Louis XIV's face, nor the midface/maxilliary retrusion that can be associated. This is not necessarily indicative that Louis lacked Habsburg genes. The gene produced the trait haphazardly in the Habsburgs. The genetic defect was an unpredictable problem for the Habsburgs that stayed silent in some members but then erupted on the faces of some of their sisters, brothers, and children in a range of extreme to hardly noticeable ways and only began to be physically present at puberty.

A 2019 study by Román Vilas et al. drew conclusions about whether the Habsburg jaw (mandibular prognathism) is related to inbreeding and to investigate its genetic basis. To do that, the study used sixty-six paintings of Habsburg family members to judge the frequency and severity of the trait of mandibular prognathism.

The Vilas study concluded that, as has always been theorized, inbreeding led to increased instances of the trait in the Habsburg family. In the past, many journal articles on Habsburg inherited facial features, particularly mandibular prognathism, have come to the conclusion that a major dominant gene caused the trait to appear. But Román Vilas says that another possibility for the frequency of the trait's appearance in the family is the random creation in some family members of copies of the gene that is associated with mandibular prognathism, so that the abnormal facial trait may be due not to an issue of dominance or recessivity (the inherent nature of the gene that is transmitted) but is due to the effect of a family member getting two copies of the same gene, in other words, a random mistake rather than an essential mistake.[590]

Dr. Donatella Lippi, who did a skeletofacial analysis of Joanna of Austria (1547–1578), Louis XIV's great-grandmother, listed some typical Habsburg facial traits in her analysis of the duchess' skull.

> Examination of the abundant portraits of the Habsburg family shows, in addition to mandibular prognathism (Angle class III malocclusion, sometimes called the Habsburg jaw), a thick, everted lower lip, a large, often misshapen nose with a prominent dorsal hump, a tendency to flattening of the malar [cheek] areas, and mild eversion of the lower eyelid.[591]

Marie Thérèse, Louis XIV's first wife, was a Habsburg princess and therefore had genes for the "Habsburg jaw," however she did not have a protruding jaw. Her father, Anne of Austria's brother, however, had one of the most extreme examples of mandibular prognathism in any Habsburg family member. The first child born to Marie-Thérèse and Louis XIV, a son, Louis, the *Grand Dauphin*, did not show visible signs of the trait, although he certainly had the gene from his mother, nor did any of his children or grandchildren. The *Grand Dauphin's* sisters and brothers died before the prognathism would have developed after puberty. We will never know if Marie-Thérèse's genes, undoubtedly passed to those sadly short-lived babies, would have caused visible deformities of the lower jaw.

Where our thesis of substitution is supported is that mandibular prognathism did not appear in any of Louis XIV's offspring by his mistresses. None of the mistresses were Habsburgs and so the controlling factor for the appearance of the Habsburg jaw would be Louis XIV's genes, that were either Habsburg...or not.

It seems logical that if Louis XIV had Habsburg genes on both his maternal and paternal side, as his family tree shows, then he would have had chil-

CHAPTER 19. A FOOTED BOWL

dren or grandchildren with the "jaw" by mistresses. If the scientific studies that have been completed over the last fifty years are a guide, there should have been at least one descendant of Louis XIV with the trait. Yet it disappeared with Louis XIV...completely disappeared from his line, both by his legitimate wife and by his mistresses.

However, in his brother's line, the Habsburg features and the protruding jaw appear with regular, although diminishing frequency. Philippe d'Orléans, the king's brother, had a daughter by his first wife (with Habsburg genes) who had a large jaw and Habsburg facial features but whose sister did not have outward signs of the trait. A daughter by his second wife (not a Habsburg) had a daughter (i.e. Philippe's granddaughter) with a large jaw and Habsburg facial features.

Figure 19.5: Marie-Antoinette of the Habsburg house of Austria, was a descendant of Philippe d'Orléans. Her full chin and protruding lower lip (some- times reduced by artists in formal portraits during her reign but visible here) are soft signs of the Habsburg trait of mandibular prognathism. Marie Antoinette au Tribunal révolutionnaire detail (engraving by Alphonse François, from a painting by Paul Delaroche) (1857). A reproduction on display at the Conciergerie, Paris. Photo by the author.

Differences In Character Between Louis D'Auger De Cavoye And Louis XIV

If we look at *differences* in personality between Louis and Louis, the facility of deception comes to mind first. Louis de Cavoye was said to be a very honest person and the king was known by diplomats from foreign governments to be a liar when it suited him. He was also deceptive in general about his life, his decisions, and his preferences. This stark contrast could be attributed to the difference in the social and political stations of the two men. Louis *Dieudonné* from birth was trained to rule a country, a responsibility that requires some lying from time to time in order to steer the nation into safety or war when need be, and the Marshal of the Lodgings of the King was a soldier, an officer, and head of a large family, and would have not had the headwinds for honesty that the king had.

The two men had wives of very different temperaments and backgrounds. Louis XIV was married twice and Louis de Cavoye only once. Cavoye had been in the sights of his future wife for years but he had not wanted a wife. The king finally had enough of Cavoye's reluctance and offered him the position of Grand Marshal of Lodgings of the King in 1677 if he would marry her. Their marriage was happy. Professor Nancy Segal, American twin specialist, thinks more research should be done on why twins pick their partners because so far, twin study results have been "mixed" on similarity of partners.[592]

List Of Similarities In The Life Events And Personalities Of Louis D'Auger De Cavoye And Louis XIV

Handwriting

The signatures of Louis and Louis look somewhat similar. The signatures of Louis XIV always have a right-facing loup on the first letter. The signature of Louis d'Auger de Cavoye always has a left-facing loup on the first letter. There are many signatures of Louis XIV available to historians but few of Louis d'Auger de Cavoye. Above is an image of Eustache d'Auger de Cavoye's and Louis d'Auger de Cavoye's signature and a signature of the king. For both men the letter L is connected with the rest of the letters in the name. The king's handwriting looks more compressed than Cavoye's and has a flourish...a curved stroke under his name that is unconnected to the name. Cavoye also wrote a small, straight flourish to complete the end of the descending stroke of the y at the end of his surname.

Scientists who compare environmental and genetic causes of human differ-

CHAPTER 19. A FOOTED BOWL

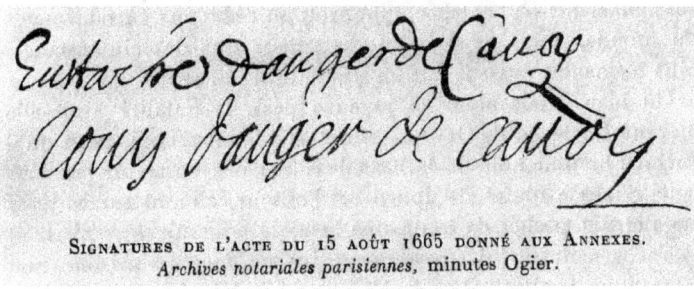

Figure 19.6: Top, "Signatures de l'acte du 15 août 1665 donné aux Annexes. Archives notariales parisiennes, minutes Ogier." The document was notarized by "Ogier", probably François Ogier, a notary active in Paris at the time of the signing, and perhaps a relative of the d'Auger de Cavoye family. The image was copied from the book by Maurice Duvivier, Le Masque de fer, Paris: Librairie Armand Colin, 1932, page 139. Bottom, Signature of Louis XIV, 1682. PD-US

ences often are pleased to find identical twins who have been separated at birth because their genetics are one hundred percent identical but they are raised in different environments by different sets of parents.[593] If they were twins, Louis and Louis would fit into that study category, although in their case the environment in which they were raised as very young children was nearly the same because Louis de Cavoye was one of the set of little boys who were playmates of the king, and then he was a court page at age seven. In his adolescence he was away from the king more than at any other time, then as an adult he was a soldier, *aide-de-camp*, and Grand Marshal of Lodgings of the King from 1677 to September 1715, a post he received directly from the king as a present. All these positions brought him into the constant close presence of Louis XIV.

Similarities Between Louis XIV And Louis D'Auger De Cavoye That Might Indicate They Were Twins

It is possible that Louis XIV and Louis d'Auger de Cavoye were twins. Scientists do not think that having identical twins is a genetically passed trait but that fraternal twins result from the trait of over ovulation in the mother and is passed from mothers to daughters. Madame Marie d'Auger de Cavoye had twin girls, Constance and Charlotte, born probably in 1629, both of whom became nuns. Marie baptized the twins at Sérignan in 1630.[594] Henriette, Marie's oldest daughter, had three sons, two of whom were twins. We do not know if either of these two sets of twins were identical.

- Louis XIV and Louis de Cavoye were both born in the month of September. Cavoye's birth year has always been printed as 1639 or 1640. We have no birth certificate for him. Louis XIV was born on September 5, 1638.
- Both were named Louis.
- Both boys' fathers died before the boys were old enough to know them: Louis XIV was four and a half years old when his father died of chronic illness and Louis de Cavoye was one year old when his father was killed in battle.
- Cavoye was placed in group of playmates of the young king by Marie d'Auger de Cavoye and Anne of Austria.
- Cavoye became a court page at age seven so he continued to spend his days near the king to one degree or another.
- Both men had extensive training in the arts of war, swordsmanship, equitation, and in courtly manners.
- They looked enough alike to cause courtiers to recognize the similarity. They had the same facial characteristics, height, stance, and tone of voice.[595]
- Both had a cool attitude of superiority.
- They had small differences in public manners. Cavoye was more animated than the king.[596]
- Neither had formal schooling.
- Both men were extremely heterosexually active.
- Cavoye was appointed *aide-de-camp* (personal staff member having a variety of duties) to the king, so in his adulthood he was in constant contact with the king.
- Cavoye had an affair with Hortense Mancini, a sister of Marie Mancini that the king was in love with; both girls were nieces of Mazarin.[597]
- Huguet, Cavoye's biographer, says that it was rumored at court that Cavoye and the king were both having an affair with the comtesse de Gramont in the same months of 1678. Sévigné reports the king's liaison with the comtesse and Scudéry wrote to Bussy-Rabutin about Cavoye and the comtesse.[598]

CHAPTER 19. A FOOTED BOWL 331

- Cavoye was on unusual terms of familiarity with the king. His social position at court ordinarily would not have allowed the familiarity with which the two men interacted.

- The sculptor Bernini, who studied the king's face carefully for a bust he carved of Louis XIV, said that some of his facial features were different on either side of the midline.[599]

- Both supported writers at court; Cavoye was a good friend of Racine and the king also liked Racine very much and invited him to private audiences when Racine would read to him.

- The signatures of Louis and Louis are similar, with the loups in the capital L being in reverse directions, the king's louping right and Cavoye's louping left.

- Cavoye was appointed by the king to be Grand Marshal of Lodgings of the King in 1677, a job which required Cavoye's constant presence at court and nearness to the king. Cavoye did not buy the position. The king presented it to him.

- The king was very opposed, even angry, when Cavoye asked to sell his position and retire from court (he said) because of poor health.

- In 1696 the king finally allowed Cavoye to sell the position but would not let him leave court, forcing Cavoye to remain active in his post.

- A few months previous to the king's death, Cavoye again asked permission to leave court and again Louis XIV refused to let Cavoye retire. He stated publicly his reason: "Mourons ensemble!" "Let us die together!"

- One of the dying king's last requests *in extremis* was that a box inside of which (the king said) was a map of Vincennes should be given to Cavoye.

Cavoye was at Versailles on 27 August 1715 when the dying king, in taking care of some preparations for the guard and lodging of the king-to-be, the little dauphin, for whom there would be a caretaker government until he came of age to rule, said that the boy's next home should be Vincennes castle on the east of Paris, an ancient, fortified, small citadel with modern lodgings fit for the court, and he ordered that as soon as death came, the regent should immediately take the dauphin there, and Louis' next thought was that the Grand Maréchal des Logis, Louis de Cavoye, was not familiar with the lodgings available at Vincennes because the court had not been there in a very long time (the master of lodging was the person who decided where the elite chosen few could have apartments), and that therefore

Cavoye would need a map of the large complex of towers, chapel, gardens, and stables of Vincennes and of the apartments in the King's wing and the Queen's wing, two facing small palaces at the south end of the fortress that would be domiciles for Louis XV and his court. The king had such a map in a box and told an aide where it was and ordered that the box should be given to Cavoye.

The valet of the marquis Louis d'Auger de Cavoye had been allowed to sit with the Chancellor of France, two close family members, and Madame de Maintenon, the king's wife, in the dying king's antechamber next to his bedroom for days leading up to his death on September 1.

Louis d'Auger de Cavoye's biographer says of this highly unusual departure from protocol:

> It was surprising that this servant, who stayed in the outer room of the king's bedchamber in company with the princesses, the prince de Rohan, the chancellor Voysin, and very few others, was allowed to enter the room of the king until 30 August in the name of Monsieur de Cavoye although in those last days almost no one could be in the king's presence. Each day the valet returned to M. de Cavoye in Paris to tell him about the king's status. We can only guess that his presence was accepted because he and the king had always had a frank and personal friendship from the time that they were children, sixty-nine years before.[600]

Louis d'Auger de Cavoye wrote his will on September 2, 1715, which was the day after the king's death, and died five months later in his *hôtel* on the rue des Saints Pères[601] on Monday, February 3, 1716. He was buried on February 5 in the Saint-Charles Borromeo side chapel at the *église* Saint-Sulpice, his parish church. (Email to the author from the office of Art, Culture et Foi, Saint-Sulpice, Paris. September 30, 2021.) His wife, Louise-Philippe de Coëtlogon (1641–1729) was with him while he died and mourned for him respectfully until her death.

Although Louis d'Auger de Cavoye's birth year is given on official documents as 1639 and his brother Armand's birth year is always given as 1638, it is likely that Marie de Cavoye, the mother of these two boys, trying to conceal the donation of a baby to the queen in 1638, switched the birth years of Louis and Armand in public notifications. We do not have the birth certificate for Louis d'Auger de Cavoye. In her will, Marie made the designation for primary family executor to be Louis rather than Armand who should have been executor if he was the older brother, and she said in her will that she did this for reasons known only to her.

20. Philippe D'Orléans

> The little man of ribbons, rouge, jewelry, and mincing ways had reached his greatest hour and proven himself to be a Bourbon, the grandson of Henry IV, the son of Louis XIII, and the cousin of the great Condé.
>
> —John Wolf

Penetrating, astute articles have recently been published that show the similarities between the Iron Mask story and the frequent story in literature of brothers who are at odds with each other and the various permutations of the characters, usually women, who lost or found abandoned babies repeated from the Bible and mythology. Mathieu Da Vinha, Alexandre Maral, and Nicolas Milovanovic in their edited volume *Louis XIV l'image et le mythe* saw the Mask story as useful for a study on the mythical hero and the "double," using Otto Rank's theories. I am too familiar with the story of Eustache Dauger to see in it anything but a tragic imposition of adverse circumstances on an innocent human being, partly due to deficiencies in medical science in past times and partly due to human cruelty.

These are the only "doubles" that I find in this story: Eustache Dauger and Eustache d'Auger de Cavoye were put in prison by the brothers, Louis XIV and Louis d'Auger de Cavoye, because they were inconvenient and dangerous to their families. They were marginalized because they were misfits...they each had a stigma: Eustache d'Auger de Cavoye was a homosexual and an alcoholic and Eustache Dauger had a face with an unnatural opening. The other "double" is that Louis XIV and Louis de Cavoye might have been twins. It is a historical fact they *looked* like twins. They didn't replace each other or switch parts, they did what twins do: stay tightly together and have the same preferences, the same women, the same education, and they died together in the same environment within months of each other.

If Marie de Cavoye was a surrogate mother of the baby that was designated dauphin of France in 1638 with the full cooperation, perhaps design, of Queen Anne of Austria and historians find DNA of any of the actors that confirms the thesis, there will be multiple new reassessments of French history of the seventeenth century. It is not the intent of the author to guess

Figure 20.1: Philippe de France, Duc d'Orléans. Engraving. De Larmessin. Between 1677 and 1701. Courtesy Bibliothèque Nationale de France.

what reaction historians would have to proof by DNA testing of the surrogacy theory.

To solve the question of whether Louis XIV was a son of Louis XIII and Anne of Austria with Medici, Habsburg, and Bourbon ancestors, DNA analysis of his remains must be done. If it is, I expect to find gene-genealogy mismatches that imply extra-pair paternity (EPP) in Louis XIV's DNA.

If Louis XIV's DNA cannot be obtained, DNA analysis of the remains of

CHAPTER 20. PHILIPPE D'ORLÉANS

Louis d'Auger de Cavoye might give some important information, at least as to whether Cavoye had a twin, which the September 2021 work of Dr. Jenny van Dongen at the Vrije Universiteit Amsterdam showed would leave a mark on the DNA.[602] His DNA might be easier to find and test than Louis XIV's but still not easy: Cavoye is buried under a sealed chapel in the Saint-Sulpice church in Paris.

In practice the process of testing DNA of historical figures is very complicated, ruled by mathematics, chemistry, the expertise of magnificently trained scientists, and good luck, entwined with the rights and wishes of the owners of whatever property physically holds the remains in which DNA rests and of the surviving family members of the deceased if any can be found. It might be predicted that the clerics of Saint-Sulpice would not welcome a geneticist with a jackhammer digging holes under their Saint-Charles Borromeo chapel.

As in any case where DNA is examined there is the ethical problem of genetic privacy...rights of family members to keep their secrets. Who in this case would that be? France? The current Orléans prince?

So far nothing much has been said about Philippe d'Orléans, Louis XIV's brother. The entire story is about him because, if Louis XIV was not legitimately king, Philippe should have been king, should have been crowned, and was not. Philippe's birth does not need investigating. He was born on November 21, 1640, and he was a child of Anne and Louis XIII. For Louis XIII the appearance of the future Louis XIV gave Louis XIII the extreme pleasure and relief of producing a first child. The stress of childlessness that the king and queen had struggled under for so many years was dissolved, and I think a pregnancy was the result. They had had pregnancies before; this one was the first that went to term. Philippe, therefore, was the first son born to Anne and Louis XIII and should have been the dauphin and eventually king.

Philippe Erlanger's biography of Philippe says that after Philippe's heroic performance on the field of battle in 1677 at Cassel, Louis XIV, jealous of his brother's victory over William of Orange and the consequent glowing compliments Philippe got from the court and the press, took revenge by never giving his brother a command again.

> After this brief triumph, Phillipe saw himself cast into an invisible prison, captive of boredom, of ceremony, of forced pleasure. At age thirty-seven he ended his life.[603]

He was the victim, as Erlanger put it, of "a monstrous injustice."

Justice has come to Philippe over and over again for three hundred years because it is his line, the d'Orléans line, that has lasted and produced Europe's royalty. Philippe is the grandfather of Catholic Europe. He had for direct descendants: Louis XV, Louis XVI, Marie Antoinette, Louis XVIII, Charles X, Philippe-Egalité, Louis-Philippe, le duc d'Enghien, Joseph II, Marie-Louise, the King of Rome, François-Joseph, Victor-Emmanuel, the sovereigns of Belgium from Léopold II, Alphonse XIII, Ferdinand of Bulgaria and many others.

What is the consequence of Louis XIV's situation, if it was as we describe? Maybe there is none. He was, as the memoirist Saint-Simon said, an average person who could have bettered himself. He ran France for a long time and had a few successes. It could have been worse for France if Philippe had been king. Anne and Jules Mazarin may have been right about that. But that leaves a gigantic lie, if there was a surrogacy, in the middle of France's history. Does that matter?

It is not a theory to say that Louis XIV's fear and the gifts he gave himself to assuage that fear—the stupendous cost for building palaces for himself and his family, the luxuriating in mistresses, producing and legitimizing his bastard children, and most of all, his war making—assured a future state that was not concerned with its people, was suspicious of them, too in love with splendor, spendthrift, corrupt, dictatorial, and in not too many years that state could not hold and fell to the people whose bigotry and lawlessness was copied from Louis XIV's playbook. The citizens overturned what they hated in a way that imitated what they hated—secretive, anti-democratic, rude, hurried, and rigid.

This book is about the consequences of a choice. About how a choice someone else made affects your life or about your own choice at a crossroads that turns the future dark but must be tolerated. It is about living with what relatives and friends have done before you that mark you in a way you are not comfortable with.

It is about power, jealousy and anger mixed. About perceived righteous actions that are illegal and immoral, and the consequence of having to make more illegal and immoral choices on top of the first ones, and on and on. When do your choices really matter? How do people get power and how do they keep it? If someone knows the crime, are they complicit for not announcing it or are they right to keep their family and children safe? Must the rules be absolutely kept or can they be crossed if a disaster is imminent? Ethics. Purity. Is the pure always the best or should it be tainted sometimes in the best interests of everyone?

Readers are invited to form their own theories about why two men, not genetically related but related by chance, physical disability, and family dysfunction, Eustache Dauger and Louis XIV, who did not know each other, were tightly bound together. The mystery of the Man in the Iron Mask is not a story about twins and musketeers, although these have a part; it is a story of family tragedy that, when mixed with revenge, hate, pity, and pride, becomes a nation's tragedy. Its theme is that of Corneille's *El Cid*, Sophocles' *Oedipus Rex*, Shakespeare's *Macbeth*...heads of state who bring tragedy to their children by prioritizing the lesser rather than the higher moral good. I think the reason this story has never ceased to fascinate is that people sense the presence of a great tragedy and they respect that fullness, that ripeness, as a story that needs to be told and will be told, if we are patient.

Medical/Clinical References

Akcam, Okan M. et al. "Dental anomalies in individuals with cleft lip and/or palate." *European Journal of Orthodontics* (March 2010): 207–213.

Anderson, Trevor. "Medieval Example of Cleft Lip and Palate from St. Gregory's Priory, Canterbury." *Cleft Palate-Craniofacial Journal* 31, no. 6 (November 1994): 466–472.

Aramany, M. A. "A History of Prosthetic Management of Cleft Palate: Paré to Suersen." *The Cleft Palate Journal* 8 (October 1, 1971): 415–430.

Bardach, Janusz and Court Cutting. "Anatomy of the Unilateral and Bilateral Cleft Lip and Nose." In Janusz Bardach and Hughlett L. Morris. *Multidisciplinary Management of Cleft Lip and Palate Section X. Nasal Airway, Otologic, and Audiologic Problems Associated with Cleft Lip and Palate.* Philadelphia: W.B. Saunders Company, 1990, 150–159.

Brophy, Truman W. *Cleft Lip and Palate*. Philadelphia: P. Blakiston's Son & Co., 1923.

Buren, Alec. "3D printing helps build upper jaw prosthetic for Indian cancer patient." (Oct. 20, 2014). Accessed February 19, 2016. https://loc8.cc/ss/alex_buren_2014

Cabanès, Augustin. *Les Morts mysterieuses de l'histoire. Nouvelle édition... Deuxième série : rois, reines et princes français, de Louis XIII à Napoléon III.* Paris: Albin Michel, 1911.

Calafell, Francesc and Maarten H. D. Larmuseau. "The Y chromosome as the most popular marker in genetic genealogy benefits interdisciplinary research." Human Genetics 136 (2017): 559–73.

Clarren, Sterling K. et al. "Feeding Infants with Cleft Lip, Cleft Palate, or Cleft Lip and Palate." *The Cleft Palate Journal* 24, no. 3 (July 1987): 244–49.

Dagher, Danielle and Eleanor Ross. "Approaches of South African Traditional Healers Regarding the Treatment of Cleft Lip and Palate." *The Cleft Palate-Craniofacial Journal* 41, no. 5 (2004): 461–69.

Derderian, Christopher A. "Bilateral Cleft Lip and Palate." Webpage of Christopher A. Derderian, M.D. https://loc8.cc/ss/drderderian_2016. Accessed May 13, 2016.

Dixon, M. J., M. L. Marazita, T. H. Beaty, and J. C. Murray. "Cleft lip and palate: understanding genetic and environmental influences." *Nature Reviews Genetics* 12, no. 3 (2011): 167–78.

Friedman, Susan Hatters, Amy Heneghan, and Miriam Rosenthal. "Characteristics of Women Who Deny or Conceal Pregnancy." *Psychosomatics* 48, no. 2 (March–April 2007): 117–22.

Garvey, M. Thérèse, Hugh J. Barry, and Marielle Blake. "Supernumerary Teeth — An Overview of Classification, Diagnosis and Management." *Journal of the Canadian Dental Association* 65, no. 11 (December 1999): 612–16.

Gélis, Jacques. *History of Childbirth: Fertility, Pregnancy and Birth in Early Modern Europe*. Translated by Rosemary Morris. Cambridge, U. K.: Polity Press, 1996.

Gilbert, Ruth. "Strange notions: treatments of early modern hermaphrodites." In *Madness, Disability and Social Exclusion, the Archaeology and Anthropology of 'Difference'*. Edited by Jane Hubert. London; New York: Routledge, 2000.

Gould, George M. and Walter L. Pyle. *Anomalies and Curiosities of Medicine*. New York: Sydenham Publishers, 1937.

Grabb, William C., Gerald P. Hodge, Reed O. Dingman, and Robert M. O'Neal. "The Habsburg Jaw." *Plastic & Reconstructive Surgery* (November 1968): 442–45.

Guillemeau, Jacques. *La chirurgie françoise, recueillie des Anciens Médecins et Chirurgiens avec plusieurs figures des Instrumens necesseres pour l'opération. Manuelle par Jacques Guillemeau D'Orléans, Chirurgien du Roy et Juré à Paris*. Paris: Nicolas Gilles, 1594.

Guillemeau, Jacques. *Œuvres de chirurgie*. Rouen: Jean Viret, François Vaultier, Clément Malassis, and Jacques Besogne, 1649.

Hanson, James W. and Jeffrey C. Murray. "Genetic Aspects of Cleft Lip and Palate." In Janusz Bardach and Hughlett L. Morris. *Multidisciplinary Management of Cleft Lip and Palate Section X. Nasal Airway, Otologic, and Audiologic Problems Associated with Cleft Lip and Palate*. Philadelphia: W.B. Saunders Company, 1990, 121–24.

Hart, Gerald D. "The Habsburg Jaw." *Canadian Medical Association Journal*

104, no. 4 (April 3, 1971): 601–603.

He, Binfeng et al. "Analysis of High-Altitude De-Acclimatization Syndrome after Exposure to High Altitudes: A Cluster-Randomized Controlled Trial." *Plos One* 8, no. 5 (May 2013): 1–11.

Hodge, Gerald P. "A Medical History of the Spanish Habsburgs." *JAMA* 238, no. 11 (September 12, 1977): 1169–174.

Hughes, T. E. et al. "The teeth and faces of twins: providing insights into dentofacial development and oral health for practising oral health professionals." *Australian Dental Journal* 59(s1) (October 2, 2013): 101–16.

International Craniofacial Institute Cleft Lip and Palate Treatment Center. "Bilateral cleft lip and alveolus." http://loc8.cc/ss/craniofacial_2014. Accessed November 18, 2014.

Jenkins, Angela, Simon Millar, and James Robins. "Denial of Pregnancy: a literature review and discussion of ethical and legal issues." *Journal of the Royal Society of Medicine* 104 (2011): 286–91.

Knijff, Peter de. "On the Forensic Use of Y-chromosome Polymorphisms." *Genes* 13, 898 (2022): 1–14.

Kuriakose, Justin et al. "Long face pattern." *Revista Latinoamericana de Ortodoncia y Odontopediatría* (2013). http://loc8.cc/ss/ortodoncia_2013.

Larmuseau, Maarten M. H. D., Philippe Delorme, Patrick Germain, Nancy Vanderheyden, Anja Gilissen, Anneleen Van Geystelen, Jean-Jacques Cassiman, and Ronny Decorte. "Genetic genealogy reveals true Y haplogroup of House of Bourbon contradicting recent identification of the presumed remains of two French Kings."

European Journal of Human Genetics (2013): 1–7. doi:10.1038/ejhg.2013.211.

Larmuseau, Maarten H. D., K. Matthijs, and T. Wenseleers. "Long-term Trends in Human Extra-Pair Paternity: Increased Fidelity or Adaptive Strategy? A Reply to Harris." *Trends in Ecology and Evolution* 31, no. 9 (September 1, 2016): 663–65.

Larmuseau, Maarten H. D. and Martin Bodner. "The biological relevance of a medieval king's DNA" (Review Article). *Biochemical Society Transactions* 46, no. 4. (August 2018): 1013–1020.

Letra, A. et al. "Defining subphenotypes for oral clefts based on dental development." *Journal of Dental Research* 86, no. 10 (October 2007): 986–91.

Lim, Paul. "Cleft Lip Repair." *PAACS (Pan African Academy of Christian Surgeons) Bulletin* 3 (2013): 19. Accessed May 17, 2016. http://loc8.cc/ss/lim_paul_2016.

Lippi, Donatella, Felicita Pierleoni, and Lorenzo Franchi. "Retrognathic maxilla in 'Habsburg jaw' – Skeletofacial analysis of Joanna of Austria (1547–1578). *Angle Orthodontist* 84, no. 4 (2012): 387–95.

Lorot-Marchand, A. et al. "Frequency and socio-psychological impact of taunting in school-age patients with cleft lip-palate surgical repair." *International Journal of Pediatric Otorhinolaryngology* 79, no. 7 (July 2015): 1041–1048.

Marazita, M. L. "Subclinical features in nonsyndromic cleft lip with or without cleft palate (CL/P): review of the evidence that subepithelial orbicularis oris muscle defects are part of an expanded phenotype for CL/P." *Orthodontics and Craniofacial Research* 10, no. 2 (2007): 82–87.

Millard, Ralph D. *Cleft Craft: The Evolution of its Surgery. I. The Unilateral Deformity*. Boston: Little, Brown and Company, 1976.

Nanda, R. S. and S. K. Nanda. "Considerations of dentofacial growth in long-term retention and stability: is active retention needed?" *American Journal of Orthodontics and Dentofacial Orthopedics* 101, no. 4 (April 1992): 297–302.

Neiswanger, K, S. M. Weinberg et al. "Orbicularis oris muscle defects as an expanded phenotypic feature in nonsyndromic cleft lip with or without cleft palate." *American Journal of Medical Genetics Part A* 143A, no. 11 (June 1 2007): 1143–149.

Neville, Brad W., Douglas D. Damm, Carl M. Allen, and Angela C. Chi. *Oral and Maxillofacial Pathology*. 5th ed. Saint Louis, Missouri: Elsevier, 2024.

Paget, Stephen. *Ambroise Paré and His Times 1510–1590*. New York; London: G. P. Putnam's Sons, 1897.

Paré, Ambroise. *Les Œuvres de M. Ambroise Paré... : avec les figures & portraicts tant de l'anatomie que des instruments de chirurgie, & de plusieurs monstres*. Paris: Gabriel Buon, 1575.

Paré, Ambroise. *The workes of that famous chirurgion Ambrose Parey translated out of Latine and compared with the French by Thomas Johnson*. Translated and edited by Thomas Johnson, Thomas Cecil, and George Baker. London: Thomas Cotes and R. Young, 1634.

Paré, Ambroise. *Œuvres complètes d'Ambroise Paré*. 3 vols. Edited by J. -F. Malgaigne. Paris: J. -B. Baillière, 1840–1841.

Plomin, Robert. *Blueprint, How DNA Makes Us Who We Are*. Cambridge, Mass; London: MIT Press, 2019.

Randall, Peter. "History of Cleft Lip Nasal Repair." *Cleft Palate-Craniofacial Journal* 29, no. 6 (November 1992): 527–30.

Reilly, Sheena, et al. "ABM Clinical Protocol #17: Guidelines for Breastfeeding Infants with Cleft Lip, Cleft Palate, or Cleft Lip and Palate." *Breastfeeding Medicine* 8, no. 4 (2013): 349–53.

Rogers, Blair O. et al. "Palate surgery prior to von Graefe's pioneering staphylorraphy (1816): an historical review of the early causes of surgical indifference in repairing the cleft palate." *Plastic and Reconstructive Surgery* 39, no. 1 (January 1967): 1–19.

Romero, Martin and José Miguel Saez. "Scope of Western Surgical Techniques to Correct Clift Lip and Palate Prior to the 18th Century." *Cleft Palate-Craniofacial Journal* 51, no. 5 (September 2014): 497–500.

Schendel, Stephen et al. "The long face syndrome: vertical maxillary excess." *American Journal of Orthodontics* 7, no. 4 (August 1976): 399–400.

Segal, Nancy L. "Twin Research Perspective on Human Development." In *Uniting Psychology and Biology, Integrative Perspectives on Human Development*. Edited by Nancy L. Segal, Glenn E. Weisfeld, and Carol C. Weisfeld. Washington, D. C. American Psychological Association, 1997, 145-73.

Segal, Nancy L. "The Closest of Strangers." *New York Times*. May 23, 2014. Accessed June 11, 2014. Sunday Review.

Segal, Nancy L. *Twin Mythconceptions: False Beliefs, Fables, and Facts About Twins*. London: Academic Press, 2017.

Segal, Nancy L. *Deliberately Divided: Inside the Controversial Study of Twins and Triplets Adopted Apart*. Lanham; Boulder; New York; London: Rowman & Littlefield, 2021.

Segal, Nancy L. "Mysteries of Monozygosity: Theories and Breakthroughs/Twin Research: Rare Case of Lost Twins; Developing a National Twin Registry; Twins' Language and Gesture Delays; DNA Testing for Vanishing Twins/Media Reports: Identical Twins Discordant for COVID Vaccination; World's Oldest Identical Twins; Olympic Athlete Stand-in; Fraternal Twin Football Players." *Twin Research and Human Genetics* (2022): 1-5. doi:10.1017/thg.2021.51.

Talapeneni, Ashok Kumar et al. "Interceptive orthopedics for the correction of maxillary transverse and sagittal deficiency in the early mixed dentition period." *Contemporary Clinical Dentistry* 2, no. 4 (2011 October–December): 331–36.

Van Dongen, Jenny, Scott D. Gordon, Dorret I. Boomsma, et al. "Identical twins carry a persistent epigenetic signature of early genome programming." *Nature Communications* 12, 5618 (September 28, 2021): 1–14.

Vieira, A. R. "Unraveling human cleft lip and palate research." *Journal of Dental Research* 87, no. 2 (February 2008): 119–25.

Vilas, Román et al. "Is the 'Habsburg jaw' related to inbreeding?" *Annals of Human Biology* 46, no. 7–8 (2019): 553–61.

Watkins, Stephanie E. et al. "Classification, Epidemiology, and Genetics of Orofacial Clefts." *Clinics in Plastic Surgery* 41, no. 2 (January 4, 2014): 149–63. Accessed October 1, 2015.

Weinberg, S. et al. "Face shape of unaffected parents with cleft affected offspring: combining three-dimensional surface imaging and geometric morphometrics." *Orthodontics & Craniofacial Research* 12, no. 4 (2009): 271–81.

Wessel, J., A. Gauruder-Burmester, and C. Gerlinger. "Denial of pregnancy–characte of women at risk." *Acta Obstetricia et Gynecologica Scandinavica* 86 (2007): 542–46.

History, Sociology, Cultural References

Albanese, Ralph. *Initiation aux Problèmes Socioculturels de la France au XVIIe siècle*. Montpellier: Etudes Sociocritiques, 1977.

A.R.B.R.E.S. Remarquables. https://www.arbres.org.

Archives Diplomatiques du Ministère des Affaires Etrangères (ADMAE)

Mémoires et Documents: France, Anonymous letter. "*Plaintes de la Reine mère contre Monsieur le Cardal.*" October 1630. PO 3716, p. 358v.

Auger-Saint-Vincent webpage. "Un village à découvrir." http://loc8.cc/ss/augerstv.

Ballon, Hilary. *The Paris of Henri IV, Architecture and Urbanism*. Boston: Architectural History Foundation and the Massachusetts Institute of Technology, 1991.

Ballon, Hilary. *Louis Le Vau: Mazarin's Collège, Colbert's Revenge*. Princeton, New Jersey: Princeton University Press, 1999.

Bardin, Etienne Alexandre and Nicholas Charles Victor Oudinot. *Dictionnaire de l'armée de terre ou recherches historiques sur l'art et les usages militaires des anciens et des modernes*. 8 vols. Paris: Perrotin, 1841.

Bates, A. W. *Emblematic monsters; unnatural conceptions and deformed births in early modern Europe*. Amsterdam and New York: Editions Rodopi B. V., 2005.

Batiffol, Louis. *Le Louvre sous Henri IV & Louis XIII: La Vie de la Cour de France au XVIIe Siècle*. Paris: Calmann-Lévy, Editeurs, 1930.

Batiffol, Louis. *Autour de Richelieu: sa fortune, ses gardes et mousquetaires, la Sorbonne, le château de Richelieu*. Paris: Calmann-Lévy, 1937.

Bauer, Robert. *The Fourth Man*. New York: Hachette Books, 2022.

Bély, Lucien. *Les secrets de Louis XIV: mystères d'Etat et pouvoir absolu*. Paris: Tallandier, 2013.

Bergasse, Jean-Denis. *Le Masque de fer: Louis XIV, Nouveau regard, fin d'énigmes?* Cessenon, France: Jean-Denis Bergasse, 2008.

Bertière, Simone. *Louis XIII et Richelieu: La "Malentente."* Paris: Fallois, 2016.

Berville, Saint-Albin and Jean-François Barrière. *Collection des Mémoires relatifs à la Révolution Française: Mémoires de Linguet sur la Bastille et de Dusaulx sur le 14 Juillet.* Paris: Baudouin Frères, 1821.

Bocher, Héloïse. *Démolir la Bastille, l'édification d'un lieu de mémoire.* Paris: Vendémiaire, 2012.

Bonnaffé, Edmond. *Les Amateurs de l'Ancienne France: Le Surintendant Fouquet.* Paris: J. Rouam; London: Remington & Co., 1882; La Vergne, Tenn.: Kessinger Publishing, 2010.

Boswell, James. *The Kindness of Strangers: The Abandonment of Children in Western*

Europe from Late Antiquity to the Renaissance. New York: Pantheon Books, 1988.

Boucher, Philip P. *The Shaping of the French Colonial Empire: A Bio-Bibliography of the Careers of Richelieu, Fouquet, and Colbert.* New York and London: Garland Publishing, Inc., 1985.

Bourgeois, Emile. *Le grand siècle, Louis XIV, les arts, les idées, d'après Voltaire, Saint-Simon, Spanheim, Dangeau, Madame de Sévigné, Choisy, La Bruyère, Laporte, le* Mercure de France, *la Princesse Palatine, etc.* Paris: Hachette, 1896.

Bourgeois, Loyse, dite Boursier. *Récit Veritable de la Naissance de Messeigneurs et Dames Les Enfans de France. Instruction à Ma Fille et autres textes.* Edited by François Rouget and Colette H. Winn. Genève: Droz, 2000.

Braudel, Fernand. *The Identity of France.* vol 1. *History and Environment.* Translated by Siân Reynolds. New York: Harper & Row, 1986.

Brisson, Isabelle. "Le Mont-Saint-Michel sera sauvé des sables." *Le Figaro.* France/Société. Samedi 19–Dimanche 20 Février 2005.

Brockliss, L. W. B. "The Development of the Spa in Seventeenth-century France."

The Medical History of Waters and Spas. Medical History. Edited by Roy Porter. Supplement No. 10. 1990.

Brockliss, Laurence and Colin Jones. *The Medical World of Early Modern*

France. Oxford: Clarendon Press; New York: Oxford University Press, 1997.

Brocher, Henri. *Le Rang et l'Etiquette sous l'Ancien Régime: à la Cour de Louis XIV*. Paris: Librairie Félix Alcan, 1934.

Brown, Elizabeth A. R. *The Monarchy of Capetian France and Royal Ceremonial*. Brookfield, Vermont: Gower, 1991.

Brugnon, Stanislas. "Identité de l'homme au masque de fer." In *Il y a trois siècles... le Masque de Fer... Actes du Colloque international sur la célèbre énigme, 12–13 Septembre 1987*. Deuxième édition. Cannes: la Direction des Affaires Culturelles de la Ville de Cannes, 1996.

Burckhardt, Carl J. *Richelieu, His Rise to Power*. New York: Random House, 1964.

Cabanès, Augustin. *Les Morts mysterieuses de l'histoire. Nouvelle édition... Deuxième série: rois, reines et princes français, de Louis XIII à Napoléon III*. Paris: Albin Michel, 1911.

Caire, M. Bernard. "Eustache et Son Secret." In *Il y a trois siècles... le Masque de Fer... Actes du Colloque international sur la célèbre énigme. 12–13 septembre 1987*. Deuxième édition. Cannes: la Direction des Affaires Culturelles de la Ville de Cannes, 1996.

Carlhian-Ribois, Fernand. "Séjour du 'Masque de fer' à Briançon." In *Il y a trois siècles... le Masque de Fer... Actes du Colloque international sur la célèbre énigme. 12–13 Septembre 1987*. Deuxième édition. Cannes: la Direction des Affaires Culturelles de la Ville de Cannes, 1996.

Carlier, Claude. *Histoire du duché de Valois: ornée de cartes et de gravures: contenant ce qui est arrivé dans ce pays depuis le temps des gaulois, & depuis l'origine de la monarchie françoise, jusqu'en l'année 1703*. 3 vols. Paris: Guillyn, 1764.

Caroly, Michelle. *Le Corps du Roi-Soleil, grandeur et misères de sa majesté Louis XIV*. Paris: Imago/Les Editions de Paris, 1990.

Carré, Henri. *The Early Life of Louis XIV (1638–1661)*. Translated by Dorothy Bolton. London: Hutchinson & Co., 1951.

Castelot, André. *La Reine Margot*. Paris: Perrin, 1993.

Castelot, André. *Madame de Maintenon: La reine secrète*. Paris: Perrin, 1996.

Chatelain, U. V. *Le Surintendant Nicolas Foucquet, Protecteur des Lettres, des Arts et des Sciences*. Paris: Perrin et Cie, 1905.

Châtellier, Louis. *L'Europe des dévots*. Paris: Flammarion, 1987.

Chéruel, Adolphe. *Dictionnaire historique des institutions, mœurs et coutumes de la France*. 2 vols. Paris: L. Hachette et cie, 1855.

Choisy, François-Timoléon de. *Mémoires pour Servir à l'Histoire de Louis XIV*. Edited by Georges Mongrédien. Paris: Mercure de France, 1966.

Christ, Yvan. *Le Louvre et les Tuileries: Histoire Architecturale d'un Double Palais*. N.P.: Editions "Tel", 1949.

Colbert, Jean Baptiste. *Lettres, instructions et mémoires de Colbert*. 6 vols. Edited by Pierre Clément. Vol. 2, part 1. Paris: Imprimerie impériale, 1861–1873.

Cooper-Marsdin, A. C. *The History of the Islands of the Lerins, the Monastery, Saints and Theologians of S. Honorat*. Cambridge, England: Cambridge University Press, 1913.

Corroyer, Edouard. *Histoire et Légendes du Mont Saint-Michel*. Paris: Jean de Bonnot, 1982.

Cottret, Monique. "La Légende En Action, Le Masque de Fer Contre l'Arbitraire."
In *Il y a trois siècles... le Masque de Fer... Actes du Colloque international sur la célèbre énigme. 12–13 Septembre 1987*. Deuxième édition, Cannes: la Direction des Affaires Culturelles de la Ville de Cannes, 1996.

Cousin, Victor. *Madame de Hautefort, Nouvelles Etudes sur les Femmes Illustres et la Société du XVIIe Siècle*. Quatrième Edition. Edited by M. Barthélemy Saint-Hilaire. Paris: Libraire Académique Didier et Cie, Libraires-Editeurs, 1874.

Dauphin, Jean-Luc. "Bénigne Dauvergne, Dit Saint-Mars, Seigneur de Palteau et Dixmont, ou Le Vrai Père du Masque de Fer." *Etudes Villeneuviennes, Bulletin des Amis du Vieux Villeneuve-sur-Yonne, Société Historique, Archéologique, Artistique et Culturelle du Villeneuvien*. No. 33. Printemps 2005.

Dauphin, Jean-Luc. *Découvrir Villeneuve-sur-Yonne et le Villeneuvien*. Villeneuve-sur-Yonne: Conseil Général de l'Yonne, 2004.

Dauphin, Jean-Luc. "Deux Documents Inédits sur le Passage en Villeneuvien du Masque de fer." *Etudes Villeneuviennes, Bulletin des Amis du Vieux Villeneuve-sur-Yonne, Société Historique, Archéologique, Artistique et Culturelle du Villeneuvien*. No. 39. Printemps 2008.

Dauzat, Albert. *Dictionnaire Etymologique des noms de famille et prénoms de*

France. Paris: Librairie Larousse, 1980.

Da Vinha, Mathieu. *Le Versailles de Louis XIV. Le fonctionnement d'une résidence royale au XVIIe siècle*. Paris: Perrin, 2009.

Delort, Joseph. *Histoire de la Détention des Philosophes et es Gens de Lettres à la Bastille et à Vincennes, Précédée de celle de Foucquet, de Pellisson et de Lauzun, avec tous les Documents Authentiques et Inédits*. Vol. 1. Paris: Firmin Didot Père et Fils, Libraires, 1829.

Delort, Joseph. *Histoire de l'homme au masque de fer, accompagnée des pièces authentiques et de facsimile*. Paris: Delaforest, 1825.

De Maupeou, Jacques, Vicomte. *Histoire des Maupeou*. Fontenay-le-Comte: P. and O. Lussaud frères, 1959.

De Maupeou, Jacques, Vicomte. "Marie de Maupeou, Mère du surintendant Fouquet, l'illustration authentique d'une sainte. Extrait de l'ouvrage du Vicomte Jacques de Maupeou, *Histoire des Maupeou*." *Bulletin de l'Association les Amis du Vieux Maincy*. No. 7. 1985.

Depping, G. B. *Correspondance Administrative sous le Règne de Louis XIV*. Vol. 2. *Administration de la Justice, Police, Galères*. Paris: Imprimerie Nationale, 1851.

Delalex, Hélène. *Louis XIV intime*. Versailles: Gallimard/Château de Versailles, 2015.

Delort, Joseph Père. *Histoire de l'homme au masque de fer, accompagnée des pièces authentiques et de facsimile*. Paris: Delaforest, 1825.

Delort, Joseph. *Histoire de la Détention des Philosophes et es Gens de Lettres à la Bastille et à Vincennes, Précédée de celle de Foucquet, de Pellisson et de Lauzun, avec tous les Documents Authentiques et Inédits*. Vol. 1. Paris: Firmin Didot Père et Fils, Libraires, 1829.

De Noailles, Paul, duc de. *Histoire de Madame de Maintenon et des principaux évènements du règne de Louis XIV*. Vol. 1. Paris: Comptoir des Imprimeurs-Unis, 1849–1858.

De Paul, Vincent. *Saint Vincent de Paul Correspondence, Conferences, Documents*. Vol. 1. Correspondence 1607–1639. 6 vols. Translated, edited, and annotated from the 1920 edition of Pierre Coste Congregation of the Mission (C.M.), Sr. Jacqueline Kilar, Disciples of Christ (D.C.), Sr. Helen Marie Law, D.C., Sr. Jean Marie Poole, D.C., Reverend James R. King, C.M., Rev. Francis Germovnik, C.M, Reverend John W. Carven, C.M. New York: New

City Press, 1985.

Depping, G. B. *Correspondance Administrative sous le Règne de Louis XIV*. Vol. 2, Administration de la Justice, Police, Galères. Paris: Imprimerie Nationale, 1851.

Delorme, Philippe. *Marie de Médicis*. Series Histoire des Reines de France. Paris: Pygmalion/Gérard Watelet, 1998.

Denis, Théophile. "Etienne de Fay, dit le 'Vieux sourd-muet d'Amiens'." *Bulletin mensuel de la Société d'histoire et d'archéologie du Vimeu*. Vol. 1, 1905–1907. Séance 13 August 1905. Saint-Valéry-sur-Somme: Société d'histoire et d'archéologie du Vimeu, 55–60.

Desprat, Jean-Paul. *Madame de Maintenon, 1635–1719, ou le prix de la réputation*. Paris: Perrin, 2003.

Desprat, Jean-Paul. *La France du Grand Siècle, 1589–1715*. Paris: Tallandier, 2012.

Dessert, Daniel. *Fouquet*. Paris: Fayard, 1987.

Dessert, Daniel. "Pouvoir et finance au XVIIe siècle: La fortune du Cardinal Mazarin." *Revue d'histoire moderne et contemporaine* 23 (1976): 161–81.

Dijol, Pierre-Marie. "L'Homme au Masque de fer." In *Il y a trois siècles... le Masque de Fer... Actes du Colloque international sur la célèbre énigme (12–13 septembre 1987)*. La Direction des Affaires Culturelles de la Ville de Cannes. Cannes: la Direction des Affaires Culturelles de la Ville de Cannes, 1996.

Dinan, Susan E. *Women and Poor Relief in Seventeenth-Century France, the Early History of the Daughters of Charity*. Aldershot, Hampshire, England: Ashgate Publishing Limited, 2006.

D'Ormesson, Olivier Lefèvre. *Journal d'Olivier Lefèvre d'Ormesson et extraits des mémoires d'André Lefèvre d'Ormesson*. Edited by M. Chéruel. Vol. 2. Paris: Imprimerie Impériale, 1860–1861.

Douthat, Ross. "Jeffrey Epstein and When To Take Conspiracies Seriously." *The New York Times* online edition. August 13, 2019. http://loc8.cc/ss/douthat_2019. Accessed August 14, 2019.

Druon, Maurice. *Les Rois Maudits. I: Le Roi de Fer*. Paris: Livre de Poche, 1970.

Duchêne, Roger. *Les Précieuses, ou Comment l'Esprit Vint aux Femmes*. Paris: Fayard, 2001.

Dufour, Valentin. *La danse macabre des Saints-Innocents à Paris.* Paris, 1874.

Dufour, Valentin. *Recherches sur la dance macabre peinte en 1425 au cimetière des Innocents.* Paris: L. Willem, 1875.

Du Fresne, Jean. *Journal des principales audiences du Parlement, avec les arrêts qui y ont été rendus. Nouvelle edition, revûë, corrigée et augmentée de plusieurs questions & reglemens placez selon l'ordre du temps depuis l'année 1622 jusqu'en 1661.* Vol. 1. Paris: Rollin fils, 1733.

Du Junca, Etienne. *L'estat de prisouniés [sic] qui sont envoiés par l'ordre du Roy à la Bastille, à commenser [sic] du mescredy honsiesme du mois d'octobre, que je suis entré en possecion [sic] de la charge de lieutenant de roy, en l'année 1690. 24 octobre 1690–26 août 1705.* 18 September 1698. MSS 5133, vol. 1, fol. 37 v^e. Archives of the Bastille. Arsenal Library, Paris, France.

Du Junca, Etienne. *L'estat de prisounies qui sortet de la Bastille, à commenser [sic] du honsiesme du mois d'octobre, que je suis entré en possecion [sic], en l'année 1690. 24 octobre 1690–15 juillet 1705.* 19–20 November 1703. MSS 5134, vol. 2, fol. 80 v^e. Archives of the Bastille. Arsenal Library, Paris, France.

Dulong, Claude. *Anne d'Autriche, Mère de Louis XIV.* Paris: Hachette littérature, 1980.

Dulong, Claude. *Mazarin et l'argent, banquiers et prête-noms.* Paris: Ecole des Chartes, 2002.

Dumas, Alexandre. *Louis XIII et Richelieu.* Paris: Les Belles Lettres, 1998.

Dunlop, Ian. *Royal Palaces of France.* London: Hamish Hamilton, 1985.

Durant, Will. *The Reformation: A History of European Civilization from Wyclif to Calvin: 1300–1564.* New York: Simon and Schuster, 1957.

Dutilleul, J. "Auger, Edmond." *Dictionnaire d'Histoire et de Géographie Ecclésiastique.* Edited by Mgr Alfred Baudrillart. Vol. 5. Paris: Letouzey et Ané, 1931.

La Bastille ou "L'enfer des vivants." Exposition Bibliothèque de l'Arsenal. November 9, 2010 to February 11, 2011. Paris: Bibliothèque nationale de France, 2010.

Duvivier, Maurice. *Le Masque de fer.* Paris: Librairie Armand Colin, 1932.

Eco, Umberto. *Name of the Rose.* Translated by William Weaver. Boston; New York: Mariner Books Houghton Mifflin Harcourt, 2014.

Ekberg, Carl J. *The Failure of Louis XIV's Dutch War*. Chapel Hill: University of North Carolina Press, 1979.

Elassar, Alaa. "A teen raised $10K to install a community baby box. Less than a year later, a newborn was found inside." CNN. January 25, 2020. http://loc8.cc/ss/elassar_2020. Accessed January 27, 2020.

Erlanger, Philippe. *Richelieu*. Translated by Patricia Wolf. New York: Stein and Day, 1968.

Erlanger, Philippe. *Monsieur, Frère de Louis XIV*. Paris: Librairie Académique Perrin, 1981.

Esnault, Pierre. "Histoire: Le mystère de la sépulture de Nicolas Foucquet, Vicomte de Vaux et de Melun, seigneur de Maincy." *Bulletin de l'Association les Amis du Vieux Maincy*. No. 9 (1987): 42–51.

Fabiani, Jean-Noël. *La fabuleuse histoire de l'hôpital du moyen âge à nos jours*. Paris: Pocket, 2018.

Farge, Arlette et Michel Foucault, eds. *Le désordre des familles, lettres de cachet des Archives de la Bastille au XVIIIe siècle*. Collection Archives dirigée par Pierre Nora et Jacques Revel. Saint-Amand (Cher), France: Editions Gallimard, Julliard, 1982.

Fauirat, Léon. "La Forêt d'Halatte et sa Capitainerie." *Senlis Compte Rendus et Mémoires* 1, series 3, (1886): 83.

Félibien, André. *Les Fêtes de Versailles*. Paris: Editions Gallimard, 2012.

Fierro, Alfred. *Historical Dictionary of Paris*. Trans. Jon Woronoff. Historical Dictionaries of Cities, No. 4. Lanham, Md.: The Scarecrow Press, Inc., 1998.

Fine, Agnès. "L'héritage du nom de baptême." *Annales, Economies, Sociétés, Civilisations*. 1987.

Foisil, Madeleine. *L'Enfant Louis XIII*, Paris: Perrin, 1996.

Fontaine, Marie Madeleine. "Plaisirs, hospitalité et profit : La maison des champs dans la littérature de la Renaissance française." In *Maison des Champs dans l'Europe de la Renaissance*. Edited by Monique Châtenet. Paris: Editions A. et J. Picard, 2003, 9–48.

Formanoir, Guillaume-L. de Palteau. "Lettre à Elie Catherine Fréron sur l'homme au masque de fer." *L'Année littéraire* 4 (1768) Microfilm m. 26 (19).

Foucault, Michel. *Folie et déraison: Histoire de la folie à l'âge classique*. Paris:

Plon, 1961.

Fougeret, W. A. *Histoire générale de la Bastille, depuis sa fondation en 1369, jusqu'à sa destruction, 1789*. Vol. 1. Paris: Gauvain, 1834.

Fouquet, Marie de Maupeou. *Les Remèdes charitables de Mme Fouquet pour guérir à peu de frais toute sorte de maux tant internes qu'externes, invétérez et qui ont passés jusques à présent pour incurables, expérimentez par la même Dame*. Lyon: Jean Certe, 1685.

Freidel, Nathalie. *La conquête de l'intime: public et privé dans la Correspondance de Madame de Sévigné*. Paris: Champion, 2009.

Funck-Brentano, Frantz. *Le Drame des poisons*. Paris: J. Tallandier, 1977.

Furneaux, Rupert. *The Man Behind the Mask: The Real Story of the "Ancient Prisoner."* London: Cassell & Company, Ltd, 1954.

Gay, Peter. *Voltaire's Politics, The Poet as Realist*. New Haven: Yale University Press, 1988.

Glaser, Christophe. *Traité de la chymie, enseignant par une briève [sic] et facile méthode toutes ses plus nécessaires préparations*, Paris: 1663.

Goffman, Erving. *Stigma: Notes on the Management of Spoiled Identity*. Englewood Cliffs, N.J.: Prentice-Hall, Inc., 1963.

Goldstein, Claire. *Vaux and Versailles: The Appropriations, Erasures, and Accidents That Made Modern France*. Philadelphia: University of Pennsylvania Press, 2008.

Goslinga, Cornelis Christiaan. *The Dutch in the Caribbean and on the Wild Coast, 1580–1680*. Assen, Netherlands; Dover, N.H., U.S.A.: Van Gorcum & Company, N.V., 1971.

Goubert, Pierre. *Louis XIV et Vingt Millions de Français*. Paris: Fayard, 1991.

Gould, Cecil. *Bernini in France, An Episode in Seventeenth-century History*. Princeton: Princeton University Press, 1982.

Gowing, Laura. "Secret Births and Infanticide in Seventeenth-century England." *Past and Present, A journal of historical studies* No. 156. Oxford Press for the Past and Present Society, (August 1997): 87–115.

Grell, Chantal. "Anne d'Autriche et ses juges." In *Anne d'Autriche, Infante d'Espagne et reine de France*. Edited by Chantal Grell. Paris: Perrin, CEEH (Centro de Estudios Europe Hispánica), Centre de Recherche, Château de

Versailles, 2010, 349–97.

Griffet, R. P. *Traité des différentes sortes de preuves qui servent à établir la vérité de l'histoire*. Liege: J. F. Bassompierre, 1769.

Griffiths, Arthur. *In Old French Prisons*. New York: Dorset Press, 1992.

Grünberg, Tristan. "Louis XIV et le Masque de fer: figures littéraires et cinématographiques du double." In *Louis XIV, l'image et le mythe*. Edited by Mathieu Da Vinha, Alexandre Maral, and Nicolas Milovanovic. Rennes: Presses universitaires de Rennes et Centre de recherche du Château de Versailles, 2014.

Guigard, Joannis. "Notice sur la mort d'Antoine Leonor Lhoste, Seigneur de Beaulieu." December 1700 *Mercure de France. Indicateur du Mercure de France, 1672–1789: contenant, par ordre alphabétique, les noms des personnages sur lesquels on trouve, dans cette collection, des notices biographiques et généalogiques, avec renvoi aux années, tomes et pages*. Paris: Librairie Bachelin-Deflorenne, 1869.

Guinot, Norbert. *Initiation à l'étude des noms de lieux*. Bourbon-Lancy, France: Editions de la Croix de Pierre, 1984.

Halbert, Philippe. "An African Prince at the Court of the Sun King." *The Monitor*. (Summer 2011): 9–10.

Harding, Vanessa. *The Dead and the Living in Paris and London, 1500–1670*. Cambridge; New York: Cambridge University Press, 2002.

Herbert, Baron Edward of Cherbury. *The Life of Edward, Lord Herbert of Cherbury*. London: Whittaker, Treacher and Arnot, MDCCCXXX (1830).

Héroard, Jean. *Journal de Jean Héroard sur l'enfance et la jeunesse de Louis XIII (1601–1628)*. 2 vols. Paris: Librairie de Firmin Didot Frères, Fils et Cie, 1868.

Hibbert, Christopher. *The French Revolution*. London: Penguin, 1980.

Hillairet, Jacques. *Les 200 Cimetières du Vieux Paris*. Paris: Les Editions de Minuit, 1958.

Hillairet, Jacques. *Dictionnaire Historique des rues de Paris*. 2 Vols. Paris: Les Editions de Minuit, 1963.

Hillairet, Jacques. *La Rue de Richelieu*. Paris: Les Editions de Minuit, 1966.

Hillairet, Jacques. *L'Ile Saint-Louis*. Paris: Les Editions de Minuit, 1967.

Huguet, Adrien. *Le Marquis de Cavoye 1640–1716: Un Grand Maréchal des Logis de la Maison du Roi.* Paris: Librairie Ancienne Honoré Champion, 1920.

Iung, Théodore. *La Verité sur le Masque de Fer (Les Empoisonneurs) d'après des documents inédits des Archives de la Guerre et autres depôts public.* Paris: Henri Plon, Imprimeur-Editeur, 1873.

Jacobé, Émile. *Un internement sous le Grand Roi: H. Lomenie de Brienne à Saint-Lazare.* Paris: Revue de Pathologie Comparée et d'Hygiène générale, 1929.

Jal, A. *Dictionnaire critique de biographie et de l'histoire. Errata et Supplement pour tous les Dictionnaires Historiques d'Après de Documents Authentiques Inédites.*

Deuxième Edition. Paris: Henri Plon, 1872.

Keller-Dorian, Georges. *Antoine Coysevox (1640–1720) Catalogue raisonné de son oeuvre.* Paris: Georges Keller-Dorian, 1920.

Kleinman, Ruth. *Anne of Austria, Queen of France.* Columbus, Ohio: Ohio State University Press, 1985.

Labbé, Jean. "Maltraitance des enfants – Perspective historique." *Santé, Société et Solidarité* 1 (2009): 17–25.

Lagarde, André et Laurent Michard, eds. *XVIIe Siècle, les grands auteurs français du programme; Anthologie et histoire littéraire.* Paris: Bordas, 1985.

Laget, Mireille. "Childbirth in Seventeenth- and Eighteenth-Century France: Obstetrical Practice and Collective Attitudes." *Medicine and Society in France: selections from the annales, économies, sociétés, civilisations.* 6 vols. Baltimore: Johns Hopkins University Press, 1980, 137–76.

Lair, Jules. *Nicolas Foucquet, Procureur Général, Surintendant des Finances, Ministre d'Etat de Louis XIV.* 2 vols. Paris: Librairie Plon, 1890.

Lambeau, Lucien. "L'ancien cimetière Saint-Paul et ses charniers, l'église Saint-Paul, la grange et la prison Saint-Eloi." *Annexe au procès-verbal de la séance du 9 novembre 1910*, 1910. (This document is at the library of the history of Paris, Hôtel Lamoignon.)

La Porte, Pierre de. "Mémoires de P. de La Porte premier valet de chambre de Louis XIV contenant plusieurs particularités des règnes de Louis XIII et de Louis XIV." *Nouvelle collection des Mémoires pour servir à l'histoire de France.* Paris: Michaud et Poujoulat, 1839.

Larcade, Véronique. "Versailles sous Louis XIV ou le tombeau des cadets de Gascogne?" *Bulletin du Centre de recherche du château de Versailles.* June 14, 2008. http://loc8.cc/ss/larcade_2008; DOI: 10.4000/crcv.5623, 11. Accessed February 14, 2019.

Laurent, Emile. *Ruelles, salons et cabarets: histoire anecdotique de la littérature française.* 2 vols. Paris: E. Dentu, 1892.

Lavisse, Ernest. *Louis XIV, Histoire d'un Grand Règne 1643–1715.* Paris: Librairie Hachette, 1908. Paris: Editions Robert Laffont, S.A., 1989.

Le Guillou, Jean-Claude. *Versailles avant Versailles au temps de Louis XIII.* Paris: Perrin, 2011.

Leroi, Armand Marie. *Mutants: on the Form, Varieties and Errors of the Human Body.* New York, N.Y: Harper Perennial, 2005.

Le Tellier, François-Michel, Marquis de Louvois to Monsieur de Saint-Mars from Saint-Germain-en-Laye. July 19, 1669. Archives Nationales, Paris, France. K//120/A/f° 67.

Le Tellier, François-Michel, Marquis de Louvois to Monsieur de Saint-Mars from Saint-Germain-en-Laye. September 10, 1669. Archives Nationales, Paris, France. K//120/A/f° 68.

Le Tellier, François-Michel, Marquis de Louvois to Monsieur de Saint-Mars from Saint-Germain-en-Laye. September 25, 1669. Archives Nationales, Paris, France. K//120/A/f° 69.

Levantal, Christophe. "Louis XIV et la *Gazette*, ou le roi publié." In *Louis XIV, l'image et le mythe.* Edited by Mathieu Da Vinha, Alexandre Maral and Nicolas Milovanovic. Rennes et Versailles: Presses Universitaires de Rennes; Centre de Recherche du Château de Versailles, 2014.

Levron, Jacques. *La vie quotidienne à la cour de Versailles.* Paris: Hachette, 1965.

Lhoste, Jean-Marie, avocat en la cour de Parlement, demeurant à Paris, rue de l'Hôtel des Ursins, paroisse Saint-Landry, et Marguerite de Bailly, sa femme: donation mutuelle. Notice n° 1303. Archives nationales (annuaire du service) [site web d'origine]. Identifiant de l'unité documentaire: Châtelet de Paris. Date: 1652 - 1652 Y//188-Y//190 - fol. 307. Insinuations (3 mars 1651–10 mars 1654).

Long, Irvin. *Exploring the Loire Chateaux.* Philadelphia: Dorrance and Company, 1963.

Lopez, Denis. "L'éducation du prince au XVIIe siècle: regards sur l'enfance."

Regards sur l'enfance au XVIIe siècle: Actes du colloque du Centre de recherches sur le XVIIe siècle européen (1600–1700). Edited by Anne Defrance, Denis Lopez, et François-Joseph Ruggiu. 24–25 Novembre 2005. Université Michel de Montaigne—Bordeaux 3. Tübingen: Gunter Narr Verlag Tübingen, 2007, 61–113.

Louis XIV. *Manière de montrer les Jardins de Versailles*. Edited by Simone Hoog. Paris: Editions de la Réunion des Musées Nationaux, 1982.

Louis XIV. *Mémoires de Louis XIV, le métier de roi*. Edited by Jean Longnon. Paris: Tallandier, 1978, 1983, 2001.

Madry, Sarah. "The Valet: The Marquis de Louvois's Invited Guest in the Mystery of the Man in the Iron Mask." *Cahiers du Dix-Septième: An Interdisciplinary Journal* 17 (2016) http://loc8.cc/ss/madry_2016.

Mallick, Oliver. "Clients and Friends: The Ladies-in-Waiting at the Court of Anne of Austria." In *The Politics of Female Households, Ladies-in-Waiting Across Early Modern Europe*. Edited by Nadine Akkerman and Birgit Houben. Leiden; Boston: Brill, 2014.

Mancini, Hortense and Marie Mancini. *Memoires d'Hortense et de Marie Mancini*. Edited by Gérard Doscot. Paris: Mercure de France, 1965.

Maral, Alexandre. *Les Derniers Jours de Louis XIV*. Paris: Perrin, 2014.

Maral, Alexandre. *Le Roi-Soleil et Dieu*. Paris: Perrin, 2012.

March, Eric. "Here's What 5 Years in Solitary Confinement Does To a Person. It's Not Pretty." *Upworthy. Things That Matter. Pass 'em On.* Accessed October 15, 2014.

Markale, Jean. *La Bastille et l'énigme du Masque du Fer*. Paris: Pygmalion/G. Watelet, 1989.

Mast, Marie-Madeleine. *Le Masque de fer, une solution révolutionnaire*. Paris: Tallandier, 1974.

Maupeou, Jacques, Vicomte de. *Histoire des Maupeou*. Fontenay-le-Comte: P. et O. Lussaud frères, 1959.

Maupeou, Jacques Vicomte de. "Marie de Maupeou, Mère du surintendant Fouquet, l'illustration authentique d'une sainte. Extrait de l'ouvrage du Vicomte Jacques de Maupeou, *Histoire des Maupeou*." *Bulletin de l'Association les Amis du Vieux Maincy* No. 7(1985): 121–24.

Maurel, Christian. "Prénomination et parenté baptismale du Moyen-Age à la Contre-reforme. Modèle religieux et logiques familiales." *Revue de l'histoire des religions* 209, no. 4 (1992): 394 and 402.

McClure, Ellen M. *Sunspots and the Sun King: Sovereignty and Mediation in Seventeenth-Century France.* Urbana and Chicago: University of Illinois Press, 2006.

Méro, Alain. *Eustache Le Sueur (1616–1655).* Paris: Athena, 1987.

Meyer, Jean. *Colbert.* Paris: Hachette, 1981.

Meyer, Jean. *La naissance de Louis XIV.* Bruxelles: Editions Complexe, 1989.

Mezzadri, Luigi. *Vincent de Paul (1581–1660).* Translated by Jean-Pierre Bagot. Paris: Desclée de Brouwer, 1985.

Miller, Naomi. *Heavenly Caves, Reflections on the Garden Grotto.* New York: George Braziller, Inc., 1982.

Ministère de l'Instruction Publique et des Beaux-Arts. *Archives des Missions Scientifiques et Littéraires, choix de rapports et instructions.* vol. 15. Paris: Ernest Leroux, 1889.

Mitford, Nancy. *The Sun King, Louis XIV at Versailles.* New York: Crescent Books, 1966.

Mongrédien, Georges. *Le Masque de Fer.* Paris: Hachette, 1952.

Mongrédien, Georges. *Louis XIV.* Paris: Editions Albin Michel, 1963.

Montclos, Jean-Marie Perouse de. *Vaux-le-Vicomte.* Paris: Editions Scala, 2002.

Montpensier, Anne-Marie-Louise d'Orléans, duchesse de. *Portraits littéraires.* Edited by Christian Bouyer. Paris: Editions Séguier, 2000.

Moote, A. Lloyd. *Louis XIII the Just.* Berkeley; Los Angeles; London: University of California Press, 1989.

Morand, Paul. *Fouquet, ou Le Soleil offusqué.* Paris: Gallimard, 1961.

Moriceau, Jean-Marc et Gilles Postel-Vinay. *Ferme entreprise famille, grande exploitation et changements agricoles, les Chartier, XVIIe-XIXe siècles.* Paris: Editions de l'Ecole des Hautes Etudes en Sciences Sociales, 1992.

Motteville, Françoise Bertaut. *Mémoires de Mme de Motteville sur Anne D'Autriche et Sa Cour, Nouvelle Edition d'après le manuscrit de Conrart avec une annota-*

tion extraite des écrits de Monglat, Omer Talon, de Retz, Gourville, Leret, Mlle de Montpensier, etc., des éclaircissements et un index par M. F. Riaux et une notice sur Mme de Motteville par M. Sainte-Beuve. Vol. 1. Paris: Bibliothèque-G. Charpentier, 1904.

Mousnier, Roland. *Paris Capitale au temps de Richelieu et de Mazarin*. Paris: Editions A. Pedone, 1978.

Mueller, Eugene. *Environs de Senlis*. Senlis: Th. Nouvain, 1896.

Murat, Inès. *Colbert*. Paris: Fayard, 1980.

Nabonne, Bernard. *Les grandes heures de Saint-Germain-en-Laye*. Paris: Sfelt, 1950.

Noailles, Paul de. *Histoire de Madame de Maintenon et des principaux évènements du règne de Louis XIV*. Vol. 1. Paris: Comptoir des Imprimeurs-Unis, 1849–1858.

Noone, John. *The Man Behind the Iron Mask*. Gloucester: Alan Sutton Publishing, 1988.

Pagnol, Marcel. *Le secret du Masque de Fer: Une enquête policière*. N.p.: Editions de Provence, 1973.

Palatine-Simmern, Sophia, Electress of Brunswick-Lüneburg. *Memoirs of Sophia, electress of Hanover, 1630–1680*. Translated by H. Forester. London: R. Bentley & Son, 1888.

Patria, Ettore. "Benigno de Saint-Mars, Géolier du Masque de Fer." In *Il y a trois siècles... le Masque de Fer... Actes du Colloque international sur la célèbre énigme. 12–13 Septembre 1987*. Deuxième édition, Cannes: la Direction des Affaires Culturelles de la Ville de Cannes, 1996.

Perdrizet, Paul. *Le Calendrier Parisien à la fin du Moyen Age d'après le Bréviaire et les livres d'heures*. Paris: Les Belles Lettres, 1933.

Pérouse de Montclos, Jean-Marie. *Vaux-le-Vicomte*. Paris: Editions Scala, 2002.

Petit, Jacques-Guy et al. *Histoire des galères, bagnes et prisons, XIIIe–XXe siècles*. Toulouse: Bibliothèque Historique Privat, 1991.

Petitfils, Jean-Christian. *L'Homme au Masque de Fer*. Paris: Librairie Académique Perrin, 1970.

Petitfils, Jean-Christian. *Le Véritable d'Artagnan*. Paris: Librairie Jules Tallandier. 1981.

Petitfils, Jean-Christian. *Louis XIV*. Paris: Perrin, 1995.

Petitfils, Jean-Christian. "Louis XIII, un grand roi méconnu." *Versalia*. No. 3 (2010): 159–71.

Pevitt, Christine. *Philippe duc d'Orléans, Regent of France*. New York: Atlantic Monthly Press, 1997.

Piat, Colette. *Le Père Joseph, le maître de Richelieu*. Paris: Bernard Grasset, 1988.

Pigaillem, Henri. *Tallemant des Réaux, l'homme des Historiettes*. Saintes, France: Le Croît Vif, 2010.

Pincas, Stéphanie. *Versailles: The History of the Gardens and Their Sculpture*. New York: Thames and Hudson, 1996.

Pillement, Georges. *Paris Inconnu, Itinéraires Archéologiques*. Paris: Bernard Grasset Editeur, 1965.

Plessis, Armand Jean duc de Richelieu, et al. *Archives curieuses de l'histoire de France....* 2e série. Vol. 5e. Paris, 1838.

Pougin, Paul. *Mémoires et Correspondance de la Marquise de Courcelles publiés d'après les manuscrits avec une notice des notes et les pièces justificatives*. Paris: P. Jannet, Libraire, MDCCCLV (1855).

Primi Fassola di San Maiolo, Giovan Battista Feliciano. *Mémoires sur la cour de Louis XIV, 1673–1681*. Paris: Librairie Académique Perrin, 1988.

Quétel, Claude. *La Bastille, Histoire vraie d'une prison légendaire*. Paris: Robert Laffont, 1989.

Quétel, Claude. *La Bastille devoilée par ses archives*. Paris: Omnibus, 2013.

Quétel, Claude. *Une ombre sur le roi Soleil: L'affaire des Poisons*. Paris: Larousse, 2010, 104.

Raatschen, Gudrun. "Merely Ornamental? Van Dyck's Portraits of Henrietta Maria." In *Henrietta Maria: piety, politics and patronage*. Edited by Erin Griffey. Aldershot: Ashgate Publishing, 2008.

Rabutin-Chantal, Marie. *Correspondance. Marie de Rabutin-Chantal, marquise de Sévigné, 1626–1696*. Vol. 1. Edited by Roger Duchêne. Paris: Gallimard, 1972.

Radier, Jean François du Dreux. *Mémoires historiques, critiques, et anecdotes sur les reines et régentes de France: Avec la continuation jusqu'à nos jours, par un professeur de l'Académie de Paris.* Vol. 6. Paris: P. Renouard, 1827.

Rady, Martyn. *The Habsburgs: To Rule the World.* New York: Basic Books, 2020.

Raillicourt, M. D. de la Barre de. "Notes sur l'hôpital général à Paris." In *Il y a trois siècles... le Masque de Fer... Actes du Colloque international sur la célèbre énigme. 12–13 Septembre 1987.* Deuxième édition, Cannes: la Direction des Affaires Culturelles de la Ville de Cannes, 1996, 200–201.

Ranum, Orest. *Artisans of Glory: Writers and Historical Thought in Seventeenth-Century France.* Chapel Hill: University of North Carolina Press, 1980.

Ranum, Orest. "Jeux de Cartes, Pédagogie et Enfance de Louis XIV." *Les Jeux à la Renaissance, Actes du XXIIIe Colloque International d'Etudes Humanistes Tours – Julliet 1980.* Edited by Philippe Ariès et Jean-Claude Margolin. Paris: Vrin, 1982, 553–62.

Recueil de titres originaux, copies, extraits, armes et tombeaux, concernant des abbayes et prieurés de France, formé par Gaignières et rangé par ordre alphabétique des monastères, du IXe au XVIIe siècle. VII. Detail from a list of names of abbots of Nanteuil-en-Vallée. http://loc8.cc/ss/gallica.

Regnault. *Quatrième requête de messire Louis Bruant des Carrières contre madame Colbert et les enfants et héritiers de... M. Colbert. Au Roi et à Nosseigneurs de son conseil. / (Signé : Regnault [3 mars 1684].)* Bibliothèque nationale de France, département Manuscrits, Z THOISY-125 . p. 26. http://catalogue.bnf.fr/ark:/12148/cb367220578. Accessed August 29, 2023.

Renaudot, Théophraste, ed. "Paris news." *Gazette.* February 12, 1661, 156.

Renaudot, Théophraste, ed. "De Meaux le 23 d'Aoust, 1631." *Recueil des Gazettes de l'année 1631.* Cote NUMP-827. Microfilm-M-197. Vue 96, 4.

Renaudot, Théophraste, ed. *Gazette.* N°s. 3, 6, 11, 12, 14, 20, 23, 26, 35. Paris: Bureau d'adresse. 1643.

Richardt, Aimé. *Louvois (1641–1691).* Paris: ERTI, 1990.

Richelieu, Armand Jean du Plessis duc de et al. *Archives curieuses de l'histoire de France....* 2e série. vol. 5e. Paris, 1838.

Richelieu, Armand Jean du Plessis duc de. *Lettres, instructions diplomatiques et papiers d'état du cardinal de Richelieu.* Edited by M. Avenel. Vol. 6. Paris: Imprimerie impériale [puis] nationale, 1853–1877.

Robrie, Jean de la. "Hypothèse sur la confusion du nom de Rougé." *Bulletin de la Société Archéologique et historique de Nantes et de Loire-Atlantique* 113 (1974): 32–39.

Rosellini, Michèle. "Pourquoi écrire des poèmes en prison ? Le cas de Paul Pellisson à la Bastille." *Les Dossiers du Grihl: Groupes de Recherches Interdisiplinaires sur l'Histoire du Littéraire*. Online since 23 December 2011. http://dossiersgrihl.revues.org/4939. Accessed August 30, 2014.

Roujon, Jacques. *Louvois et son maître*. Paris: Editions Bernard Grasset, 1934.

Rousset, Camille. *Histoire de Louvois et de son administration politique et militaire*. Paris: Didier, 1873.

Roux-Fazillac, Pierre. *Recherches historiques et critiques sur l'Homme au masque de fer, d'où resultent des notions certaines sur ce prisonnier, ouvrage rédigé sur des materiaux authentiques*. Paris: Valade, an IX (1801).

Ruggieri, Eve. *L'Honneur retrouvé du Marquis de Montespan*. Paris: Perrin, 1992.

Russell, Phillips. *William the Conqueror*. New York & London: Scharles Scribner's Sons, 1933.

Safford, Philip L. and Elizabeth J. Safford. *A History of Childhood and Disability*. London & New York: Teachers College Press, 1997.

Saint-Amour, Amédée De Caix de. "Mémoire sur l'origine de la ville et du nom de Senlis." *Comptes rendus et mémoires – Comité archéologique de Senlis*. Senlis: Société d'histoire et d'archéologie de Senlis (1862): 3–21.

Saint-Foix, Germain-François Poullain de. *Réponse de M. de Saint-Foix au R. P. Griffet, et recueil de tout ce qui a été écrit sur le prisonnier masqué*. Paris; London: Vente, 1770.

Saint-Mars (Bénigne Dauvergne). 26 septembre 1708. Testament olographe de Bénigne Dauvergne de Saint-Mars, en date du 21 août 1704, apporté par Michel Ancel Desgranges, maître des cérémonies à Jean Le Camus, lieutenant civil, et déposé pour minute par ce dernier à Me Louis Durant, notaire, le 26 septembre 1708. Minutes de Louis DURANT (MC/ET/XCVI/191 - MC/ET/XCVI/301). Minutes. 1708, juillet–1708, septembre (MC/ET/XCVI/203). Archives Nationale MC/ET/XCVI/203.

Saint-Simon, Louis de Rouvroy, duc de. *Mémoires de Saint-Simon*. Edited by J. -G. L. de Boislisle, et al. Vol. 2. Paris: Hachette, 1879–1931.

Saint-Simon, Louis de Rouvroy, duc de. *Mémoires (1714–1716) Additions au*

Journal de Dangeau. Edited by Yves Coirault Vol 5. Paris: Gallimard, 1983.

Sangoï, Jean-Claude. "Forename, Family, and Society in Southwest France (Eighteenth-Nineteenth Centuries)." *The History of the Family* 4, no. 3 (September 1999): 239–59.

Sauval, Henri. *Histoire et recherches des antiquités de la ville de Paris.* Vol. 1. Paris: Charles Moette and Jacques Chardon, 1724.

Schama, Simon. *Citizens: A Chronicle of the French Revolution.* New York: Vintage Books, 1989.

Schwartz, Lita Linzer and Natalie K. Isser. *Endangered Children: Neonaticide, Infanticide, and Filicide.* Boca Raton; London; New York; Washington, D.C.: CRC Press, 2000.

Service Historique de la Défense. Vincennes, France. *1669–Minutes–Juillet–Aoust.* 234, series A1. Microfiche GR A 1 234, 271, 272.

Shahar, Shulamith. *Childhood in the Middle Ages.* London; New York: Routledge, 1990.

Sinsoilliez, Robert. *Tombelaine, l'îlot de la baie du Mont-Saint-Michel.* Saint-Malo, France: Editions L'ancre de marine, 1989.

Snyder, Timothy. *The Road to Unfreedom, Russia, Europe, America.* New York: Tim Duggin Books, 2018.

Soll, Jacob. *The Information Master: Jean-Baptiste Colbert's Secret State Intelligence System.* Ann Arbor: University of Michigan Press, 2009.

Sonnino, Paul. *The Search for the Man in the Iron Mask, a Historical Detective Story.* Lanham, Maryland: Rowman & Littlefield, 2016.

Soudan, Cécile, ed. *Mercure François.* Groupe de Recherches Interdisciplinaires sur l'Histoire du Littéraire, CNRS (Centre National de la Recherche Scientifique) 22, (1637–1638). http://mercurefrancois.ehess.fr/picture.php?/20302/category/108. Accessed November 29, 2016.

Spanheim, Ezéchiel. *Relation de la Cour de France en 1690.* Edited by Emile Bourgeois. Paris: Mercure de France, 1973.

Tapié, Victor Lucien. *La France de Louis XIII et de Richelieu.* Paris: Flammarion, 1967.

Tassé, H. "La Duchesse d'Aiguillon (1604–1675)." *Mon Magazine.* (September 1929): 34–35.

Tellier, Luc-Normand. *Face aux Colbert: Les Le Tellier, Vauban, Turgot... et l'Avènement du Liberalisme*. Sillery, Québec: Presses de l'Université du Québec, 1987.

Thompson, Harry. "La Théorie d'Eustache Dauger de Cavoye". In *Il y a trois siècles... le Masque de Fer... Actes du Colloque international sur la célèbre énigme. 12–13 Septembre 1987*. Deuxième édition, Cannes: la Direction des Affaires Culturelles de la Ville de Cannes, 1996, 123–131.

Thompson, C. J. S. *The Mystery and Romance of Alchemy and Pharmacy*. London: The Scientific Press, Limited, 1897.

Thompson, Harry. *The Man in the Iron Mask, a historical detective investigation*. London: Weidenfeld and Nicolson, 1987.

Tillinac, Denis. *L'ange du désordre, Marie de Rohan duchesse de Chevreuse*. Paris: Robert Laffont, 1989.

Tiollais, Madeleine. *Le Masque de fer, enquête sur le prisonnier dont le nom ne se dit pas*. Edition Cheminement, 2003.

Topin, Marius. *L'homme au masque de fer*. Paris: E. Dentu; Didier, 1870.

"Trouvée dans un champ: on lui donne le patronyme de Deschamps." Archives départemental de Pas-de-Calais 5 MIR 829/2, Fonds et collections. Archives de l'état civil et notariales, Les insolites de l'état civil. Published January 21, 2014. Accessed September 30, 2017.

"Un surnom singulier pour un baptême atypique." Archives départemental de Pas-de-Calais 3 E 275/2, Fonds et collections. Archives de l'état civil et notariales, Les insolites de l'état civil. Published December 12, 2011. Accessed September 30, 2017.

Vallouit, Arnaud de. "Un portrait éclaté de Louis XIV: la représentation fragmentaire du souverain dans les *Mémoires* inédits de Philibert de La Mare." In Mathieu Da Vinha, Alexandre Maral and Nicolas Milovanovic. *Louis XIV, l'image et le mythe*. Rennes et Versailles: Presses Universitaires de Rennes; Centre de Recherche du Château de Versailles, 2014.

Van Rensselaer, Mrs. John King. *The Devil's Picture-Books, a History of Playing Cards*. New York: Dodd, Mead, and Company, 1890.

Vauban, Sébastien Le Prestre de. *Vauban: sa famille et ses écrits, ses "Oisivetés" et sa correspondance*. Edited by Eugène-Auguste-Albert de Rochas d'Aiglun, Vol. 2. Paris: Berger-Levrault, 1910.

Vergé-Franceschi, Michel. *Le Masque de Fer, Enfin Démasqué*. Paris: Fayard,

2009.

Vigarello, Georges. *Le propre et le sale: l'hygiène du corps depuis le Moyen Age.* Paris: Le Seuil, 1985.

Vizetelly, Ernest Alfred. *The Favourites of Louis XIV.* London: Chatto & Windus, 1912.

Voltaire (François-Marie Arouet). *Le Siècle de Louis XIV*. Vol. 1. Frankfurt: Knoch & Eslinger, 1753.

Voltaire (François-Marie Arouet). "On the certainty of history." *Encyclopédie, ou dictionnaire raisonné des sciences, des arts et les métiers* 8. Edited by Denis Diderot and Jean le Rond d'Alembert, 1765.

Voltaire (François-Marie Arouet). "Letter to the Abbé Dubos from Cirey, 30 October 1738," *Oeuvres de Voltaire ; 51–52, 54–70. Correspondance.* Vol. 53. Edited by Adrien-Jean-Quentin Beuchot. Paris: Firmin Didot frères; Werdet et Lequien fils, 1830–1834. Accessed April 26, 2015.

Von der Pfalz, Elisabeth-Charlotte de Bavière, duchesse d'Orléans. *Die Briefe der Liselotte von der Pfalz, Herzogin von Orléans.* Ebenhausen-München: Langewiesche-Brandt, 1914.

Von der Pfalz, Elisabeth-Charlotte de Bavière, duchesse d'Orléans. *A Woman's Life in the Court of the Sun King, Letters of Liselotte von der Pfalz, 1652–1722.* Translated by Elborg Forster. Baltimore and London: Johns Hopkins University Press, 1984.

Wharton, Edith. *Edith Wharton Abroad, Selected Travel Writings, 1888–1920.* Edited by Sarah Bird Wright. New York: St. Martin's Press, 1995.

Wilson, Dudley. *Signs and Portents, Monstrous Births from the Middle Ages to the Enlightenment.* London and New York: Routledge, 1993.

Wilson, Peter. "European Warfare 1450–1815." In *War in the Early Modern World 1450–1815.* Edited by Jeremy Black. Westview Press, 1999.

Witkowski, Gustave Joseph. *Accoucheurs et Sages Femmes Célèbres: esquisses biographiques.* Paris: G. Steinheil, 1891.

Witkowski, Gustave Jules. *Les Accouchements à la cour.* Paris: G. Steinheil, n.d.

Wittkower, Rudolf. *Bernini's Bust of Louis XIV. Charlton Lectures on Art Delivered at King's College in the University of Durham, Newcastle upon Tyne.* November 22, 1950. London; New York; Toronto: Geoffrey Cumberlege, Oxford

University Press, 1951.

Wolf, John B. *Louis XIV*. New York: W.W. Norton & Company, Inc., 1968.

Endnotes

[1]Copies of the text of the death certificate were reproduced by R. P. Griffet in *Traité des différentes sortes de preuves qui servent à établir la vérité de l'histoire* (Liège: J. F. Bassompierre 1770); and in the monograph by Germain-François Poullain de Saint-Foix, *Réponse de M. de Saint-Foix au R. P. Griffet, et recueil de tout ce qui a été écrit sur le prisonnier masqué* (Paris and London: Vente, 1770), and in Marius Topin's *L'homme au masque de fer*.

[2]Germain-François Poullain de Saint-Foix, *Réponse de M. de Saint-Foix au R. P. Griffet, et recueil de tout ce qui a été écrit sur le prisonnier masqué* (Paris and London: Vente, 1770), 8–9.

[3]The estimation of the spelling of the false name varies among historians who have seen the original manuscript.

[4]Etienne du Junca, *L'estat de prisounies qui sortet de la Bastille, a commenser du honsiesme du mois d'octobre, que je suis entre en possession, en l'annee 1690, 24 octobre 1690–15 juillet 1705, 19–20 novembre 1703*, MSS 5134, vol. 2, fol. 80 v^e, Manuscripts of the Bibliothèque de l'Arsenal, Journal de du Junca, registres des entrées.

[5]Marius Topin. *L'homme au masque de fer*. (Paris: E. Dentu, 1870), 179. Marius Topin gave the location of the burial certificate as, "Archives de l'Hôtel de Ville, Registres du secrétariat de la maison du roi, Archives impériales (nationales). Registre des baptêmes, mariages, et sépultures de la paroisse de Saint-Paul, 1703 à 1705, t. II, no. 166." In 2018 the location was: Archives nationales, Registre des baptêmes, mariages et sépultures de la paroisse de Saint-Paul, 1703 à 1705, Département des Manuscrits, Collections généalogiques, Fr. 32591. Volumes reliés du Cabinet des titres: recherches de noblesse, armoriaux, preuves, histoires généalogiques. Paris. Diocèse: Marguillerie de Saint-Paul, registres. VII Paroisse de Saint-Paul. Cote de consultation en salle de lecture: MF 7630. Cote de la matrice (pour commander une reproduction): R 108425.

[6]Most of the books on this subject are in French but six very good ones are in English: Rupert Furneaux's *The Man Behind the Mask: The Real Story of the "Ancient Prisoner"* (1954); Harry Thompson's *The Man in the Iron Mask, a Historical Detective Investigation* (1987); John Noone's *The Man Behind the Iron Mask* (1988); Roger McDonald's *The Man in the Iron Mask: The True Story of the Most Famous Prisoner in History and the Four Musketeers* (2005); Paul Sonnino's *The Search for the Man in the Iron Mask, a Historical Detective Story* (2016); and Josephine Wilkinson, *The Man in the Iron Mask, the True Story of Europe's Most Famous Prisoner* (2021).

[7]The Saint-Paul church, destroyed after the French Revolution, was on the rue Saint Paul two blocks from the rue Saint-Antoine. One element of the north tower is extant.

[8]Harry Thompson, *The Man in the Iron Mask, a Historical Detective Investigation* (London: Weidenfeld and Nicolson, 1987), 11.

[9]Vanessa Harding, *The Dead and the Living in Paris and London, 1500–1670* (Cambridge, United Kingdom and New York: Cambridge University Press, 2002), 9. Arcades on the rue de la Ferronnerie at #6 are at the point of entrance to the old cemetery, which is now part of the *Les Halles* district.

[10]Yvan Christ, *Eglises Parisiennes actuelles et disparues* (Paris: Editions "Tel," 1947), 43. The mural was possibly commissioned by the Duc de Berry (1340–1416), brother of King Charles V of France.

[11]See Abbé Valentin Dufour, Recherches sur la dance macabre peinte en 1425 au cimetière des Innocents (Paris: L. Willem, 1875). A woodcut was made of this mural and reproductions were printed. https://gallica.bnf.fr/ark:/12148/bpt6k64621602.

[12]Harding, 102. Forty-six euros in today's money or about $56.00 U.S. dollars.

[13]The Valois branch of the ruling Capet family became extinct in 1589. The genealogists had to back up hundreds of years on the Capet family tree to the revered Saint Louis (Louis IX, 1214–1270) and go out on a thin branch to find Henri, the Protestant king of Navarre of the house of Bourbon. He had the only legitimate claim to the French throne, but only Catholics were allowed to sit on it. To prevent his becoming king, the ongoing Wars of Religion between Protestants and Catholics intensified, and parts of France were stripped of their wealth and population by dukes and squires carrying the flags of Christ into battles that bloodied the

meek of the earth and forced them to feed on roots and bark until Henri of Navarre agreed in 1593 to a personal conversion to Catholicism in order to stop the carnage and ruination of the country. He was crowned King Henri IV in Chartres cathedral on February 27, 1594.

[14] The street was widened twice again in 1797 and 1838.

[15] Dufour, *Recherches sur la dance macabre*, 78.

[16] The *dévots* (the devoted, the devout) were fervent Counter Reformation Catholics committed to eliminating Protestantism and to supporting hospitals, monasteries and other charities.

[17] Simon Schama, *Citizens: A Chronicle of the French Revolution* (New York: Vintage Books, 1989), 407. Schama, I think, did not mean that there had been no madness, no chains, no long, dreary days in black cells for hundreds of Bastille prisoners.

[18] Dutray-Lecoin, Elise, Danielle Muzerelle. *La Bastille ou "L'enfer des vivants."* Exposition, Paris, Bibliothèque de l'Arsenal, 9 November 2010 to 11 February 2011. Paris: Bibliothèque nationale de France, 2010.

[19] Christopher Hibbert, *The French Revolution* (London: Penguin, 1980), 81–82.

[20] Héloïse Bocher, *Démolir la Bastille, l'édification d'un lieu de mémoire* (Paris: Vendémiaire, 2012), 209.

[21] At the end of the day, someone remembered that there might still be prisoners in the cells. They found seven, but to free them, the invaders had to remove the doors to the cells because all the keys had been snatched by rioters who were by then miles away: two counterfeiters; a madman, put away on request of his family who had thought he would be better taken care of at the Bastille than in a madhouse; the comte de Solages, imprisoned for incest; and a person named Tavernier who, compromised in the affair Damiens (an attempt in 1757 on the life of Louis XV), had been in the Bastille for thirty years. These seven were set free but the counterfeiters were imprisoned again the next day.

[22] Theodore Iung, *La Verité sur le Masque de Fer (Les Empoisonneurs) d'après des documents inédits des Archives de la Guerre et autres depôts public* (Paris: Henri Plon, Imprimeur-Editeur, 1873), 51–52.

[23] Calais, France is a port city that is very near the English city of Dover, only twenty-one miles (thirty-four kilometers) of choppy English Channel water between them. It is in the Hauts-de-France region, department Pas-de-Calais.

[24] The letters of Madame de Sévigné, *née* Marie de Rabutin-Chantal, from Paris to her daughter in Provence tell us an immense amount about people and events at Louis XIV's court.

[25] La Mousse was also the name of a friend of Madame's who often visited her at Les Rochers, so she is using the same words for two different meanings.

[26] Marie de Rabutin-Chantal, *Correspondance. Marie de Rabutin-Chantal, marquise de Sévigné, 1626–1696*, ed. Roger Duchêne (Paris: Gallimard, 1972), 1:365–66.

[27] Versailles was not the principal home of the king and the seat of government until 1682. In 1669 it was one of many small châteaux that the king owned, albeit favored by Louis XIV because it had been the favorite hunting retreat of his father, Louis XIII.

[28] Alexandre Maral, *Le Roi-Soleil et Dieu* (Paris: Perrin, 2012), 62–64. These two services were held each Sunday and all courtiers were expected to attend.

[29] Service Historique de la Défense (SHD).

[30] Louis XIV to Captain Alexandre de Vauroy, Saint-Germain-en-Laye, July 28, 1669, *1669–Minutes–Juillet–Aoust–Volume*, series A1, vol. 234, Microfiche GR A 1 234, 271. Archives of the SHD, Vincennes, France.

[31] Maurice Duvivier, *Le Masque de fer* (Paris: Librairie Armand Colin, 1932), 120. This is also Duvivier's opinion as to why the master letters are extant.

[32] Louis XIV to Saint-Mars, Saint-Germain-en-Laye, July 28, 1669, *1669–Minutes–Juillet–Aoust–Volume*, series A1, vol. 234, Microfiche GR A 1 234, Archives of the SHD, Vincennes, France, 272.

[33] Marcel Pagnol, *Le secret du Masque de Fer: Une enquête policière* (n.p.: Editions de Provence,

1973), 123–24.

[34] Pagnol, 124.

[35] Pagnol, 124.

[36] Pagnol, 125.

[37] Pagnol, 123. Pagnol estimates that Vauroy received the warrant on 1 August and made the arrest on the next day. In this as in many other guesses on timing of events, there is variation among historians.

[38] Brugnon is one of the authors of the collected lectures on the subject of the Man in the Iron Mask called *Il y a trois siècles* (*Three Centuries Ago*) given at a conference held in Cannes, France in 1987.

[39] Michel Vergé-Franceschi, *Le Masque de fer, enfin démasqué* (Paris: Fayard, 2009), 261.

[40] Pierre Roux-Fazillac, *Recherches historiques et critiques sur l'Homme au masque de fer, d'où resultent des notions certaines sur ce prisonnier, ouvrage rédigé sur des materiaux authentiques* (Paris: Valade, an IX [1801]), 105.

[41] Vergé-Franceschi says that the original August 21, 1669 letter of Saint-Mars was burned in the fires set by the Paris Commune in 1871 and we have a transcript only because Roux-Fazillac read the original when doing research for his book and quoted it, so we cannot know whether Saint-Mars wrote "Dauger" or "d'Auger." Louvois's and Saint-Mars's other letters for which we have the originals spell it "Dauger." Vergé-Franceschi, 267.

[42] Vergé-Franceschi, 267–68.

[43] François-Michel Letellier marquis de Louvois to Saint-Mars, Saint-Germain-en-Laye, July 19, 1669, Archives Nationales, Paris, France, Microfilm K//120/A, 67.

[44] Saint-Mars eventually made many severe mistakes in his guard of the prisoner but despite these, the king never fired him.

[45] The Saint-Paul cemetery was closed in 1791; the church was destroyed in 1799.

[46] Jacques Hillairet, *Dictionnaire Historique des Rues de Paris*. (Paris: Les Editions de Minuit, 1963), 2:479.

[47] Jacques Hillairet, *Les 200 Cimetières du Vieux Paris* (Paris: Les Editions de Minuit, 1958), 77.

[48] Duvivier, 2.

[49] Paul Sonnino, *The Search for the Man in the Iron Mask, a Historical Detective Story* (Lanham, Maryland: Rowman & Littlefield, 2016), 155.

[50] Eustache lived in the lower tower of the prison at Pignerol.

[51] This 19 July letter was found in the National Archives by Father Joseph Delort during his research for his book *Histoire de l'homme au masque de fer*, published in 1825.

[52] Louvois to Saint-Mars, July 19, 1669.

[53] Pierre-Marie Dijol, "L'Homme au Masque de fer," *Il y a trois siècles...le Masque de Fer...Actes du Colloque international sur la célèbre énigme (12–13 September 1987)* (Cannes: La Direction des Affaires Culturelles de la Ville de Cannes, 1996), 51.

[54] Monique Cottret, "La Légende En Action, Le Masque de Fer Contre l'Arbitraire,"
Il y a trois siècles...le Masque de Fer... Actes du Colloque international sur la célèbre énigme (12–13 Septembre 1987) (Cannes: la Direction des Affaires Culturelles de la Ville de Cannes, 1996), 233.

[55] Georges Mongrédien, *Le Masque de Fer* (Paris: Hachette, 1952), 23.

[56] Napoléon I also ordered that the Bastille records be searched for the identity of the Mask.

[57] Iung, 55.

[58] Chevalier assumed that Dauger was forced to wear a mask, but there is no evidence to warrant that conclusion.

[59] The du Junca volumes are books of records of prisoners of the Bastille made by Lieutenant du Junca, officer of the Bastille, separately from the *Great Register*. The du Junca volumes will

be described further in the next chapter.

[60] Iung, 56.

[61] Sébastien Le Prestre de Vauban, *Vauban: sa famille et ses écrits, ses "Oisivetés" et sa correspondance*, ed. Eugène-Auguste-Albert de Rochas d'Aiglun (Paris: Berger-Levrault, 1910), 2: XI.

[62] Henri Griffet [Reverend Father], *Traité des différentes sortes de preuves qui servent à établir la vérité de l'histoire* (Paris: J. F. Bassompierre, 1770), 311.

[63] Jacques Roujon, *Louvois et son maître* (Paris: Editions Bernard Grasset, 1934), 24. Literally this is translated into English as, "They stirred all the sauces"; the meaning is that these two operatives were put to work wherever the king needed them.

[64] Daniel Dessert, "Pouvoir et finance au XVIIe siècle: La fortune du Cardinal Mazarin," *Revue d'histoire moderne et contemporaine* 23 (1976): 164.

[65] Sonnino, 110–29.

[66] Roujon, 150.

[67] Roux-Fazillac, 105.

[68] Vergé-Franceschi, 256.

[69] See the *Gazette* article in chapter 4 describing La Rivière's origins and his baptism in Paris on February 6, 1661. His godmother was Marie de Maupeou Fouquet.

[70] Daniel Dessert, *Fouquet* (Paris: Fayard, 1987), 50.

[71] H. Tassé, "La Duchesse d'Aiguillon (1604–1675)," *Mon Magazine* (September 1929): 35.

[72] The leaders and founders of Montréal were M. de Chomedey de Maisonneuve (1612–1676), recruiter, fundraiser and Governor of Ville-Marie, Jeanne Mance (1606–1672), a nurse, credited with founding the hospital, and Saint Marguerite Bourgeois (1620–1700), who founded the first school in Montréal.

[73] The *Séminaire des Missions pour les pays étrangers* is at 128 rue du Bac in Paris.

[74] Luigi Mezzadri. *Vincent de Paul (1581–1660)*, trans. Jean-Pierre Bagot (Paris: Desclée de Brouwer, 1985), 100.

[75] Giovan Battista Feliciano Primi Fassola di San Maiolo. *Mémoires sur la cour de Louis XIV, 1673–1681* (Paris: Librairie Académique Perrin, 1988), 137.

[76] Fouquet eventually bought the island of Belle-Ile that lies to the southwest of the Brittany peninsula from Pierre de Gondi (1602–1676), the older brother of Cardinal Jean-François-Paul de Retz, the Frondeur, and began his shipping enterprise.

[77] Robert Sinsoilliez, *Tombelaine, l'îlot de la baie du Mont-Saint-Michel* (Saint-Malo, France: Editions L'ancre de marine, 1989), 170.

[78] Corroyer, 371.

[79] Personal conversation with M. Jean-Luc Leservoisier, archivist of the Avranches library, at Avranches city hall, May 2012.

[80] Madame Scarron's second husband was Louis XIV.

[81] The Palais des Tournelles had been destroyed on orders of Catherine de' Medici to punish it for being the location of a jousting match in which her husband, King Henri II, was accidentally killed. For a medical assessment of the eye wound that killed Henri II, see Kian Eftekhari, "The Last Ride of Henry II of France: Orbital Injury and a King's Demise," *Survey of Ophthamology* 60, no. 3 (May–June 2015): 274–278.

[82] Duvivier, 138. "Not enough air between the head and the hat."

[83] Jean Markale, *La Bastille et l'enigme du Masque du Fer* (Paris: Pygmalion/G. Watelet, 1989), 51.

[84] The Saint-Antoine Hospital is at 184, rue du Faubourg Saint-Antoine, 75012 Paris.

[85] Henri Sauval, *Histoire et recherches des antiquités de la ville de Paris* (Paris: Charles Moette and Jacques Chardon, 1724), 1:41.

[86] Jacques Hillairet, *Dictionnaire Historique des rues de Paris* (Paris: Les Editions de Minuit,

1963), 1:155.

⁸⁷Bocher, 119.

⁸⁸The abbé Jean-Baptiste Dubos (1670–1742) was a historian and diplomat.

⁸⁹Voltaire, "Letter to the Abbé Dubos from Cirey, 30 October 1738," in *Oeuvres de Voltaire* ; 51–52, 54–70. *Correspondance*, ed. Adrien-Jean-Quentin Beuchot (Paris: Firmin Didot frères; Werdet et Lequien fils, 1830–1834), 53:305, accessed April 26, 2015.

⁹⁰Voltaire said he had seen people who had "served him." Maybe Dauger had been given a servant at the Bastille. We know that at the third prison he lived in, Sainte-Marguerite, a person lived in an antichamber of his cell but we do not know anything about that person. Perhaps someone served Dauger at the Bastille who was still alive in the 1720s and could have talked to Voltaire? But we have many testimonies that only Saint-Mars, Rosarges, and Rû saw the prisoner.

⁹¹Louis XIV's birth and death dates are September 5, 1638 and September 1, 1715 and his dates of rule are May 14, 1643 to September 1, 1715.

⁹²Voltaire's dates of incarceration in the Bastille were May 21, 1717 to April 14, 1718, and from April 17 to 26, 1726.

⁹³Jules Mazarin, born Giulio Mazzarino in Rome in 1602, died at Vincennes in 1661, was Anne of Austria's chief minister and counselor during her regency, godfather to Louis XIV.

⁹⁴"Saint-Mars" is a military nickname; many soldiers had one. The fighting name that Louis XIV chose for himself as a child when he played war games with his friends was "La Fleur," which in this context means the finest, the best, the most glorious.

⁹⁵Voltaire, *Le Siècle de Louis XIV* (Frankfurt: Knoch & Eslinger, 1753), 1:311–312.

⁹⁶Pignerol and Exilles at the time of the Mask's incarceration were French possessions.

⁹⁷Cannes and the Lérins Islands are in the French department Alpes-Maritimes in the region of Provence-Alpes-Côte-d'Azur.

⁹⁸Traveling chairs carried by human porters were a common form of transportation in France at that time, particularly where the road was bad enough that a carriage might wreck or, in the mountains, might go over into the valley below.

⁹⁹Peter Wilson, "European Warfare 1450–1815," in *War in the Early Modern World 1450–1815* ed. Jeremy Black (Westview Press, 1999), 196. The League of Augsburg was a group of principalities that had joined to oppose Louis XIV (1688–1697).

¹⁰⁰Vergé-Franceschi, 324.

¹⁰¹Joseph Delort, *Histoire de l'homme au masque de fer, accompagnée des pièces authentiques et de facsimile* (Paris: Delaforest, 1825), 282.

¹⁰²Delort, *Histoire de l'Homme*, 284.

¹⁰³Jules Lair, *Nicolas Foucquet, Procureur General, Surintendant des Finances, Ministre d'Etat de Louis XIV* (Paris: Librairie Plon, 1890), 1:387.

¹⁰⁴Agde is on the Mediterranean Gulf of Lion southwest of Marseilles in the modern French province of Occitanie, department of the Hérault, but in 1687 the province was called Languedoc.

¹⁰⁵The Fortress of Oblivion was one of the most famous prisons in antiquity located in Persia (Iran).

¹⁰⁶Letter from Bishop Louis Fouquet, September 4, 1687, no recipient given. Bibliothèque Sainte-Geneviève Reserve (manuscripts). Vol. 1477 f396v. Some capitalization, accent marks, and punctuation have been added to help the reader parse the text. The volume 1477 in which the letter is bound doesn't have a title. It is a compiled and bound volume of letters and relations without organization and often without date or recipient. All letters and relations in the volume are dated 1686 or 1687. The book of letters is a collection of various sorts of communications: epitaphs, recipes against illness, *le mal caduc*, by example (p. 144r). One letter is to Nicolas Fouquet's former personal secretary Paul Pellisson (p. 184r).

¹⁰⁷She was the daughter of Charles I Louis, Elector of the Palatinate, the area in southwest

Germany around and including Heidelberg, Germany.

[108] Elisabeth-Charlotte de Bavière von der Pfalz, duchesse d'Orléans, *Die Briefe der Liselotte von der Pfalz, Herzogin von Orléans* (Ebenhausen-München: Langewiesche-Brandt, 1914), 323.

[109] Vergé-Franceschi tells that Madame must have meant the would-be assassin of William III called Fenwick...that she must have misread or misunderstood the name, because the Duke of Berwick had an honorable career and never attempted the assassination of anyone. Vergé-Franceschi, 26. Once more we see that an errant vowel or consonant can cause a cascade of mistakes in the history of this mystery.

[110] Griffet, 317.

[111] Saint-Foix wrote light theatrical works and had published a book about Paris called *Essais historiques sur Paris* in 1754.

[112] Pagnol, 57.

[113] Claude Quétel, *La Bastille, Histoire vraie d'une prison légendaire* (Paris: Robert Laffont, 1989), 248–49.

[114] Guillaume-Louis Formanoir de Palteau, "Lettre à Elie Catherine Fréron sur l'homme au masque de fer," *L'Année littéraire* 4 (1768), Microfilm m. 26 (19): 351–54. Villeneuve-le-Roi is now called Villeneuve-sur-Yonne.

[115] Eric March, "Here's What 5 Years in Solitary Confinement Does To a Person. It's Not Pretty," *Upworthy. Things That Matter. Pass 'em On*, http://www.upworthy.com/heres-what-5-years-in-solitary-confinement-does-to-a-person-its-not-pretty?c=huf1, accessed October 15, 2014.

[116] Saint-Mars had willed the estate to the father of de Palteau. It is south of Sens in the department of the Yonne in the region of Bourgogne-Franche-Comté.

[117] Harding, 80.

[118] Lucien Lambeau, "L'ancien cimetière Saint-Paul et ses charniers, l'église Saint-Paul, la grange et la prison Saint-Eloi," *Annexe au procès-verbal de la séance du 9 novembre 1910* (1910): 14. This document is at the library of the history of Paris.

[119] Jean-Luc Dauphin died before *Second Son* was published, a source of great sorrow to the author. My only consolation is that, not knowing he was ill, I sent him a copy of the draft chapter about Saint-Mars a few months before he died, so that he was assured that, as the last line of his article proclaims, "*La recherche continue donc!*" I owe him my deepest thanks for his help.

[120] Georges Mongrédien, *Le Masque de Fer*, (Paris: Hachette, 1952), 45.

[121] Jean-Luc Dauphin, "Deux Documents Inédits sur le Passage en Villeneuvien du Masque de fer," *Etudes Villeneuviennes, Bulletin des Amis du Vieux Villeneuve-sur-Yonne* (Société Historique, Archéologique, Artistique et Culturelle du Villeneuvien, no. 39, (Printemps 2008): 40.

[122] Jean-Luc Dauphin, "Deux Documents Inédits sur le Passage en Villeneuvien du Masque de fer," 38.

[123] Dauphin, "Deux Documents Inédits sur le Passage en Villeneuvien du Masque de fer," 40.

[124] Dauphin, "Deux Documents Inédits sur le Passage en Villeneuvien du Masque de fer," 41.

[125] An almoner might be described as a supervisor of the religious practices of the household.

[126] The Bastille lieutenant, in charge of day-to-day operations, was second in rank to the governor.

[127] Father Griffet's Jesuit religious order was expelled from France in 1764. He went to Brussels, where he wrote his book, published in 1769. It is doubtful he would have dared to publish the entries in du Junca's journal if he had been in France. As far as how he found the journal, it would seem logical that he noticed the journal volumes in a storage room or office of the Bastille on a shelf at some point while he worked at the Bastille and in his spare time began reading them...and copying them.

[128] General Theodore Iung's translation of this word in his book on the Mask published in

1873 was "*sud*" ("south") and this translation persisted into modern times. In my examination of the page at the Arsenal library, I saw that the word was "*seul*" ("alone"). "*Seul*" makes far better sense because it shows that du Junca had been told to put the prisoner in a cell by himself, which was a sign of deference and adherence to Dauger's previous management. The towers were never named according to their locations on the compass.

[129] Etienne du Junca. *L'estat de prisouniés [sic] qui sont envoiés par l'ordre du Roy à la Bastille, à commenser [sic] du mescredy honsiesme du mois d'octobre, que je suis entré en possecion [sic] de la charge de lieutenant de roy, en l'année 1690. 24 octobre 1690–26 août 1705.* September18, 1698. MSS 5133, vol. 1, fol. 37 v^e. Archives of the Bastille, Bibliothèque nationale, Paris, France.

[130] Etienne du Junca, *Journal*, November 19–20, 1703.

[131] Vergé-Franceschi, 50–51.

[132] The two volumes are large books, about 20 inches tall by 16 inches wide, each covered in light brown hard covers with thick, stiff, yellowed sheets of paper inside filled from top to bottom with du Junca's handwriting. (I was determined to see the two volumes by du Junca. I wanted a reward for spending many years of my life on this project. The Arsenal library curator wanted me to be satisfied with microfiche and was not going to allow me to see these two books but I insisted because I wanted to assess their size and check the actual text against previously printed texts of the journal. The archivist finally relented after twenty minutes of questioning me and making me fill out extra forms, but the *président de la salle* limited me to an hour with them, I couldn't photograph them, and I was told I could see them once but never again! I would have to use microfiche next time.)

[133] Lagrange-Chancel had been dead for ten years in 1768 but this is the date of *Père* Griffet's publication and of de Palteau's letter so perhaps Elie Fréron, the editor of *l'Année littéraire*, pulled Lagrange-Chancel's 1758 letter out of the archives to help rehash the mysterious prisoner's existence.

[134] Reverend Father Henri Griffet, *Traité des différentes sortes de preuves qui servent à établir la vérité de l'histoire* (Liege: J. F. Bassompierre, 1770), 311.

[135] Griffet, 318.

[136] Griffet, 312.

[137] La Borde was *premier valet de chambre* of Louis XV.

[138] Lair, *Nicolas Foucquet*, 2:454.

[139] Markale, 271.

[140] Mrs. John King van Rensselaer, *The Devil's Picture-Books, a History of Playing Cards* (New York: Dodd, Mead, and Company, 1890), 161.The word "Knave" in Old English meant a boy and only much later took on a connotation of a slippery character.

[141] The third rank picture card in the other suits are the *Valet de Coeurs* (Hearts), the *Valet de Trèfles* (Clubs), and the *Valet de Carreaux* (Diamonds).

[142] Van Rensselaer, 101.

[143] Orest A. Ranum, *Artisans of Glory: Writers and Historical Thought in Seventeenth-Century France* (Chapel Hill: University of North Carolina Press, 1980), 17.

[144] Van Rensselaer, 167–68.

[145] Adrien Huguet, *Le Marquis De Cavoye, 1640-1716: Un Grand Mar:raw-latex:'é'chal Des Logis De La Maison Du Roi*, (Paris: H. Champion, 1920), 298-99.

[146] Sarah Brandes Madry, "The Valet: The Marquis de Louvois's Invited Guest in the Mystery of the Man in the Iron Mask," *Cahiers du Dix-Septième: An Interdisciplinary Journal* 17 (2016), http://se17.bowdoin.edu/2016-volume-xvii/2016-volume-xvii. The afternoon *rendezvous* occurred sometime in the spring of 1668.

[147] Pougin, 21.

[148] Cardinal Jules Mazarin (1602–1661) was born Giulio Mazzarino in Rome and became a masterful diplomat who came to the French court just before the death of Louis XIII in spring 1643. See chapter 10.

[149] Markale, 289.

[150] Vaux-le-Vicomte is in the Seine-et-Marne department, near Maincy and Melun, in the region of Ile-de-France.

[151] Fouquet also owned a Paris town house (destroyed) formerly belonging to a previous superintendant of finances, Particelli d'Hémery. It was at the junction of the rue Croix-des-Petit-Champs and the rue Vide-Gousset, on the location of the place des Victoires.

[152] Jean-Marie Perouse de Montclos, *Vaux-le-Vicomte* (Paris: Editions Scala, 2002),76–77.

[153] Jacques Hillairet, *La Rue de Richelieu* (Paris: Les Editions de Minuit, 1966), 20.

[154] Georges Keller-Dorian, *Antoine Coysevox (1640–1720) Catalogue raisonné de son oeuvre* (Paris: Georges Keller-Dorian, 1920), 53–57.

[155] Hilary Ballon, *Louis Le Vau: Mazarin's Collège, Colbert's Revenge* (Princeton, New Jersey: Princeton University Press, 1999), 125.

[156] *Equivoco* in Italian means equivocal, ambiguous, dubious, shady, fishy, shifty.

[157] Claude Dulong, *Mazarin et l'argent, banquiers et prête-noms* (Paris: Ecole des Chartes, 2002), 237.

[158] Inès Murat, *Colbert* (Paris: Fayard, 1980), 61–62.

[159] Quiberon is on the northwestern coast of France in the Morbihan department in Brittany.

[160] Philip P. Boucher, *The Shaping of the French Colonial Empire: A Bio-Bibliography of the Careers of Richelieu, Fouquet, and Colbert* (New York and London: Garland Publishing, Inc., 1985), 111.

[161] Murat, 95–96.

[162] Jean de la Robrie, "Hypothèse sur la confusion du nom de Rougé," *Bulletin de la Société Archéologique et historique de Nantes et de Loire-Atlantique* 113 (1974), 32–39. Le Tellier's written instructions to d'Artagnan for the arrest of Fouquet say that he was lodging at the Hôtel de Rougé, which has been assumed to be a townhouse of Madame de Rougé, the marquise du Plessis-Bellière, Fouquet's close friend, but an article in the 1974 edition of the *Bulletin de la Société Archéologique et historique de Nantes et de Loire-Atlantique* takes up the question and says that "sounds like" spelling is responsible for a mistake. The townhouse where Nicolas Fouquet stayed was the Manoir de la Chézine owned by François-Joseph Rogier, a Breton magistrate and colleague of Fouquet. There was not a Hôtel de Rougé in Nantes. And the Manoir de Chézine fits the description given by a person who visited Fouquet at the house: beside the river, within the town, but far from the cathedral. Le Tellier heard "Rogier," and printed "Rougé," just as Basile Fouquet heard "Saint-Mars," but printed "Cinq Mars." I am grateful to a friend, originally from Nantes, who found this article in the Nantes archives.

[163] Paul Morand, *Fouquet, ou Le Soleil offusqué* (Paris: Gallimard, 1961), 117. One possible answer to Morand's question is that Fouquet felt safe from arrest because the king had told him an outright lie to seduce him to Nantes and to immunize him against any rumors that he was in danger.

[164] Neither Fouquet nor his lawyers were ever allowed to see the papers to prepare a defense for Fouquet at his trial, only an inventory of the papers made by the prosecutors. The documents disappeared, were lost, a few were saved. It was a tragic loss for historians, not to mention Fouquet.

[165] "Monsieur" was the traditional nomenclature for the first brother of the king.

[166] Jean Baptiste Colbert, *Lettres, instructions et mémoires de Colbert*, ed. Pierre Clément, 2, (1), (Paris: Imprimerie impériale, 1861–1873), p. XI.

[167] Notre-Dame-des-Anges is now the United Protestant Church of the Marais.

[168] Jacques Hillairet, *Les 200 Cimetières du Vieux Paris* (Paris: Les Editions de Minuit, 1958), 77. Among many other famous people buried in the Saint-Paul cemetery were: François Rabelais (d. 1553); the partner and leading actress of Molière, Madeleine Béjart (d. 1672); two of the greatest architects in France's history, François Mansart (d. 1666) and his nephew Jules-Hardouin Mansart (d. 1708); and the famous courtisan Marion Delorme (d. 1650). Dauger's jailers Saint-Mars and Antoine Ru were also buried there.

[169] Iung, 293–294. "*Vous me ferez plaisir de garder jusqu'à mon retour la*

cassette qui vous sera remise chez feu Nallot, et Carpatry vous fera encore porter un lit dont je vous prie de faire de même et de prendre soin qu'il ne se gâte."

[170] Hillairet. *Dictionnaire*, 2: 112. He died supposedly of a natural death due to a laboratory explosion. His laboratory was at #4 impasse Maubert in the fifth arrondissement.

[171] An excellent book in English on the poison scandal is Anne Somerset, *The Affair of the Poisons: Murder, Infanticide and Satanism at the Court of Louis XIV*.

[172] Iung, 335–336. Iung says the crime of du Colombier had something to do with the religious orders of Saint-Lazare and Saint-Esprit. This false monk was conspiring with a number of foreign agents and interior agents from Turin, Lyon, and Brussels.

[173] Georges Vigarello, *Le propre et le sale: l'hygiène du corps depuis le Moyen Age* (Paris: Le Seuil, 1985), 70.

[174] Claude Quétel. *Une ombre sur le roi Soleil: L'affaire des Poisons*. Paris: Larousse, 2010, 104.

[175] Aimé Richardt, *Louvois (1641–1691)* (Paris: ERTI, 1990), 274.

[176] Tonnerre is in the Yonne department of the Bourgogne-Franche-Comté region.

[177] According to Luc-Normand Tellier in his book *Face aux Colbert: Les Le Tellier, Vauban, Turgot... et l'Avènement du Liberalisme* (Sillery, Québec: Presses de l'Université du Québec, 1987), 19, "[T]he armes parlantes come from 'd'azur à trois lézards d'argent posés en pal au chef cousu de gueules, chargés de trois étoiles d'or. In latin 'lizard' is *stellio* and star is *stellifer*... when you take out the letters s and f of these words you get tellio and tellier."

[178] Louvois fell from a horse in 1679 and his leg never healed properly, causing him to walk with a limp.

[179] Bile is a fluid produced in the liver. Black bile and green bile are two of the four humours of Hippocratic medicine which were thought in Louvois' time to cause health problems if they became unbalanced.

[180] Ezéchiel Spanheim, *Relation de la Cour de France en 1690*, ed. Emile Bourgeois, (Paris: Mercure de France, 1973), 154–63.

[181] Except for the year between 1671 to 1672.

[182] Roujon, 129.

[183] Eugène Vaillé,(*Le Cabinet Noir*. Paris: Presses Universitaires de France, 1950), 102. The Cabinet Noir (the Black Room) is a gracious phrase for the opening of the mail by the French government to spy on its citizens.

[184] Louvois' Paris house is gone but the square on which it stood is called the square Louvois. It is directly opposite one of the entrances on the rue de Richelieu to the Bibliothèque Nationale, where sleuths have gone for centuries to look for clues to the mystery Louvois helped create.

[185] They left Paris on August 3 and arrived at Briançon on the 7th, from where they rode mules with special custom-made saddles to cross the last Alpine miles.

[186] Joseph Delort, *Histoire de la Détention des Philosophes et es Gens de Lettres à la Bastille et à Vincennes, Précédée de celle de Foucquet, de Pellisson et de Lauzun, avec tous les Documents Authentiques et Inédits*. (Paris : Firmin Didot Père et Fils, Libraires, 1829), 1:167–168.

[187] Vergé-Franceschi, 285.

[188] Vergé-Franceschi, 285.

[189] Madeleine Tiollais, *Le Masque de fer, enquête sur le prisonnier dont le nom ne se dit pas* (Edition Cheminement, 2003), 249.

[190] François-Timoléon de Choisy, *Mémoires pour Servir à l'Histoire de Louis XIV*, ed. Georges Mongrédien (Paris: Mercure de France, 1966), 173.

[191] Noone, 262–63.

[192] A free company (*compagnie franche*) was a cohort of paramilitary men responsible only to their leader, who handpicked them; they were not bound by the rules of the army.

[193] Norbert Guinot, *Initiation à l'étude des noms de lieux* (Bourbon-Lancy, France: Editions de la Croix de Pierre, 1984), 39.

[194] The corps was named for the grey and white horses they rode.

¹⁹⁵Pierre-Marie Dijol, "L'Homme au Masque de fer," *Il y a trois siècles... le Masque de Fer... Actes du Colloque international sur la célèbre énigme (12–13 septembre 1987)*, ed. La Direction des Affaires Culturelles de la Ville de Cannes (Cannes: la Direction des Affaires Culturelles de la Ville de Cannes, 1996), 56.

¹⁹⁶Adolphe Chéruel, *Dictionnaire historique des institutions, mœurs et coutumes de la France*, Part 2 (Paris: L. Hachette et cie, 1855), 868.

¹⁹⁷Véronique Larcade, "Versailles sous Louis XIV ou le tombeau des cadets de Gascogne?," *Bulletin du Centre de recherche du château de Versailles*, 2008, posted June 14, 2008. http://journals.openedition.org/crcv/5623; DOI: 10.4000/crcv.5623, p. 11, accessed February 14, 2019.

¹⁹⁸Dijol, "L'Homme au Masque de fer," 58.

¹⁹⁹This title was formed from Saint-Mars' fighting name, and was not, as would be usual, formed from the name of a property because Saint-Mars did not own a property that would qualify for a status of nobility in 1673.

²⁰⁰Jean-Luc Dauphin. "Bénigne Dauvergne, Dit Saint-Mars, Seigneur de Palteau et Dixmont, ou Le Vrai Père du Masque de Fer." *Etudes Villeneuviennes, Bulletin des Amis du Vieux Villeneuve-sur-Yonne, Société Historique, Archéologique, Artistique et Culturelle du Villeneuvien.* No. 33, Printemps 2005, p. 12.

²⁰¹Dauphin., 65.

²⁰²Dauphin, 62.

²⁰³The dragoons were created in the middle of the seventeenth century. They could fight either on foot or on horseback.

²⁰⁴Dijol, "L'Homme au Masque de fer," 65–66.

²⁰⁵Dijol, "L'Homme au Masque de fer," 73. The battle of Landau occurred during the War of the Spanish Succession, Louis XIV's last war.

²⁰⁶Jean-Luc Dauphin. *Découvrir Villeneuve-sur-Yonne et le Villeneuvien*. Villeneuve-sur-Yonne: Conseil Général de l'Yonne, 2004, p. 37.

²⁰⁷Dauphin, *Découvrir Villeneuve-sur-Yonne*, 36.

²⁰⁸"Testament olographe de Bénigne Dauvergne de Saint-Mars, en date du 21 août 1704, apporté par Michel Ancel Desgranges, maître des cérémonies à Jean Le Camus, lieutenant civil, et déposé pour minute par ce dernier à Me Louis Durant, notaire, le 26 septembre 1708." Minutes de Louis DURANT (MC/ET/XCVI/191 - MC/ET/XCVI/301), 1708, juillet–1708, septembre (MC/ET/XCVI/203), Archives Nationales de France MC/ET/XCVI/203.

²⁰⁹Duvivier, 208. Presidents were the chief magistrates of the Paris *Parlement*, which consisted of eight chambers: a *Grand'Chambre* [sic], five chambers of investigation, and two chambers of appeal. The chambers each had counselors to make judicial decisions and presidents to preside over sessions of court. The presidents in the *Grand'Chambre* ranked higher than other presidents and to distinguish themselves, they wore a black velvet hat with two gold stripes that had on top a flat disk similar to a mortar board. They were called *présidents à mortier*.

²¹⁰Joseph Delort, *Histoire de la Détention des Philosophes et es Gens de Lettres à la Bastille et à Vincennes, Précédée de celle de Foucquet, de Pellisson et de Lauzun, avec tous les Documents Authentiques et Inédits.* (Paris: Firmin Didot Père et Fils, Libraires, 1829), 1: 69..

²¹¹Pagnol, 47. Skepticism is appropriate.

²¹²There are numerous testimonies that the governor respected Dauger.

²¹³Vergé-Franceschi, 267–68.

²¹⁴Delort, *Histoire de la Détention des Philosophes* 1: 102-103.

²¹⁵Arthur Griffiths, *In Old French Prisons* (New York: Dorset Press, 1992), 54–55.

²¹⁶Rupert Furneaux, *The Man Behind the Mask: The Real Story of the "Ancient Prisoner"* (London: Cassell & Company, Ltd, 1954), 51.

²¹⁷Carl J. Ekberg, *The Failure of Louis XIV's Dutch War* (Chapel Hill: University of North

[218] Théophraste Renaudot, "Paris news," *La Gazette*, February 12, 1661, 156.

[219] Vergé-Franceschi, 311.

[220] The letters were the business of the minister of war, Louvois, so they went to the ministerial archives after his death and remained there. Today it is called the *Service Historique de la Défense* (SHD).

[221] The last five years of his detention were in Paris and no letters were written then because Saint-Mars was locally accessible.

[222] Delort, *Histoire de la Détention des Philosophes* 1:103–104.

[223] Delort, *Histoire Détention des philosophes* 1: 105–106.

[224] Delort, *Histoire Détention des Philosophes* 1: 123.

[225] There was no nickname for Monsieur Nicolas Fouquet. His presence at Pignerol was not a secret so perhaps that is why Louvois and Saint-Mars did not hesitate to frequently use Fouquet's name in their correspondence.

[226] This is a sarcastic criticism of Saint-Mars. Louvois had learned from a spy at the prison that Saint-Mars had talked to someone about the arrival of his new prisoner, which was forbidden. Louvois is telling him not to do this again.

[227] François-Michel Le Tellier marquis de Louvois to Monsieur de Saint-Mars, 10 September 1669 from Saint-Germain-en-Laye, Archives Nationales de France, K//120/A/f° 68.

[228] François-Michel Le Tellier marquis de Louvois to Monsieur de Saint-Mars, 25 September 1669 from Saint-Germain-en-Laye, Archives Nationales de France, K//120/A/f° 69.

[229] Delort, *Histoire Détention des Philosophes* 1: 204.

[230] Rupert Furneaux, *The Man Behind the Mask: The Real Story of the "Ancient Prisoner,"* (London: Cassell & Company, Ltd, 1954), 13.

[231] Jacques Hillairet, *L'Ile Saint-Louis* (Paris: Les Editions de Minuit, 1967), 70.

[232] The Lot-et-Garonne department is in the Nouvelle Aquitaine region.

[233] Etienne Alexandre Bardin and Nicholas Charles Victor Oudinot, *Dictionnaire de l'armée de terre ou recherches historiques sur l'art et les usages militaires des anciens et des modernes*. (Paris: Perrotin, 1841), 2: 730.

[234] Dauger's escort was Vauroy and three other soldiers.

[235] Delort, *Histoire Détention des Philosophes*, 1: 179–80.

[236] Delort, *Histoire Détention des Philosophes*, 1: 180–181.

[237] Delort, *Histoire Détention des Philosophes*, 1: 186.

[238] Delort, *Histoire Détention des Philosophes*, 1: 241.

[239] Delort, *Histoire Détention des Philosophes*, 1: 327–28.

[240] Petitfils, *L'Homme*, 158–59.

[241] Delort, *Histoire Détention des Philosophes*, 1: 233–34.

[242] Louvois wrote to Saint-Mars in November 1671 just after Lauzun arrived that he should provide Lauzun with the same quality of linens and clothing that Fouquet had, but they should not be elaborate. "Furnish his room with a good bed, chairs, tables, fireplace utensils and a Bergamo tapestry, *"propre et honneste."* Delort, *Histoire Détention des Philosophes,* 1: 177–178. Bergamo tapestries were constructed of yarn and wool, very different from expensive tapestries from Flanders. Jean-Claude Le Guillou, *Versailles avant Versailles au temps de Louis XIII* (Paris: Perrin, 2011), 156.

[243] The old theory that originated in 1825 that Dauger was a valet in his past life is, in this present book at least, not credible; Louvois' comment about Dauger was a play on words and not the name of his profession. If Dauger had been a valet in the past, the issue of trying to decide if he could valet Fouquet or not would never have come up; Louvois would simply have ordered Saint-Mars to use Dauger as he liked for a servant.

[244] Drinking wine without mixing it with water was coarse and not usually done.

[245] Pagnol, 198–99.

[246] Petitfils, *L'Homme*, 455.

[247] This did not occur. Marie-Thérèse died at age forty-four in 1683. Out of six children, five died in infancy or before the age of five. She gave birth to a baby with black skin who was quickly pronounced dead but was in fact put into seclusion and became a nun called the Mooress of Moret but no one knows who the father was. The king and Mme de Maintenon used to visit her occasionally.

[248] The secret meetings of Fouquet and Lauzun occurred at night and Dauger went to his own room at night, presumably. It was therefore La Rivière who stood guard over the forbidden conversations.

[249] Delort, *Histoire Détention des Philosophes*, 1: 278.

[250] Delort, *Histoire Détention des Philosophes*, 1: 280.

[251] La Reynie was the lieutenant of police.

[252] Claude Quétel, *La Bastille devoilée par ses archives* (Paris: Omnibus, 2013), 268–269.

[253] Petitfils, *L'Homme*, 210.

[254] C. J. S. Thompson., *The Mystery and Romance of Alchemy and Pharmacy* (London: The Scientific Press, Limited, 1897) 56.

[255] Fouquet's daughter had been allowed to stay with her father at Pignerol in a room they set up for her but it didn't turn out well. She and Lauzun began an affair and it hurt Fouquet immensely.

[256] Delort, *Histoire Détention des Philosophes*, 1: 317–318.

[257] Petitfils, *L'Homme*, 210. *Salut* can mean various things but here it means Barrail retired from public life and made deliberate efforts to admit to and atone for sins and follow legal and church teachings in a methodical way. For some people, memories of past irregular life habits brought on a need to make things right before dying.

[258] Louis Batiffol, *La Vie de Paris sous Louis XIII*. (Paris: Calmann-Lévy, 1932), 1.

[259] Saint-Germain-en-Laye was the seat of two royal chateaux, an old chateau and a new one, both on the same plain looking over the Seine north of Paris.

[260] Gilbert Colbert, marquis de Saint-Pouenge, d. October 22, 1706.

[261] Occitanie region.

[262] Iung, 103.

[263] Dessert, *Fouquet*, 296.

[264] Lair, 2: 461. *Euphrasia officinalis* is a flowering herb with the common name eye-bright that has been promoted since the 1300s for improving and restoring sight.

[265] Frantz Funck-Brentano, *Le Drame des poisons*, (Paris: J. Tallandier, 1977), 24.

[266] Christophe Glaser, *Traité de la chymie, enseignant par une briève [sic] et facile méthode toutes ses plus nécessaires préparations* (Paris, 1663), 177.

[267] Alchemists thought the planets could influence metals.

[268] Glaser, 179–80.

[269] Marie de Maupeou Fouquet, *Recueil de receptes où est expliquée la maniere de guerir à peu de frais toute sorte de maux tant internes, qu'externes inveterez, & qui ont passé jusqu'à present pour incurables* (Lyon: Jean Certe, 1675), 361–62.

[270] Laurence Brockliss and Colin Jones, *The Medical World of Early Modern France* (Oxford: Clarendon Press; New York: Oxford University Press, 1997), 153–54. A troche is a suspension containing powders.

[271] Edmond Bonnaffé, *Les Amateurs de l'Ancienne France: Le Surintendant Foucquet* (Paris: J. Rouam; London: Remington & Co., 1882; La Vergne, Tenn.: Kessinger Publishing, 2010), 79–80.

[272] Chalon-sur-Saône is a town in southern Burgundy approximately half way between Pignerol and Paris. Amboise is in the Loire Valley nears Tours.

[273] Marius Topin, *L'homme au masque de fer* (Paris: E. Dentu; Didier, 1870), 329–30.

²⁷⁴Philippe Delorme, *Marie de' Médicis*, Series Histoire des Reines de France (Paris: Pygmalion/Gérard Watelet, 1998), 16.

²⁷⁵The "Jacobin" was a Dominican monk, arrested in 1673, who preyed on women using his knowledge of philosophy and alchemy as bait. He lost his mind while in Pignerol.

²⁷⁶Dubreuil was a spy, possibly a former military officer, who went mad at Pignerol. Iung thinks he died at Saint-Marguerite prison in 1697.

²⁷⁷Ercole Mattioli was a secretary of the Duke of Mantua, who was arrested on May 2, 1679. He died insane, a prisoner at Sainte-Marguerite.

²⁷⁸Ettore Patria, "Benigno de Saint-Mars, Géolier du Masque de Fer," in *Il y a trois siècles... le Masque de Fer... Actes du Colloque international sur la célèbre énigme, 12–13 Septembre 1987*. (Cannes: la Direction des Affaires Culturelles de la Ville de Cannes, 1996), 147.

²⁷⁹Edith Wharton, *Edith Wharton Abroad, Selected Travel Writings, 1888–1920*, ed. Sarah Bird Wright (New York: St. Martin's Press, 1995), 88.

²⁸⁰Furneaux, 93.

²⁸¹Furneaux, 94.

²⁸²Furneaux, 94–95. Louvois was referring to Rosarges.

²⁸³Furneaux, 94.

²⁸⁴Furneaux, 94–95.

²⁸⁵Furneaux, 97.

²⁸⁶Mongrédien, *Masque de Fer*, 112.

²⁸⁷Fernand Braudel, "History and Environment," in *The Identity of France*, trans. Siân Reynolds (New York: Harper & Row, 1986), 117.

²⁸⁸Vergé-Franceschi, 333.

²⁸⁹The comte de Guitaut was the nephew of François de Guitaut who had been captain of the guards for Louis XIII and Anne of Austria.

²⁹⁰Fernand Carlhian-Ribois, "Séjour du 'Masque de fer' à Briançon," in *Il y a trois siècles... le Masque de Fer... Actes du Colloque international sur la célèbre énigme, 12–13 Septembre 1987*. (Cannes: Direction des Affaires Culturelles, 1996), 135–42.

²⁹¹Neither Monsieur Carlhian-Ribois' article nor the archives of Briançon say whether the family of Saint-Mars was with him. Perhaps they traveled separately from the troops.

²⁹²Carlhian-Ribois, 140.

²⁹³Vergé-Franceschi, 324. This mention of expenses is a subtle hint that he would like to be reimbursed.

²⁹⁴A.C. Cooper-Marsdin, *The History of the Islands of the Lerins, the Monastery, Saints and Theologians of S. Honorat* (Cambridge, England: Cambridge University Press, 1913), 34.

²⁹⁵Iung, 167.

²⁹⁶Iung, 168.

²⁹⁷Iung, 176–77.

²⁹⁸Today the name of the small street is rue de la Bastille.

²⁹⁹Iung, 173–174.

³⁰⁰Hilliaret, *Dictionnaire*, 1: 153.

³⁰¹In 1761, an apartment building was built at the far end of the court opposite the main entrance, making two courtyards out of one. The lieutenant, major, and doctor of the institution had apartments there and there was a conference room where prisoners were registered and interrogated but the courtyard was undivided when Eustache Dauger was in the Bastille.

³⁰²The *dauphin* was the man who would become king upon the death of the present king, almost always the king's firstborn or surviving oldest son.

³⁰³Saint-Albin Berville et Jean-François Barrière, *Collection des Mémoires relatifs à la Révolution*

Française: Mémoires de Linguet sur la Bastille et de Dusaulx sur le 14 Juillet (Paris: Baudouin Frères, 1821), 65–66.

[304] W. A. Fougeret, *Histoire générale de la Bastille, depuis sa fondation en 1369, jusqu'à sa destruction, 1789* (Paris: Gauvain, 1834), 1: 15–16.

[305] Michèle Rosellini, "Pourquoi écrire des poèmes en prison ? Le cas de Paul Pellisson à la Bastille," in *Les Dossiers du Grihl: Groupes de Recherches Interdisiplinaires sur l'Histoire du Littéraire*. 2011–01 | 2011, http://dossiersgrihl.revues.org/4939, accessed August 30, 2014.

[306] Berville, 75.

[307] Quétel, *La Bastille, histoire vraie*, 53.

[308] Quétel, *La Bastille, histoire vraie*, 53–54.

[309] Image of Charles V of Spain. Etching by Daniel Hopfer and Hieronymous Hopfer. circa 1520. Printed 1684. Courtesy National Gallery of Art, Washington, D.C., USA.

[310] The wing was expanded much later. In Queen Anne's time, it was still a single stalk of rooms with windows on either side.

[311] "*Monsieur de Montagu, que voilà, sait ce qu je dois à Dieu, les grâces qu'il m'a faites et les grandes miséricordes dont je lui suis redevable.*"

[312] Dulong, *Anne*, pp. 389–391. For her final instruction to Louis XIV, see also Radier, Jean François du Dreux. *Mémoires historiques, critiques, et anecdotes sur les reines et régentes de France: Avec la continuation jusqu'à nos jours, par un professeur de l'Académie de Paris*. Vol. 6. Paris: P. Renouard, 1827, p. 165.

[313] An excellent biography of Anne of Austria in English is by Ruth Kleinman, *Anne of Austria, Queen of France*. Columbus, Ohio: Ohio State University Press, 1985.

[314] Henri Carré, *The Early Life of Louis XIV (1638–1661)*, trans. Dorothy Bolton (London: Hutchinson & Co., 1951), 25.

[315] October 1630 was just a month before the Day of the Dupes when Louis XIII decided he could not let his mother, Marie de' Medici, chase Richelieu from his service.

[316] Les Archives Diplomatiques du Ministère des Affaires Etrangères (ADMAE)
Mémoires et Documents: France, Anonymous letter, "*Plaintes de la Reine mère contre Monsieur le Cardal*," October 1630, PO 3716, 358v.

[317] Sonnino, 56. Paul Sonnino says that Augier was a French Huguenot.

[318] Tillinac, *Ange du désordre*, 165.

[319] Richardt, 23.

[320] Chantal Grell, "Anne d'Autriche et ses juges," in *Anne d'Autriche, Infante d'Espagne et reine de France*, ed. Chantal Grell (Paris: Perrin, CEEH (Centro de Estudios Europe Hispánica), Centre de Recherche, Château de Versailles, 2010), 389.

[321] "*Fronde*" is the nickname given to the French civil war of 1649–1653, and it means slingshot. Unruly young Parisians showed their support for the resistance to the crown by launching rocks at the local police force. Mazarin spent almost the entire year of 1651 in exile, staying for many months at the château of Brühl owned by the Elector of Cologne.

[322] Val-de-Grâce was a convent on the rue Saint-Jacques that Anne of Austria, early in her reign, vowed to sustain as sign of her dedication to the Virgin Mary and the Virgin Birth. She rebuilt it and kept a permanent apartment there. Its large Baroque chapel and some of its dependencies remain on the top of the rue Saint-Jacques, facing the university and the river at the bottom of the hill.

[323] Françoise Bertaut, Dame de Motteville (1615–1689), widow of a chief justice in Rouen, whose place in Anne's life was as close friend and confidante, was fluent in Spanish, which made the two women close and facilitated conversation between them. Much of what we know about Anne of Austria and her regency is from Madame de Motteville's diary, a detailed, frank, and well written description of the court and all its members.

[324] In the middle of the 14th century Count Humbert of Vienne in the province of Dauphiny

gave his lands to the oldest son of the king of France. Humbert's arms bore a dolphin (in French *dauphin*). The styling of the oldest son of the king as *dauphin* was kept.

[325] The name "*Dieudonné*" had been given before in France to a royal infant that would be known in adulthood as Philippe-Auguste (b. 1165) because he had been long awaited and was very much needed to secure the Capet line.

[326] Will Durant, *The Reformation: A History of European Civilization from Wyclif to Calvin: 1300–1564*, New York: Simon and Schuster, 1957, 25.

[327] Meyer, *Colbert*, 162.

[328] Meyer, *Colbert*, 162.

[329] Meyer, *Naissance*, 113, 120, 147. Also, Ralph Albanese. *Initiation aux Problèmes Socioculturels de la France au XVIIe siècle*. Montpellier: Etudes Sociocritiques, 1977, 41.

[330] Anne-Marie-Louise d'Orléans, duchesse de Montpensier, *Portraits littéraires*, ed. Christian Bouyer (Paris: Editions Séguier, 2000), 75–76.

[331] Primi, 115 and 138.

[332] Spanheim, 32–37.

[333] Hélène Delalex, *Louis XIV intime* (Versailles: Gallimard/Château de Versailles, 2015), 8.

[334] De Choisy, 30.

[335] Primi, 34–35.

[336] Niort is in the Nouvelle-Aquitaine region of France, department of Deux-Sèvres.

[337] André Castelot, *Madame de Maintenon: La reine secrète* (Paris: Perrin, 1996), 30.

[338] Christophe Levantal, "Louis XIV et la *Gazette*, ou le roi publié," in *Louis XIV, l'image et le mythe*, eds. Mathieu Da Vinha, Alexandre Maral et Nicolas Milovanovic (Rennes et Versailles: Presses Universitaires de Rennes; Centre de Recherche du Château de Versailles, 2014), 158.

[339] Levantal, 156.

[340] Primi, 27.

[341] Alfred Fierro, *Historical Dictionary of Paris*, trans. Jon Woronoff. Historical Dictionaries of Cities, No. 4. (Lanham, Md.: The Scarecrow Press, Inc., 1998), 61. In 1701, when this street merchant was a concern of the king, the Comédie-Française had moved from the rue Jacques-Callot and was located in the rue de l'Ancienne-Comédie.

[342] G. B. Depping, *Correspondance Administrative sous le Règne de Louis XIV, Administration de la Justice, Police, Galères* (Paris: Imprimerie Nationale, M DCCC LI. 1851), 2:739–40.

[343] Louis de Rouvroy, duc de Saint-Simon, *Mémoires (1714–1716) Additions au Journal de Dangeau*, ed. Yves Coirault (Paris: Gallimard, 1983), 5: 471.

[344] De Choisy, 24.

[345] De Choisy, 106.

[346] Petitfils, *Louis XIV*, 688.

[347] The church of the Jesuits is on the rue Saint-Antoine and is called the church of Saint-Paul and Saint-Louis, usually shortened to Saint-Paul.

[348] Alexandre Maral, *Les Derniers Jours de Louis XIV* (Paris: Perrin, 2014), 209.

[349] François de Neufville, 2nd maréchal de Villeroy (1644–1730) had been a childhood friend of Louis XIV.

[350] Théophraste Renaudot, "De Meaux le 23 d'Aoust, 1631," *Recueil des Gazettes de l'année 1631*, Cote NUMP-827, Microfilm-M-197, Vue 96, 4.

[351] Others who have thought the Mask was a son of either Anne of Austria or Louis XIII by adultery are Michel de Dorat-Cubières-Palmézeaux, Marie-Madeleine Mast, and Jean Aillon.

[352] Jean-Paul Desprat, *La France du Grand Siècle, 1589–1715* (Paris: Tallandier, 2012), 120.

[353] Jean Héroard, *Journal de Jean Héroard sur l'Enfance et la Jeunesse de Louis XIII (1601–1628)* (Paris: Librairie de Firmin Didot Frères, Fils et Cie, 1868), 2:11.

[354] Bernard Nabonne, *Les grandes heures de Saint-Germain-en-Laye* (Paris: Sfelt, 1950), 56–57.

[355] Hillairet, "rue de la Ferronnerie," *Dictionnaire*, 1:521.

[356] Hillairet, "rue de Seine," *Dictionnaire*, 2: 510. Queen Marguerite's forty-acre parcel had the Seine river for north boundary and was limited to the east by the rue de Seine, to the south by the rue Jacob and de l'Université, and to the west by the rue du Bac. The parcel was sold in 1623 to five developers for 1,315,000 *livres tournois*.

[357] Roland Mousnier, *Paris Capitale au temps de Richelieu et de Mazarin* (Paris: Editions A. Pedone, 1978), 100.

[358] Héroard, 256.

[359] The medical term for low body fluid drainage is hypohidrosis.

[360] Victor Lucien Tapié, *La France de Louis XIII et de Richelieu* (Paris: Flammarion, 1967), 280.

[361] Dulong, 149.

[362] The *Tribunal* was on the south end of the *salle des Caryatides*, a very large multi-use space for celebrations and musical performances.

[363] The raised *Tribunal* platform was removed in 1808 and the area where it stood was merged into the *salle des Caryatides* to make one space. The stone columns holding up the little orchestral platform are (this musicians' stage still stands) carved in the form of caryatides, ladies in antique full-body veils, a theme taken from the Erechtheion temple on the Acropolis in Athens, Greece.

[364] Yvan Christ, *Le Louvre et les Tuileries: Histoire Architecturale d'un Double Palais* (N.P.: Editions "Tel", 1949), 9. Yvan Christ, a Louvre history specialist, says it was under Saint Louis (1214–1270) that the forerunner of today's salle des Caryatides was created in the fortified medieval palace, a *grande salle* where he and his successors rendered justice and where receptions and festivities took place. When King François I decided to start dismantling the old medieval Louvre castle in 1528 to update his Paris fortress to the new Renaissance style, he started with the wing in which the grand reception rooms of the palace had traditionally been, the west wing of the courtyard.

[365] Louis Batiffol, *Le Louvre sous Henri IV & Louis XIII : La Vie de la Cour de France au XVIIe Siècle* (Paris: Calmann-Lévy, Editeurs, 1930), 146. The princesse de Conti was a very good friend of Marie de' Medici. She had an apartment on the second floor of the new quarters of the Louvre.

[366] A. Lloyd Moote, *Louis XIII the Just* (Berkeley; Los Angeles; London: University of California Press, 1989), 146.

[367] Héroard, 106.

[368] Edward Herbert of Cherbury, *The Life of Edward, Lord Herbert of Cherbury* (London: Whittaker, Treacher and Arnot, MDCCCXXX (1830)), 116.

[369] Dulong, 24.

[370] Dulong, 24.

[371] Dulong, 25.

[372] Literature on the genetics of cleft lip/palate generally agree that the first gene conclusively associated with the malformation (in non-syndromic patients) was interferon regulatory factor 6 (IRF6). Genome-wide association studies (GWAS) have identified numerous loci associated with the malformation in populations of European and Asian ancestry. See J. A. Vel:raw-latex:'á'zquez-Arag:raw-latex:'ó'n M. A. Alc:raw-latex:'á'ntara-Ortigoza, B. Estandia-Ortega, M. E. Reyna-Fabi:raw-latex:'á'n, C. D. M:raw-latex:'é'ndez-Adame, and A. Gonz:raw-latex:'á'lez-del Angel, "Gene Interactions Provide Evidence for Signaling Pathways Involved in Cleft Lip/Palate in Humans," *Journal of Dental Research* 95, no. 11 (2016): 1257–64. Other regions found by scientists are on chromosome 9q21 and a subsequent fine-mapping study suggested the forkhead box E1 (FOXE1) gene (homeotic gene) as responsible for the linkage signal and two restriction-length polymorphisms at the TGF-a (transforming growth factor alpha) locus. E. Mangold, K. U. Ludwig, M. M. Nothen, "Breakthroughs in the genetics of orofacial clefting," *Trends in Molecular Medicine* 17, no. 12 (2011): 725–33. These are but a few of the loci

in human DNA that are suspected by geneticists for cleft lip/palate but we, in this book, are not concerned with the complicated details of DNA gene mapping. We are, though, telling a family story where cleft lip/palate has caused pain, and thus we should appreciate the work of researchers who are finding the genetic causes of this birth defect, their goal being to predict and perhaps one day, prevent, cleft lip and palate.

[373] Arnaud de Vallouit, "Un portrait éclaté de Louis XIV: la représentation fragmentaire du souverain dans les *Mémoires* inédits de Philibert de La Mare," in Mathieu Da Vinha, Alexandre Maral and Nicolas Milovanovic, *Louis XIV, l'image et le mythe* (Rennes et Versailles: Presses Universitaires de Rennes; Centre de Recherche du Château de Versailles, 2014), 191.

[374] M. Thérèse Garvey, H. J. Barry, M. Blake, "Supernumerary Teeth — An Overview of Classification, Diagnosis and Management," *Journal of the Canadian Dental Association* 65, no. 11 (December 1999): 612.

[375] M. J. Dixon, M. L. Marazita, T. H. Beaty, J. C. Murray. "Cleft lip and palate: understanding genetic and environmental influences," *Nature Reviews Genetics*
12, no. 3 (2011): 170.

[376] Chronic eye tearing, ironically, can be caused by lack of moisture in the eye; the tear production ducts work overtime to respond to the dryness and the tears overflow without being absorbed by the eye.

[377] Madeleine Foisil, *L'Enfant Louis XIII* (Paris: Perrin, 1996), 38–39.

[378] Augustin Cabanès, *Les Morts mysterieuses de l'histoire. Nouvelle édition... Deuxième série : rois, reines et princes français, de Louis XIII à Napoléon III* (Paris: Albin Michel, 1911), 2.

[379] M. L. Marazita, "Subclinical features in nonsyndromic cleft lip with or without cleft palate (CL/P): review of the evidence that subepithelial orbicularis oris muscle defects are part of an expanded phenotype for CL/P," *Orthod Craniofac Res* 10, no. 2 (2007): 82.

[380] K. Neiswanger, S. M. Weinberg et al., "Orbicularis oris muscle defects as an expanded phenotypic feature in nonsyndromic cleft lip with or without cleft palate," *American Journal of Medical Genetics Part A* 143A, no. 11 (June 1 2007), 1143.

[381] J. Kuriakose, P. Kamath, A. Kumar, R. Scindhia, and M. B. Raghuraj, "Long face pattern," *Revista Latinoamericana de Ortodoncia y Odontopediatría* (2013).
https://www.ortodoncia.ws/publicaciones/2013/art-34/.

[382] Elizabeth A.R. Brown, *The Monarchy of Capetian France and Royal Ceremonial* (Brookfield, Vermont: Gower, 1991), 256.

[383] Armand Marie Leroi, *Mutants: on the Form, Varieties and Errors of the Human Body* (New York, N.Y: Harper Perennial, 2005), 286–87.

[384] Voltaire, "On the certainty of history," *Encyclopédie, ou dictionnaire raisonné des sciences, des arts et les métiers*, eds. Denis Diderot and Jean le Rond d'Alembert 8 (1765).

[385] Jean-Denis Bergasse, *Le Masque de fer: Louis XIV, Nouveau regard, fin'd'énigmes?* (Cessenon, France: Jean-Denis Bergasse, 2008), 20.

[386] Louis-François-Armand de Vignerot du Plessis, (1696–1788), great nephew of Cardinal Richelieu.

[387] Delort, *Histoire de l'homme au masque de fer*, 19.

[388] Topin, 11–12.

[389] Jean Markale, *La Bastille et l'énigme du Masque du Fer* (Paris: Pygmalion/G. Watelet, 1989), 314.

[390] Vergé-Franceschi, 20.

[391] Erving Goffman, *Stigma: Notes on the Management of Spoiled Identity* (Prentice-Hall, Inc.: Englewood Cliffs, N. J.) 1963, 16.

[392] Voltaire, *Le Siècle de Louis XIV* (Frankfurt: Knoch & Eslinger, 1753), 1:312.

[393] Iung, 44.

[394] Jean-Christian Petitfils, *L'Homme au Masque de Fer* (Paris: Librairie Académique Perrin,

1970), 19. Some other translations and quotations of this sentence use "sound" where "tone" is more correct. There is a distinct difference between "sound" and "tone." Absolute clarity on this medical assessment is necessary because it has perhaps a stronger clue for solving part of the mystery than any other.

[395] Dauger's strange speech might have been the reason for his nickname, "*La Tour*" (the Tower). De Palteau's uncle Blainvilliers told him that the prisoner was only known at Sainte Marguerite and at the Bastille as "*La Tour*." His cell at Pignerol in the *tour d'en bas*, the largest, oldest tower of the prison, was the original reason for the nickname, but "*La Tour*" could have referred to the Bible story of the Tower of Babel in the Book of Genesis that explains that there are different languages because the descendants of Noah tried to build a tower to reach heaven. To temper their pride, God decided to give them new challenges by altering their speech so they couldn't understand one another and therefore had to give up their tower building project and move apart. If Dauger couldn't speak well, the staff might have given him this nickname as a double reflection of his attributes.

[396] Saint-Mars had willed the estate to his nephew, the father of de Palteau. It is south of Sens in the department of the Yonne in the region of Bourgogne-Franche-Comté.

[397] Brad W. Neville, Douglas D. Damm, Carl M. Allen, and Angela C. Chi. "Developmental Defects of the Oral and Maxillofacial Region." *Oral and Maxillofacial Pathology*. 5th ed., 1.

[398] Stephanie E. Watkins et al., "Classification, Epidemiology, and Genetics of Orofacial Clefts," *Clinics in Plastic Surgery* 41, no. 2 (April 2014):152.

[399] Watkins, 153.

[400] James W. Hanson and Jeffrey C. Murray, "Genetic Aspects of Cleft Lip and Palate," in Janusz Bardach and Hughlett L. Morris, *Multidisciplinary Management of Cleft Lip and Palate Section X. Nasal Airway, Otologic, and Audiologic Problems Associated with Cleft Lip and Palate* (Philadelphia: W.B. Saunders Company, 1990), 121.

[401] Janusz Bardach and Court Cutting, "Anatomy of the Unilateral and Bilateral Cleft Lip and Nose," in Bardach and Morris, 152.

[402] A. Lorot-Marchand et al., "Frequency and socio-psychological impact of taunting in school-age patients with cleft lip-palate surgical repair," *International Journal of Pediatric Otorhinolaryngology* 79, no. 7 (July 2015), 1041.

403

A. Lorot-Marchand et al., 1046.

404

A. Lorot-Marchand et al., 1042.

405

A. Lorot-Marchand et al., 1042.

[406] Romero and Saez, 498.

[407] Henri II (1519–1559), François II (1544–1560), Charles IX (1550–1574), and Henri III (1551–1589).

[408] Ambroise Paré, *Œuvres complètes d'Ambroise Paré.*, ed. J.-F. Malgaigne (Paris: J.-B. Baillière, 1840–1841). There are many editions of Paré's *Œuvres*, but the above nineteenth-century edition may be the most helpful for those who want to get the broadest view of this great surgeon's life and work. This edition has critical notes and an introduction on the origin and progress of surgery in the West from the sixteenth to the seventeenth century and a history of the life, travels, and works of Ambroise Paré. It is in French. An English translation made in 1634 by Thomas Johnson is cited below. Also see Ira Rutkow, *Empire of the Scalpel* (New York: Scribner, 2022).

[409] Jacques Guillemeau, *La chirurgie françoise, recueillie des Anciens Médecins et Chirurgiens*

avec plusieurs figures des Instrumens necesseres pour l'opération. Manuelle par Jacques Guillemeau D'Orléans, Chirurgien du Roy et Juré à Paris (Paris: Nicolas Gilles, 1594).

[410] Laudanum and opium were available for those who could afford them, and traditional healers and specialists in herbs had some natural materials for pain, but no really effective surgery pain relief would come until the middle of the 1800s.

[411] Guillemeau, *La chirurgie françoise*, 13. Guillemeau was Paré's son-in-law and is known for his advanced work on opthamology and obstetrics.

[412] Romero and Saez, 499.

[413] Rogers et al., 16.

[414] Ambroise Paré, *The workes of that famous chirurgion Ambrose Parey translated out of Latine and compared with the French by Thomas Johnson*, trans. and ed. Thomas Johnson, Thomas Cecil, and George Baker (London: Thomas Cotes and R. Young, 1634), 874.

[415] R. S. Nanda and S. K. Nanda, "Considerations of dentofacial growth in long-term retention and stability: is active retention needed?" *American Journal of Orthodontics and Dentofacial Orthopedics* 101, no. 4 (1992): 297.

[416] Ambroise Paré, *The workes of that famous chirurgion Ambrose Parey translated out of Latine and compared with the French by Thomas Johnson*, eds. Thomas Johnson, Thomas Cecil, George Baker (London: Thomas Cotes and R. Young, 1634), 869–873.

[417] M. A. Aramany, "A history of prosthetic management of cleft palate: Paré to Suersen," *Cleft Palate* 8: 415; and Sterling K. Clarren, Barbara Anderson, Lynn S. Wolf, "Feeding Infants with Cleft Lip, Cleft Palate, or Cleft Lip and Palate," *Cleft Palate Journal* 24, no. 3 (July 1987), 246.

[418] George M. Gould and Walter L. Pyle, *Anomalies and Curiosities of Medicine* (New York: Sydenham Publishers, 1937), 256.

[419] A book in English by James Snell, *Observations on the History, Use, and Construction of Obturateurs, Or Artificial Palates Illustrated by Cases of Recent Improvements to Which Are Added Numerous Cases of Deficiency of the Lower Jaw, Lips, Nose, etc. With the Most Efficient Means of Restoring the Parts Artificially*, gives a readable and thorough history of the development of obturators up to the mid 1700s. Second edition. (London: Callow and Wilson, 1828). Jean Héroard, Louis XIII's doctor who kept such good notes on the king's health, was known to Jacques Guillemeau through Guillaume Héroard, Jean's uncle, who had helped Jean get established as a doctor in Paris.

[420] Information from Dr. David Zajac, February 16, 2012.

[421] The trip originated at the Exilles fort, but Exilles was not typically used as a prison, so it was assumed the origination was Pignerol, a known state prison.

[422] Letter from Bishop Louis Fouquet,4 September 1687, no recipient, n.p., Bibliothèque Sainte-Geneviève Reserve MSS, 1477 f396v. The French phrase used in the letter is "*ayant un masque d'acier sur la visage.*" Acier is steel.

[423] Louis Fouquet, "... *que tous les gens que le public croit morts, ne le sont pas.*"

[424] Simone Bertière, *Louis XIII et Richelieu: La Malentente* (Paris: Fallois, 2016), 17–18.

[425] Binfeng He et al., "Analysis of High-Altitude De-Acclimatization Syndrome after Exposure to High Altitudes: A Cluster-Randomized Controlled Trial," *Plos One* 8, no. 5 (May 2013):9.

[426] Lair, 2:454.

[427] Roux-Fazillac's caution was quoted in chapter 1.

[428] Ross Douthat, "Jeffrey Epstein and When To Take Conspiracies Seriously," *New York Times* online edition, August 13, 2019, accessed August 14, 2019.

[429] Théophraste Renaudot, ed, *La Gazette*, Paris: Bureau d'adresse, no. 3 (1643): 20. Kings of France were thought able to influence God to cure a person they touched.

[430] Théophraste Renaudot, ed., *La Gazette,* Paris: Bureau d'adresse, no. 6 (1643), 40.

[431] Théophraste Renaudot, ed., *La Gazette*, Paris: Bureau d'adresse.,no. 11 (1643), 72.

[432] Théophraste Renaudot, ed., *La Gazette*, Paris: Bureau d'adresse, no. 12 (1643), 73.

[433] Théophraste Renaudot, ed., *La Gazette*, Paris: Bureau d'adresse, no. 14 (1643), 92.

[434] Théophraste Renaudot, ed., *La Gazette*, Paris: Bureau d'adresse, no. 20 (1643), 132.

[435] Théophraste Renaudot, ed., *La Gazette*, Paris: Bureau d'adresse, no. 23 (1643), 151.

[436] Théophraste Renaudot, ed., *La Gazette*, Paris: Bureau d'adresse, no. 26 (1643), 172.

[437] Théophraste Renaudot, ed., *La Gazette*, Paris: Bureau d'adresse, no. 35 (1643), 232.

[438] The Roussillon was a historic county contested between Spain and France on the southern border of France. It is approximately the present day department of Pyrénées Orientals in the region of Occitanie.

[439] Nabonne, 124.

[440] Motteville, 1:102.

[441] Motteville, 1:122–23.

[442] Roujon, 18.

[443] Motteville, 1:123–24.

[444] Roujon, 17.

[445] Vergé-Franceschi, 45.

[446] Peter Gay, *Voltaire's Politics, The Poet as Realist* (New Haven: Yale University Press, 1988), 24.

[447] Gustave-Joseph Witkowski, *Accoucheurs et Sages Femmes Célèbres; Esquisses Biographiques* (Paris: G. Steinheil, 1891), 28–29.

[448] Susan Hatters Friedman, Amy Heneghan, Miriam Rosenthal, "Characteristics of Women Who Deny or Conceal Pregnancy," *Psychosomatics* 48, no. 2 (March–April 2007): 117.

[449] Angela Jenkins, Simon Millar, James Robins, "Denial of Pregnancy: a literature review and discussion of ethical and legal issues," *Journal of the Royal Society of Medicine* 104 (2011): 287.

[450] Jenkins, 286–87.

[451] J. Wessel, A. Gauruder-Burmester, and C. Gerlinger, "Denial of pregnancy–characteristics of women at risk," *Acta Obstetricia et Gynecologica Scandinavica* 86 (2007): 542–46.

[452] See chapter 11 of this volume for an analysis of physical descriptions of Dauger by eyewitnesses that indicate he had cleft lip and palate.

[453] Jacques Gélis, *History of Childbirth: Fertility, Pregnancy and Birth in Early Modern Europe*, trans. Rosemary Morris (Cambridge, U.K.: Polity Press, 1996), 263–264. See also Ruth Gilbert, "Strange notions: treatments of early modern hermaphrodites," in *Madness, Disability and Social Exclusion, the Archaeology and Anthropology of 'Difference'*, ed. Jane Hubert (London; New York: Routledge, 2000), 148.

[454] Philip L. Safford and Elizabeth J. Safford, *A History of Childhood and Disability* (London & New York: Teachers College Press, 1997), 2.

[455] Ambroise Paré, *Des Monstres et prodiges* (Genève: Librairie Droz, 1971) [first published 1573], 4.

[456] Paré, *Des Monstres et prodiges*, 35.

[457] Arlette Farge et Michel Foucault, eds., *Le désordre des familles, lettres de cachet des Archives de la Bastille au XVIIIe siècle*, Collection Archives dirigée par Pierre Nora et Jacques Revel (Saint-Amand (Cher), France: Editions Gallimard, Julliard, 1982), 183–84.

[458] Lucien Bély, *Les secrets de Louis XIV: mystères d'Etat et pouvoir absolu* (Paris: Tallandier, 2013), 386.

[459] Susan E. Dinan, *Women and Poor Relief in Seventeenth-Century France, the Early History of the Daughters of Charity* (Aldershot, Hampshire, England: Ashgate Publishing Limited, 2006), 4.

[460] In a previous chapter it was noted that Louis XIV paid the pension for the room and board (captivity) of the "Mooress of Moret," a girl with dark skin that was born to Marie-Thérèse, the king's wife. He was assumed to be the father.

[461] Safford and Safford, 34.

[462] Jean Labbé, "Maltraitance des enfants – perspective historique," *Santé, Société et Solidarité* 1 (2009), 19–20.

[463] The Baccarat Museum is now at 11, place des Etats-Unis, Paris 75116.

[464] Eustache Dauger was the name the authorities used from his arrest. They must have had a good reason for using this name in his arrest warrant. When, in the future, there is clarification about the identity of his parents, it will become clear whether this was the only name he ever had. Soon after his arrest the prisoner's name began to fade from his official record. Eustache's name finally died on the day that Fouquet died; Eustache officially ceased to exist...became a white crow, and what does not exist has no name.

[465] Christian Maurel, "Prénomination et parenté baptismale du Moyen-Age à la Contre-reforme. Modèle religieux et logiques familiales," *Revue de l'histoire des religions* 209, no. 4 (1992): 394.

[466] Maurel, 398.

[467] Maurel, 401–405.

[468] Jean-Claude Sangoï, "Forename, family, and society in southwest France (Eighteenth-nineteenth centuries)," *The History of the Family* 4, no. 3 (September 1999): 246. Also Maurel, 411

[469] Maurel, 395.

[470] Claude Mollet (circa 1564–1649) was a landscape designer for Henri IV and Louis XIII.

[471] Auguste Jal, *Dictionnaire critique de biographie et d'histoire* (Paris, 1867), 152. The port Saint-Paul was a small dock on the Seine at the intersection of the rue Saint-Paul and the river.

[472] Alain Mérot, *Eustache Le Sueur (1616–1655)* (Paris: Athena, 1987), 113.

[473] Mérot, 113.

[474] Agnès Fine, "L'héritage du nom de baptême," *Annales, Economies, Sociétés, Civilisations* (1987), 869.

[475] Paul Perdrizet, *Le Calendrier Parisien à la fin du Moyen Age d'après le Bréviaire et les livres d'heures* (Paris: Les Belles Lettres, 1933), 74.

[476] Boulogne-sur-Mer is in the Pas-de-Calais department, region of Hauts-de-France, on the far northeast coast of France. It is about nineteen miles (thirty kilometers) from Calais.

[477] These phrases are anagrams. Anagrams are codes in which a name or message is hidden by mixing up the letters to make new words.

[478] Archives départemental de Pas-de-Calais, Fonds et collections, Archives de l'état civil et notariales, Les insolites de l'état civil, "Trouvée dans un champ: on lui donne le patronyme de Deschamps," 5 MIR 829/2, January 21, 2014, accessed September 30, 2017.

[479] Archives départemental de Pas-de-Calais, Fonds et collections, Archives de l'état civil et notariales, Les insolites de l'état civil, "Un surnom singulier pour un baptême atypique," 3 E 275/2, December 12, 2011, accessed September 30, 2017.

[480] Pierre Roux-Fazillac, 105. The only copy of this letter from Saint-Mars to Louvois is in the 1801 book by Roux-Fazillac because the original was in the Paris city hall records that were burned by the Paris Communards in 1871. Roux-Fazillac wrote "d'Auger." Did he take liberties with the spelling of Dauger to make it "d'Auger" or was that the spelling he saw on Saint-Mars' letter? Whether Saint-Mars wrote the name "d'Auger" or "Dauger," we cannot know because spelling of names was approximate in 1801 when Roux-Fazillac wrote his book, as it was in 1669, but since in all the other letters between the king, Louvois, and Saint-Mars in 1669 the spelling was "Dauger," I think one can wonder whether Roux-Fazillac added the apostrophe and it was not in Saint-Mars' original.

[481] "Sézanne," Wikipedia, https://fr.wikipedia.org/wiki/Sézanne, accessed February 29, 2020. Also J. Dutilleul, "Auger, Edmond," *Dictionnaire d'Histoire et de Géographie Ecclésiastique*, ed. Mgr Alfred Baudrillart (Paris: Letouzey and Ané, 1931), 5: 378.

[482] The French government on January 1, 2016 created the region of Hauts-de-France, which

includes most of the former Picardy except some territories that passed into the region of the Nord-Pas-de-Calais.

[483] Louis Graves, *Notice archéologique sur le département de l'Oise: comprenant la liste des monumens de l'époque celtique, de l'époque gallo-romaine et du moyen âge*, (Beauvais: A. Desjardins, 1839), 83.

[484] Léon Fauirat, "La Forêt d'Halatte et sa Capitainerie," *Senlis Compte Rendus et Mémoires* 1, series 3 (1886), 83.

[485] Auger-Saint-Vincent webpage, "Un village à découvrir," https://augersaintvincent.fr.

[486] Fauirat, 6.

[487] Saint-Vincent of Saragossa was revered from the first half of the first milennium. Childebert (496–558) brought the saint's cloak back to Paris from Spain, and he and his wife Ultragothe founded the basilica of Saint-Vincent and Sainte-Croix on the left bank of Paris, which was eventually renamed Saint-Germain-des-Prés for the bishop Saint-Germain (c. 496–576).

[488] Fauirat, 86.

[489] Auger-Saint-Vincent webpage.

[490] Eugene Mueller, *Environs de Senlis*. (Senlis: Th. Nouvain, 1896), 186. Auger-Saint-Vincent in the Middle Ages was the center of a brotherhood of Saint-Caprais, martyr and the first bishop of Agen.

[491] Claude Carlier, *Histoire du duché de Valois : ornée de cartes et de gravures : contenant ce qui est arrivé dans ce pays depuis le temps des gaulois, & depuis l'origine de la monarchie françoise, jusqu'en l'année 1703* (Paris: Guillyn, 1764), 1:177–178.

[492] Carlier, 176–77. Carlier criticized map makers who changed the original spelling of Oger to Auger, and perhaps it would have been easier for mapmakers and detectives of the Man in the Iron Mask if Oger had never been changed to Auger, but the spelling of Auger or Augier (d'Auger or d'Augier) outlasted the original. However, Oger the Dane is never named Auger the Dane.

[493] Albert Dauzat, *Dictionnaire Etymologique des noms de famille et prénoms de France* (Paris: Librairie Larousse, 1980), 455. The name Oger, Ogier, Oge, comes from the German *od-gari* (*od-*, rich; *gari*, lance).

[494] Today the gated entrance to Mont Cornon from the village of Plessis-Cornefroy is accessed by a street called rue de Oger le Danois.

[495] Carlier, 1: 178.

[496] For Orest Ranum's comments on this tradition, see his *Artisans of Glory: Writers and Historical Thought in Seventeenth-Century France* (Chapel Hill: University of North Carolina Press, 1980), 5.

[497] Sonnino,190–91.

[498] Charlemagne's residence in the Valois is attested to in official charters.

[499] Carlier, 1: 183.

[500] Parc aux Dames is literally translated as Park of the Ladies but a translation that is closer to the meaning of the name is the Ladies' Preserve. The property is privately owned and does not allow visitors.

[501] Carlier, 2: 3–4.

[502] The remains of the abbey of Longpont are close to La Ferté-Milon in the Valois.

[503] Carlier, 2:6.

[504] *Recueil de titres originaux, copies, extraits, armes et tombeaux, concernant des abbayes et prieurés de France, formé par Gaignières et rangé par ordre alphabétique des monastères, du IXe au XVIIe siècle*, 1201–1800, 7:87. http://gallica.bnf.fr/ark:/12148/btv1b9062258g/, accessed September 30, 2017.

[505] Auger-Saint-Vincent webpage.

[506] Jacques de Maupeou, *Histoire des Maupeou* (Fontenay-le-Comte: P. et O. Lussaud frères,

1959), 139.

[507] Jacques de Maupeou, "Marie de Maupeou, Mère du surintendant Fouquet, l'illustration authentique d'une sainte. Extrait de l'ouvrage du Vicomte Jacques de Maupeou, *Histoire des Maupeou*," Bulletin de l'Association les Amis du Vieux Maincy, no. 7 (1985), 124.

[508] Gaignières, 87.

[509] The Cassini maps were created in the mid eighteenth century by four generations of the Cassini family, particularly Jean-Dominique Cassini (1677–1756) and his son César-François Cassini (1714–1783). They show topography, government and religious institutions, chateaux, towns, villages, parks, and other aspects of all the departments of France.

[510] Oise department, Hauts-de-France region. Senlis is 35 miles northeast of Paris (56.4 kilometers).

[511] "Manoir de Beaulieu-le Vieux" Base Merimée, Ministère de la Culture, Plate-forme ouvert du patrimoine (POP), https://www.pop.culture.gouv.fr/search/list?mainSearch=%22beaulieu%22&type=%5B%22Manoir%20de%20Beaulieu-le-Vieux%22%5D/ accessed July 30, 2015 and September 7, 2023.

[512] Marie Madeleine Fontaine, "Plaisirs, hospitalité et profit : La maison des champs dans la littérature de la Renaissance française," in *Maison des Champs dans l'Europe de la Renaissance*, ed. Monique Châtenet (Paris: Editions A. and J. Picard, 2003), 38.

[513] Base Merimée, "*Manoir de Beaulieu-le-Vieux.*"

[514] We have 1155 letters from Madame de Sévigné, 764 of them to her daughter, which were released for publication from 1725 to 1754, amputated and "corrected" by the family.

[515] Marie de Rabutin-Chantal, *Correspondance. Marie de Rabutin-Chantal, marquise de Sévigné, 1626–1696*, ed. Roger Duchêne (Paris: Gallimard, 1972), 1:364–66.

[516] Richardt, 122.

[517] The house is now the town hall of Sucy-en-Brie. Sucy-en-Brie is a commune 9.5 miles (15.4 km) to the southeast of Paris in the Ile-de-France region, Val-de-Marne department.

[518] Emile Gérard-Gailly, *Madame de Sévigné* (Paris: Hachette, 1971), 50.

[519] Picpus is in the twelfth arrondissement in Paris in the southeastern part of the Right Bank.

[520] Les Rochers is in the Ille-et-Vilaine department, region of Brittany.

[521] Adhémar is in the Drôme department, region of Provence-Alpes-Côtes d'Azur.

[522] "*Hélas! J'aurais grand besoin de cet homme noir pour me faire prendre un chemin dans l'air. Celui de terre devient si épouvantable que je crains quelquefois que nous ne soyons assiégés ici par les eaux.*" Rabutin-Chantal, *Correspondance*, Duchêne, 1: 364.

[523] There are multiple mentions in this letter of *La Mousse*. In this instance it refers to a friend of Madame de Sévigné's, who often went with her to Les Rochers, called by his friends *La Mousse*. *Mousse* is translated to English as foam.

[524] Rabutin-Chantal, *Correspondance*, 1: 365–366.

[525] Rabutin-Chantal, *Correspondance*, 1: 1178.

[526] *Mousse* means foam in English, so the appearance of a ghost or mirage would be sort of like a mousse, half there and half not… full of air and yet there.

[527] Vergé-Franceschi, 136.

[528] Gérard-Gailly, 65–66. We don't know the house number but it was probably on the west side of the rue du Temple because it was next to the manor of the Saint-Martin-des-Champs priory while the houses on the east side were continuous to each other.

[529] Louis Bourdaloue, Jesuit orator (1632–1704).

[530] Marie-Madeleine de Castille-Villemareuil (1635–1716), second wife of Nicolas Fouquet.

[531] Jeanne-Françoise Frémiot, baronne de Chantal (d. 1641). Beatified by Pope Benedict in 1751 and canonized by Clement XIII sixteen years later.

[532] Nathalie Freidel, *La conquête de l'intime: public et privé dans la Correspondance de madame de*

Sévigné (Paris: Champion, 2009), 365–67.

[533] Renaudot was the editor of the two major newpapers in Paris, *La Gazette* and *Le Mercure François*.

[534] Rabutin-Chantal, *Correspondance*, 1: 367–68.

[535] Philippe Halbert, "An African Prince at the Court of the Sun King," *The Monitor* (Summer 2011), 9–10.

[536] "*Elle avait soupé comme à son ordinaire, et elle se promena au clair de lune jusqu'à minuit.*" Quoted in Frantz Funck Brentano, *Le drame des poisons* (Paris: Tallandier, 1928), 236.

[537] Rabutin-Chantal, *Correspondance*, 1: 118.

[538] *Gallica* is the name of the online collection of documents in France's Bibliothèque Nationale. https://gallica.bnf.fr/.

[539] I also spent two hours in the reading room of the French Military Archives pulling books off the shelves and using the services of the room president who helped me look for information on the *Gentilshommes à Bec de Corbin*. The search did not turn up much, but was very enjoyable.

[540] A *corbin* is a word for a jay, a magpie, a raven or other prominently beaked bird.

[541] Bardin and Oudinot, 2: 730. The same volume of Bardin and Oudinot says lengths of the shank of the *bec de corbin* arm were between four and a half feet and six feet, p. 730.

[542] André Castelot, *La Reine Margot* (Paris: Perrin, 1993), 34.

[543] Vergé-Franceschi, 193. For the revelations of the Adhémar family connections I am grateful to the research of Professor Vergé-Franceschi, whose research in his book on the *Masque de fer*, published in 2009, presented them.

[544] Olivier Le Fèvre d'Ormesson. *Journal d'Olivier Lefèvre d'Ormesson et extraits des mémoires d'André Lefèvre d'Ormesson*, ed. M. Chéruel (Paris: Imprimerie Impériale, 1860–1861), 2: 50.

[545] Lair, 2: 181–82.

[546] Jean-Marie Lhoste, avocat en la cour de Parlement, demeurant à Paris, rue de l'Hôtel des Ursins, paroisse Saint-Landry, et Marguerite de Bailly, sa femme: donation mutuelle. Notice n° 1303. Archives nationales (annuaire du service) [site web d'origine]. Identifiant de l'unité documentaire: Châtelet de Paris. Date: 1652–1652 Y//188-Y//190 - fol. 307. Insinuations (3 mars 1651–10 mars 1654). https://francearchives.fr/facomponent/40c10d1eb6b819791c6e1fbd2bd32b7da4ab2b29. The rue de l'Hôtel des Ursins was opened on the place formerly occupied by the Hôtel des Ursins, a large townhouse that overlooked the Seine River and was torn down in 1637. It is in the fourth arrondissement on the north side of the Ile de la Cité looking over the river to the Marais. Hillairet, *Dictionnaire*, 2: 587.

[547] Some references say that Claude Lhoste was Fouquet's lawyer but that is not true. Both the Montargis and Beaulieu Lhoste families used the first names Claude and Antoine repeatedly over generations and the Montargis Lhoste were a very respected family in which many of the males were high-ranking officials in local Montargis government. Antoine Lhoste of Montargis (1578–1623) was counselor of the king, civil and criminal lieutenant general of Montargis and the surrounding areas, beginning in 1604. By his wife Catherine Gassot he had children: Catherine, Antoine, and Claude. His father was named Claude. The notoriety of Antoine Lhoste of Montargis and the family's repeated use of the same first names of Claude and Antoine almost certainly have something to do with the mistake that names Claude Lhoste as one of Fouquet's lawyers. It is also possible the families were related. The archivist of the department of the Loiret, in which Montargis is located, did not find a familial connection. More research is needed.

[548] Louis Châtellier, *L'Europe des dévots* (Paris: Flammarion, 1987), 117.

[549] Saint Vincent de Paul, *Saint Vincent de Paul Correspondence, Conferences, Documents*, vol. 1, correspondence 1607–1639, trans., ed., and annotated from the 1920 edition of C. M. Pierre Coste, S. R. Jacqueline Kilar, D. C., S. R. Helen Marie Law, D. C., S. R. Jean Marie Poole, D. C., Rev. James R. King, C. M., Rev. Francis Germovnik, C. M., Rev. John W. Carven, C. M (New

York: New City Press, 1985,) 1: 339–40.

[550] Email from Archives départementales de l'Oise to the author, July 30, 2015.

[551] Jean-Marc Moriceau et Gilles Postel-Vinay, *Ferme entreprise famille, grande exploitation et changements agricoles, les Chartier XVIIe-XIXe siècles* (Paris: Editions de l'Ecole des Hautes Etudes en Sciences Sociales, 1992), 48.

[552] Joannis Guigard, "Notice sur la mort d'Antoine Leonor Lhoste, Seigneur de Beaulieu," *Mercure de France. Indicateur du Mercure de France, 1672–1789: contenant, par ordre alphabétique, les noms des personnages sur lesquels on trouve, dans cette collection, des notices biographiques et généalogiques, avec renvoi aux années, tomes et pages*, December 1700 (Paris: Librairie Bachelin-Deflorenne, 1869), 176.

[553] Hillairet, *Dictionnaire*, 1: 230–31. This address is now one of a series of service entrances to nearby stores, a few blocks north of the Pont Neuf.

[554] Regnault, *Quatrième requête de messire Louis Bruant des Carrières contre madame Colbert et les enfants et héritiers de... M. Colbert. Au Roi et à Nosseigneurs de son conseil. / (Signé : Regnault [3 mars 1684].)* Bibliothèque nationale de France, département Manuscrits, Z THOISY-125 . p. 26, http://catalogue.bnf.fr/ark:/12148/cb367220578, accessed August 29, 2023).

[555] Chapelle des Prêtres et des Frères de la Congrégation de la Mission. 95, rue de Sèvres 75006, Paris, France; Maison-Mère des Filles de la Charité, 140, rue du Bac 75007, Paris, France, https://www.filles-de-la-charite.org/en/where-we-are/.

[556] The location of the prison of Saint Lazare was slightly to the west of the present entrance to the Gare de l'Est railway station in Paris' 10th arrondissement.

[557] This street is on the hill that the ruins of the Paris antique Roman outdoor theater are on, *Les Arènes*, ruins that were completely hidden by centuries of soil and trash when de Paul's abandoned children lived across the street. It was discovered when putting through the rue Monge from 1860 to 1869.

[558] Mezzadri, 117.

[559] Mezzadri, 189.

[560] Marie de Maupeou Fouquet, *Les Remèdes charitables de Mme Fouquet pour guérir à peu de frais toute sorte de maux tant internes qu'externes, invétérez et qui ont passés jusques à présent pour incurables, expérimentez par la même Dame* (Lyon: Jean Certe, 1685).

[561] Phillips Russell, *William the Conqueror* (New York & London: Scharles Scribner's Sons, 1933), 126.

[562] Shulamith Shahar, *Childhood in the Middle Ages*, (London; New York: Routledge, 1990), 148.

[563] Vergé-Franceschi, 311.

[564] Edgar Leoni, *Nostradamus: Life and Literature* (New York: Exposition Press, 1961), 161. This quotation is Nostradamus' prediction made in *Les Premières Centuries ou Prophéties* around 1555. The first stanza has never been fully understood. Historians have said that the first line refers to a fable told about Olympias, the mother of Alexander the Great, who had found a serpent in her bed, causing her husband, Philip the Great, to be wary of sleeping with her. What is problematic are the next lines: "It" will be done by the lady and no one will discover it." Lines three and four are easier to interpret. Scholars traditionally say they refer to Louis XIV's birth.

[565] Huguet, 30. Huguet says the ancestral lands of the Cavoye were in Picardy, near the village of Epagny, near Chauny. The mid eighteenth-century Cassini map names this village "Chaussoy." "Chaussoy" derives from the Latin root "salix" meaning willow. Information courtesy of Roland Seené, Archives départementales de la Somme, November 28, 2017.

[566] Emile Bourgeois, *Le grand siècle, Louis XIV, les arts, les idées, d'après Voltaire, Saint-Simon, Spanheim, Dangeau, Madame de Sévigné, Choisy, La Bruyère, Laporte, le Mercure de France, la Princesse Palatine, etc.* (Paris: Hachette, 1896), 11.

[567] Albanese, 41–42.

[568] Orest Ranum, "Jeux de Cartes, Pédagogie et Enfance de Louis XIV," in *Les Jeux à la Renis-*

sance, Actes du XXIIIe Colloque International d'Etudes Humanistes Tours – Julliet 1980, eds. Philippe Ariès et Jean-Claude Margolin (Paris: Librairie Philosophique J. Vrin, 1982), 554.

[569] The chief of Louis XIII's guards (and after Louis XIII's death, chief of Anne of Austria's guards) was the uncle of the comte Guillaume de Comminges de Guitaut (d. 1685) whose job as Sainte-Marguerite prison governor Saint-Mars took in 1687.

[570] Roland Mousnier, *Paris Capitale au temps de Richelieu et de Mazarin* (Paris: Editions A. Pedone, 1978), 100. Mousnier says that the medieval east wing of the Louvre with this ancient gate was not destroyed until after 1652.

[571] Ruth Kleinman.,*Anne of Austria, Queen of France* (Columbus, Ohio: Ohio State University Press, 1985), 106.

[572] Sainte Marguerite of Antioch, a third-century martyr, was swallowed by a dragon but the dragon could not stomach her purity and faith and so he threw her up. She was thought to be protective for women who were pregnant and in labor. The belt of Saint Marguerite was kept in the abbey of Saint-Germain-des-Prés in Paris.

[573] Witkowski, *Les Accouchements à la cour*, 54.

[574] The *mesdames* Condé, Vendôme, and Soissons were wives of Louis XIII's cousins. The duchesse de Boüillon-la Mark was of the house of de La Tour d'Auvergne, rulers of the principality of Sedan, the *vicomté* of Turenne, and the duchy of Bouillon. Louis XIV's great general Turenne was of this house.

[575] Nabonne, 119.

[576] Madame Peronne Du Moutier was a midwife certified by the Paris city department at *Châtelet* that oversaw the training of midwives and issued certifications. She was well thought of, widow of Monsieur de la Planche, living in rue Saint-Honoré, "near the Palais-Cardinal" (after Richelieu's death the name was changed to Palais-Royal). Anne of Austria sent Dame Peronne to Exeter, England, in June 1644 to attend Queen of England Henriette-Marie in the delivery of her baby Henriette, when the English queen was fleeing from Cromwell's soldiers. That she sent her into a dangerous situation in a foreign country awash in revolution shows her trust of Madame Peronne and Madame's returned fidelity to Anne, her queen, neighbor, and employer. Madame died in 1648 and the queen paid for her funeral expenses.

[577] Mireille Laget, "Childbirth in Seventeenth- and Eighteenth-Century France: Obstetrical Practice and Collective Attitudes," in *Medicine and Society in France: selections from the annales, économies, sociétés, civilisations* (Baltimore: Johns Hopkins University Press, 1980), 6:140.

[578] Meyer, *Naissance*, 138–139.

[579] Soudan, 291–92.

[580] *Note*: Another man who was not so adverse to physical contact with his wife, or at least who was living in the same bedroom as his wife, could not have been manipulated by this plot. Louis XIII's absence from her that had been a large part of her inability to become pregnant for so long now worked in her favor.

[581] Soudan, 293.

[582] Grell, 373.

[583] The judgements of the likenesses and differences in facial traits of the Bourbon, Medici, and Habsburg people in this chapter are those of the author.

[584] Grell, 365.

[585] The Palais Mazarin is part of the Bibliothèque Nationale in Paris.

[586] Cecil Gould, *Bernini in France, An Episode in Seventeenth-century History* (Princeton: Princeton University Press, 1982), 81.

[587] Gould, 82.

[588] Gould, 82.

[589] Rudolf Wittkower, *Bernini's Bust of Louis XIV. Charlton Lectures on Art Delivered at King's College in the University of Durham, Newcastle upon Tyne*, November 22, 1950 (London; New

York; Toronto: Geoffrey Cumberlege, Oxford University Press, 1951), 12.

[590] Román Vilas et al., "Is the 'Habsburg jaw' related to inbreeding?" *Annals of Human Biology* 46, no. 7–8 (2019), 557, accessed December 13, 2019.

[591] Donatella Lippi, Felicita Pierleoni, and Lorenzo Franchi, "Retrognathic maxilla in 'Habsburg jaw' – Skeletofacial analysis of Joanna of Austria (1547–1578)," *Angle Orthodontist* 82, no. 4 (2012), 392.

[592] Nancy L. Segal, *Deliberately Divided: Inside the Controversial Study of Twins and Triplets Adopted Apart* (Lanham: Boulder and New York; London: Rowman and Littlefield, 2021), 168.

[593] Robert Plomin, *Blueprint, How DNA Makes Us Who We Are* (Cambridge, Mass; London: MIT Press, 2019), 5.

[594] Bergasse, 76.

[595] Huguet, 166.

[596] Huguet, 166.

[597] Hortense Mancini and Marie Mancini, *Memoires d'Hortense et de Marie*, ed. Gérard Doscot (Paris: Mercure de France, 1965), 214.

[598] Huguet, 328–29.

[599] Gould, 82.

[600] Gould, 413. "Each day" would mean the 28th, 29th, and 30th.

[601] The beautiful town mansion of Louis d'Auger de Cavoye on the rue des Saint-Pères has been cared for since his death, and is still in private ownership.

[602] Jenny van Dongen, Scott D. Gordon, Dorret I. Boomsma, et al., "Identical twins carry a persistent epigenetic signature of early genome programming," *Nature Communications* 12, 5618 (28 September 2021): 1–14. https://doi.org/10.1038/s41467-021-25583-7.

[603] Philippe Erlanger, *Monsieur, Frère de Louis XIV* (Paris: Librairie Académique Perrin, 1981), 196.

www.ingramcontent.com/pod-product-compliance
Lightning Source LLC
Chambersburg PA
CBHW060937230426